THE CAPITAL UNDERGROUND

By

Ron Ruthfield

Names, places, characters, and occurrences in this book have been purposely altered by the authors. Any comparisons to actual people, times, locations, or events contained herein are totally coincidental and should not be construed to be historically factual. This book may not be reproduced in whole or in part, by photocopies or any other means, without written permission from the publisher except in the case of brief quotations embodied in critical articles and reviews.

Copyright © 2009 by RAZ Partners Publishing, LLC. All rights reserved.
First Edition

Copyright © 2025 by RAZ Partners Publishing, LLC. All rights reserved.
Second Edition

Manufactured in the United States of America
Available as an e-book
ISBN: 979-8-9928998-0-1 (paperback)
ISBN: 979-8-3154229-3-8 (hardcover)
Library of Congress Control Number: 2010906365
ronruthfield.com

Publify Publishing
Lampasas, TX

Acknowledgements

The author wishes to acknowledge the millions of U.S. citizens who have become, and continue to be, casualties of America's War on Drugs.

One day, hopefully in the not-too-distant future, those in power will recognize the mistakes of the past, accede to the wishes of the nation's Founding Fathers, and restore the public trust between government and its citizens.

"The liberties of our country, the freedoms of our civil Constitution are worth defending at all hazards, And it is our duty to defend them against all attacks. We have received them as a fair inheritance from our worthy ancestors. They purchased them for us with toil, danger, and expense of treasure and blood. It will bring a mark of everlasting infamy on the present generation - enlightened as it is - if we should suffer them to be wrested from us by violence without a struggle, or to be cheated out of them by the artifices of designing men."

Samuel Adams, American political leader, philosopher, author, and advocate of the Boston Tea Party

FOREWORD

As of this writing, the fentanyl crisis in the United States has escalated into a public health emergency, particularly among Americans aged 18 to 45. This synthetic opioid has become the number one killer in this demographic, claiming 108,300 lives in 2023 alone. As the crisis deepens, it's clear that the United States' southern border plays a pivotal role in the trafficking of fentanyl, raising concerns about national security, public safety, and international cooperation.

At the heart of the crisis is the fact that most illicit fentanyl entering the U.S. is smuggled through the southern border. Contrary to common assumptions about illegal immigration, a large portion of this deadly substance is brought into the country by U.S. citizens who use Ports of Entry (POEs) as their main points of smuggling. This method of trafficking allows for vast quantities of fentanyl to slip through the cracks of U.S. border security, despite heightened measures and increased surveillance.

Ports of Entry are complex, bustling hubs of legitimate trade and travel. However, they have also become ground zero for the smuggling of fentanyl and related substances. U.S. Customs and Border Protection (CBP) has been overwhelmed by the sheer volume of traffic, with the majority of illicit fentanyl being hidden among the thousands of legal shipments passing through each day. While human smuggling and illegal immigration are often the focus of political debate, it is these legal crossings where the drug crisis finds its primary entry point into American communities.

The drug's potency is one of the key reasons it has emerged as the leading cause of death for so many Americans. Fentanyl is up to 100 times stronger than morphine and 50 times more potent than heroin. Even small amounts can be lethal, and drug dealers often lace other narcotics with fentanyl to increase their potency, leading to accidental overdoses. With its high profit margin and extreme potency, fentanyl has become the drug of choice for traffickers, making it a particularly dangerous substance for anyone who comes into contact with it, whether they are seeking it out or not.

China has emerged as the primary source of fentanyl and related precursor chemicals. These substances are often shipped in small quantities via international mail and express consignments, making it difficult for authorities to detect and intercept them. Despite attempts by the U.S. government to curb these shipments, China remains the main origin point for the fentanyl that is ultimately trafficked into the United States. The Chinese government has faced criticism for not doing enough to crack down on the production and export of these chemicals, despite their commitment to international cooperation in combating the drug trade.

However, China is not the only player in this crisis. Once fentanyl precursors arrive in Mexico, they are often processed into the final product by drug cartels. These cartels then transport the fentanyl across the U.S.-Mexico border, using sophisticated smuggling techniques to evade detection. The involvement of Mexican cartels has further complicated the situation, as they have the infrastructure and networks to distribute fentanyl on a massive scale, ensuring that the drug reaches nearly every corner of the U.S.

Addressing the fentanyl crisis requires a multifaceted approach. Border security plays a critical role, but the solution goes beyond simply reinforcing the southern border. While enhanced surveillance, better detection technology, and increased manpower at Ports of Entry are necessary, they are not sufficient on their own. International cooperation, particularly with China and Mexico, must be strengthened to tackle the issue at its source.

Diplomatic pressure on China to more rigorously control the export of fentanyl elements is essential. The U.S. must also continue to work closely with Mexican authorities to disrupt the operations of cartels that are central to the trafficking of fentanyl. At the same time, tackling domestic demand for fentanyl through better education, rehabilitation programs, and addiction treatment will be crucial to stemming the tide of overdose deaths.

The sheer scale of the fentanyl crisis means that no single solution will suffice. It is a national tragedy that demands the attention of policymakers, law enforcement, and international partners alike. The southern border has become a conduit for fentanyl entering the United States, but the true scope of the problem is global, with roots in Chinese chemical factories and Mexican drug cartels. To truly address this crisis, a comprehensive strategy that tackles every point in the supply chain, from production to distribution to demand, is essential.

The hundreds of thousands of deaths are a stark reminder of the human toll of this crisis. Fentanyl has become a weapon of mass destruction, devastating families and communities across the U.S. and unless there is a coordinated, sustained effort to curb its trafficking and reduce demand, this death toll will continue to rise, with fentanyl cementing its status as the number one killer of young Americans.

The time for action is now, before even more lives are lost to this silent epidemic.

CONTENTS

Acknowledgements .... *iii*

Foreword .... *v*

Chapter 1 - **THE BOMB** *1*

Chapter 2 - **BAD NEWS, WORSE NEWS** *6*

Chapter 3 - **ARI, SANDRA AND THE FLORIDA BAR** *10*

Chapter 4 - **WELCOME TO CLUB WitSec** *18*

Chapter 5 - **ARI AND THE SUNTAN MAN** *22*

Chapter 6 - **SURPRISE, SURPRISE** *35*

Chapter 7 - **PLANNING THE PLAN** *39*

Chapter 8 - **ARI MAKES THE LIST** *44*

Chapter 9 - **TAKE THE MONEY AND RUN** *55*

Chapter 10 - **MILKING THE COW** *62*

Chapter 11 - **THE WAR BEGINS** *70*

Chapter 12 - **THE STARBUCKS EXPRESS** *75*

Chapter 13 - **THE DEADWOOD DEAL** *86*

Chapter 14 - **LET'S HAVE ANOTHER CUP OF COFFEE** *102*

Chapter 15 - **UNCLE MIKEY** *111*

Chapter 16 - **THE DETROIT SPECIAL** *118*

Chapter 17 - **THE MOTOR CITY SHOWDOWN** *124*

Chapter 18 - **JOINT TASK FORCE MEETING – THE INTRODUCTIONS** *133*

Chapter 19 - **JOINT TASK FORCE MEETING – COURTROOM CHAOS** *151*

Chapter 20 - **JOINT TASK FORCE MEETING – DUDU THE DUDE** *162*

Chapter 21 - **JOINT TASK FORCE MEETING – BEFORE THE CALL** *171*

Chapter 22 - **JOINT TASK FORCE MEETING – TWO CALLS LATER** *176*

Chapter 23 - **JOINT TASK FORCE MEETING – THIRD TIME'S A CHARM** *185*

Chapter 24 - **JOINT TASK FORCE MEETING – PREPARATION H** *192*

Chapter 25 - **ASSEMBLY TIME** *202*

Chapter 26 - **THE REUNION** *210*

Chapter 27 - **THE ROOM WITH NO VIEW** *218*

Chapter 28 - **CODE BLUE**	227
Chapter 29 - **SPECIAL DELIVERY**	238
Chapter 30 - **THE PIZZA PARTY**	246
Chapter 31 - **ENTER THE BARON**	255
Chapter 32 - **THE FACTS FAX**	264
Chapter 33 - **THE SMITH COURTSHIP**	271
Chapter 34 - **DOCUMENTED HISTORY AND THE HIRSCH CONNECTION**	282
Chapter 35 - **THE DUDES**	291
Chapter 36 - **SAY GOOD-BYE TO THE POLISH GUY**	300
Chapter 37 - **STRATEGIC DEVELOPMENT**	305
Chapter 38 - **TAKING CARE OF BUSINESS**	310
Chapter 39 - **THE UPDATE**	315
Chapter 40 - **MEANWHILE, BACK AT THE MANSION**	322
Chapter 41 - **ALL ABOARD**	327
Chapter 42 - **TO HELL AND BACK**	331
Chapter 43 - **THE FLYING FEDS**	336
Chapter 44 - **ARRIVAL TIME**	340
Chapter 45 - **INFORMATION PLEASE**	347
Chapter 46 - **ZANY ZURICH**	363
Chapter 47 - **COURT TIME**	371
Chapter 48 - **WHERE THERE'S A WILL THERE'S A WAY**	378
Chapter 49 - **FULL-COURT PRESS**	394
Chapter 50 - **RECESS OVER**	404
Chapter 51 - **BANK SHOT**	412
Chapter 52 - **COUNTDOWN**	420
Chapter 53 - **JUDGMENT DAY**	425
Chapter 54 - **DON'T COUNT YOUR CHICKENS**	432
About The Author	440

CHAPTER ONE

"Every friend of freedom must be as revolted as am by the prospect of turning the United States into an armed camp, by the vision of jails filled with casual drug users and of an army of enforcers empowered to invade the liberty of citizens on slight evidence."

Milton Friedman,
Nobel Prize-winning American economist

3:00 PM, Friday, June 17, 1988

THE BOMB

Ari's sweat-soaked shirt stuck to his black-leather swivel chair when he heard a voice on the other end of the phone telling him he was going to die, albeit painlessly, with the twist of a switch. It was at that very moment he knew he should have taken a furlough from the War on Drugs.

It wasn't the death threat making him perspire so profusely. It was the hazy Florida sun that could drive a lazy man crazy. It had been a particularly hot Friday in Fort Lauderdale, a seasonal nuance that almost always occurred less than a week before the summer scorch started to melt even the thickest asphalt. At 3:00 PM, he arrived at the parking lot outside his downtown office building, at eighteen stories the tallest in Broward County, He was returning from a lengthy client meeting in congested Miami that had begun at nine o'clock that morning.

Ari grabbed his navy-blue pinstriped suit jacket draped on the passenger seat and escaped from the cool air of his metallic silver Jaguar, He flung the garment over his white-shirted shoulder as the ninety-seven-degree temperature outside smothered him like a sausage sautéing in a hundred-and-fifty-degree chafing dish.

It was a forty-five-second walk from his car to the entrance, but there was enough mixture of humidity and solar power to drown his clothes quickly in perspiration.

Once inside, he took the elevator to the penthouse floor. He opened one of the double doors to "Hirsch & Hirsch, Attorneys-at-Law" then went breezing past his receptionist and into his well-appointed office. After grabbing a bottle of cold Evian from his private half-size fridge, Ari sat down to confront the mess on his desk and sifted through papers that had become intermingled with piles of pink message slips. It had been a long, blistering week. Ari thought about heading home a bit early and jumping in the pool at his condo complex. Everyone in the office except Stacy, the twenty-eight-year-old who worked the front office, had already left for the day. Although Fridays at the firm in the summer months meant working till noon only, the receptionist had stayed on to finish filing some papers. A short twelve minutes later, Ari's private phone rang. The call dashed his plan to splash. He didn't know it would become the most important call of his life. Or alternatively, death.

"Mr. Hirsch, Robert Sewell from the FBI is on the phone. Line four."

Ari knew this call was urgent, particularly because "line four" was for Emergency Use Only. "This is Ari Hirsch."

"Ari, Bob Sewell. Are you alone?" He put on his best bureau voice, one that reflected a sense of great urgency.

"Yes, Bob. Nobody's in my office but me. How can I help you?"

"I'm here to help you, Ari, not the other way around."

"Well then, Bob, please. Assist me," Ari responded, a bit condescendingly.

"Look, Hirsch. I feel the same way about you as you do about me," Sewell answered in an inflection slightly more than intense. "So, let's forego the unsociable gestures." Hirsch held no distinct fondness for the FBI, primarily because its agents had exercised extraordinary statutory means to arrest and testify against dozens of his legal patrons.

In the nine years Sewell held the post of top cop in that part of the country, he and Hirsch had a rather vast number of unfriendly run-ins during court sessions. By 1988, Hirsch had represented more than one hundred accused criminals arrested by local police, deputy sheriffs, and state and federal agencies for drug-related crimes.

Many of them had received complimentary "get-out-of-jail-free" cards, including those dealt by the FBL. Those were dished out when clients agreed to testify against their accomplices and enter WitSec, the Federal Witness Protection Program.

Even with smuggling illegal drugs into the country and, in some cases committing multiple murders, the hoodlums hid behind an opaque veil of secrecy in villages, towns, and cities across America. Ari's experience spoke volumes, He knew quite well that many governmental entities, including those with more letters in their acronyms than the Hawaiian alphabet - particularly those fighting the War on Drugs - had disgraced themselves by becoming as corrupt as the traffickers they were trying to arrest.

There were ugly ones, those who became the fat-layered underbellies in many government agencies always hungry for money and willing to do almost anything to get it. Crooked officials became the symbols of the system. They locked their paws on more dollars than had ever been printed by the U.S. Mint, and more deutschemarks, francs, and gold than Switzerland had laundered for the Nazis.

There was credence to Ari's belief that there were drug-thugs on every petal of the poppy plant. Despite what the government had told the public for decades, he knew it was all about the money and power. Both had become permanent motives of the culture that involved occupants of the crack house and the penthouse, the jail house and the White House. Trying to stop that machine would be like attempting to halt an Earth-bound meteor with a water pistol filled with Jell-O.

To be sure, Ari had gotten a number of calls on his private phone, but this one from Sewell, chief of the bureau's South Florida office, was different. "Shoot." Ari didn't mean that literally.

"Dino Morelli is planning to put a bomb in your Jag and take you out."

"What the hell are you talking about? Where'd that come from? Attempting to intimidate a lawyer defending his client is out of bounds. Sewell, it's not going to work," Ari said impatiently.

"Ari, this is one situation that's as serious as colon cancer, and your ass is on the operating table. Morelli thinks you're going to sell him out at the grand jury hearing on Monday." There was a thunderous silence as Ari thought about what he had just heard. He knew Morelli was looking at up to twenty-five years for getting nabbed with coke that had a street value of $10 million, but Ari would never have sacrificed his attorney- client privilege or told anyone where the "bodies were buried." He was dumbfounded that Morelli wouldn't know that.

"You feds never stop harassing us, do you?" In the creases of his mind, Hirsch thought something this serious might or could actually happen, but he was still surprisingly shocked, He had represented Morelli in two other drug cases and there was never a problem between them. He owed Ari his freedom for horse-trading with government agencies, including the IRS and DEA."

Pay the income tax on the drug profits and I'll try to cut a deal," Hirsch had told Morelli, a dope-smuggling wise guy who was also a professional crackhead. Both times, Ari was successful with the feds and Morelli skated from doing time.

"So why would Morelli now want me dead?" he asked himself.

He knew standing in for someone that high up in organized crime certainly had its financial rewards. He also knew of its many personal pitfalls, and this was, without question, one of them.

Those kinds of deals were second nature to Ari because he knew the system so well. He didn't spend seven years as a Special Agent for the U.S. Internal Revenue Service and waste his time learning zip.

"How'd you get this information, Bob?" Hirsch asked in a slightly friendlier, more moderate spirit. He knew he needed to keep calm; it was the only way he would be able to decrease the severity of the literal jolt.

"Got it on tape, Ari. The bureau's had a wiretap on his phone ever since he was jammed up."

Two months prior, Morelli had posted a five hundred-thousand-dollar bond within hours of his apprehension by the feds and the seizure of the cocaine. He was once again a free man but confronting almost certain indictment during the upcoming special session of a federal grand jury. "We recorded it two hours ago. The conversation is between Morelli and Jimmy Spazzini, one of his goombahs. Wanna hear it?" Ari Hirsch didn't give it a second thought, nor did he care if the tap was legal or illegal. "I'm all ears."

"I'll call you back in a few minutes. Stay put. Do not leave your office. Make sure you lock the doors. If you don't do as I say, you're a dead man."

CHAPTER TWO

"Amid the clichés of the drug war, our country has lost sight of the scientific facts. Amid the frantic rhetoric of our leaders, we've become blind to reality. The War on Drugs, as it is currently fought, is too expensive, and too inhumane. But nothing will change until someone has the courage to stand up and say what so many politicians privately know, The War on Drugs has failed."

Walter Cronkite, American broadcast journalist

42 Minutes Later-3:42 PM, Friday, June 17, 1988

BAD NEWS, WORSE NEWS

Immediately after the call, Ari told Stacy to take off the rest of the day, slumped in his chair and became as still as the Florida air. He had carefully locked the door behind her as his eyes followed her happily wiggle her way to the elevator foyer. But now he was in the office and frighteningly alone.

His entire body tensed but managed to cool down from the air conditioning that almost all south Floridians used year-round, Beads of cold worry-sweat appeared across his forehead and dripped down his cheeks until they fell off the edges of his face.

The tick of the clock resting on Hirsch's desk appeared to get louder and louder with each passing second as he nervously waited for the phone to ring. When "line four" finally did, he immediately grabbed the receiver.

"Ari Hirsch speaking."

"Yeah, Ari, it's Bob. Are you ready to listen to the tape?"

"Go ahead, Bob."

As Sewell started the recorder, Hirsch got a sharp pain in the pit of his stomach, a sign of his being unready for what he was about to hear. As the tape began to roll, it felt as though someone had jabbed him with a pointy object, like a six-inch, stainless-steel ice pick.

"Hey, Spazzini, is that you?"

"Yeah, who's this?"

"It's Morelli. No small talk. Just listen. We have a problem that needs to be taken care of."

"What kinda problem?"

"Hirsch."

"Ari Hirsch?"

"No, Hershey Bar. What the fuck is wrong with you? Yeah, Ari Hirsch! He's trouble."

"What's the beef?"

"You remember what happened to Carmine Nardelli in Providence last year? I want the same thing to happen to Hirsch." Morelli was alluding to one of the heads of the New England mob who one year before was blown to miniscule fragments by a bomb rigged to detonate when he started his two-month-old stretch Cadillac de Ville.

The police found a bloody hand and head more than a hundred feet from where the explosion occurred. Nardelli's carcass was missing both. Ten fingers and a frowning face lying on the ground in pools of rusty-colored blood.

"Are you fuckin' nuts? That guy's helped you more than your own mother!"

Despite the mild protest, Morelli knew Spazzini – appropriately baptized Jimmy "The Fuse" because of his expertise in pyrotechnics – would carry out his demand, He had too much on him and Jimmy knew it. Besides, killing people was Spazzini's regular day-and-night job, including weekends.

"I think Hirsch is gonna sing on me come next week."

"Flip on ya? You're flippin' on yourself! Hirsch never gave up anyone!"

"Do it tonight, Spazzini. Do it tonight. You know where he lives. In his Jag, and make sure it's the right car. You owe me, Jimmy."

"What's in it for me?"

"Ten grand."

"I'll get it done."

Simple enough for someone who loved money more than life itself.

The jaw-dropping, brazen conversation between the two gangsters clicked off as Sewell unhooked the connection between the tape recorder and the phone.

"Do you believe me now, Ari?" asked Sewell. Once he played the taped conversation, the fifty-eight-year-old with thirty-one years of agency experience, knew Hirsch would be petrified. At least enough to get Ari to agree with what the FBI had in mind.

Hirsch recognized a grave situation. This one came with a shovel.

"What do I do from here?"

"It's bad news, worse news, Ari, and you only have the two choices, First, the worse news. You can do nothing and die. The bad news is that we can put you into witness protection."

"WitSec? Over my dead body, Sewell!" Jesus, that was the wrong thing to say.

"That's still the worse news, Ari. Take it from me. Your life as a lawyer is over. So, take advantage of us helping you start a new one in a different part of the country. You know the game and all its rules. Get to a new location so we don't have to scrape your flesh and bone fragments from your driveway."

Ari thought of a third alternative but quickly dismissed it. "I could find a hiding spot on my own, but they'll get me for certain," He knew Morelli's hit squad wouldn't rest until Hirsch became dust. The option of being in the Federal Witness Protection Program, commonly called WitSec, came as no surprise to Ari. Not at all. He was aware that any honorable federal agent who had knowledge of a potential murder was, by government policy, compelled to notify the person in danger and offer sanctuary.

What they were not obligated to do was reveal where or when someone entering the program would be hidden. Nor did they have to tell anyone the disposition of charges against the conspirators, in this case Morelli and Spazzini.

Living in the open and not being murdered would be difficult, After all, the kingpin of Colombia's Medellin drug cartel, Pablo Escobar, had assassinated more than twelve-hundred people throughout his years of running 80 percent of Latin America's trafficking, His butchers had eradicated more than two-hundred judges, including many who sat on the bench of his country's Supreme Court, top-ranked police officials, dozens of journalists, and three of Colombia's presidential candidates.

Even Escobar's own attorneys died on his orders,

How could Ari Hirsch think he might be safe? He didn't. And Sewell's cold, straightforward manner made him feel even less secure.

"You really mean WitSec, don't you?" Hirsch inquired.

"You know that's exactly what I mean, Ari. WitSec is the only way you're going to stay alive. And you know as well as anyone that it's always the last choice in keeping someone breathing. But before I call in the U.S. Marshals, you need to make the decision to get in or stay out, and you don't have much time."

"How much time?"

"It's already run out."

CHAPTER THREE

"Prohibition will work great injury to the cause of temperance. It is a species of intemperance within itself, for it goes beyond the bounds of reason in that it attempts to control a man's appetite by legislation and makes a crime out of things that are not crimes. A Prohibition law strikes a blow at the very principles upon which our government was founded."

Abraham Lincoln, Sixteenth President of the U.S.

6 Years and 11 Months Earlier - 9:15 PM, Friday, May 8, 1981

ARI, SANDRA, AND THE FLORIDA BAR

If Aristotle Einshtein Hirsch had been born a horse, he'd have been a Thoroughbred. He wasn't only hot-blooded but possessed agility, speed, spirit, and strength. He never ever quit - not even after he crossed the finish line whether it was in the classroom or on the athletic field. Any of his high school, college or law school classmates could have told you Ari was the ultimate competitor. For that matter, his drug-smuggling clients would have testified to that as well. Sixty-two of them, in fact, had become permanent fixtures in WitSec after agreeing to sweetheart plea deals. Most of them served little or no time behind bars because of negotiations executed and finalized between Ari and various policing agencies.

In return, the buyers of his services were willing to testify against the overlords and more important figures in drug organizations. Typically, they also agreed to plead guilty to lesser charges of federal income tax evasion. They entered WitSec and completely avoided the greater risk of being murdered in an out-of-control drug war. Since the program had been authorized in 1970, no witness out of the approximately seventy-five hundred who had become WitSec members had ever been assassinated – if all the strict rules had been followed.

In addition to being an officer of the court, Ari Hirsch was a legal commando who had smoother moves than a toreador's cape. He was fearless. Not numb-and-dumb fearless, simply fearless. He demanded attorneys, including him, uphold the U.S. Constitution. At all times. In all cases, No passes, No free rides.

But the War on Drugs eventually took its toll. With vast amounts of money involved, the legal system became insanely corrupt. High standards quickly eroded and dribbled off the lips of the scales of justice. That spillage included large numbers of venal and dishonest government agencies, courts, bureaucrats, and politicians. It especially affected South Florida where the media had endless headlines and broadcasts of police, judges and other public officials arrested for bribery and other felonies related to the illicit junk trade.

"Government is a trust, and the officers of the government are trustees; and both the trust and the trustees are created for the benefit of the people." That quote, spoken by U.S. Senator, Speaker of the House, and brilliant orator, Henry Clay, was Ari's Holy Grail.

He had engraved a brass-and-wood plaque with those words and hung it on his office wall next to his law degree to serve as a reminder to live up to the maxim voiced by the nineteenth century American statesman.

"Trust everybody but make sure you cut the cards," was another way Ari operated; he played with an honest hand and wanted to keep his adversaries scrupulous as well. Nevertheless, he always saved the aces inside his sleeve for uncommon occasions.

In the 1970s and 1980s Ari had a blue-chip reputation as one of the best tax lawyers east of the Western Continental Divide, He had graduated near the top of his law school class. He also held the title of Certified Public Accountant.

A seven-year stint as an Internal Revenue Service Special Agent permitted him the distinct ability of completely understanding the most complicated of cases from every vantage point of the legal roundtable, an edge not enjoyed by most prosecutors, defense attorneys or even judges.

If his heart was the bullet in a gun, his brain was the trigger. In addition, it certainly didn't hurt that he had an intelligence level that qualified him to become a member of MENSA. His strength came from the gene pool of his Eastern European ancestors. They were the ones who had to fight and claw their way to self-determination to escape nationally sponsored hatred of Jews and friendly neighbors who thought the Chosen People needed to suffer and die for their heresy.

They made their way to America during the wave of nineteenth-century immigration and passed their genetic predisposition for survival to their kids. One of the youngsters was Murray Hirsch, Ari's dad. Murray was tougher than a fifty-nine-cent stick of beef jerky. As a member of Company B, Seventh Division of the highly respected U.S. Cavalry, he served his country well.

Stationed at Fort Riley, Kansas, in 1920 he was among the last of America's warriors to ride horseback. He had the distinct ability to shoot a weapon while atop his steed galloping at full speed. When he returned in 1923 to Camp Dix in his home state of New Jersey, Murray captured the Golden Gloves Championship in the U.S. Army's lightweight division.

But he was no lightweight out of the ring. In 1948, when a couple of miscreants called him a "dirty Jew bastard" in front of eight-year-old Ari, Murray pummeled the punks with the ferocity of a trio of elephants trampling through a circus audience. Nobody but nobody screwed with Murray Hirsch. If someone did, they never forgot.

Ari never forgot, either. The lessons he learned from that single encounter were twofold. First, be proud of your heritage and second, stand tall and stick to your principles. He knew his father stayed true to his ideals, true to his beliefs and true to his commitments.

The incident invaded Ari's psyche and made him that much more aware of his father's resolve. He closely guarded photos of Murray handsomely attired in full Army regalia atop his Cavalry chestnut. How Ari loved looking at Murray's perfectly erect posture on his horse, his leather leggings wrapped around his pegged pants, and garter belts surrounding his muscular arms. To cap it, Murray wore his World War I campaign hat held tightly by a chinstrap.

Two other photos showed his dad and his opponent squaring off in the pugilism competition, which at that time required intense endurance because the matches had unlimited numbers of rounds.

One couldn't tell if the photos were of Murray or Ari since both looked like Kinko's had duplicated them. Both had long, strong facial features, with deep-set hazel eyes that glinted when light hit them at certain angles. Their eyebrows were as thick as full-grown moustaches, and their heads of brown, frizzy, French Poodle-like hair always rejected all but the most toothless of combs.

His Uncle Sidney's Purple Heart was also part of Ari's memorabilia collection of his family, along with the wallet that was in his uncle's back pocket when he got blown to scraps by a World War II Nazi projectile, He had been one of the first ground troops to land in Italy in 1943, Murray's brother had paid the ultimate price in service to America by sacrificing his life under the command of General George S. Patton. Patriotism came easy but living came hard for the Hirsch family, Murray, not well-schooled himself, made the inevitable decision that his offspring would be the recipients of the best possible education, which he thought was the second most important thing to mortal beings.

First was family.

He did everything he could do to provide for the household, which included driving a laundry truck to make ends meet when the family moved to Miami from New Jersey in 1950. He taught his sons to be independent and close to one another. They returned the favor in kind by becoming successful lawyers and business partners. Enough to make a dad's chest pop the buttons off his shirt.

Unfortunately, the younger son, Stan, died tragically when a cement truck went out of control and rolled his Corvette in a head-on collision in the mid 1980s. Adversity aside, Ari thrived, but his first marriage didn't. Financial success came easy, but coping with the trials and travails of his constant contact with narcotics characters while juggling his personal life and professional obligations became a tale of woe. He and Barbara decided to remove their respective wedding bands sixteen years and two kids later.

Ari began living his life alone, except for the times when he positively thought he could break the record of basketball legend Wilt Chamberlain by scoring more loose women in a lifetime than he did hooping free throws. Considering that Ari married quite young and was now free of connubial bliss, he took care not to rebound. After some years of being more peripatetic than the Harlem Globetrotters, Ari met Sandra. One Friday evening in the middle of spring 1981, after spending several months dating women who wore short shorts and flaunted varicose veins, he walked into a busy South Florida cocktail lounge. Ari made his way through the crowd to the bar and sat down next to what he perceived was a "person of interest."

"Hi. My name's Ari and my recently deceased aunt left me $20 million in a trust fund, I can't touch the money unless I get married by the end of next month. Care to talk, beautiful?"

"Sure," said Sandra without cracking the slightest smile, while her girlfriend sitting next to her swallowed an ice cube whole, "but the hundreds might get in the way of my two-thousand ounces of gold bullion. Besides, my Rottweiler is guarding the vault, and no one can get near it except me. Unless, of course, you have the balls of a pit bull. Do you, Ari?"

"Before we talk about cojones, can you at least tell me your name?" Ari asked with a smile.

"Sandra. Not Sandy. Sandra."

"Got it. And by the way, Sandra, who are you here with?"

"Your aunt's money" she said, then followed it with a bountiful laugh.

"So, tell me about your nerve, Ari. If you really have it, flaunt it. Not the money. The audacity."

"I'm really not that audacious," Ari whispered after taking a swallow of his Harvey Wallbanger, noticing Sandra was not wearing a gold band or diamond ring on the fourth finger of her left hand. "Only determined. Tell me, are you here looking for Mr. Right?"

"No, Mr. Wrong, I'm here with my girlfriend relaxing, And you? Why are you here?"

"It's more comfortable than staying home alone." Ari was surprised and uncomfortable with his own honesty. "How often do you stay home alone?" That question dug deep, primarily because Ari rarely stayed in his oceanfront condo by himself.

"Probably not enough," Ari admitted.

The conversation became a bit more probing as Ari and Sandra opened it up to a much deeper and more intense conversation. Sandra's girlfriend, Victoria, picked up quickly on the situation. Her sensitivity told her the two were getting into a much more sober-sided exchange and there was no way she wanted to be a spoiler. Victoria finished her drink, paid her tab, and departed – "excuse me but I have to go home and water my terrarium" – leaving the two of them alone.

Victoria had been right. Ari and Sandra instinctively knew they had stumbled on a new relationship that wasn't about to begin and end at the Florida bar. In fact, it never ended.

Within sixty days, they were playing house in Ari's condo, and had fallen impossibly in love with one another. Neither of them knew they would wind up putting their lives into the clutches of the U.S. government some seven years later.

When Sandra Elizabeth Hayes was eight, her parents packed the house, took their Snow White and drifted south over the Canadian U.S. border. Sandra was thirteen years younger than Ari but looked twenty years younger because of her petite, athletic appearance, and wrinkle-free face. She had lived in the United States for more than two decades.

Her family traded bitter-cold winter mornings along Nova Scotia's Bay of Fundy, maple leaves and hockey pucks for sunshine and tropical beaches, palm fronds and the War on Drugs in South Florida. After graduating high school in the "Venice of America" – Fort Lauderdale got the nametag because of its manmade parallel canals like its Italian sister city – Sandra spent two years at Florida State University in Tallahassee studying Beer Swigging 101.

Her fundamentalist Baptist parents urgently requested Sandra to find her messiah in the form of a husband and become an ordained housewife. Much to their chagrin, she didn't bear that cross. When Sandra's mom died in 1986 from cancer, Alvin Tucker Hayes did what he thought was Biblically correct; he married his widow's sister nine months after she passed. Alvin was Biblically correct since the holy book mandates that a man marry his deceased brother's widow.

Even though he was befuddled at times, Alvin was a self-taught engineer for one of the world's largest jet aviation manufacturers but thought education for women was a waste of precious resources. All women really needed were Jesus, marriage, and their husbands to lord over.

Sandra must not have paid close attention. She dropped out of college and successively become a hairdresser, bartender, commodities' broker, and headhunter. Not the kind who shrank from the top one places in management and executive positions. Her ability to match candidates with clients led to more success than she'd ever experienced.

But dad wasn't happy with his daughter. Not because she withdrew from college, but after all that experience, she still hadn't found a spouse. Besides, she served liquor to strangers, Rumor was she even drank the Devil's Brew herself occasionally.

Sandra had an abundance of traits that could have qualified her for becoming another Mother Teresa, Joan of Arc, Dian Fossey, or a lion tamer. She could have charmed the stripes off a zebra or the tail of a rattlesnake, easy assignments for a woman who was born under the sign of Leo. Ambitious, confident, and generous to a fault, her loyalty was as unwavering as a guide dog. Although she may have been stubborn at times, Sandra was by contrast encouraging with Ari, a quality that fit her personality as easily as a T-shirt, jeans and sandals fit her body and feet.

Her happiness came from knowing she was totally capable of being independently successful but recognized the need for periodic reinforcement and someone special like Ari by her side. To him, Sandra was the ultimate friend, someone who was eminently forgiving, and who perennially lifted him spiritually and emotionally. Sandra was hard not to like. There was no tension, no personal agenda, no dwelling on things she couldn't fix. She also had a keen sense of people's differences, making her accepting of almost anyone. In return, everyone embraced her for who she was and not who they wanted her to be.

Her warmth and enthusiasm immediately attracted people. Allies were Sandra's specialty because of her desire to help, whether it was personally or in whatever endeavor or task she undertook.

Whomever Sandra met acknowledged her joie de vivre, her sense of balance, her ultimate friendship.

Determined never to fail at anything, Sandra had more pride than a family of lions. She ruled over a kingdom that she avidly protected and cherished. That included her business life and her existence with Ari.

He was attracted to her wit and charm, but she was also very easy on the eyes. Intuitively, he knew he could never make her better than she was because of her insistence on doing it herself. Sandra wanted to be the best at everything she did, including her attempts to make all things right.

Ari knew quickly that Sandra would make an excellent partner because she gave him almost total affection and communicated a deep love, he had never experienced but that made him feel good about his reason for being. At times, she may have been stoic, but was kind, supportive, flexible, and had a desire for adventure like no other woman he had ever met, Between the two, there was enough passion to make their heads spin like a twister in the middle of Nebraska, enough energy to take their relationship to new levels, and enough fire to light up the stage at a Rolling Stones concert. The bottom line was that she loved Ari deeply and, in a way, she had never loved anyone else in her life.

She wasn't about to let that go.

CHAPTER FOUR

"Western governments...will lose the war against dealers unless efforts are switched to prevention and therapy...All penalties for drug users should be dropped...Making drug abuse a crime is useless and even dangerous...Every year we seize more and more drugs and arrest more and more dealers but at the same time the quantity available in our countries still increases...Police are losing the drug battle worldwide."

Raymond Kendall, Former Secretary-General of Interpol

6 Years and 11 Months Later - 4:44 PM, Friday, June 17, 1988

WELCOME TO CLUB WITSEC

Sandra answered the phone at the condo, "Sweetheart, we need to talk. Anyone else at home other than you?" Ari was calling from his office.

"Nope. No one here except me and the cockroaches. "Florida was famous for those creepy invertebrates. "What do we need to talk about?"

"Us," Ari suggested somberly.

"What about us?" Sandra asked, "This sounds wonderfully mysterious."

"A moment ago, I hung up with the FBI chief for South Florida. You're not going to like what he told me, Sandra," he said in a notably heavy timbre.

"Pray tell me, Ari." Sandra never knew when he was teasing.

"They want to put me into WitSec," he responded quietly.

"What the hell is WitSec?" she asked.

"It's the Federal Witness Protection Program."

"What are you talking about? Is this a joke?" Now, she was palpably disturbed and agitated. She knew Ari had many clients who might have broken the law, but she knew nothing of how deeply he was involved in defending them. Notably drug traffickers.

"It's as serious as my life," Ari said in a tone Sandra had never heard from him. "One of my clients is going to be indicted for drug smuggling in three days and is planning to put a bomb in my car, similar to the one that took out Carmine Nardelli last year."

"How could that possibly be," Sandra questioned, "when you're his attorney?" She remembered Ari telling her about the infamous Nardelli case. She had actually seen the aftermath of the assassination on the evening network news the day it happened.

"I may be his lawyer, but this is for real, Sandra, The South Florida FBI chief called a little while ago and played a tape the bureau recorded on a phone tap. The client was talking to one of his gang associates and told him I knew too much, that he couldn't leave himself exposed for fear I might testify against him and tell what I know.

"He's afraid he'll go away for twenty-five years if the feds uncover the information I have. They were planning to plant the bomb tonight, like terrorists!"

"You're really serious about this, aren't you Ari?"

"Unfortunately, I am."

"Doesn't this guy know you wouldn't say a word? What the hell is going to happen to us? Are they taking you into protective custody? How long will you be gone? How did you get into this, anyway? Shit, Ari, didn't you know the risks? What the hell were you thinking?" Sandra fired questions at Ari faster than he could respond.

"You're asking too many questions, Sandra, and there's not enough time to answer them all. The FBI is telling me to leave right now, tonight. If I don't, my life is over. Maybe not by a car bomb, but they'll find another way sooner or later." This was the scariest moment of his life, and Sandra knew it. "My folks will fall apart if they see another son die – by a Mafia hit man, no less."

"Where are they taking you?"

"I don't know yet, Sandra. Right now, I'm in danger, can't even come home and I have no idea where I'm going, All I know is that I have to get out of here fast and not look back. Once I get into WitSee, I can't get out."

"Ari, I'm going with you," Sandra demanded, "You are not leaving me behind."

"No way, Sandra. Being in hiding is no way for you to live. That's crazy. You might never see your father or sister or friends again. Get on with your life, Sandra. You can do a lot better than staying with me."

"I didn't get into this relationship for a temporary fling. My future is with you, Ari, and I'm staying with you for as long as it takes to get our lives together. You have no choice." "My life has no meaning right now, Sandra, and yours does," Ari said unconvincingly, "I have no idea where or how I'm going, what I'll be doing, when or if I'm ever coming back, and I can't pull you into this bottomless pit.

"There's a drug war going on, and there are dragnets everywhere. I need to bail out to keep my sanity and my earthly existence. If this client doesn't get me, another paranoid, coke-crazed one will. I can't take you with me, Sandra."

"The hell you can't! I'm packing some bags and we're leaving together you son-of a-bitch, and don't ever tell me what to do or who and how to love."

Within hours, Ari and Sandra were passengers in exile on a jet plane flying to an unknown destination with the FBI acting as federal agents, travel agents and chaperones.

And for what might be the only time in American history, a CPA, attorney, and former IRS Special Agent, all rolled into one character, entered WitSec. He and Sandra began new lives and remained self-muzzled and incognito more than twenty years later.

What led to the banishment, however, had begun almost a decade-and-a-half earlier.

CHAPTER FIVE

"Alcohol didn't cause the high crime rates of the 20s and 30s, Prohibition did. And drugs do not cause today's alarming crime rates, but drug prohibition does."

James C. Paine, U.S. District Court Judge

14 Years and 2 Months Earlier - 1:05 PM, Sunday, April 14, 1974

ARI AND THE SUNTAN MAN

The Bronze-Tone sales representative permanently colored Ari's life, and in return, Ari saved his skin. Before he ever began representing an endless wave of clients involved in the drug war, the thirty-four-year-old legal whiz had become a highly skilled, versatile tax attorney handling high-profile cases. He administered corporate mergers, acquisitions, and spin-offs as seamlessly as he planned the transition of multimillion-dollar estates.

He was proficient at formulating pension plans and tax shelters. Plus, he was every doctor's financial best friend since he knew how to make medical professionals judgment proof. That all changed when Kenny Cooper topped ten miles over the speed limit in tiny Golden Beach, a spit of land in Dade County one mile long and four blocks wide with a grand total of nine-hundred-thirty-two, money-flushed residents,

The townspeople didn't take well to people driving more than the twenty-five-miles-an-hour speed limit through their tiny barrier island, bordered on the east by the Atlantic Ocean and the west by the Intracoastal Waterway.

Hallandale Beach pointed due north and the condo canyon of North Miami Beach and Sunny Isles lay south.

Inhabitants of the upscale coastal enclave paid their cops well to stop anyone from putting the pedal to the metal, even if it was a gentle push to twenty-six miles an hour. Most outsiders in the area knew if their speedometer went beyond the legal requirements in Golden Beach, they'd wind up paying a substantial fine, not to mention a hefty increase in their insurance premiums. Strangers rolling along A1A, the ocean road that ran through the middle of town, became easy bullseyes in the speed trap and Kenny Cooper was the ultimate stranger. He had never even heard of Golden Beach, much less crossed its boundaries.

It turned out to be the most bizarre Sunday afternoon drive he had ever taken.

As the needle on his speedometer hit thirty-five-miles-an-hour, he saw the red lights atop a squad car swirling in his rear-view mirror and a reflection of what was in store. "License and registration," boomed the voice of the constable as Cooper rolled down the driver's side window of the bright-white, bucket-seated 1974 Pontiac Bonneville ragtop he was driving.

"Did I do somethin' wrong, officer?"

"Hold the questions for the judge and step out of the car."

Cooper, the Key West rep for Bronze-Tone – which promised both sexes the "The Most Stunning Fun-Tan Under The Sun" – knew this cop spelled and smelled trouble. He located the registration in the cars glove compartment, exited the car, then pulled out his billfold from a back pocket and fumbled for his license.

"Thank goodness it's valid, "Cooper muttered to himself as he handed it over.

The man in blue – in truth, the police wore short-sleeve white shirts in Golden Beach – stuck his head inside the vehicle to look around for anything suspicious. It wasn't what he saw but what he sniffed that grabbed his attention.

The heavy and distinct odor of high-grade marijuana was quite familiar to the officer, who had engaged in taking a toke or two every now and then with some of his police pals. Most of what they smoked was easily "borrowed" from a couple of low-level pot dealers they knew as off-duty officers. But now he was on the job and had to enforce the law.

Like the schmuck that he was, Cooper had smoked a joint on the jaunt and didn't bother to open the windows or put down the convertible top to air out the vehicle. Bad Kenny, bad.

"Put your hands behind your back," the cop bellowed as he grabbed the suspect by his collar and threw him against the car. Cooper complied. He had no choice. This was his first arrest, and he didn't even know why. There was zero evidence of "Mary Jane" in the interior of the car, and he felt secure the only thing he could get detained for was a speeding violation.

As much as he tried to convince himself there was nothing to be concerned about, he was petrified when they slapped the adjustable silver-colored hoops on his hairy, boney wrists. The officer searched inside the car for any leftover grass, roaches or seeds and pushed the interior switch that unlatched the trunk. It was then the cop unearthed the jackpot, but it wasn't cannabis or any form of it. There, sitting in neatly stacked piles and rubber-banded, were more twenty-dollar bills than either one of them had ever seen.

"Shit, officer, it's not even my car. What the hell is all that cash doin' in there? It's not mine, damn it. I swear to God it's not mine! Hey, take these cuffs off. They're killin' me. Come on, cut me a break here."

He might as well have been talking to a granite headstone.

Two back-up officers arrived faster than they could say "Look at those Andrew Jacksons," assessed the situation after sealing off the town with "Police Crime Scene - Do Not Cross" yellow ribbons cut from a spool, then began counting the money.

Right there on the side of the road. Peeling off bill after bill and enumerating aloud, they wrote down the amount contained in each mound and tossed them into police-issued duffel bags.

Twenty minutes later, traffic began to back up both north and south of Golden Beach. Irate drivers began blowing their horns. That was always a sign of impatience and arrogance by New Yorkers. The ones who made the annual "snowbird" pilgrimage to that area to roast in the sun and visit family and friends who had moved there to escape the crime, pollution, traffic jams, and people honking their horns.

A couple of them cursed at the police trying to control traffic and were cited for "verbal abuse of a police officer," a no-no in the hamlet. Some of them were unlucky enough to get on-the-spot citations for breaking the anti-noise ordinance, while others received them for making illegal U-turns. All required court appearances or the payment of a large fine plus court costs. Whoops! There go the insurance rates.

It was enough money to fill the ticket quota of the City of Hallandale Beach for a month, and a sizable bonus for Dade County deputies at the other end of Golden Beach.

After five-and a-half hours and hundreds of onlookers and stalled cars later, the trinity of cops stopped counting at exactly $1.5 million after finally running out of crisp, green bills.

The "cash register" was empty and so was the feeling Cooper had in his stomach.

He sat in the hot police car until they finished the detailed accounting, hands behind him still clasped together with chromium shackles.

By the time they reached the mid-point in tallying, there were journalists from every newspaper, TV, and radio station in Dade and Broward Counties clamoring to chronicle the events and claim their fifteen minutes of fame, or infamy. The story made it all the way to the three dominant national networks, which aired the events on their evening newscasts. Several television stations sent up their two-seater Bell helicopters to record the action in full, vivid color.

At the time, the incident was one of the biggest money-busts in the history of South Florida, but puny as compared to later takedowns.

"Chaotic, unruly and comical" was how one reporter described it on the eleven o'clock news, accompanied by aerial views of three-mile-long caravans of vehicles on both sides of town. Golden Beachers Find Green Gold screamed a headline in one of the dailies, while another announced Cops Cop Cash, Can't Cop Crop, an obvious reference to the police's inability to find any illegal substances anywhere at the "crime" scene.

Poor Cooper couldn't catch a hungry catfish in a ten-gallon aquarium using jumbo shrimp as bait on a drop-line hook.

He was always an empty bottle in the suntan lotion industry, and for that matter any business in which the forty-three-year-old *schlemiel* was ever employed; there were at least a dozen. He could barely explain what SPF meant, which was perhaps one of the many reasons he was the lowest producer among one-hundred-sixty-seven Bronze-Tone reps across fifty states minus Alaska. The company had given him one of the hottest suntan markets in America, the Florida Keys or as the locals called it, "The Conch Republic." But he was such an inferior salesman he might as well have been peddling the greasy tan oil to the nomads of Lapland.

A likeable enough guy, Cooper often picked up some extra bucks doing odd jobs. Sometimes really odd. Like this one. A small-time weed hustler Cooper knew asked him if he'd like to make a quick five grand. He also told the lotion "specialist" he would forgive the past-due debt for fourteen joints of potent pot that Cooper had bought from him.

"Are you trying to be funny? Five grand? Tell me what I have to do," Kenny urged his pal, "My rent is two weeks late and I don't have it. This'll get me healthy." Cooper could never get healthy. The two-hundred-twenty pounds clinging to his five foot-seven-inch frame was enough beef to cause some serious cardiac damage. Especially with a daily diet of mayonnaise-soaked eggs, one-hundred-fifty-one proof Bacardi Añejo rum, random amounts of pocket rocket, and no exercise, although he believed chasing women was a noteworthy part of physical training.

"Tomorrow morning, I want you to take a car to the Sea Point Plaza high-rise in Hallandale Beach and park it in the underground garage in spot number 145. I'll give you the address in the morning. You'll see a bright red, 1973 Chevy Impala in parking place number 146. The keys will be in the ignition. All you gotta do is swap out the Pontiac for the Chevy and bring it back. I'll give you the five grand when you return. Got it?"

Cooper bobbed his head north and south and wrote down the information so he wouldn't get confused. He was also speechless thinking that amount of cash would be in his hands in less than a day.

"Whatever you do, do not look in the trunk of the car because you'll break a special seal that's placed inside. If the wrong people find out you poked your nose in the wrong spot, there could be trouble. You don't want to disappoint them, do you Coop?" Cooper quickly shook his head side to side as his shoulder-length, bleached-blonde hair slapped back and forth over his shoulders and ears.

Cooper, dressed in white-tattered beachcomber shorts, palm-fronded tropical shirt and teal-blue flip-flops picked up the Pontiac the next morning. He jotted down the street address and directions and headed north along the Overseas Highway for the four-and-a-half-hour jaunt to Hallandale Beach.

Too bad he had to drive through Golden Beach before he got there. The array of tagged, twin-locked bags landed in the police vehicles, as did Coop. Headquarters was two short blocks away and that's where the human and financial contents got driven. One of the cops took the Bonneville to the precinct and parked it in the small, beach-sand-coated parking lot.

The last thing the residents of the wealthy settlement wanted was a lot of publicity, The chief of police summoned the sixty-two-year-old mayor, who had been enjoying Sunday evening cocktails and dinner at his chichi country club three miles away with his wife and another couple who lived in the exclusive ghetto.

"Hizzoner" appeared at the station house wearing the mandatory cuff-less madras pants, light blue golf shirt-with-alligator-logo, and dark blue Arnold Palmer Palm Beach blazer. His white, patent leather shoes matched his belt to perfection.

"We have to get rid of this money." The mayor was more than slightly serious, "Call the sheriff's office and have them take it off our hands. We don't need any more exposure. And for God's sake, get it out of the jail cell – and him, too!" he hollered as he waved his right-hand index finger at Cooper who by now was sitting quietly with the cuffs still on his wrists.

Yes, the big blue duffels and the Coop were behind bars, all incarcerated and causing prison overcrowding. There was nowhere else to put the cash except in one of the two six-by-nine-foot cells; they could barely squeeze anybody in the one stall bathroom when the structure was built twenty years prior, let alone have a safe big enough in which to stuff that amount of bagged money. The police vault was slightly smaller than a sixty-nine-dollar microwave oven.

Cooper sat there in silence until the cops began to throw question after question at him, Other than saying he wanted an attorney, he refused to talk, Clammed up tighter than an over-size cork in a bottle of champagne. Nevertheless, he was charged with a few misdemeanors but nothing more serious than speeding. Yeah, he had a lot of money in the car, but that wasn't a crime.

Within an hour, Dade County sheriffs' vehicles came screaming into Golden Beach, moved the cash into an evidence van and Cooper into a Ford cruiser.

They deposited Cooper in a holding cell at the county corrections center, and stowed the cash filled bags in the property room. A deputy sheriff put the funds into the department's official account the next morning, figuring the department would hold it in trust for whoever owned it.

That would later turn out to be a bad move for the sheriff and a great maneuver for Cooper. A bank officer informed the Miami office of the IRS about the large deposit, which was standard operating procedure in these kinds of cases. In turn, the tax guys served "jeopardy assessment" papers, under Section 6851 of the Internal Revenue Code, on the Dade County Sheriff's Department.

The IRS wanted its "rightful share" of the taxes due on the money, which was immediately frozen, and that was that. If the agency deemed the money came from unknown sources, the money had to be taxed at the highest possible rate. If no one claimed the cash, the government would keep all of it. Orders for the assessment came directly from the heads of field offices for the Internal Revenue Service, which had intelligence, audit and collection specialists spread throughout the area to determine if the agency was in danger of losing tax money. One such occurrence made international headlines.

When a heavyweight championship boxing match took place in a Dade County arena, federal meddlers heard that one of the fighters was about to be paid in cash and might leave the United States without forking over the taxes that were due.

He was victorious in the fight for the crown, but knocked out by the feds when they confiscated his entire purse of more than $1 million stashed in his suitcase at the Miami International Airport. The new champ was waiting to catch his flight to Europe.

He went home with the championship boxing belt but had no need for a money belt because his pockets were as empty as his previously filled suitcase. Dead broke, the champ never recovered as much as a kroner.

Meanwhile, a cell became Cooper's part-time coop. With zero cash – his "delivery service" fee hadn't been paid – he couldn't even post bail. He didn't have enough cash to buy another joint or get himself out of the joint.

At Monday's 9:30 AM arraignment, the presiding judge appointed Martin Markell, a public defender, to represent Cooper. Charges against Cooper included speeding and reckless driving. Markell, a fifty something idealist who soon would become a financial mercenary, filed a motion for delay. He notified the presiding judge he needed more time to find and consult with a tax attorney to evaluate the cash seizure by the sheriff's office and the IRS.

Most judges didn't enjoy stepping on the stubby, grubby fingers and toes of the federal revenue department. However, this case was different.

Upon careful examination of the file, Judge Paul Fields determined there were sufficient funds in control of the government, and a bond on minor traffic violations was "outrageous." The assistant state attorneys ground their teeth when the judge released Cooper. Fortunately for Kenny, there was no evidence to charge him with any other crime.

The very next morning, a lawyer friend of Markell suggested he contact Ari Hirsch who he described as a "former IRS Special Agent, CPA, and tax attorney who knew all the machinations of jeopardy assessment cases from both sides of the legal fence."

"Good morning, Hirsch and Hirsch. How may I help you?"

"Ari Hirsch, please."

"May I ask who's calling?"

"Martin Markell from the Dade County Public Defender's office."

"One moment please, I'll see if he's available."

Markell wondered if this was another one of his legal colleagues who was always "in a meeting" but who he had to call several times before Hirsch would grant him the courtesy of a conversation.

"Mr. Markell, this is Ari Hirsch."

Somewhat surprised at the quick response, Markell said, "Thank you for taking my call, Mr. Hirsch. I'd like to make an appointment to see you with a client of mine who desperately needs help."

"Can you tell me a little about the case?"

"It's pretty involved, but here's the scenario."

Markell summarized the situation in a bit more than five minutes. Ari had it figured out before the public defender, known by his associates and clients as "the M&M man" because of his initials, even finished his explanation of what Hirsch had already perceived to be a simple case.

"I'll have my receptionist give you the address and directions. Can you and your client be in my office this afternoon at three?" Ari asked.

"On the dot," Markell replied.

At precisely 3:00 PM, Markell and Cooper entered the top floor suite of Hirsch & Hirsch, introduced themselves to the receptionist, then took side by side seats while she proclaimed their presence to Hirsch after knocking on and opening Ari's closed office door.

"Have them come right in, please," Hirsch told her, as he stood up to formally greet them.

After the usual business amenities – "Nice to meet you; please sit down; thanks for seeing us in such an expeditious manner; care for a cold drink?" – they got down to money business. Within thirty minutes, Markell articulated full details of the case. Cooper chimed in with irrelevancies whenever he felt it was necessary, which was about every fifteen seconds, until his counselor politely told him not to speak. Ari determined Cooper's intelligence level was twenty cents short of a dollar and that he appeared to be a never-was has-been.

"What I failed to mention on the phone, Mr. Hirsch, is that Mr. Cooper has absolutely no cash," Markell offered, "He's also going to be out of a job because of this occurrence." Cooper nodded in agreement. Markell explained that Cooper was staying with him and his wife for the time being. They had taken him in as a result of his dire straits, that of being a resident of Tap City. Neither did they want him wandering the streets or standing in line at the Brothers of the Good Shepherd homeless shelter.

Nice guy that Markell.

What Markell also mentioned was that regardless of his public defender status, Mr. Cooper had promised him a share of the proceeds.

Was Markell crazy? How could he get away with that? No law license pulled? Why was he telling Hirsch? Ari figured he was another one of the locals on two payrolls he had heard about so often. What he didn't figure was that Markell would soon leave his public defender post and become personal counsel to Cooper.

"We're going to attempt to recover Mr. Cooper's money," said Ari with an air of confidence, "and I think we'll be successful." He had lots of experience in these kinds of cases and knew exactly what buttons to push to get the money out of the IRS "pawn shop."

"First, we have to determine whose money it is and if it's not yours" – Ari was looking straight at Cooper – "I need to know who I'm representing. In addition, the IRS has close to five hundred different forms to recover the million-and-a-half. We have to identify the right one and have it signed by the owner of the cash, Barring that, the government will deny the claim and keep the money. We're going to presume it belongs to Mr. Cooper," Markell said. "But if it's drug money, how is he going to claim it?"

"That's the way Al Capone and other criminals got away with it," Hirsch answered. "He voluntarily reported his vast, illegally obtained income every year and filed it under 'Miscellaneous Income' on Schedule E. He was more religious about filing his taxes correctly than he was at attending church,"

By allowing Capone to file in this manner, it set a precedent for other tax cheats, including some of Ari's bookmaker clients, "Lots of people earn money and don't report to the IRS how they made it. As long as the agency gets its money, it couldn't care less where it came from." His clients had few worries that the revenue service would ever seize their assets.

Drug dealers and smugglers, whose activities in the early 1970s began to garner millions upon millions in cash, also paid their taxes to the federal government via the same method as Capone.

As their business boomed, so did Ari's.

Over the years Hirsch liked telling his clients a tongue in cheek story about his dad helping Capone with "laundering" but never divulging it wasn't "money laundering "The mobster used Murray Hirsch's pick-up laundry and dry-cleaning service when "Scarface" stayed at his winter home on Palm Island off the MacArthur Causeway on Miami Beach, Capone was the biggest tipper on Murray's route.

"Mr. Cooper…"

"You can call me Kenny or Coop. Mr. Cooper sounds too stuffy."

"Coop, the owner needs to file a special return for a partial tax year under an obscure IRS code which allows him or her to prepay income tax on the seized money and explain how it was earned," Hirsch said, knowing it was probably way over Cooper's level of understanding.

"Huh?" grunted Cooper. Comprehending what Ari illustrated was about at the same level of Kenny's understanding of Greek mythology.

"I get it," said Markell. "I'll explain it to you later, Coop. Right now, we need to move ahead with Mr. Hirsch's advice. Please continue Mr. Hirsch."

"Once I prepare an income tax return disclosing miscellaneous income of $1.5 million, l will file it with the Internal Revenue, arrange for payment of the taxes, secure a final settlement, and obtain a refund. The balance, minus legal fees and expenses, will go to the rightful owner. If it's you, Coop, you'll have to sign the filing declaring you're the owner."

The "refund" was more money than Cooper could even calculate.

It was then that Cooper finally came clean about the ownership, "There are some guys in the Keys it belongs to, but they'll flee to Central

America if I tell 'em they must sign a tax document to get the money back. Who knows what they'll do to me for getting them into this mess?"

"Explain the situation to them," Ari suggested, "and let them know this is their only choice. Get back to me after you speak and meet with them, and we'll proceed accordingly."

"Meet with 'em, hell! They'll kill me on the spot!"

"No, they won't, Coop. They're not going to risk their freedom by signing a document affirming ownership of the car in which the money was found," said Ari. "They also know they can't get the money without claiming it belongs to them and they won't want any part of that. Getting rid of you does them no good at all because then they'll have a murder rap to deal with.

"Neither do they want their pictures hanging on post office walls saying Wanted for Murder, Dead or Alive, $50,000 Reward."

"Mind if Mr. Cooper and I have a confidential talking your conference room?" Markell asked.

They followed Ari into the cherry-paneled meeting quarters and took seats in two of the twelve leather swivel chairs surrounding the oval table. Exactly enough seats for a jury and enough privacy to discuss the alternatives.

Ari went back to his office.

"Look, Coop, if Hirsch says nothing is going to happen, take him at his word. Don't give me a hard time on this or I'll walk away from the deal. Agree to it or I sail."

He knew he had his client in a corner. Cooper appeared disturbed enough to leap from the eighteenth floor. He didn't answer. He got up from his chair, paced the forest-green carpet for several minutes, then told Markell he would try it "Hirsch's way." The two men returned to Ari's office and consented to the process. Cooper was too chicken to commit suicide and besides, it might hurt.

"Fine," said Ari, "Go back into the meeting room for about an hour while I prepare documents for your friends to sign. The receptionist will get you some cold Cokes. There's a TV behind the pull-down screen, so go in and relax."

"Relax? How the fuck can I relax? "Cooper asked Hirsch.

Seventy minutes later, Cooper and Markell left the office with the documents Hirsch had drawn and cruised to Markell's house where Coop called his drug buds. They already knew what had happened from TV reports and they were more than a bit pissed.

Cooper told one of them he needed to speak with them face-to-face. They agreed to meet with him in one of their bungalows in Key West the next afternoon,

Markell had managed to recover the Bonneville from the Golden Beach cops that very morning, a much easier task than dealing with either the sheriff's office or the feds particularly since the town wanted nothing to do with the case. Determining there were no drugs in the vehicle, the department quickly gave in to Markell's demand of returning it.

Cooper asked Markell for fifty bucks, enough to fill and refill the tank in the event he needed to get it back to Broward County from Key West.

"At least if I'm still breathing," he asserted. He had a few dollars left over for a box of Twinkies and a six-pack for the trip home. A six-pack of Seven-Up, that is. After taking ten milligrams of Valium he pilfered from his host's medicine cabinet, Cooper got a decent night's sleep and awakened at 6:30 AM.

After showering, shaving, and getting dressed, he walked out of Markell's house, hopped in the car, and headed straight toward a McDonald's for two cups of black coffee; one to drink there and one to take with him as he headed south to the Keys.

Slowly.

CHAPTER SIX

"The government is good at job creation. Every arrest of a drug dealer creates a new high-paying job opening."

Pete Guither, American drug policy reformer

3 Days Later - 1:30 PM, Wednesday, April 17, 1974

SURPRISE, SURPRISE

When Cooper arrived at the seaside cottage, he didn't have to knock. His "friends" were expecting him, and he was right on time. As he entered, his three pals made him take off every stitch of clothing. Standing there as naked as the day he was born.

Coop was searched from his hair to his toenails and every body cavity in between.

They weren't looking for drugs, but a bug, not the kind you kill with Raid but the type that records voices. Finding nothing in the empty spaces but skin and hair, they informed Cooper they didn't know anything about the money.

"How could they not know anything?" Cooper asked himself. As long as they didn't whack him, he wasn't probing. They never even asked Cooper to explain what happened. They already knew enough from watching the tube.

"We were doing a favor for a friend, and he's already back in Costa Rica We had no idea what was in the car except from the television reports," one of them said.

"Is he serious?" reasoned Cooper silently. As long as he was off the hook, that's what mattered most. Eliminating him was now off the table.

"He paid us fifteen grand to get it delivered, and we were gonna give you five to get it done. Now, you get nothin' and we're keepin' it all 'cause you fucked-up the score. We searched you because we wanted to make sure you didn't rat us out."

"How could I squeal on you when I didn't know any of this?" Cooper asked.

"This is your puzzle now, Coop, so put the pieces together," one of them said. "We don't know anything, and we don't wanna. We're gonna make believe it never happened. No fuckin' way we're gettin' involved with the feds, and we'll deal with our Costa Rican friend later."

"Well, then, the least you can do is sign a paper transferring the ownership of the car to me.," Cooper said but not without a quiver in his voice.

"There's been enough trouble with the cops already. I don't need another highway stop and not be able to prove I own the car. If one of you takes the car and gets pulled over, you're gonna be right back where you started and cause yourselves a lot of grief."

Cooper stood there scratching his facial stubble waiting for a response.

"What do we have to sign?" someone in the group asked Cooper.

"I'm goin' out to the car to get the transfer of title documents." Cooper walked outside to the car. From the glove compartment he pulled the papers Ari had prepared and walked back into the house.

"It's a formality. Sign it with your friend's name," Cooper said. The spokesman for the trio immediately scribbled a name on the documents, which not only transferred the ownership to Cooper but waived all rights to the contents of the vehicle.

Perhaps Cooper wasn't as dumb as he projected. He now owned the car and its contents, "owned" being the operative word. A few days before, he was trying to sell suntan lotion to drug stores, souvenir shops and tourist traps, and now he was ready to become the not-so-humble winner of a $1.5 million payoff, although still in the possession of the IRS.

Even Cooper couldn't believe how he got so luck struck. For the first time in his years on the planet, he thought he was heading for the bonanza window, the one that had a sign over it declaring Winners Line. After he got the necessary signature, he said "bye-bye" to his three associates who by now were delighted with getting themselves out of a potentially giant predicament. Cooper was waiting to tell someone about the secret sting and get his hands on the money.

He didn't know how much he'd wind up with, but he knew it would be a better payoff than he'd ever received in his life.

Cooper never bothered to go back to his own one-room apartment. Instead, he got into the Bonneville, steered it to the closest gas station to fill the tank, headed for the nearest pay phone, dropped a couple of coins in the slot, and dialed a Broward County number.

"Marty, I'm comin' back right now! Wait till you hear what happened. You're not gonna believe this one!"

"Hold it a second, Coop. You've only been down there for a couple of hours. Give me a hint about what happ—"

Before he could finish the word, Marty heard a click He sat back patiently in his office, scratched his mostly bald, silver-edged pate, and wondered what had occurred two-hundred miles away, He decided to go home and await Cooper's arrival.

The entire ride back, Kenny couldn't stop thinking about the loot he was going to have. He'd lowered the convertible top and was singing his favorite song, *Blowin' in the Wind*, which was a perfect description of how his hair was acting.

He glided along U.S. 1, then took I-95 north to Hollywood Boulevard, turned west five blocks and hung a right into the upscale community of Emerald Hills. He pulled into Mr. and Mrs. Martin Markell's driveway at 6:47 PM.

Marty was already at the front door to greet him.

CHAPTER SEVEN

"Making our whole society a prison would not bring success to this floundering War on Drugs. Sinister motives of the profiteers and gangsters along with prevailing public ignorance, keep this futile war going, Illegal and artificially high-price drugs drive the underworld to produce, sell and profit from this social depravity. Failure to recognize that drug addiction, like alcoholism, is a disease rather than a crime, encourage the drug warriors in efforts that have not and will not ever work."

Rep. Ron Paul, R-Texas, Physician, author, and U.S. Presidential candidate.

1 Day Later - 7:05 AM, Thursday, April 18, 1974

PLANNING THE PLAN

The very next day, Ari's office phone rang a few minutes past 7:00 AM.

"Mr. Hirsch? Marty Markell. We need to see you right away. For obvious reasons, I don't want to be too late getting to my own office. Can we come over now?"

Ari was used to going to work early practically every day. He didn't require more than a few hours' sleep a night, and because of his active practice, he was always trying to play catch-up on his workload. He didn't expect the majority of the firm's partners and staff to match his daily 7:00 AM arrival time so he usually was alone for at least an hour-and-a-half before others began to show up for work.

"Yes, Marty. I was expecting your call, but not so soon."

"Seems like Cooper has what we need to get it done. He showed up at the house last night and we're ready to come over to see you. How 'bout it? We can be there in twenty to thirty minutes."

"Fine. I'll clear my desk and meet you downstairs. The doors to the building stay locked until eight o'clock. See you in a bit." Ari had to review more briefs than a Hanes underwear assembly line inspector but wanted to wrap up the Cooper caper as quickly as possible.

It meant a lot of money to the firm. Not that Hirsch & Hirsch was hurting financially, but the capital infusion meant it might be able to take on a sixth partner and grow the practice even more. At the age of thirty-four, Ari knew he and his brother could create a much larger firm than the thirty-one employees they already had.

He believed they were still in the embryonic stage of augmentation. They were two of the best tax and securities legal professionals in the state, and South Florida was populating faster than builders could construct housing, schools, and highways for the massive and growing vehicular traffic.

And the drug traffic.

Ari walked downstairs at seven thirty and saw Cooper and Markell heading for the front entrance of the glass clad edifice. He unlatched the front door, and the three of them got in a waiting elevator, which lifted them to the top floor in less than fifteen seconds.

They went into the privacy of Ari's office. Cooper hurriedly communicated the story to Ari who intuitively knew what the results would be. Although he predicted the bottom line, he still thought the way it went down was like watching and cackling through a Three Stooges routine.

"You're a fortunate man, Cooper. I guess you'll never have to worry about selling Bronze-Tone again. How'd you get messed up in this thing anyway?" asked Ari.

"To tell you the truth, Mr. Hirsch, I'm so hopelessly in debt I had to make some money. When five grand was on the table, I couldn't turn it down. I suspected somethin' was wrong with the deal, but I really didn't have a clue about what was in the trunk. I've never been involved with anything like this.

"When I came to you a few days ago, it was the first time in my life I was ever in an attorney's office, except when I got divorced. What an awful feelin' I had bein' in trouble with the law.

"Locked up like an animal in the zoo. Except $1.5 million was sitting next to me! I didn't know what the hell to think. Thank goodness for Marty findin' you.

"Both of you now know I was the fall guy if anything had gone wrong, but now it looks like it might work out. I can tell you I'm still broke but I feel like there's some light at the end of this black hole I've been sucked into' cause of you and Marty doin' what you're doin' for me."

"As long as Marty and I get your full cooperation, I don't think there'll be any hitches, but you have to do as we say or it'll fall apart," Ari said.

"Mr. Hirsch, right now l owe my life to you, I'll do anything you say."

"The compliment's not necessary, but I appreciate it, Kenny. What I'd like you to do now is sign a current income tax return confirming a gross income of $1.5 million with a tax liability of six-hundred-thousand dollars. The return also shows the IRS seized $1.5 million in prepaid income tax, but if we fork over the tax on the income, you'll get a refund of nine-hundred thousand.

"Our fees and expenses total approximately a quarter-of-a-million, meaning that if we do collect, you'll receive a check for around six-hundred-fifty thousand. Not bad for a few days' work and overnight shelter in jail."

"Not bad? How 'bout in-fucking-credible? From five grand to six-hundred-fifty grand cause I was over the speed limit! How fucked up is that? Ha! I think I'll zoom through Golden Beach again," Cooper said playfully.

He immediately signed the tax return, the fee arrangement agreement, and the assignment of the tax refund for deposit into the Hirsch & Hirsch trust account. Cooper also inked his signature on a limited power of attorney authorizing Ari to represent him in front of the IRS.

Hirsch explained one last issue. Civil, Criminal and Collection Division IRS agents would interview Cooper as owner of the cash. He also might have to appear before an attorney from the Department of Justice.

"What are they gonna ask me and what should I tell them?" Cooper was catching the drift.

"Give them your name and social security number *only*," Ari said. "Don't answer any other questions. If they ask any, I'll object and invoke your Fifth Amendment right to remain silent. You won't have to say anything else. You'll simply sit there and let me take care of it."

"I've heard of the Fifth Amendment, but what does it actually say?" For all intents and purposes, Cooper couldn't tell anyone what any amendment said.

"Let me read it to you, Kenny" Ari pulled a sheet of paper out of a desk drawer and recited it verbatim:

"No person shall be held to answer for a capital, or otherwise infamous crime, unless on a presentment or indictment of a Grand Jury, except in cases arising in the land or naval forces, or in the Militia, when in actual service in time of War or public danger; nor shall any person be subject for the same offense to be twice put in jeopardy of life or limb; nor shall be compelled in any criminal case to be a witness against himself, nor be deprived of life, liberty, or property, without due process of law; nor shall private property be taken for public use, without just compensation."

Ari disclosed to Markell and Cooper a private revenue ruling issued by the IRS, which permitted the federal taxing authority to presume that the collection of tax is in jeopardy if an individual is in physical control of more than ten-thousand dollars in cash or its equivalent.

"That money can be legally seized," Hirsch said. "As specified in Section 1 of the Internal Revenue code, it's likely to be treated as gross income and taxed at the highest possible rate." Cooper's head was spinning like he had terminal vertigo. He had never experienced anything of this magnitude or this complicated. He had gone from meaningless job to less-meaningless job feeling like the abject failure he was.

He arrived in Key West days after he had quit selling city tours in Charleston, South Carolina. Partying every night, Cooper took in the sunsets with several Tequila Sunrises and futilely tried selling suntan lotion to people who wanted to buy it as much as they wanted to suffer third-degree sunburns.

Now, he felt his life had taken an incredible turn of one-hundred-eighty degrees, twice the average summer temperature in Key West.

The paperwork signed, Ari called the IRS representative in the agency's collection department, as well as the Southern District Tax Section Chief of the U.S. Department of Justice. He arranged for the filing of a short period return and the turning over of the excess taxes. Hirsch also gave his assurance that Cooper would be available to both agencies for questioning. The arrangement included an immediate refund of the excess taxes paid on the reported income. Ari checked his calendar and made an appointment to meet with the two government reps, with Cooper and Markell in tow, at the IRS office in Miami at 1:30 PM the next day.

This might be over sooner than anyone thought.

CHAPTER EIGHT

"The prestige of government has undoubtedly been lowered considerably by the Prohibition law, For nothing is more destructive of respect for the government and the law of the land than passing laws which cannot be enforced."

Albert Einstein, American physicist and Nobel Prize Laureate

1 Day Later - 1:20 PM, Friday, April 19, 1974

ARI MAKES THE LIST

Marty knew the location of the IRS offices and drove there with Cooper as his passenger, Ari took his own wheels. Both cars pulled into the parking lot ten minutes before the scheduled meeting, giving the occupants a few moments to review the strategy Ari had established.

"Don't answer any questions beyond your name and social security number. Remember that, Cooper, and it'll go effortlessly." Hirsch told Kenny in an attempt to keep him calm.

Cooper appeared as edgy as an outlaw about to hang from a tree branch, but as long as his two legal "rabbis" surrounded him, he felt blessed and a bit more comfortable. They walked into the revenue service's front door and introduced themselves to the receptionist who led them to the interview room. It was large enough to seat a least ten and Spartan enough to feel like military barracks.

A rather stiff-looking six-footer about forty years old walked in and described himself as "U.S. Attorney Roger LaSalle. I'm head of the district Tax Section for the DOJ."

Hirsch was expecting only IRS agents, but they decided to bring in a Department of Justice back-up hitter, all dressed up in Ivy League finery. Hirsch was completely surprised, but not rattled, that they had brought in a heavy weapon.

LaSalle's presence signified this was an important case, certainly large enough to warrant inserting one of the department's most respected tax experts. A combo attorney and CPA, LaSalle took the lead on very special assignments and proceedings that would put the DOJ in the national spotlight and further his own career. Who knew? One day he might even become the U.S. Attorney-General. His ambitions were obvious, given his philosophy of always locking up as many citizens as he could.

Ari, Marty, and Cooper introduced themselves but the unambiguous chill in the air made the room feel like a January day in Maine. This was clearly not a meeting among good friends. A moment later, in came the civil- and criminal-investigation IRS agents. They went through the same meaningless exercise of telling everyone in the room who they were.

Prior to being duly sworn in, Ari took Cooper aside to tell him the interview was being audio- and video-taped, and that Kenny was paying a court reporter out of his potential proceeds to record the conversations and have them transcribed.

The reporter sat about four feet in back and adjacent to the table with her stenotype machine perched atop a skinny metal stand, high enough for everyone in the room to guess she was about a twenty-five-year-old natural blonde. Her tight blue skirt stopped four inches above her knees. She displayed a prime pair of legs in a county that prided itself on female attributes.

Her waist was so tiny that her enormous breasts housed behind her white, partially buttoned blouse cast a shadow over her reporting equipment. What made it difficult for her to type were those long, beautifully manicured nails, but who cared if it distracted the attention of the IRS and DOJ?

Naturally, Ari had hired her, He had always employed various people based on not only their skills, but also how they might look. He called it "softening the market. "In this case, it was probably hardening the market."

The interview began.

LaSalle asked Cooper his name and Cooper, for the record, said,

"Kenneth J. Cooper. The J stands for Joseph."

"Why did you have so much cash in the car, Mr. Cooper?"

Ari immediately injected, "My client wishes to invoke his Fifth Amendment rights and remain silent. He will answer no questions other than his name and social security number."

They knew trying to get him to talk would be about as useful as putting a sweater on a penguin.

The three feds suspended the interview, got up to leave and told Hirsch, Markell, and Cooper they would be back in fifteen minutes.

Building relationships with both sides of the law were crucial. Hirsch knew his alliances with policing agencies and his clients had to have a foundation of trust even if it was shaky. There were times it was difficult to achieve, but it was a continuing process, not a one-time occurrence, that would persuade each side to reach an outcome best for all involved. With a bit of luck, the results would manifest themselves even prior to the adversaries' head-to-head meeting.

Recognition of one's own power and the circumvention of becoming docile and deferential were meaningful. Ari remembered those things from law school. *"Illegitemi non carborundum"* one of his litigation professors would tell him, "Don't let the bastards grind you down. Find the best and most correct information you can dig up and use it."

Ari's thinking went from wanting approval to getting approval from state and federal agencies whenever he made deals on behalf of his clients. Finding out how they worked from the inside out was one of Ari's strongest advantages, having worked nationwide for years as an IRS

Special Agent. That experience embellished his chances for successful negotiations. He had the insight to understand the upside and the downside prior to discussing a deal and expected mutual respect, which often was difficult to get from government bureaucrats.

Their sense of give-and-take was "you give us what we want, and we'll take it." He rarely conceded because he knew it would destroy his ability to carve out settlements in the future thereby reducing his worth to clients.

LaSalle returned twenty minutes later and presented Ari with an envelope. Inside was a cashier's check for nine-hundred-thousand dollars payable to Hirsch's trust account and authorized by the head of the Internal Revenue Service's South Florida office, The final words were a "thank you" from Hirsch to the agents.

Cooper almost fainted and Markell practically urinated in his pants. Now it was a reality.

Once Ari cut Cooper a check, he would be filthy rich. He could hardly contain his emotions when he and Markell got back to their car. Once inside, Cooper screamed, "I'm fucking rich! Do you hear me, Marty? I'm fucking rich!" He repeated the same phrase no less than twenty-five times.

Markell didn't mind the noise. He knew his client could and would parlay the money into a lot more and by default make much more for him. All Coop needed was some "seed" money to begin his next career, His recently acquired assets were enough to feed a lot of pigeons.

As Ari left the IRS complex, LaSalle followed him to his car. Before Hirsch could open the door and get in, the DOJ attorney pointed his index finger in Ari's face.

With his teeth clenched as tight as the stenographer's skirt, LaSalle said in a restrained but diabolical voice, "You're now officially on our hit list, Hirsch. We're going to get your ass, and you know when we say were going to get you, we always do. How you can possibly protect someone like that scumbag is beyond all comprehension.

"And lining your pockets while you're doing it! Remember, make one tiny mistake and you're as good as gone, That's a government promise."

Those words would come back to haunt Ari Hirsch. Many times.

Without fluttering an eyelash, Ari got behind the wheel and pulled out of the yellow-striped, asphalt parking lot. He returned to his office prior to Markell and Cooper and instructed his bookkeeper to make out a check in the amount of six-hundred-forty-nine-thousand dollars to Kenneth J. Cooper.

He also gave her the government's check for nine-hundred thousand dollars and instructed her to deposit it into his escrow account "immediately." Within five minutes, Markell and Cooper arrived, all smiles. Ari gave Cooper the check and asked him not to deposit it "until Monday afternoon, after the government's check clears my bank."

Hirsch took no chances with federally issued financial instruments. He knew they could bounce the same height as any other rubber check. He also told Cooper he had deducted one thousand dollars for expenses from the settlement.

Cooper and Markell left Ari's office and headed straight for the nearest bar. Even though it was only three-fifteen, they started their weekend celebration early. Marty paid the tab since Cooper still didn't have enough to pay for a beer on tap. "Besides," thought Marty, "Cooper's going to be my client for a long, long time."

Monday morning Cooper headed back to Key West. With more than six-hundred-thousand dollars in his control, he was already planning his financial future. Even with having to fork over fifty-grand to Markell, he was loaded beyond his wildest dreams.

At three o'clock, he arrived at the Key West Bank of Commerce where he had a balance of forty-one dollars and twenty cents in his account upon which he had written a batch of bad checks. He walked over to an enclosed office, introduced himself to a very attractive, youthful looking bank officer whom he had never met, and asked her to cash the check.

She looked at the phone number for Hirsch & Hirsch on the check, called the signatory, one Ari Hirsch in Fort Lauderdale, and received his vocal authorization to "cash the six-hundred-forty-nine-thousand-dollar check." Seeing he was a Florida attorney, she granted his request but not before calling Hirsch's bank to determine its validity.

"What denominations would you like that in, Mr. Cooper?" she asked after Ari's banker said, "It would be fine to cash Mr. Hirsch's check."

"All hundreds," answered Cooper in a cheery and very polite manner, "but please keep eight-hundred dollars in my personal account. I need to cover some checks I've written."

"I'll be happy to give you a receipt for the check, Mr. Cooper, because it's going to take us the rest of today and part of tomorrow to obtain that amount of cash and count it. Would it be convenient for you to come back at about 1:00 PM tomorrow?"

He had no choice but to accept the receipt and have the bank tackle what was an apparently large and cumbersome task. The bank had already been given Ari and his bank's approvals to cash it. Cooper didn't want to go through the same process with another financial institution, predominantly because the Bank of Commerce was the only one with which he had an account.

He put the receipt in his knock off Gucci wallet and walked a couple of blocks to Duval Street to get a rum and Coke at Sloppy Joe's Bar, one of America's best-known watering holes.

It was the very same establishment where Ernest Hemingway used to mix with the locals, the tourists, and the copper-bodied fishermen whose ancillary occupations became loading and unloading containers with the kinds of drugs that lots of Americans simply loved – from whacky weed to snort to Frisco speedballs.

The drug trade in the Keys was the industry of choice because of the fortunes it offered. It was easier than having to chum or throw nets into the salty sea to gather up a school of snapper, grouper, or stone crabs. Besides, drugs didn't smell nearly as bad as dead inhabitants of the ocean depths.

Cooper sat down next to a "conch" he knew by the nickname of "Alfie".

"Coop," as the drug meisters called the lotion vendor, "wanna make a big score with some of that cash you nabbed? There's a load coming in Friday night near Big Pine Key that's gonna have nose powder filled to its gunwales. Two-hundred-twenty-five kilos of the best quality cocaine anywhere – uncut, near-pure and the quality is unbeatable."

"I've never done anything like that, Alfie! Anyway, who's got that kind of money?"

Cooper purposely didn't want *anyone* to know how flushed with cash he was going to be the very next day. If someone found out, Cooper thought, morsels of his body could become more than two-hundred pounds of bait at the sharp end of fishing hooks, and his haul would be gone.

Besides, everyone knew that Cooper always had less money than the average citizen of Haiti.

"Come on, Coop. Just 'cause we live down here at the end of Florida don't mean we didn't see the news on the Golden Beach bust. You looked like you had a case of diarrhea sittin' in the squad car," he said with a chuckle.

"Knowin' you and dumb luck, I figure you walked away with somethin' specially cause you're out of the slammer. Coulda been big. You want a part of the deal or not?"

"How much a kilo?" Cooper inquired.

"Two grand,"

"Let me see if I can find a source for you. Wait here." Even if Cooper paid that amount and the deal went south, he'd still have almost a hundred-fifty thousand in his pocket if he paid for the whole load. He'd never have to worry about being in suntan lotion sales again. He walked to the Bronze-Tone office a few doors away, unlocked the street-front venue, walked in, picked up the phone, and called his manager who was headquartered in Myrtle Beach.

"Bronze-Tone. This is Tommy Draper. Can I help you?"

"No, you can't Tommy. This is Kenny Cooper. I quit my job as of three seconds ago. I'd rather throw the lotion in the ocean 'cause even the sun-in-the-fun stores ain't buyin' the greasy crap. I'll mail you the keys to the office, and any money you owe me, keep it."

He hung up the phone and never gave Tommy a chance to articulate another syllable. After locking the office door behind him – he didn't want folks to merely walk in and take their pick of *Designer Tropical Tanning Cream, Shangri-La Lotion* or *Pacific Breeze* in the handy squeeze bottle – he returned to Sloppy Joe's and his cordial companion.

Now, Cooper had another occupation and enough money to make him an overnight success. He knew that profit percentages on illegal drug sales were higher than those of the major oil companies. Besides, the best drug contacts hustled the streets of Key West as prolifically as the flesh peddlers who walked Miami's Biscayne Boulevard.

"I think I might be able to take the whole load," Cooper said.

"Hah! I knew it! A bunch of us figured you scored the big bucks."

"You're all wrong. I got some more partners. Now tell me where and when to pick it up."

"It's gonna come in on the north side of Big Pine. Friday night at eleven-forty-five. I'll take you in my van. You're gonna need to bring four-hundred-fifty thousand. Cash. No marked bills, no wires, no leaks, or they'll kill ya as fast as the cops blew away John Dillinger in front of that Chicago movie theater."

"Toss in the van and I'll do the transaction." Cooper knew Alfie was getting a big chunk for making the connection, so why not get another set of wheels for himself?

"Done. I'll pick you up at your place at nine. There might be a little traffic headin' to Miami for the weekend. I don't wanna miss the buy and neither do you,"

Cooper and his buddy stayed at the alcohol palace for a few more Cubalibres, then left the open-air bar very happy. This was going to be an illustrious and lucrative contract for both. They shook hands symbolically sealing the deal and parted ways.

Although "good fortune" was a mild idiom for what was transpiring, Cooper thought the phrase sounded a bit too oriental. He preferred to think about it as a hefty investment he had helped create, one that would provide a wonderful return.

After going home with those self-absorbed thoughts, he threw three eggs in a water-filled pot on his hotplate stove and boiled them for fifteen minutes. He cracked the shells, removed the contents, then mashed them with "mayo, hold the lettuce" and made himself a sandwich on white bread.

He turned on the tube, tuned in to continuously running episodes of The Fugitive, Gunsmoke, and I Love Lucy, then drifted off with pleasant dreams of having a vanload of money the next afternoon and a boatload of blow a few days later.

The next morning at ten, Cooper awakened with great anticipation and left his apartment feeling as though life couldn't have dealt him a better hand than the one he was holding. He strolled along the palm tree-lined streets and passed some of the restored 1920-era homes with large, sometimes lacquered terraces made of Dade pine.

He arrived at his favorite breakfast spot on Truman Avenue where he ordered the Huevos Rancheros special – he just loved eggs – and two cups of coffee.

Cooper's eyes kept focusing on his watch to make sure he'd be at the bank at exactly one o'clock. Only two hours to go. He bought the Florida Keys Keynoter and spent an hour or so reading about the previous day's drug raids as far north as Key Largo, then went on to more intellectual pursuits by reading Peanuts, Blondie, Sad Sack, and working the Jumble word puzzle.

When he returned to his apartment, Cooper pulled two mismatched, hard-sided, large empty suitcases from under his twin bed, brought them downstairs and tossed them in the trunk of his car.

It took him less than two minutes to reach the bank.

"Is the money ready?" he asked his new blonde banker-friend. "I brought a couple of suitcases with me to put it in."

"It is, Mr. Cooper. We've secured it in our vault. I'll be happy to take you in so you can transfer it."

There was no need to total it. The bank already did that, and the tabulating machine was not prone to making mistakes. This time was no different.

Cooper could barely walk out of the bank without getting a hernia because of the apparent weight of the baggage. He lugged them to the edge of the trunk of his car and struggled to get them in, but not before looking around see if there were any "spotters" a common practice among drug traffickers. They were all over the Keys looking to rip off drugs, money, or both.

He took home the two suitcases, barely made it up the stairs, and shoved them under his twin bed. The spread was king-size and flopped over the sides, hiding what was underneath. He turned on the television again and spent the rest of the afternoon playing couch potato. At six o'clock, he decided to go to the waterfront to see the always-spectacular Key West sunsets and wasn't disappointed.

At least not until he returned home.

He found his door wide open! He ran up the flight of stairs to his second-floor studio, instantly dropped to the floor to look under the bed – and discovered the suitcases were missing! Disappeared! Gone! Stolen! Taken by some "lowlife" who followed him to the bank but stayed out of sight while Cooper was inside stowing the currency.

Cooper merely smirked a smirk that only Cooper could smirk.

A "spotter" indeed had followed him to the bank, but what the invisible burglar didn't see was the switch. Instead of putting the money in the suitcases, Cooper had the bank store all of it in its biggest safe with his name on each stack of hundred-dollar bills.

He had tugged and dragged the valises and pretended they were as heavy as marble slabs, a good way to make an unwanted observer believe there was a copious amount of money locked inside.

The banker couldn't understand why Cooper hadn't taken the loot with him. He had told her he changed his mind and to "please keep the money in the vault." She was even more bewildered when he acted like the suitcases were heavier than high-density lead.

Yes, Cooper might have had the intellect of a lobotomized turtle, but those gut impulses paid off, even if they hadn't surfaced in his cranium when the Golden Beach authorities seized him. Now he figured the danger was over because the person who tried to rob him knew Coop was onto their little game of ripping the money from his grip.

Cooper drove back to the bank and asked the "sweet young thing" bank employee to put the money in large, unmarked canvas bags, similar to those found in Wells Fargo and Brinks armored cars. It would take fifteen satchels to hold all the bills, including the fifty thousand he agreed to pay Markell and the thousand he needed for pocket change. The balance would stay in the vault. Coop informed his new-found, shapely banker he would return at 4:30 PM Friday, thirty minutes before the bank closed, to haul off the load.

Honest friends were hard to come by in Key West. Cooper had but one. A city cop, Juan de la Vega, who knew Cooper might have smoked some herb but never trafficked. Juan always cut him some slack, and Cooper gave his friend a few joints for personal use every now and then, unless he was broke. Instinctively, they trusted one another.

"Juan, I'd like you to accompany me to my bank late Friday afternoon. I have a large sum of cash in fifteen bags I want to put into my trunk, and I think I might need some protection. Would you mind?"

"Course not, Coop. What bank?"

"Bank of Commerce."

"*No problema*. What are you going to do with the dinero?"

"I've got an all-cash investment to make, Juan, and I don't want to talk about it right now. After we pick up the dough from the bank, I'd appreciate your hanging around with me until ten o'clock in front of my apartment so no one will even think of coming close."

"*Bueno*. You got it, amigo. You know you can always count on me."

"Let's meet at the bank at four-forty-five."

"*Seguro*, Coop, sure, but be careful, Things can get rough doing deals like that, I don't want to see anything happen to you."

"Not to worry, mi amigo. Everything's cool."

For the next several days, Cooper made a series of calls to Miami. He knew he needed to capitalize on his new product line by reaching the necessary contacts to do specifically that.

CHAPTER NINE

"Have you checked out...the endless loss of individual rights in the name of the drug war? When reformers point to the flaws and problems of the drug war, the warriors answer is to do more of it. More money, More guns. More authoritarian control. Isn't that the response of all addicts?"

Bill Masters, Sheriff, San Miguel County, Colorado

3 Days Later - 4:45 PM, Friday, April 26, 1974

TAKE THE MONEY AND RUN

Juan wheeled his white-with-blue-trim #567 squad car to the bank and parked directly in front to prevent any potential criminal act. A purposeful nullification. Written along both front fenders of the vehicle were the words Protecting Paradise.

Most civilians who saw it didn't know how right that was. Paradise could mean many different things to lots of different people. Within a minute, Cooper came walking around the corner, acknowledged Juan with a nod and a thumbs up, entered the one-inch-thick, glass-door entrance to the bank, and traipsed toward "Ms. Lovely-To-Look-At."

The Key West cop stayed outside and opened his trunk so it could swallow the bags of cash. Inside, Cooper dipped into one of the satchels and took out fifty-one thousand dollars – fifty for his attorney and one for him – and stuffed it into a big laundry sack he brought with him.

Within ten minutes, Cooper was rolling a flatbed trolley laden with the fifteen canvas duffels and the laundry tote out the bank's front door. He loaded them into the deep back bay of the police cruiser.

The cop looked warily around at anyone walking or driving along the street. No harm, no foul. Everything was ticking along as smoothly as a handcrafted Swiss timepiece.

The six-foot-two Juan slammed the lid shut and the pair jumped into the front seat. Two minutes later, they arrived at Cooper's two-story wooden-clad structure that was in bad need of repair. At ninety bucks a month rent, Kenny wasn't complaining.

They sat in the car and took turns going to the bathroom. The first time Cooper went up to use the "john," he filled his Mr. Coffee with water and ground beans so they'd have something to keep them from dozing off during the wait. Since Juan was now off duty and there was no rush to get the car back to the police station, he could have stayed there until the next day if necessary.

But it wasn't.

At 9:57 PM, the single occupant of a seven-year-old midnight blue Chevy van pulled behind the police car. Alfie sat motionless behind the wheel. He was somewhat uneasy and unsure if this was a set-up until Cooper got out of the passenger side of the cop cruiser, walked to the van, and told him not to be concerned.

Juan was a friend of his, he explained, and he had the money in the trunk. Alfie had little to worry about anyway because there was nothing incriminating in his vehicle or on his person. Alfie and Juan stepped out of their respective vehicles at the same moment. The three men transferred the cash-filled bags into the Chevy, Juan headed to the precinct parking lot and Alfie and Cooper headed to U.S. 1 for the half-hour trip north to Big Pine Key.

The talc-like pharmaceuticals would soon arrive aboard a fifteen-hundred-seventy-five-horse-powered, specially rigged, forty-two-foot

Cigarette that glided along the turquoise waters between The Bahamas and the lower tip of Florida.

There was heavy traffic heading both north and south on the skinny strip of highway. Some of it was the result of weekend visitors to the Keys from throughout South Florida. Others were tourists returning home or catching flights out of Miami International heading for destinations throughout the world. Still others were local residents going to Miami, Fort Lauderdale, or other cities in Florida for either personal or business reasons.

When the van arrived at Big Pine Key, Alfie took a left turn across U.S. 1 and followed the road that led to a desolate beach at the northeast corner of the island. There were twenty-nine surrounding islands, which made it difficult to navigate by boat, but they served as visual impediments to any water- or land-based police patrols.

He parked behind a thicket of scrub bushes and sea grape trees and shut the lights. Both engaged in relatively idle conversation until their synchronized watches read 11:40 PM. It was then they spotted the streamlined, custom-painted, yellow-and-red forty-two-foot watercraft. They could barely hear the three, 525-horsepower Mercruisers because the captain had purposely slowed it down to about ten knots. No sense in attracting attention.

One-third of the Cigarette ran up and partially beached itself. Alfie took hold of the two-inch-diameter hawser aboard and anchored the vessel by tying the thick rope around a large jetty boulder.

"Money first," the captain said. He was wearing a Greek fisherman's cap that made him look like the coach of a championship sponge-diving team.

Alfie opened the back door of the van. He and Cooper began throwing the sacks aboard while two of the mates, dressed in jean shorts and dark T-shirts, opened them, and began to count the stacks, already numbered with the total amount in each. Cooper was careful to leave the laundry bag inside the vehicle. The crew quickly ruffled and fanned the bills to make sure all of them were a hundred bucks each.

Satisfied it was the right amount, the two helpers offloaded the two-hundred-twenty-five kilos – at two-point-two pounds per kilo, it added up to four-hundred-ninety-five pounds – they had retrieved from hidden compartments underneath the wooden slats of the deck.

The square-shaped bundles, tightly bound in thick layers of pink Saran Wrap, made them appear lipstick red. Alfie slit open one of the packages with the tip of a pocketknife and plunged it into the coke. Licking the toot off the blade to determine if it was the real thing or a powdery substitute, Alfie declared, "Best shit I've ever tasted."

The mates tossed the dream dust into the back of the van, then pushed the bow of the boat to shove it back into the Gulf of Mexico. They jumped on the craft as they immersed themselves into knee-deep water. The anonymous captain slowly made his way to the open sea and took off like a drenched Richard Petty heading for the white-and-black checkered flag on a flooded racetrack, topping out at a speed of a hundred-and-eighteen miles per hour.

The two recipients of the bounty hopped into the van and directed it back to Key West. Cooper dropped off Alfie at Sloppy Joe's, then headed back to U.S. 1 and made his way north again, only this time all the way to Dade County.

It was slow going since the traffic had not quite subsided. Getting pulled over for a minor traffic violation was not an option, Once was enough. The "sneeze"-for-cash transaction set up by Cooper by phone the day before was a mere two days after he and Juan had gone to the bank. During his seventy-two-hour wait for the coke, Cooper located a couple of dauntless drug dealers who made frequent trips to the Keys and whom he had met at an all-night stimulant feast at a friend's house months before.

When he informed them of what he was getting his hands on, they subscribed to take it all at fifteen thousand a kilo. As major-leaguers, they knew they could hit a grand slam by cutting it and doubling their money.

Cut, re-cut and re-cut again, the profit on that amount of "candycaine" became bigger than the gross domestic product of many small, independent nations.

It was what the marketplace wanted, and this was what the industry giants felt compelled to provide.

Cooper pulled into a three-car garage attached to a residence at the end of a cul-de-sac in a gated community in Kendall, a burgeoning upper-middle-class neighborhood south of Miami. He knew he had the right address because his customers told him there would be a yellow ribbon wrapped around a ponytail palm tree planted to the right of the garage. The ribbon not only served as a symbol for Cooper but honored the soldiers who had not yet returned from the Vietnam War.

He parked inside the one open space and turned off the engine; the overhead door closed automatically. Two men came walking through the entrance leading from the kitchen to the garage.

The two recipients of the bounty hopped into the van and directed it back to Key West. Cooper dropped off Alfie at Sloppy Joe's, then headed back to U.S. 1 and made his way north again, only this time all the way to Dade County. It was slow going since the traffic had not quite subsided. Getting pulled over for a minor traffic violation was not an option.

Once was enough.

The "sneeze"-for-cash transaction set up by Cooper by phone the day before was a mere two days after he and Juan had gone to the bank.

During his seventy-two-hour wait for the coke, Cooper located a couple of dauntless drug dealers who made frequent trips to the Keys and whom he had met at an all-night stimulant feast at a friend's house months before.

When he informed them of what he was getting his hands on, they subscribed to take it all at fifteen thousand a kilo. As major-leaguers, they knew they could hit a grand slam by cutting it and doubling their money.

Cut, re-cut and re-cut again, the profit on that amount of "candycaine" became bigger than the gross domestic product of many small, independent nations.

It was what the marketplace wanted, and this was what the industry giants felt compelled to provide.

Cooper pulled into a three-car garage attached to a residence at the end of a cul-de-sac in a gated community in Kendall, a burgeoning upper-middle-class neighborhood south of Miami.

He knew he had the right address because his customers told him there would be a yellow ribbon wrapped around a ponytail palm tree planted to the right of the garage. The ribbon not only served as a symbol for Cooper but honored the soldiers who had not yet returned from the Vietnam War.

He parked inside the one open space and turned off the engine; the overhead door closed automatically. Two men came walking through the entrance leading from the kitchen to the garage.

After the mandatory handshaking, they asked Cooper if he had the goods. It was understood they wanted to make this quick. The side door to the van glided open as Cooper pulled the handle to show them the two-hundred-twenty-five kilos.

"Great," said Chuck, the taller of the two. "I'll go get the cash while Troy unloads."

While Troy removed the cocaine – he also acted as vice-president of quality control by putting it through a taste test – Chuck walked back into the house and began bringing out medium-size, unsealed, corrugated cartons with "Allied Van Lines" logos on them. Ten of them. All packed with more money than Cooper ever knew existed.

He quickly sorted through each of the boxes, sealed them with a packing tape gun provided by his joint-venture capitalists, then loaded them in the back of the van making sure he could see out the back window. He had to be careful not to alert a cop to any driving transgressions.

Within fifteen minutes, the pact was complete. They quickly shook hands again and thanked each other for the agreeable deal. Cooper backed out of the garage, turned right, arrived at U.S. 1 within five minutes, then headed south for his trip back to Key West with $3.75 million keeping him company. Plus, the fifty-one grand in the ditty bag.

Cooper began to laugh aloud as he thought about being a multimillionaire and the pitiable life-without-money he had lived all those years. The big bowl of cherry coke wasn't bad for a dope dealer who had minutes before cured his virginity, but now he thought about another issue. How was he going to pay the taxes on the income and shelter the money? He knew he was going to have to get that done as quickly as possible.

It didn't take much time to ask for help from Ari Hirsch. In fact, after Coop boasted about what a great "legal mouthpiece" and "cool counselor" Ari was, the young attorney's reputation among the drug rings, syndicates, alliances, organizations, and individuals began spreading faster than a Florida wildfire in August. While Ari was changing their lives, the government was beginning to change his. The words of Roger LaSalle, the DOJ attorney at Cooper's IRS hearing, rang true.

The feds had Hirsch on its "hit list" and wouldn't rest until they ripped him apart chunk by chunk. They knew there would be plenty of opportunities to do just that. The IRS, DEA and DOJ soon recognized that Ari was becoming the leader of a legal movement against the War on Drugs. By getting dozens upon dozens of his junk-peddling clients to voluntarily pay income taxes, they largely avoided long jail stretches.

How could the U.S. government allow that? What about all the other drug dealers who might use the same ploy and walk away with scads of money by importing and selling illicit narcotics? That simply couldn't and wouldn't stand. "Not another radical movement for this country" was the consensus in Washington. The nation had been through enough with Vietnam, so the theory went. The government, determined to impede legal tax payments and institute a new war – this one against hallucinogens – used Ari and his clients as the brake system.

But what never stopped was the drug war itself or the rapidly escalating importing of illegal substances. Throughout the years, instead of collecting billions in taxes from the traffickers, the feds chose to pour a trillion or more dollars into an unwinnable armed conflict.

With Ari Hirsch, other attorneys with the same world view, and most of their clients silenced, the feds thought they could terminate the crusade of allowing legal income tax payments by drug smugglers and handing out financial penalties but scant prison time. It might also censor the voices of those who were opposed to the ever-increasing and costly drug war.

It worked for twenty years. Despite its attempts, the government could not suppress the social and political discourse of free-thinking people. The feds would find that out in due time.

Particularly about Ari Hirsch.

CHAPTER TEN

"It is nonsense that we should be devoting so many law-enforcement resources to marijuana. I am skeptical of a society that is so tolerant of alcohol and cigarettes should come down so hard on marijuana use and send people to prison for life without parole...Prison terms in America have become appallingly long, especially for conduct that, arguably, should not be criminal at all...Only decriminalization is a sure route to a lower crime rate..."

Judge Richard Posner, U.S. Court of Appeals, Seventh Circuit

20 Days Later - 11:00 AM, Thursday, April 26, 1974

MILKING THE COW

After scoring big and carousing twenty-two hours a day for more than two weeks, Cooper made an appointment to see his tax counselor. Not for more social diversion but to seek advice on what the financial impact on the income would be. Both in the short-and long-term, he thought it would be best to err on the side of safety. Peculiar that Cooper could make a conscious decision like that.

Realistically, he didn't want any additional involvement with the IRS. Who would?

Now he could pay for Ari's advice. Markell, who drove to Key West the prior week to pick up his all-cash side-fee from Coop, endorsed Ari's consultation compensation of one-hundred dollars an hour. The return on investment and prudent advice would soon prove to be well worth the expenditure.

"I'll send Cooper to see you," Markell told Hirsch after the ex-Bronze-Tone man mentioned he thought he needed Ari's input. "Be sure to keep me in the loop. I need to know what's going on so that I can time my resignation appropriately. You knew I was going to become his full-time counsel, didn't you, Ari?"

"Yes, Marty, I had a notion you would. Are you sure that's a good idea? Shouldn't you stick it out until your retirement and not get so involved? What's your family going to think?"

"My wife's a shrew, Hirsch. All she cares about is money. This will give me an opportunity to shut her up for once. Besides, everyone I know who's ever quit this public defending shame-and-blame-game has gotten wealthy. As in multimillionaire wealthy. As in eight-figure wealthy. At my age, I finally want to be a part of something bigger than this. My days of benevolence are over."

Markell was unprepared for Cooper being his client for less than a year. He resigned his public defender's post, became Cooper's personal legal loophole, and enmeshed himself in the hallucinogenic consumables trade.

Trapped in a huge money-laundering sting initiated by the IRS and DEA in 1977, he lost his license to practice law and spent four years at the federal prison camp in Eglin, Florida.

Divorce papers were tossed into his "accommodations" after a year in the slammer, and when he was finally released, Markell became a pariah among his family, friends, and former clients.

Destitute and physically and psychologically broken, Marty Markell, the M&M man, melted. He took his own life after three months on the street by overdosing on a mixture of crack, Valium and a fifth of cheap scotch, not at all like the Chivas Regal that had always been his libation of choice.

Cooper showed up on time for his 11:00 AM appointment at the offices of Hirsch & Hirsch. Now he was dressed in a yellow, short-sleeve silk shirt and a pair of navy-blue linen slacks tightly held up by a black, lizard-skin belt. All of it had been bought at the most expensive men's boutique in Key West. He was wearing Italian loafers without socks and a fourteen-karat gold rope chain around his neck. His new cologne had him smelling like roadkill.

"When Marty and I were here a few weeks ago, Mr. Hirsch, both of us heard you talkin' to one of your clients about saving tax money. Didn't mean to snoop. The phone in the conference room was off the hook and we heard you speakin' to a client about cows that could save him some tax money."

"How many times do I have to tell that receptionist to put the phone on the hook after she calls me from that room?" Ari thought, without denigrating her aloud.

"Exactly what did you hear, Mr. Cooper?"

"Nothin' more than that, Mr. Hirsch. I assure you. It wasn't anything I did intentionally. Neither did Marty."

"Okay, Kenny. I understand. By the way, call me Ari. No need to be so formal anymore. Other than the $1.5 million on which you paid the taxes, how much have you earned this year?"

"Well, I earned a hundred-seventy-seven-fifty in commissions on the suntan lotion I sold," Cooper replied. His voice stalled for about five seconds. "Course, that didn't include what they owed me, which I told them they could keep. Bronze-Tone never did send me the check."

"And...?" Ari solicited an answer.

"Well, a bit more from a recent investment."

"Kenny, you're paying me a hundred an hour. Don't you want your money's worth?"

"Course I do!"

"Then quit playing games and tell me how much more you made this year!"

"Well, I took four-hundred-fifty thousand from the money I got from the IRS – incidentally, did I thank you for what you did for me?"

"Yes, you did, Kenny. Six or seven times. Continue."

"I turned that amount into $3.375 million, minus expenses of course."

Ari dropped his burgundy, twenty-four-karat-gold-tipped-and-barrel-banded fountain pen on his desk at the same time his mouth dropped almost to the same ink spot on which the Mont Blanc landed.

"Holy shit. I'm not even going to ask you how!" That wasn't like Ari. His decorum was highly professional, and cursing was not his normal style. "What do you mean 'less expenses'?"

"Well, I had to spend about five bucks on gas."

"Forget the five bucks. And what you overheard was not 'cows' but cattle."

"Isn't that the same thing?"

"Yes and no, but let's not worry about the distinction. My firm is part of a syndicate – call it a business enterprise – that buys feeder cattle. They can be cows, bulls, steers, heifers. They can have horns or udders. That doesn't matter.

"Here's what matters, and I want you to pay attention. Close attention."

"I always listen to you, Mr. Hirsch."

"Sure, you do, Cooper. Is that why you're still calling me 'Mr. Hirsch.'?"

Ignorance is bliss but only to the ignorant.

"Whoops, sorry Ari. Please tell me about the cows."

"We take a trip to South Texas for a week every year on behalf of some clients. We purchase mature cattle, old enough to take to a feed yard so we can fatten them up. Once they get to the desired poundage, we sell them.

"We also buy enough corn and grain in advance and deduct from your income tax the full cost of the commodities at the time you bought them. That offsets all the reported income, and you wind up paying zero taxes to the IRS for that year.

"We sell the cattle three or four months later essentially for the same amount we paid for them. Then we defer the cost of the cattle and the feed into the next tax year which for all intents and purposes is the money you've made this year.

"We've been doing this for a couple of years for some high-net-worth individuals. Not only does it work, but it's also legal. You're not going to make lots of money on the cattle sale, but you won't lose much either.

"The best part of 'milking the cow' is that you don't pay any income taxes on this year's earned income until next year."

"That's unbelievable, Ari. Can you explain it again?"

"That's not necessary, Kenny. It'll confuse you more. Once Marty hears an explanation on the phone, I'm sure he'll be satisfied with the arrangement."

After pressing the intercom switch, Ari asked his secretary to get Markell on the phone. Less than two minutes later, Ari heard, "Mr. Hirsch, Mr. Markell is on line two."

"Hello Marty. I wanted to get your okay on this tax shelter for Kenny."

"I was hoping you'd call. Let me hear all about it, Ari."

Hirsch outlined the shelter and answered several of Markell's questions.

"Do you mind if I put you on the speakerphone, Marty? I want both of you to hear what I'm going to say next. It's important."

"Not a problem."

Ari pushed the speaker control and adjusted the volume.

"The Federal Intermediate Credit Banking system works with bankers in the agricultural industry. I can get Kenny qualified for cattle acquisition loans and get 100 percent financing for the cost of the feed and feedlot charges, plus veterinary expenses. We then pay off the loan when we sell the cattle.

"Kenny has to put up a hundred bucks a head for cattle selling for five hundred a head. The financing of the balance of four hundred is likely to come from the South Texas Cattle Feeding Association which receives its loans from the Federal Intermediate Credit Banking system. Pretty straightforward, Marty, and the dollar-for-dollar write-off can't be beat.

"When you buy enough cattle, feed them and sell them, the federal government considers you a cattle rancher. If Kenny buys enough head, his investment will make him a cattle rancher."

"What's your take?" Markell asked Ari.

"Ten percent of the amount invested."

"Let me speak with Kenny. Privately."

"Go into the conference room and pick up line two, Kenny. And don't forget to put it back on the hook when you're through." Ari wasn't taking any more chances.

Within ten minutes, Cooper walked back into the office and gave Ari permission to invest $3.2 million in the cattle deal, thereby deferring almost all his income for 1974.

Cooper left himself with more than a hundred-thousand dollars in spending money, and paid Ari a fee of three-hundred-twenty-thousand dollars. Not too shabby for someone who worked for twenty-plus years and never made more than three grand in any one year, although "worked" might have been a stretch in describing Cooper's employment ethics and productivity.

"I'll wire-transfer you the money when I get back to Key West tomorrow, Ari."

"That'll be fine, Kenny. Here's our bank's transfer number." Hirsch handed Cooper a card with the information already imprinted. "However, right now we need to amend your return for this year because of the additional income."

Hirsch's plan for a tax loss backfired, if doubling your money is backfiring.

Cooper bought the feeder cattle at forty-two cents per-hundredweight. The price took off like a pebble in a slingshot, zooming to eighty-three cents by the following February. Cooper's money got cloned. Soybeans and grain skyrocketed in price as well but that didn't disturb the tax shelter because Cooper bought the feed in advance. It was financed 100 percent by Uncle Sam. Kenny Cooper was now sitting on more than $6.5 million. He threatened to quit the drug business and become a full-time cattle baron, but there was little chance of switching, not when the drug business had been so astoundingly lucrative.

Nothing could stop Cooper from attempting to make millions more. He immersed himself even further into the drug importing business, only on a larger scale. He made as much money in one day than many people earned in a lifetime – and even bought a home on Golden Beach, the island where he began his odyssey. He garnished the oceanfront mansion with a Rolls Royce, a Porsche and five other exotic cars, and even bought his own private jet.

The town's inhabitants finally found out who he was and did everything short of hiring a contract killer to get rid of him, but to no avail. Cooper took care of moving on his own, or at least with the help of the federal government.

When the feds learned Cooper concocted the cattle arrangement with Hirsch, you could hear them screaming "motherfuckers" all the way to San Antonio. Ari and his clients had become permanent government enemies, and agents would hound all of them for the rest of their lives.

For Cooper, who by now was a full-blown junkie, that wasn't a very long time.

After three busts for running drugs, he caved like a professional spelunker. He cut a deal, turned south on his cohorts, and forfeited his remaining assets. The feds sent him away to a minimum-security lock-up for eighteen months to get sober. Those satanic drugs dragged him into the snake pits of physical and emotional hell.

Upon his release, Cooper moved to his sister's ranch in South Carolina, one he had paid for with smuggling profits, and passed away at the age of forty-eight from an aortic aneurism. The DEA nailed Cooper's brother-in-law on the ranch for possessing a pot-load of grass. Seven years in jail for his indiscretion was a stiff penalty to pay. Another inmate, unfortunately, murdered him after only one year of confinement. Death by shiv.

There was one final irony. The FBI ultimately charged the Key West Police Department with running a criminal enterprise. They nabbed three high-ranking police officers and a number of other good citizens of the southernmost city in the contiguous forty-eight states, long after the Washington politicians declared the War on Drugs.

CHAPTER ELEVEN

"No drug, not even alcohol, causes the fundamental ills of society. If we're looking for the sources of our troubles, we shouldn't test people for drugs, we should test them for stupidity, ignorance, greed, and love of power."

P.J. O'Rourke, American satirist, journalist, author, and commentator

2 years and 10 months earlier - Noon, June 15, 1971

THE WAR BEGINS

Throughout the years since the War on Drugs had been officially decreed by President Richard M. Nixon in 1971, and almost three years before Cooper and Markell's sojourn began, Ari couldn't help but notice that local, state, and federal agencies were becoming as bloated as pregnant whales.

The call for more and more drug enforcement spread like an incurable virus, creating a race-for-the-money among those who had become cash-hungry government competitors. Initially, all of them were out to capture individuals and gangs involved in growing and smuggling the cash crop of grass.

That soon changed.

The amount of money from the sale of cannabis, cocaine, methamphetamines, and heroin was much more than the annual gross domestic products of many countries. Hirsch discerned that amount of cash triggered a business explosion and immense mercantile opportunities. Not only among contrabandists, pushers, and users, but for dirty cops and agents who started stealing, dealing, and wheeling, and even murdering their prey.

For a sharp observer like Hirsch, the facts were clear. The commercial enterprises were so incredibly lucrative that organized crime, which normally had a hands-off policy when it came to trafficking drugs, plunged in headfirst like Olympians diving into a swimming pool in want of a gold medal. Some of the drug enterprises got and kept the money, while a tidal wave of authorities on a global chase drowned some others.

The government hunters did not represent social welfare agencies which annually clamored for every penny from their respective authorities. They used it to help the poor, feed the hungry, create jobs, provide better education, and furnish financial and medical care for all citizens who needed those services.

The other side of the government coin consisted of agencies filled with egotistical, self-absorbed, dishonest, and oftentimes criminal elements, Ari knew. They were there for three reasons: money, money, and more money.

Whether by auto, train, bus, truck, air, boat, submarine, or other conveyance, drug traffic increased by quantum leaps, according to every government report that Ari laid his eyes on. So much so that agencies fought for more and more financial resources. It allowed them to snare more and more people who in turn provided more and more cash for the avaricious appetites of drug abusers and bribery-minded, badge-flaunting, and reckless double-crossers.

Hirsch was only beginning to understand what was happening – an all-out global assault on the illegal drug business was under way. Seized money was simply adding to the government waist.

Yes, Ari concluded, many cops were virtually double agents in this contentious blitzkrieg of human attrition, representing regimes on one hand and themselves on the other, all while the American public was paying a large price for the widespread carnage. In financial terms, in lost productivity by people imprisoned for long stretches, and by the rapid ablation of the U.S. Constitution. The Bill of Rights was fast becoming the Bill of Wrongs.

The War on Drugs became more than a few tough clashes, and even Common Sense got killed in action. There were loud calls from all corners of the political and social spectrum to "legalize and decriminalize" drug use. Hirsch formed the same opinion early in his career. There was a logical reason for that. Practically all his clients were being caught and thrown in jail regularly. Over time, almost all of them were apprehended.

From far-left liberals to ultra-right conservatives, from the educated to the illiterate. So many Americans, including the tens of millions who smoked pot daily, wanted to put the skids on what many considered an absurdity of the struggle to arrest, detain, incarcerate, and release those who had been caught.

Ari knew that education and treatment were answers put into practice in several nations, but those in power in the United States continued its flogging of the American mind and body. They refused to listen until it was too late. Government bureaucrats continued their indulgences, divided the spoils, and the chaos never stopped. Those accused needed representation and Ari Hirsch was willing to make certain he or she got his or her fair and speedy hearing. After all, he did take an oath to act as counsel to those who needed it, and that is exactly what the Constitution's Sixth Amendment provided:

"In all criminal prosecutions, the accused shall enjoy the right to a speedy and public trial, by an impartial jury of the State and district where in the crime shall have been committed, which district shall have been previously ascertained by law, and to be informed of the nature and cause of the accusation; to be confronted with the witnesses against him; to have compulsory process for obtaining witnesses in his favor, and to have the Assistance of Counsel for his defence."

Yes, there were large numbers of people calling for the end to this authoritarian insanity, but no government administration or agency ever listened, much less acted. Ari knew that no matter how widespread the criminal activity or how involved the "system" itself had become interwoven in nefarious and felonious pursuits, it was nearly impossible to stop the momentum.

The amount of taxpayer expenditures wasn't even the slightest concern. Neither was how many souls were put away for smoking a joint or doing a line of coke. Ari got it. Nobody with any power to discontinue the delirium took any steps to hold back the non-stop assaults on people's privacy, illegal searches and seizures and First Amendment Rights.

It had even reached the point where judges denied payment to lawyers, including Hirsch & Hirsch, by defendants if the fees due were assumed to be earned from drug transactions. For all intents and purposes, the drug war rules forced attorneys to work free to defend clients who either were – or were not – convicted.

Indeed, the acts of the government had convinced Hirsch it had become involved in its own version of drug trafficking during the infamous Iran-Contra scandal in the mid 1980s.

U.S. Marine Lt. Col. Oliver North, a member of the National Security Council, created and executed a plan to sell arms to Iran, which would in turn put pressure on its Hezbollah terror proxy to release six American hostages held in Lebanon.

Part of the proceeds from the weapons sales wound up in the hands of Nicaragua's anti-Sandinista guerilla movement, the Contras.

Some of the cash also wound up in the hands of several of Ari's clients who worked part-time for North.

At the end of the day, Hirsch and the rest of the world learned that the Central Intelligence Agency during Ronald Reagan's presidency provided support for the Contras by knowingly allowing cocaine to enter Los Angeles. The money from the drug sales, according to testimony, helped fund the anti-Sandinista movement.

Considering those historic events, it was uncanny that Reagan himself heralded phase two of the War on Drugs and appointed Vice-President George Herbert Walker Bush America's drug czar.

Isnas,, the base of operations for Iran-Contra was the White House in Washington DC, within a short walk of the Department of Justice and a solitary Starbucks.

CHAPTER TWELVE

"Narcotics police are an enormous, corrupt international bureaucracy...and now fund a coterie of researchers who provide them with 'scientific support...fanatics who distort the legitimate research of others... The anti-marijuana campaign is a cancerous tissue of lies, undermining law enforcement, aggravating the drug problem, depriving the sick of needed help, and suckering well-intentioned conservatives and countless frightened parents."

William F. Buckley, American author, publisher, and conservative TV commentator

27 Years and 1 Month Later - 1:50 AM, July 8, 2008

THE STARBUCKS EXPRESS

Elwood Frank Hutton hauled ass up I-95 enroute to the District of Columbia. Hauled ass? He was seventy-four-years-and-eleven-months old. How he could possibly haul ass was a complete mystery. Twenty minutes earlier, he had placed his Colt 45 – not the malt liquor, the automatic weapon – in a mildewed, brown-leather holster he had slid onto his five-buck Wal-Mart belt. Slowly, he ambled to his car outside his tired looking home on a quiet street in the faded resort town of Virginia Beach in the Commonwealth of Virginia.

The ex-FBI agent opened the driver's door, tossed his cane onto the back seat, and scrunched behind the wheel of his pasty, nine-year-old Ford Crown Victoria that was five years overdue for a muffler.

He really needed to make it to DC in time for a 6:30 AM meeting, followed by an 8:00 AM gathering at the Department of Justice. Hutton looked scornfully at his Timex chronograph - he thought wearing his gold-plated, hundred-and-fifty-buck Seiko was a bit too flashy-to make sure the pace of his four-hour trip was close to perfect. He didn't want to arrive too early or too late for his first encounter of the day. Neither did now-retired U.S. Federal Marshal Robert Fenwick Buggelshofer. One day prior to his jaunt to the nation's capital, he spent sixty-seven-fifty filling the gas tank of his 2001 white Jeep Cherokee for the two-hundred-ten-mile trip and made sure his Glock 40 was fully loaded with fresh ammo.

He, too, lived in Virginia Beach, but far enough from Hutton so that the one-time, sometime federal adversaries hadn't bumped into one another, not even accidentally, since they left government work in 1991.

Surrounded by family, friends and military bases neither chose to engage each other since retiring. Moreover, agency "territorial" disputes had created bad enough vibes between them already so why bother talking? Each took his own vehicle to reach DC chiefly because they didn't want to be seen in the same car. It was dicey enough they had even spoken on the phone in late June to set up their meeting.

Neither did they want to let old feuds get in the way of their July Fourth weekend they planned to spend with their kinfolk.

"Buggy," as Buggelshofer was known to everyone who had ever been in his company for more than an hour, knew he needed to take the fastest highway route. His short-term memory was slowly fading, but he understood well enough to take I-264, spill onto I-64, merge onto I-295, and then roll onto Interstate I-95 so he could make his way to I-395 and inside the Beltway.

Unlike Hutton, Buggelshofer had less hair than Yul Brynner, Telly Savalas and Howie Mandel combined. His vehicle's tires looked like his head and acted like his ego. Bald and deflated.

His twin Beltone hearing aids didn't help his disposition, either. He constantly complained about the "ringing reverberation inside my ear canals."

Buggelshofer and his now-deceased wife had bought a neat little three-bedroom, two-bath home in a middle-income neighborhood months before he called it a career. Emily took ill less than a year into seclusion. He solemnly buried her in a plot next to the one he had reserved for himself close to the beach.

He had three daughters in the area, along with seven grandchildren. As years went on, his grandkids left for college in other parts of the country, and his daughters and sons-in-law got a bit too busy to see "pop" more than once a month and on mandatory holidays.

While Buggelshofer waited for the Grim Reaper, he became more depressed than Wall Street investors in October 1929. At one point, he wanted to end it with his pistol, but he couldn't possibly face Jesus if he put a bullet through his brain. As a good Catholic, it was important for him to reach the Pearly Gates without too many blemishes.

His addiction to pain killers and Xanax were enough of a scar, but he figured the Holy Ghost would understand his affliction, despite the fact he had captured hundreds - even thousands of drug abusers and knew the damage those nasty habits caused.

He was about the same height as Hutton, with slightly less pork around his mid-section, but still twenty-nine pounds above his U.S. Marine Corps mass back in the 1950s. Buggelshofer's home-cooked meals stopped when Emily passed, and that kept his bulginess at a comfortable one-hundred-ninety-five pounds, without clothes and weapon, even with his daily consumption of two jumbo cups of Wendy's chili.

The three shots of daily bourbon nurtured him through the pain of a hip replacement, but he kept his friend, Jack Daniels Black, handy if he needed a fourth from the fifth. The two former agents were sweating from even thinking about their pending meeting the ninety-two-degree heat and 99 percent humidity certainly didn't help. They displayed distinct signs of wear and tear as both sped toward their seventy-fifth birthdays and their mutual destination, a coffee shop in the nation's capital.

During their two-minute covert phone conversation at the end of June, each acquiesced to meet at a convenient location. It was a spot within walking range of the Federal Bureau of Investigation's home quarters, the J. Edgar Hoover edifice along Pennsylvania Avenue, and within earshot of the Department of Justice. Dubbed "E.F." long ago, Hutton was tired and long retired from his FBI career seventeen years earlier.

His route would be identical to Buggelshofer's. Before he left, he took a big swig of Maalox as he swung out of his driveway. His stomach ulcers had returned more ferociously painful than ever. E.F. kept a gallon of the chalky substance in his car and one in his refrigerator chiefly because he was wound tighter than a size-six hat on a size-seven head. He felt so old he thought the medical community was going to cancel his blood type.

After parking his cucumber mobile in a public garage on the other side of the Potomac River near the Fourteenth Street Bridge, Hutton grabbed a non-descript taxi to take him to the previously agreed upon meeting at Starbucks on Seventh Street NW.

Hutton liked the offbeat routine. He knew that various federal policing agencies ever since the Cold War had successfully used "leapfrogging," a masterfully crafted and successful technique of trailing spies, their own surrogates, and "suspects" who J. Edgar thought deserved "attention" by the federal government. Hutton was completely aware this kind of surveillance was possible.

Dressed in his grey-suit FBI "uniform" that fit as snugly as O.J.'s glove, Hutton was completely aware that this kind of surveillance was possible.

He knew leapfrogging and wide-scale government observation were conducted by a vast army of precision-trained operatives who knew where, when, and how to nab a target. Hutton did not want to become the object of a Special Security Group's enterprise, even though he hadn't done a thing to warrant suspicion.

Times in DC had changed drastically since 9/11. The Federal Triangle, more heavily guarded than the Crown Jewels, consisted of seventy acres snuggled between the Capitol and the White House. The pie-shaped piece of land was home to dozens of prominent structures essentially housing every major government agency.

Buggelshofer wasn't about to become a statistic in a federal snag. It would have ruined his reputation. The fact was, two weeks prior to his retirement he had received one of the agency's highest honors, the President Rank of Distinguished Executive Award. He had been an important hub in the federal wheel by taking lead roles in helping fight the drug wars of the 1970s and 1980s.

Assigned to the South Florida multi-agency anti-drug task force meant he was where the most narcotics interventions and interceptions in the United States were taking place.

His job was to provide safe havens for witnesses whose lives were at great risk.

Hutton, about three inches shorter than a six-foot-tree, with a protruding belly from continual daily overdoses of pale ale, was revealing his age with more than deep wrinkles and liver spots. Skin tags smothered his chubby-cheeked face and flabby arms. His once-speedy gait significantly slowed because of two knee replacements that hadn't quite healed exactly as the doctors had predicted.

Now, he was shuffling with a pronounced gimpy limp in his left leg, aided by a sixteen-gauge aluminum cane capped at the bottom with a thick, vulcanized tip. The rubber nub softened the metallic noise as he placed it on the sidewalk in front of him with the conviction of a battle-worn infantryman with a chest full of medals.

His still-full head of hair had quickly turned from blonde brown to greyer than a Confederate uniform; his dandruff blended quite well. Hutton kept his heart arrhythmia concealed from everyone, including Annabelle, his wife of forty-eight years.

Neither did he tell his two sons. One, a financial analyst and consultant, lived with his wife and two sons in nearby Norfolk. The other was divorced and childless and lived in Chapel Hill, where he taught International Studies at the University of North Carolina.

Somehow, E.F. still managed to consistently complain to whoever would listen about the possibility of his heart making a secret attack on his thorax and thereby rendering him either totally useless, or worse. Unlike the financial firm of the same name, when E. F. Hutton spoke, nobody listened, especially now that he was grappling with far fewer years in front of him than those already booked. He felt like a twenty-nine-year-old Kentucky Derby winner let out to pasture. A stud he wasn't.

As far as he was concerned, he didn't care about names that his colleagues stuck on him as permanently as Gorilla Glue. Like E. F. "Mutton the Meathead." Or their E. F. "Sutton" allusion to the urban legend bank robber, Willie Sutton, who held up more financial institutions between the late 1920s and early 1950s than Bonnie Parker and Clyde Barrow could ever have hoped to pillage.

At Hutton's age and state of health, he really didn't give a twit about the fun people poked at him. He wasn't about to give up his way of life that brought him and his solid-citizen wife to within driving distance of the District of Columbia, not to mention being much closer to one of their bloodlines in a seaside community of their liking.

It was a place where they could inhale the salt air if the winds blew in the right direction and didn't affect Hutton's sinus condition. A spot where they could live out their memories and enjoy the companionship of a slew of retirees from the ranks of the U.S. government whom he endearingly called the "Fed Flock."

Buggelshofer pulled into the District and left his Jeep with a valet at a three-dollars-an-hour indoor garage in Georgetown. The attendant noticed the vanity license plate labeled EX-FED and figured "another bureaucrat's wheels."

He hailed a cab and told the hack to head straight to the coffee location. He was still early for his meeting with Hutton, who by now was sitting in a two-person booth and reading a sign that said, "No Seniors Can Use Wi-Fi Without Buying a Prune Danish." At least that's what entered his mind as he sat there sipping a hot latte made from a hearty Sumatra blend and two packs of Splenda. Before he entered Starbucks, Buggelshofer did a three-sixty to see exactly where the street cameras were. He spotted Homeland Security snoopers and snipers on several rooftops surveying the surroundings through their scopes. Buggy wasn't taking any sloppy chances, even at six-thirty in the morning. For all he knew there might also be parabolic microphones aimed at his lips to pick up every spoken word he uttered to himself. Somewhat satisfied their meeting would not be compromised, he caught a glimpse of Hutton, walked over to the counter, ordered a large regular coffee – "cream no sugar, thank you"— brought it to the booth and took the seat across from him.

He placed his broad-brimmed grey felt hat on the seat next to him, the same way Hutton had nestled his brown Fedora. Not only did they wear headgear; both men hid their eyes behind chocolate-colored sunglasses to avoid detection.

Even though Buggelshofer felt at ease about going unnoticed, he still became a bit edgy because of all the cameras focused on almost everything that moved in the Triangle. Hutton and Buggelshofer had not been very pleased. Summarily "drafted" by the Justice Department to work on what it described as a "top-secret case involving numerous agencies," both men knew it might be one that could fall apart faster than a Nigerian scam on videotape. The investigation needed handling with the "greatest of security and care" by "seasoned veterans" who knew most of the details and cast of characters involved in what had been a sensational story some twenty years back.

Suddenly, it took on significant importance. In other words, it was a jalapeño-pepper case, so hot, the boss said, that it had now become a question of "national economic security." Unfortunately for both, virtually every other federal agent who had worked on the file either had already been buried in a bone orchard or was too ill to take on this cold-case-turned-sizzling assignment. Employing an old but effective tactic, the government got the two to agree to return for an encore.

This was one time when the DOJ needed not only their skills but also contacts and informants who were still inhaling and exhaling. The pair may not have been as sharp as they once were, but their collective body of knowledge, certainly not their physiological bodies, were still superior to anyone else's in the U.S. Marshal Service or FBI.

Their former supervisors made it clear that despite all their claims of possible incontinence, inconvenience and special dietary needs, the small print in their retirement exit papers mentioned that if they failed to cooperate in investigations such as this, their pensions could stop immediately. Finished. Kaput. Nada. "In other words, if you don't agree, you'll both die slow financial deaths. So, take the deal and stay monetarily alive."

Kind of like being sent to Vietnam or Iraq for a fourth tour of duty.

Although neither man wanted to appear at the meeting, the feds waved fifty-thousand-dollar post-retirement bonuses at each of them, not to mention the current wage paid for their GS ratings. They also promised non-taxable per diems of two-hundred dollars and five-hundred dollars for domestic and international travel, respectively. They both needed the money like street addicts looking for another hit of black-tar heroin. They had lost much of their Golden Cow slush funds in the dot.com bust of 2000-01, in addition to some sucker investments. Plus, their weekly donations to the Virginia Lottery rendered them as nervous as two potbellied pigs in a bacon factory.

Arresting and charging the pair with losing their financial smarts might well have resulted in a plea of nolo contendere, no contest. Convictions would have been a certainty. Left with little choice, they quietly but grudgingly accepted the government's benevolent offer.

Sure, they could have taken jobs hustling tourists to buy time-share weeks at a couple of nearby beachfront resorts. Or they could have become private cops at various civic events, but neither really wanted to get back on a payroll unless their services were going to be well paid.

They reluctantly admitted the assignment had its risks, even though neither knew anything about it. That was the nature of the beast.

How could it not be risky? They weren't being called in to take charge of a government daycare center. But how could they possibly take a pass when they were both at the bottoms of their bank accounts?

The pair had been notified their appearances were not only urgently necessary, but legally mandatory at 8:00 AM, Tuesday, July 8, 2008, in a seventh-floor courtroom in the U.S. Department of Justice building. They were to be in the same chamber where the Foreign Intelligence Security Act-FISA-had been ruled upon after the 1970's Watergate scandal. Effectively, the act permitted the federal government to eavesdrop clandestinely on American citizens.

Little did authorities realize that within a few years of enacting FISA, there would be an epiphany and a paradigm shift among international drug smuggling operations. For all it was worth, FISA rulings helped create the beginnings of massive government corruption on a global scale. In addition, the murder rate in the U.S. surpassed all previous records.

More drug seizures occurred than those in an epileptic clinic. More prisoners were locked away than the populations of sizable metropolitan cities. Moreover, the introduction of Miami's Cocaine Cowboys made South Florida not only the Gateway to Latin America but the Gateway to Hell.

President Nixon had supported FISA by leading the way to enact a law resembling similar domination granted to the Star Chamber of merry old England in the fifteenth and sixteenth centuries. That bunch of medieval tyrants ran amok and trampled on the rights of anyone the British Establishment wanted to crucify.

Unlike previous eras, the American government had many more distinct advantages than the England of four-hundred years before. Arming agencies with sophisticated electronic devices to monitor criminal targets and ordinary citizens only took a modicum of money, some low-tech experts, and an on-off switch.

Invasion of privacy and denial of personal rights were of utmost importance. They became legal instruments during the drug war, gearing up to be one of the largest, costliest, and most useless programs in American history. Law enforcement had to win the cultural struggle at any cost, financial or human.

It was now time to eliminate the old rules and bring forth some new ones.

Prior to 1971, judges throughout the nation were handing down effective but short-term penalties for smuggling marijuana, whether it was called "Mexican Locoweed," "Zambi," "Panama Cut," or any one of hundreds of different names for the cannabis plant.

Everything changed when every drug pirate on and off the high seas learned of the combined one-hundred-eighteen-year slammer sentence slapped on the two masterminds of Florida's Black Tuna Gang. The cabal was a group of laidback hippies who had conspired to bring in hundreds of tons of grass.

Because of this draconian sentencing decision, traffickers faced additional risks and consequences of smuggling "Bobo." They also recognized the monstrous increase of profits awaiting them by illegally importing cocaine, heroin, and methamphetamines – and encountering the same penalties as smuggling "ganja."

They upped the ante.

Coke and meth labs got cooking in the forests of Colombia and virtually every nation in Latin America. By 1981, more than 70 percent of all marijuana and cocaine smuggled into the United States came through South Florida, turning it into Paradise Lost.

Hutton and Buggelshofer knew all that since they were willing or unwilling participants in trying to eliminate trafficking via the Florida coastline, whether it was grass, cocaine, meth, or any other illegal drug.

Both had been thoroughly indoctrinated and drilled in the zigs and zags of the illicit drug business and the Federal Witness Protection Program. Buggelshofer spent two-and-a-half decades as a deputy in WitSec, administered by the U.S. Marshal Service under the aegis of the Department of Justice's Criminal Division.

Hutton had been handed WitSec responsibilities by the FBI and spent ten years helping to launder money for protected witnesses, creating phony identities, profiling people entering the program, investigating their pact activities, and a host of other duties.

Both men knew each other well, but that was in another life at another time.

Each had to be supremely careful with this morning's meeting.

They wanted to avoid another probe at all costs. Their careers and retirement had been jeopardized in the late 1980s when they became subjects of two extensive investigations, one conducted by FBI Internal Affairs and the other by the Marshal Service's IA desk. The inquests involved their association with a lone "enlistee" of WitSec. Seems this protected witness popped up on law-enforcement computers across the country when, under Hutton's and Buggelshofer's protection, he made a seven-figure profit on a real estate deal within months of joining WitSec.

Strangely coincidental that both men worked closely with this protected witness, thought the IA snoops, but nobody ever found evidence of any wrongdoing.

How could they when there wasn't any? That was two decades ago, but Hutton and Buggelshofer still couldn't forget the escapade no matter how old they got.

CHAPTER THIRTEEN

"Let us face facts and let us not mince words: Our nation's policy of drug prohibition is not working. This policy is actually causing much more harm than the prohibited drugs themselves would ever be causing on their own-here and everywhere else around the world."

James P. Gray, Superior Court Judge, Orange County, California

19 Years and 9 Months Earlier - Noon - October 20, 1988

THE DEADWOOD DEAL

Transplanting a South Florida Jewish guy and his significant other in New York City would have been a gastronomic, cultural, and educational treasure chest for Ari and Sandra. Bagels and lox. Corned beef on rye. Broadway and Greenwich Village. Columbia and Fordham. Macy's and Bloomingdale's. Carnegie Hall and the Guggenheim. Yes, all would have been within taxi, bus, subway, or walking reach if they had been given sanctuary there.

But they weren't even close.

Predictably, their exile was thousands of miles from New York, Florida, and everywhere else on the East Coast. Instead of thriving in the Big Apple, they adapted to their new lives in a small city in the Upper Midwest of America's Great Plains. New York City alone had more than a dozen times the population than the entire state in which they were now abiding, and both were customary to big-city life.

Laughingly, they dubbed their new place of residency the Sour Raspberry. To be sure, lots of different fruits blossomed there despite the very cold weather. They plainly weren't of the tropical variety. Neither was it the sweetest spot in the country, but it certainly was a beautiful chunk of America, and they adjusted quite well to the "cowboy" lifestyle.

They transitioned from cotton clothing to wool sweaters, filet mignon to beefalo, beaches to farmland, sunshine to shiny western boots, from socially liberal attitudes to faith- based conservative values. It was a realistic if underappreciated postcard of Americana.

It wasn't long before the U.S. Marshal Service and the FBI gave them new identities, names that were far and apart from the ones their parents granted them at birth. Both received new passports, birth certificates, drivers' licenses, voter registration cards, and social security numbers under the names "Brian Goodman" and "Katherine Newsome."

Operatives of each federal agency made certain the two got decent jobs.

Instead of practicing law, Brian became a law professor at a small university prior to the fall semester of 1988. Katherine became a part-time used-car-and-truck salesperson, a free-lance hairdresser and an entrepreneur. She developed a direct mail business from their three-bedroom townhouse selling gemstones mined in the area.

With Ari and Sandra's incomes, in addition to the bank withdrawals the feds made on Hirsch's personal and company accounts, plus a healthy stipend from the Marshal's Service, they were financially well fixed.

It was easier to adapt to the foreign elements than Ari and Sandra originally had anticipated. It wasn't exactly a simple task to get to this place of peace. Nor was it a snap to get through each day living with the thought that someone might jump in front of you and put a metal projectile in your head. Unpleasant ideas sometimes crept into their minds, like strangers finding them at the base of a nine-hundred-foot rocky cliff, or perhaps never discovering them at all.

"Ari, if Morelli or one of his goons ever gets us, at least we'll go out together." Sandra was both fatalistic and realistic. For all she knew that could happen. She made sure she was continually aware of her surroundings, above all when she saw strange faces. Not ugly strange but unfamiliar strange.

"Strange" was an excellent word to describe parts of the process of how Ari and Sandra were immersed into WitSec.

"Do you believe that psychiatrist asked me if I believe in Armageddon?"

Sandra really didn't expect Ari to answer the question. He scratched his head as if to say, "What the hell does that have to do with being in witness protection?"

It was but one of the inquiries directed at her during a mandatory interview with a U.S. Public Health Service psychiatrist two days after she and Ari arrived at their final destination.

The "doc" was part of the shrink team the Marshals used to be sure new WitSec recruits met the program's emotional requirements. "Mentally fit to withstand the constant stress" was how it was explained to Ari and Sandra, but she thought the brain examination was farcical.

Sandra answered the doctor's question with a question. "Do you?"

"Why, yes I do, but please answer me. Do you believe in an apocalyptic catastrophe, that the end of the earth will occur from a battle between God and Satan?"

"Not the end of the earth, but the end of this ridiculous conversation. Make believe I'm Jesus and you're the devil."

"I'm sorry if I offended you but it's the protocol."

"To offend me?" asked Sandra.

"No, to ask certain questions!" The doctor wasn't usually this verbally impeded. Neither had he ever been confronted by someone in WitSec in that manner.

"Why do you want to be in the program when you don't have to be?"

A logical question awaited a cogent answer.

"Because Ari's great in bed and I don't want to miss having sex with him," snapped Sandra without a hint of a smile.

"Have you ever molested a child?" The doctor quickly changed the subject.

"Yes, but not since last week." Sandra was purposely being a smartass.

"If you don't cooperate, I'm afraid we can't continue."

"That's what I was hoping for, doctor. By the way, are you a medical doctor or a shaman?"

Without waiting for an answer, she added, "Excuse me, but I have to go back to the hotel room and have sex with Ari."

She left the office escorted by a mustachioed, rugged-looking Marshal – "Uncle Bill" she liked to call him – and returned to the temporary hotel accommodations where Ari was waiting to fulfill the sexual commitment she communicated to the man in the white coat.

Since Ari and Sandra had left South Florida, federal agents were convinced there was no threat posed. They had been quickly flown to Tampa, their first stopover city, on their journey to somewhere. They were the last passengers off the plane, and behind a pair of U.S. Air Marshals who were not only protecting the couple but everyone on the aircraft. A government car whisked them to a hotel where they checked in as "Mr. and Mrs. Andrew Sloan." Their bodyguards sat in lobby chairs while their eyes roamed to make sure no one had followed them. For ten consecutive nights, the couple slept at a different hotel in the Tampa Bay area and used a different alias each time.

Although Sandra had packed six suitcases, the feds only permitted two on board the plane, both without identification and placed in an overhead compartment. Agents sent their other bags to several different airports as a diversionary tactic before the couple arrived in the next unknown city, considered a new "home" for Ari and Sandra, or whatever their names were at the time.

Kansas City was a great place to take in a Royals game on the diamond and watch the Chiefs butt heads on the turf, but baseball season had ended a few weeks before they arrived. They did manage to obtain fifty-yard-line seats, courtesy of the U.S. government, and became cheering-but-temporary fans at a game between the Chiefs and the Raiders. The four nights they spent in "Cowtown" were pleasant enough except for the repeat performance of moving each day to another accommodation.

"Remember, guys, we want to be upgraded to a suite."

That was Ari's message upon arrival at every hotel.

"Come on, Ari, why are you making things tough on our budget?"

"Tough on your budget? What about ours? The government is too damn cheap. You're financially cramping us way too much on our daily allowance for meals. Lunch at Burger King every day? You gotta be spoofing. Get the suite!" Until they arrived at their final destination, The Odd Couple was granted the upgraded room and assorted meals served up at Long John Silver's, IHOP and Bojangles'.

Trying to find out where they would end up was difficult. The location had to be cleared and approved by Washington, and the feds couldn't make a final decision for weeks. In their past lives, Sandra and Ari had been to so many places throughout North America that their handlers were fearful someone might recognize them.

Neither had ever been to the city ultimately chosen and neither felt the threat level had ever dissipated. Whatever tranquility there was they derived from the two Marshals who rather uncomfortable and felt unprotected and antsy were in close proximity to protect them. When the security detail took a 50 percent cut in people power for "budget" reasons there was additional anxiety. Ari and Sandra became somewhat fearful. "They gossip too much," Ari remarked to Sandra one day. "What are they doing telling us about other people in WitSec?" He was incredulous. "If they're divulging names and places where they're hiding, what about us? What are they saying about us to other witnesses and their associates?"

"Oh, don't worry about it, Ari. Nobody's coming to kill us." Sandra's appeasement was as clear as crystal and Ari saw right through it. Not only were they both concerned about their safety, but their families and friends didn't learn what had happened until weeks after the couple's disappearance.

Their immediate family members received calls from federal Marshals informing them of what had transpired. However, they couldn't reveal their location. Neither could Sandra or Ari even when authorities granted them permission a couple of months later to phone most of the people who had been frantically worrying about them. Still, the couple held back out of fear.

After a month or so feeling skeptical about their decision to go underground, they bought a new rack-roofed, 4WD Jeep Cherokee, paid for by the U.S. government, to break out of the physical and psychological boundaries the couple had been living within. Granted their space by the feds to travel freely even though they didn't have round-the clock protection, they could now see a part of the country neither had ever experienced.

"Brian's" flexible class schedule and "Katherine's" part-time responsibilities gave them the opportunity to travel throughout the Upper Northwest and Upper Plains as though they were on perpetual vacation.

Very few people in WitSec were as confident and as "normal" as these two, according to the Marshals and FBI agents who were in constant contact with them. That information was also in the reports the feds had to file monthly on the couple's activities.

They wheeled their way to the majestic mountains of Montana, the High Plains prairies of Wyoming, the fourteen-thousand-foot peaks in the Colorado Rockies, the Badlands of North Dakota, and the four-faced Mount Rushmore in South Dakota.

One crispy-cold day in the fall a short three months after they arrived, Brian and Katherine took an excursion through the spectacular Spearfish Canyon rimmed with gold, red and yellow leaves dripping from the aspens, birches, and oaks. The canyon base, graced with multi-hued foliage hanging from stands of sturdy Ponderosa and Spruce pines, took their breath away.

Nothing came close to this natural, raw beauty in Florida, except perhaps for the women.

Eleven miles from their unearthing of colorful nature was Deadwood, a rundown town at an elevation of forty-five-hundred feet in South Dakota's Black Hills. The most famous people in Deadwood were just that. Dead and in wood. Wooden boxes, that is. Both Wild Bill Hickok and Calamity Jane claimed the town as their final resting place.

One assumed they were haunting the thirteen hundred townspeople from their gravesites atop Mount Mariah Cemetery which overlooked Deadwood. Folklore passed down by previous generations suggested that Lewis and Clark, Wyatt Earp, General George Armstrong Custer before his last stand, Mark Twain, and the Sundance Kid had all passed through at one time or another. They all must have been on their way to fortune, fame and a bold asterisk in the history of the town.

In 1876, gold fever made Deadwood come alive, and with it brought prospectors, saloons, casinos, prostitutes, and opium dens, turning the town into an illegal, lawless municipal enterprise of five thousand residents.

What also made Deadwood illegal was that the federal government stole the historic land from the Sioux Indians.

Deadwood died a second death three years later when more than three hundred buildings turned to ashes caused by a raging inferno that burned through town like Sherman torched and scorched Atlanta on his March to the Sea.

Despite Deadwood's spot on the National Historic Register, the town was barely surviving in the 1980s.

Shutters were the norm for most storefronts. The population was steadily declining, and its inhabitants were trying to sell their classically designed Victorian homes, along with everything else permanently affixed to the ground. The city leaders had considered putting Deadwood on life support and declaring bankruptcy. Tax revenues were barely enough to pay for trash collection.

Strolling around the town as tourists and like a pair of city slickers in their new fashion genre, Brian and Katherine saw how hard times had hit Main Street like a financial hammer. Not a Dairy Queen or a Taco Bell within sight or sound.

They were curious as to why there was zero activity. Always thinking about the next opportunity no matter where he was, Brian decided to call a local phone number he saw on a for-sale sign taped to a window of an empty store.

He found a pay phone at the closest corner and dialed.

"Hello. I'm calling about the store for sale on Main Street. May I speak to the owner?"

"You're talkin' to him," said the voice on the other end of the phone. "My name's Higginbottham. Fred Higginbottham. What's yours and where ya callin' me from?"

"My name's Brian Goodman, and I'm downtown on Main Street here in Deadwood. I was looking at your storefront and I'm interested in speaking with you about it. I have to leave town later this afternoon, but I thought I might be able to meet with you before we go. Are you available?"

"Sure. I'll meet ya in front of the store in less than five minutes." A clear sign that the sixty-something Higginbottham thought he might have himself a live one.

"Finally," he thought. It was the first nibble he had gotten about the store in more than three years.

Higginbottham's Budweiser-belly got there in three minutes and the rest of him got there in another nanosecond. The tub of guts took one look at Hirsch in his gringo outfit and the newly bleached-blonde Sandra. He was doubtful whether his only prospect was even serious, but he didn't want to blow what could be a potential sale. It might take another three years before he got another inquiry.

"You look like a couple of them fancy folks from New York," he said in a not-so-flattering way.

"No, Mr. Higginbottham. If you must know my girlfriend and I are living not too far from here and I'm looking for an investment."

Higginbottham had heard of "shacking up" but they didn't do that kind of "sinful thing" around Deadwood, regardless of the town's ancient distinction of being bawdy, rowdy, and raucous. Virtually all the citizenry attended church on a weekly basis and kept their pregnant teen-agers locked in the house. They also hid their booze from public view. It wasn't only the Baptists in the South with that frame of religious reference, but good, church-going folks in that part of the country as well.

"Well, let me take ya in and show ya 'round."

The three of them entered the store after Higginbottham unlocked the front door, fumbling with the key with his tubby thumbs and fatso fingers. Brian, when he was Ari, had represented building contractors as well as narcotics contractors, and could have discerned a construction glitch as fast as a pneumatic nail gun could spit, but he gave it only a perfunctory inspection.

The store was dusty, musty, and rusty, but that didn't deter Brian.

"What's the asking price?" he inquired.

"Twenty-five thousand as is."

"I'll take it."

"You'll what? You're gonna buy this from me?" Higginbottham was in disbelief.

"Why not?" asked Brian. "Aren't you trying to sell it? I saw the sign in the window."

"Never thought I'd sell it this quickly," Higginbotham interrupted. "It's a great surprise, that's all. Gotta speak with my two partners to make sure they agree with the sale.

Shouldn't take but a couple of phone calls."

Higginbottham thought there were a hundred or more moths flapping inside his stomach. He could not believe that on this Day of the Sabbath he might be selling this useless property on which he and his partners still had to pay taxes and carry casualty insurance.

"Good," said Brian. "I'll go handwrite a contract in my car while you make your calls. Do you have a photocopier nearby? I'll need to make several copies."

"How're ya gonna get a contract written?"

"I took a few business law courses in college and learned how to do them. Don't worry. You won't have to sign it until you pass it by your own attorney."

"Okay. After ya get the contract done, come on over to the sheriff's office and we'll get 'em copied." Higginbottham gave Ari directions to the local lock-up, which was less than two short blocks from the store.

"Son-of-a-bitch, if he ain't the strangest businessman I ever met. Buyin' this piece of crap store and writin' his own contract, my ass!"

Higginbottham did his due diligence and called the first of his two partners from the sheriff's office.

"Hank, you're not gonna believe this. I think we've got a buyer for the store, but the guy wants to write his own contract."

"Back up, Fred. Who we sellin' it to, and how can he write the agreement?"

"Dunno. Said somethin' about takin' some classes in college and says he knows how. Now I'm not promisin' anything but could be he's the real deal. All I need is your approval and I'll move ahead as far and as fast as I can. No need to call Clay since it only takes two of us to approve the sale. His name is Goodman. Sounds like a Jewboy to me."

"I don't give a shit if he's a Jew, Buddhist or one of them Hindus. If his money's green, take it. Don't worry 'bout Clay. I'll call him. How much is he offerin'?"

"The askin' price."

"Don't take me for a jackass, you big bag of worm food. Now how much we gettin'? It's been sittin' on the friggin' market for over three years and you're tellin' me we're gettin' the askin' price?"

"That's exactly what I'm tellin' ya – twenty-five grand."

"I'll believe it when I see it." Hank hung up.

Finished contract in one hand and a three-hundred-dollar brown leather attaché case in the other, Goodman walked to the sheriff's department with Katherine and found Higginbottham waiting at the copy machine.

"Did you make the calls, Mr. Higginbotham?"

"Sure did. We'll agree to your offer. You did say twenty-five thousand, didn't ya, Mr. Goodman?"

"That's correct. No sense in haggling about the price. The only contingency is that when your attorney reviews the contract and its addendum" – Goodman had both in his hand – "you and your partners must immediately sign both like I've already done.

"The addendum will assign limited ownership rights to me. I'll give you a five-thousand-dollar down payment today that your attorney can put into his trust account."

"What's the addendum about?" asked Higginbottham. He was suspicious enough already and this raised his uncertainty even more.

Hirsch handed both documents to Higginbottham who fiddled with his rimless specs so his eyes could focus through the bifocals. Picking up the handwritten papers and staring at them, Higginbottham said, "Mind if I ask what this says? Can hardly read your writin'."

"It would grant me the legal right," Brian answered, "to petition the county for a business zoning variance. It would also allow me to file papers with the South Dakota government on behalf of you and your partners for clearance to operate another type of enterprise."

"What kinda enterprise?"

"I can't tell you right now because the addendum is absolutely and irrevocably confidential. No one except you, your partners, attorney, and I can know about it."

"Well, that sounds all right. I'll need to tell my partners and attorney anyway. I'll speak to them about it. What about the down payment?"

Hirsch placed his case on the copy machine and clicked the latches to release the gold-colored clasps to open it. Inside were five pairs of Ben Franklin's eyes staring at Higginbottham. There were hundred-dollar bills in five banded rectangles for a total of twenty-five-thousand dollars. Also, inside was a receipt he had prepared.

Sort of reminded Ari about Golden Beach and Kenny Cooper, the seminal event that Hirsch believed changed his life. If it hadn't been for the Coop, he wouldn't be in Deadwood.

By now, Hirsch had spent enough time in the area and knew that folks in this part of the country were, for the most part, honest. He trusted Higginbottham enough to turn over the five grand but made sure that Higginbottham signed the receipt for the money.

"Please call me after you and your partners meet with your lawyer, Mr. Higginbottham. Set up another meeting for all of us. How long do you think it'll take?" Ari handed him a square of paper with "Brian Goodman" and his home phone number written on it.

"I'll set it up with my attorney first thing tomorrow mornin'. Dalton Jorgensen's his name. By the way, Mr. Goodman, mind if I call you Brian? You can call me Fred. I'll get back to ya quickly. My partners, Hank, and Clay, both of 'em live in Deadwood. We'd like to get the deal done as quickly as possible."

"So would I, Fred. So would I."

When Higginbottham told his partners about the addendum, they got as inquisitive as a wife finding lipstick on her husband's collar. When they met with Jorgensen on Monday afternoon, the three partners insisted he made certain the deal went through, but they also wanted his opinion on the addendum.

"I want you to keep this as quiet as a leaf falling from one of our oaks," the attorney insisted. "I found out Goodman wants to petition the state to permit small stakes gambling on Main Street. He thinks it might revitalize not only Deadwood but the entire area. But you must keep this to yourselves.

"Don't tell your wives, don't tell your kids or any kinfolk, and certainly don't tell your gossipy friends. Remember, Goodman can cancel the contract if it becomes public knowledge. Before you know it, the Centennial will get a hold of the story, not to mention the Black Hills Pioneer in Rapid City and the TV news departments. Those damn media riffraff will blow it apart."

"Listen, Dalton, we're not gonna say anything." Higginbottham responded. "But Goodman must be smokin' somethin' funny in his peace pipe. He'll never get those screwballs in Pierre to agree to an idea like that! Those shit-for-brains politicians don't want South Dakota turnin' into another Las Vegas or Reno. Look at the dang town, Dalton. It'll go under faster than a German U-Boat in World War Two unless we do somethin'."

"I know that, and you know that," the attorney said, "but let's get this done and not add a distraction. Sell the damn property and take the money. If you don't do it now, you'll never do it. Plus, you'll miss out on what could be the only opportunity to unload it.

"Call Goodman and tell him to be here tomorrow afternoon at one so we can get the contract and addendum signed. Won't take but an hour to finalize the sale."

"Brian," boomed Fred into the telephone. "Dalton and my partners are ready to sign off on the deal. Can ya make it at one tomorrow afternoon?"

"Yes, I can, Fred. I'll be there with the rest of the money. Another caveat, Fred. Remember, don't let this information leak or you will have violated the contract."

"What's a cave yacht?"

"Kah-vee-aht, Fred. Simply a mild warning about leaking the information."

"Ya got my word on that, Brian."

Hirsch appeared at 12:55 PM the next day at Jorgensen's office. Fred had given him the address the day before. It was tough to get lost in Deadwood. The law office was across the street from the sheriff.

Recognition of the frailties of human beings was one of Ari's strong suits. He had been anticipating and hoping that Jorgensen, Higginbottham and his two partners would tell everyone in Deadwood about his plan.

That's exactly what they did.

Word spread faster than the 1879 fire that destroyed the town. Everyone in Deadwood and its environs suddenly "discovered" that an investor, who talked like a "bigshot" lawyer and carried "tons of cash" in a briefcase, was planning to ask the state government to permit gambling in the vanishing town.

The town finally had its cause célèbre. "The hell with the continuing economic depression! We've had years of it and we're through!"

Their voices became so loud, so resonant, so urgent that a movement started throughout Deadwood and Lawrence County, led by the owners of the empty stores on Main Street. Even the kids marched on the Capitol building in Pierre displaying signs that read Bring Deadwood To Life With Slots and Shots, appealing to legislators to allow the town to open casinos and saloons.

Within six months of non-stop activism, a special state referendum declared victory for the pro-vice forces. South Dakota voters, by a wide margin, approved limited-stakes gambling. Speculators came in like carpetbaggers and bought every parcel of property for sale in Deadwood at prices that would have made Donald Trump envious.

Brian's property value soared like a helium-filled balloon heading for the rich-blue Dakota sky.

After eight months of holding the property, an active member of WitSec turned a $25,000 investment into $1.5 million.

The profit qualified for the lowest government-mandated capital gains tax because Ari knew the IRS rules – he had held the title for a minimum of six months.

Not only were Higginbottham and his partners infuriated about the "Jew lawyer taking advantage" of them, so were the heads of the U.S. Marshal Service and the FBI.

They needed a scapegoat for allowing the transaction to take place under their watch, one that they probably bought at a flea market which didn't keep accurate time. Their second-hand knowledge was also quite late. Both agencies immediately ordered an investigation of the transaction, but it turned out to be a rather simple case. No one knew Ari had so much cash when he entered WitSec.

What they learned later was that Ari-cum-Brian always carried a big sum of currency with him wherever he went. "Just-in-case spending money" he called it.

Agents Hutton and Buggelshofer got spilled into a French-fried-potato fryer and almost got themselves burned to a crisp. Their government "chefs" intensively questioned them as though the two had spoiled the recipe and forced them to write more reports than a high school English class. How could someone in witness protection make that much money with so little effort in so little time? Not a single agency employee would believe that it was a clean deal. They wanted to prove it by drafting the two agents assigned to look after Ari's activities into a government inquisition. The Internal Affairs investigators were not only stumped, but they called in the DEA to determine if Ari was laundering money for one of his former clients, a totally false assumption based on the single fact that there was not one grain of evidence pointing to it.

It never dawned on any of the investigators that Ari would never have contacted anyone from his past business relationships and risk losing his life.

They finally gave up the dead-end exploration. After a while, Hutton and Buggelshofer received automatic grade promotions and raises, while Ari became a legend as the most financially successful prototype of someone on active WitSec duty. He was "living proof" that not only could they keep him alive, but that a protected witness could become a millionaire within months of entering the program.

It took "professional" testimony by drug-busting police agencies and tax experts to reveal that the "financial success of this one witness protection member proves that our program works so well that America's free-market democracy is doing fine and rewards those who stay within the policy structure and confines of witness security."

"Gentlemen," said a top DEA blowhard, "that's not only an amazing accomplishment but helps us rid the nation of drug lords and illegal smuggling. We point to this case as a shining example of success within the context of this administration serving its citizens at every opportunity. Yes, this case is one more way of keeping our children safe from the evil of drugs."

Huh? That's what most lobbyists called doublespeak. Bullshit was probably a better description.

A few weeks later, both the House and Senate passed a spending bill that turned over an additional $40 million to the Marshal Service, another $30 million to the FBI, and still another $50 million to the DEA, all earmarked to fight the War on Drugs. Turning swine into pearls was no easy achievement.

Oh, yes. Today, Deadwood is very much alive, with a thriving business in eighty casinos; charming hotels and bed-and-breakfasts; a variety of tours; great restaurants; a theme park; and loads of children's attractions. Could it be that a Floridian from New Jersey burrowed in WitSec made this all possible? Murray Hirsch was sorely uncomfortable when his older son was forced into the federal program but content he had made the most of it.

Indeed, Ari had, but being around the feds continued to erode Ari and Sandra's faith in the way the system was run. Although she never really conveyed her true feelings to Ari about being in WitSec, she had enough of the freezing weather and their jobs.

One minute she felt paranoid, the next numb with fear. She thought she would never get back to Florida, but three years after being in hiding, Ari threw her a beach ball.

While having dinner at a restaurant on a weekend night, Ari told Sandra, "We're going back home. The feds say the threat level has decreased. They're also getting on my nerves by constantly asking me for tax and legal advice and telling me about their cases." Psychologists would have called it a form of Stockholm syndrome when Sandra told Ari she really didn't want to leave. "Besides, what are we going to do with those casks filled with gemstones?"

"Leave them in the basement or take them with you, Sandra. We're heading for heat."

CHAPTER FOURTEEN

"We have attempted Prohibition. All that happened was that courts became clogged with thousands of cases and small, individual users, and a generation of young people came to think of the police as their enemies. There were no resources left to fight other crime. I say legalize drugs because I want to see less drug abuse, not more. And I say legalize drugs because I want to see the criminals put out of business."

Edward Ellison, Former operational head of Scotland Yard Drugs Squad

19 Years and 9 Months Later - 6:35 AM, Tuesday, July 8, 2008

LET'S HAVE ANOTHER CUP OF COFFEE

The DOJ building passes, updated credentials, and decades-old agency badges – Buggelshofer immediately super-shined his with Tarn-X – were hand-delivered to them at their homes by FBI couriers well in advance of their Starbucks meeting.

A swift processing of the twosome by Homeland Security declared them "clean." The top-level security checks and clearances were the final items needed for both to be formally on board once again. The information at the DOJ gathering, after all, was going to include knowledge about a highly sensitive "red-folder, red-ribbon" case unlike any the U.S. had pursued in a very, very long time.

Based upon their ages and clear infirmities, the pair of seniors was not exactly ready for the task.

"If today was a fish, I'd throw it back in," Hutton whispered to Buggelshofer, making sure that no one at a neighboring table was listening. Buggy was busy tuning his hearing aids, which had become necessities from being around too many live ammo rounds fired at range and human targets in his lengthy federal career.

"This place might be littered with feds, maybe even some of the behind-the-counter employees." That paranoid thought forced them to recognize the need to keep their voices to a very low decibel level.

"I'd bet my next-to-last dollar" – Hutton had already spent his next-to-last last dollar – "this is about Ari Hirsch. He's probably holding court with them right now and waiting to get us involved. Level with me, Buggelshofer. What the fuck is going on?"

"I don't know any more than you do Hutton, and don't curse at me dumbass! How could it possibly be about Hirsch? I know he's living in Florida and making a lot of money in real estate. No way possible this case has him entangled.

"You must've forgotten he left the drug war twenty years ago and gave up his law practice. Had to. There was still a level of risk. He had enough crap twenty years ago to last him and Sandra the rest of their lives. Besides, he's almost as old as us and has no intention of getting his balls burned in a case that must be straight from hell."

Talking about their relationship with Ari and Sandra evoked a strange sense of nostalgia. It was a considerably different bond the two had experienced with the couple than they had created with the criminals and malcontents who made up most of WitSec's inductees.

Hu ton and Buggelshofer's affinity for the duo was time-tested and lasted much longer than the years spent on assignment with Ari and Sandra's case.

They got to know what made Ari go tick and tock and could depend upon cooperation and communication from both him and Sandra.

They also recognized Ari's brilliance and considered him a financial mastermind, lending credibility to their instincts and belief that this was a case as big as they came and one in which they would play principal roles.

Buggelshofer had spoken with Ari and Sandra as recently as eleven months prior. There wasn't a glint or a hint they were doing anything but keeping their lives as private as possible.

"Bottom line? We know both of them better than anyone in the program," Hutton said boastfully and emphatically. "So, I suspect that's why we've been called back to help in this case."

Buggy squeezed out of the booth, shuffled to the counter, ordered another coffee, and sat back down. He cupped his hands, turned to Hutton, and in a restrained response, said,

"You couldn't be any further from reality."

"Stubborn bastard aren't you," Hutton muttered before he got up to order another large latte, knowing the rich and tasty java would help cure his chronic constipation. "You're about as sharp as an out-of-focus photo. And how come you didn't ask me if I wanted another cup?"

He headed to the counter, got another dose of caffeine, and went back to the table.

The pair was as compatible as a thong and Depends.

"Stubborn? You were the most mulish and biggest asshole the FBI ever put on the street. Your head must be harder than dry cement," Buggelshofer said, bristling at Hutton's holier-than-thou attitude.

"Besides, how in the hell are we going to be useful at our age? I can barely walk and you're drunk eighteen hours a day. I can smell it on your breath right now! Both of us are trapped and in the dark as to why we're even here. Typical joke by our former employer."

Even though the extra money was a godsend at this time of their lives, Buggelshofer still wasn't upbeat about having to lay his life on the line once again because of the continuing War on Drugs. He needed the cash more than he needed another Xanax, which he popped in his mouth and swallowed before the word "joke" left his lips. "Fine," Hutton said as he cleared a thick glob of phlegm in his throat and swallowed it. "You always had a way of playing ostrich. I'd like to see you finally pull your head out of the sand and see what's in front of us! I can't be sure, but if this turns out to be more than I bargained for, I don't know if I'm gonna make it past the initial meeting without having more heart palpitations."

Hutton and Buggelshofer started their thirty-year law-enforcement careers thinking idealistically, that America was all that it could be.

After a short time, both determined their country was significantly less than they both believed it should be. During oftentimes hazardous assignments, they saw enough drug-induced corruption and cover-ups, lethargy, and incompetence, then they ever could have surmised.

Assignment to WitSec late in their lives spawned personal conflicts. In most cases, they were required to protect criminals who had committed the most heinous of crimes, the same ones granted immunity from prosecution if they testified against a fellow criminal or drug merchant.

Thousands of informants had put the witness protection program on overload. Hutton and Buggelshofer found it detestable to protect criminals and hand them endless amounts of unaccounted for, tax-free cash so they would take the stand on behalf of the prosecution, which in all cases was the government.

Both often discussed with Ari what they thought was a lack of government morality. Hirsch had agreed that paying taxpayers' dollars for the testimony of admitted felons undermined the integrity of the legal system and fundamental due process. That, they knew, made him a unique member of WitSec.

They also reached defining moments and pivotal points in their lives. It was their choice. They could stay and play inside the system or leave for another vocation.

Both had been recently married, started families, and had taken on an array of financial obligations. They decided to stick it out as long as they could, and hopefully reach retirement in their late fifties with an appealing pension.

This recent and sudden call-to-arms only served to prove their long-held beliefs-that the government of, for and by the people was no better than the folks pulling the strings and setting up the stings. They had seen enough twine yanked to hang a number of the crooked puppeteers.

Now, both felt they were coming to a "Butch Cassidy and Sundance Kid" moment of throwing themselves over a cliff.

It was a far cry from Hutton's early life growing up in a tiny town on a middle-of-Nebraska corn farm with his tightly knit Methodist family.

He had gotten tired of his slowpoke life, as heady youths were wont to do in the 1950s. His draft board offered him a student deferment after he decided to enter a well-known mid-West university. He matriculated with a major in criminology and a minor in accounting but had a thirst for more education. To quench it, he earned a diploma from George Washington University Law School by attending nights shortly after he first signed on with the bureau.

A courtroom match for Ari he wasn't, and neither was his legal mind as quick or as deep. Hutton did take advantage of Hirsch's superior scholarship and knowledge about the U.S. Constitution, Bill of Rights and American history, and Hirsch was delighted to share his insight.

Buggelshofer, on the other hand, had a more frenetic upbringing by an alcoholic father and sickly mother in a frowzy area of Pittsburgh.

He had enough tenacity to work his way through a local community college, then transferred to a four-year university in New England where he earned top honors studying criminal justice. He made money during school as a part-time clerk in a local police precinct and as a private security guard during his summer breaks. Both men had near-perfect credentials and the personal discipline to be fine government agents. As honorable as they were, they were equally as gullible about the system.

More than a bit shaken when reactivated, each was getting less than four hours a night sleep since that first phone call a few weeks earlier. Both became neurotic enough to land them in rubber rooms. Not surprising considering both knew the other had been in touch with Ari and Sandra multiple times in defiance of the departments' orders to "never speak with those two ever again unless you want to lose your jobs, pensions and benefits."

In an act of apparent perversion, the government now was telling the two ailing seniors they would and could still take everything away unless they came back to work on this "far-reaching case."

Although they had been at odds on many occasions over the years, they were now philosophically united against what they thought was a form of harassment. But that wasn't nearly enough to put aside their personal animosities.

Now that they were together in what was clearly a furtive exercise, they not only got snippy with one another, but became as skittish as virgins in a whorehouse.

"If Ari was here," said Hutton, "he'd have you calmed down so you wouldn't have to keep slipping those pills into your gullet. That shit can kill you!"

"Why are we talking about Ari? Why would you think he's even involved?"

"Simple." answered Hutton. "When we were told this is an exceptional and critical case, he's the first one who came to mind."

Now, Buggelshofer thought E.F. might be right. Ari was exceptional. People like Hirsch simply did not exist in WitSec.

"He's been everywhere but the electric chair and seen everything but the wind. He's not about to come out of the safe shadows no matter what this case is about. Unless, of course, our new colleagues become desperate," said E.F.

"If he is involved," Buggelshofer responded, "he'll get through it. The question is will we?"

Both remembered that Hirsch withstood some of the most extreme psychological pressure any human being could possibly endure. He was good to his caretakers as well. Both made lots of extra money in some solid investments Hirsch had led them to.

"If it weren't for him, we'd both be living in Wrinkle City, along with a bunch of other old farts. You're lucky you still have Annabelle taking care of you. If she weren't around, you'd be looking twice as old and making your own funeral plans for next weekend. Picked a plot yet?" Buggelshofer took every opportunity to lay it on.

"Always have to get the digs in, don't you? You never could leave well enough alone," Hutton said.

"You're easy to get to, Mr. Thinskin. Plus, I enjoy seeing you squirm." Buggelshofer was enjoying the rhetorical duel.

"Well, we're probably both gonna squiggle on this one, and you're the one who'll do the most wiggling, you snake!" Hutton was on his own roll. "And keep your goddamn voice down, loudmouth, or we'll be spotted as fast as you can say OxyContin!"

"We might as well leave one at a time and scoot over to DOJ," said Hutton, not realizing that the only scooting he was going to do was on a five-miles-an-hour motorized vehicle for the handicapped.

Hutton donned his hat so that the brim nearly covered his eyebrows, put on his sunglasses, snatched his cane, and reluctantly made his way toward the front door. He made sure to wipe his paper cup to clean any trace of fingerprints before he tossed it into the trash container.

Walking along Seventh Street, he turned right on "D," hung a left on Ninth Street and walked south to Pennsylvania Avenue. E.F. stood at the corner where FBI headquarters was located, waited for traffic to pass, then walked across the heavily traveled artery and into the Justice complex.

The time on his stopwatch feature showed four minutes and forty-two seconds had passed.

Although he simulated the routine, Buggelshofer took almost twice that time. His lungs ran out of breathing space a few times, forcing him to lean against a building for a couple of minutes while he added some Washington oxygen. He also had to wait for additional cars to pass as traffic began to build on Pennsylvania.

Buggy was less than enthused when he noticed approximately twenty bulletproof Chevy 4X4 Suburbans, all as black as newly poured asphalt and with dark windows. Each had an authentic, blue-and-white "U.S. Government" license plate. The autocade around DOJ headquarters was causing a giant traffic jam around the building.

The super-size vehicles were awaiting Homeland Security clearance and permission to enter the heavily fortified basement parking garage.

Buggelshofer shook his head and muttered to himself, "What a bunch of first-class lamebrains. They might as well launch a few flares and draw more attention to the meeting. "Don't they even know that Washington is a town full of spies, squealers, lobbyists, paparazzi, and gossip mongers who make a living reporting on this kind of crap?" he asked himself.

Buggy walked into the building, snarled past the two growling, leashed German Shepherds drooling saliva from their pinkish tongues, and cleared security as Hutton had done a few minutes earlier.

Both were escorted to the elevator by special Justice Department stewards who delivered them, separately, to the seventh floor. Getting there required a special key placed in a slot in the elevator's electronic panel. Once they were in the anteroom, another two sets of government eyes scanned their security documents. "If you're carrying a cell phone or recording device, make sure they're turned off," ordered one of the guards. Upon the second approval, they were ushered into the courtroom.

Both felt the safety inspections were necessary but administered a bit too harshly. Nerves in DC were getting stretched thinner and thinner day by day.

They also conceded that the United States of America, notwithstanding its constitutional protections, Bill of Rights, and alleged judicial due process, had allowed the War on Drugs to help facilitate a nation run by folks who were one hair short of being government skinheads.

Hutton and Buggelshofer had more than enough experience with who they contended had become legalized anarchists and co-conspirators, and who they knew relentlessly trailed drug smugglers even into foreign countries. If they couldn't grab them in the states, they would extort their return by tossing their relatives, without justifiable cause, into prisons throughout the U.S. without benefit of counsel or access to a phone.

In the name of justice, it wasn't unheard of to incarcerate innocent family members and friends of those the feds were looking for. That was one part of their daily grinds Buggelshofer and Hutton hated.

They had heard one-way conversations such as, "You better come back and come clean, Smith, or we're throwing your siblings and parents in jail for conspiracy," or "If you don't cooperate, Johnny, we'll take everything your folks ever owned and make sure they lose their jobs."

Not surprisingly, people caved out of planned fear created by civil servants. Even before they entered a courtroom, these victims knew their fates were inevitable. No wonder the Marshal Service established a Judicial Security Division, Buggelshofer concluded. It provided a broad range of protection to local, state, and federal judges, many of whom had received assassination threats.

In some cases, physical assaults occurred. With more than two thousand sitting federal judges situated in eight hundred plus locations in ninety-four judicial districts, sheltering them from harm had become a serious issue.

For the most part, the concept of habeas corpus no longer existed. Ari had been right all along, Hutton mused. The legal writ became a political weapon that eliminated sanctuary for those detained either lawfully or unlawfully.

Trampling upon that document was both a direct and indirect result of the disgraced President Nixon's War on Drugs, Hirsch believed. Evidence showed Nixon was a willing co-conspirator in the most notorious case of political criminality in American history. Watergate made the Teapot Dome scandal look as bland as a bowl of white rice.

By reading the paper and watching his forty-two-inch Sanyo HDTV, Hutton knew the Great Writ of Habeas Corpus had "abuse" written all over it during the War on Terror. E.F. had seen those same tactics applied in the War on Drugs.

Suspects, without being criminally indicted or charged with a crime, languished in prisons until SCOTUS, the Supreme Court of the United States, in a five-four decision rebuffed the government's attempt to trash habeas corpus, one of the essential components of the U.S. Constitution.

Hutton and Buggelshofer clearly thought the court's razor-thin decision was astounding. A more appropriate vote, they felt, would have been nine-to-zero to support what they believed to be a core value of America's most precious document.

Hutton and Buggelshofer knew that Ari would agree.

———◆———

CHAPTER FIFTEEN

"If you support the War on Drugs in its present form, then you're only paying lip service to the defense of freedom, and you really don't grasp the concept of the sovereign individual human being."

Neal Boortz, nationally syndicated conservative talk-show host

19 Years and 2 Months Earlier –

5:00 AM, Wednesday, March 15, 1989

UNCLE MIKEY

Actually, Ari did agree, most notably when it came to a client like Mike Friedman.

"Uncle Mikey" was one-fourth the physical dimensions of the Pillsbury Doughboy, but to Ari he was bigger than life. At five-foot-six and barely one-hundred-twenty pounds, Uncle Mikey looked as though a mild trade wind might knock him on his no-fat butt. Ari had a genuine affinity for the man twenty-five years his senior.

At one time, the self-made multimillionaire had even wanted to adopt his attorney and CPA as his own son. Ari knew his real dad would have frowned upon such an act and would have considered it dishonorable.

But the fact was that Ari and his Uncle Mikey had become as authentically close as father and son. There was an inherent sameness between the two which created a definitive but unidentifiable, spiritual bond.

When they first met in the rainy and smothering humid month of May in Fort Lauderdale, a tad more than a year before the U.S. bicentennial, Mike had colorful fireworks of his own with the IRS.

At fifty-nine years old, that was the last thing he needed or, for that matter, wanted. The nasty affair with the feds took him away from the daily joys of his businesses. Mike was a whisker shy of looking consumptive partly because of his three-packs-a-day, non-filtered Camel cigarette habit and in some measure by his lack of good nutrition. Peanut butter crackers and Mountain Dew were his favorite meal, followed by a Moon Pie for dessert.

But those inhibitors didn't make him any less of a financial target for the IRS. His grey beard and matching hair added to his aura, and his illuminated blue eyes, soft smile, deep tan, and sun-wrinkled skin betrayed his toughness and aggressive-but-always-gauged attitude.

One of his close friends, upon hearing of his troubles with the federal tax collectors, had suggested he call Ari.

The problems, solved handily enough, set the standard for a twenty-four-year relationship that transcended mere friendship. Together, Ari Hirsch and Mike Friedman raised cattle in Texas, speculated in commodities, negotiated multimillion-dollar business deals, and savored the times they made enormous amounts of money and had fun with the profits.

They traveled together on private jets to Las Vegas, Lake Tahoe, Aspen, The Bahamas, New York City, and most points north, south, east, and west of everywhere. They bounced around more than Anna Nicole Smith's breasts attached to an electric massager.

With Ari's financial advice and tax guidance, and Mike's entrepreneurial skills at successfully operating several businesses simultaneously, it was as good a match as Barnes & Noble.

Uncle Mikey's enterprises included three cattle ranches located in several Florida counties. Each was hundreds of acres, and each had its own aircraft landing strip. His ventures also comprised a marine engine parts and transmission shop, plus a twenty-acre, large-boat repair marina situated along the Miami River right off Brickell Avenue near the Magic City's downtown area.

The boatyard, which operated on a cash-only basis, had an uncommon competence in fixing and modifying seagoing craft that could typically outrun a slow-moving torpedo. Uncle Mikey stuffed his pouch-like pockets daily with more U.S. currency than a typical bank had on payday. His business boldness and acumen made him more money than he'd ever thought possible as a kid growing up in a Brooklyn slum.

The location for his enterprise was *sui generis*. The plethora of South Florida drug smugglers fell in love with the locale, chiefly because it was within a relatively short boat ride of reaching Biscayne Bay, Government Cut and the open waters of the Atlantic. Seeing the arrival of high-velocity boats laden with pot and coke was like viewing a war film featuring the merchant marines. Scenes were as real as the bullets in the weapons aboard the sea craft, in the guns of the Coast Guard and in the assault rifles of DEA functionaries who were continually embarrassed for not being able to keep up with the waterway drug traffic.

Ari was the economic expert for all of Mike's fiscal initiatives and increasing assets, but it didn't stop there. Hirsch also became the executor of his estate, successor trustee of his trust, business manager, legal counsel, and personal representative.

When Ari fell off the edge of the earth some fourteen years after they first met, Uncle Mikey almost lost his mind. For months on end, he attempted to locate his only "son" but no matter whom he called or asked he got an "I don't know" or "beats me" answer. He couldn't elicit information from anyone.

After Ari accepted the protection "invitation" from the FBI, he left the office without calling anyone other than Sandra.

Mike had even hired three different teams of private detectives who were known for finding anyone, anywhere and at any time, dead or alive.

After a two-month search of North America, including the most remote Caribbean islands, Canada, and Mexico, they all gave up.

That was the point of WitSec, but Mike hadn't even known Ari had gone under cover.

Nine months after Ari was embedded, Mike's home phone rang in the early hours of a Tuesday morning.

"Mike, it's Ari. I'm sorry I haven't called before-"

"Where in the hell have you been goddamnit, Ari? I haven't been this worried since my IRS troubles. Shit, I've been scared out of my wits and haven't slept for nine fucking months!"

"Mike, I can't talk long. Don't ask any questions. Hear me out. I'm in the fed's witness protection program and I need your help. I've just hit a $1.5 million jackpot and I must get the money to you for safekeeping. I'm going to---"

"WitSec? What happened? Why didn't you let me know before now? I thought I'd lost you forever. I'll do whatever you need done, Ari. Just tell me where you are."

"I can't do that Uncle Mikey. It's much too dangerous for both of us. As I was trying to say, I'm asking you to meet me at Fort Lauderdale Executive Airport three nights from now. I should be in about eleven o'clock. Please be on the tarmac with transportation because I don't want to expose myself or anybody I'll be with. It could mean big trouble.

"We're also going to need a hotel room where we can speak privately. I'll be with a couple of feds. Decent guys. Maybe you can rent three rooms: one for Sandra and me and one for each of them. If you can get a couple of hookers for them, they'll be indebted to us forever. Will you do that, Mike?"

"Will I do it? Don't you know me better than that? Of course, I'll do it. You better be there, or I'll think something happened to you. Thank goodness you're okay. Sandra's with you?" Mike asked.

"Yes, she's with me and she's fine. Don't worry, Mike, I'll be there. Gotta go."

Ari hung up the pay phone outside the convenience store from where he made the call using a credit card issued to him by government accountants. Hirsch immediately made another call, this one to

Buggelshofer who at the time was paying his periodic visit from Washington to check on Ari's safety and update case files.

"I need you to come over quickly, Buggy." Ari sounded anxious.

"Are you in danger?"

"I have to make some arrangements very quickly and need to see you here. I can't speak about it over the phone."

"I'm doing my perennial mound of paperwork in the office right now, Ari, and there's no way I can get there this minute. I can be there in a few hours."

"It can't wait three hours. Something's come up that's an emergency and I need your help right now." Hirsch knew it was Buggelshofer's responsibility to respond immediately to any requests made if the agent thought someone under government protection was in danger.

The Marshal was there in ten minutes.

"I need to be in Fort Lauderdale Thursday night, Buggy. I've got to protect some money I have, and I can only trust handing it over to a close friend. I'd like you to escort me there on a Learjet I've rented."

"A Learjet? You want me to fly on a Learjet with you to Florida so you can deliver some money? Have you lost your mind? Jesus, Mary, and Joseph, you are really trying to screw up what little career I have left! How do you think I can get away with putting your life in jeopardy and mine as well?"

"Relax, Buggy. You'll have a federal companion. I want E.F. to go as well. I know he's in town checking up on things, so have him extend his trip for a couple of days and get him to come along. It'll only be overnight.

"Among you, Hutton and even more protection I've arranged for when we get there, there won't be a security lapse. I absolutely need the both of you with me, chiefly for airport clearances."

Ari knew that field agents had broad latitude in risk assessment and could make quick, independent decisions.

By this time, Hutton and Buggelshofer had taken even more of a liking to Ari. He'd never given them a hard time or broken their stones like the "asshole criminals" in the program. Hirsch had always treated both agents with great respect. Since the two had become guardians for the survival of their witness, Buggelshofer felt it was almost obligatory to help him. In this case, he also felt his "witness" would not put himself or Sandra in a chancy position. He cautiously agreed to the proposal.

"The only thing we're going to need is clearance to take off and land at Ellsworth." Ari was referring to Ellsworth Air Force Base near Rapid City, South Dakota.

"I don't know why I'm saying 'yes' to this, but if you need Hutton and clearance, I'll accomplish both missions. If this leaks, you're going to be moved out of this federal jurisdiction and wind up in a cold cave a thousand miles from the closest gas station."

"Thanks, Buggy. I won't forget this. I give you my word no one in the service or bureau will ever find out." And no one ever did.

A quick visit to the local FBI office and Buggelshofer convinced Hutton to replicate the favor to Ari. Both immediately proceeded to the air base. They made an appointment with the commanding officer for the next day, exposed their badges upon arrival, and got consent for the round-trip takeoff and landing.

Although it was highly abnormal for a small civilian jet to land on a U.S. Air Force base, the CO made sure his personnel knew it was an "unofficial but authorized trip approved by the Air Force Chief of Staff."

At six-thirty Thursday evening, Buggelshofer and Hutton picked up Ari and Sandra and headed straight for the base. The CO left their names at the gate and security cleared them without a hitch. Within fifteen minutes a sleek, gleaming-white, red-accented Learjet 28, with a capacity of eight, two crew and six passengers, arrived between two hangars after being flagged in by an airman.

There were four air-bound hitchhikers, one with a heavy attaché case in his grip, awaiting the plane's arrival for the three-and-half-hour flight to Fort Lauderdale. They climbed aboard, buckled themselves into their kid-leather seats, and waited for the captain and co-captain to complete their routine and altitude adjustment checks prior to take-off. The plane taxied to runway thirty-one, waited for tower clearance, rumbled down the tarmac, and seconds later the mechanical bird lifted itself into the magnificent early night skies of the Black Hills, colorfully draped by a golden-red sunset that rivaled any in the world for natural artistry. The trip south was deadly silent except for the monotonous hum of the twin jets cruising at four-hundred-and-seventy miles an hour, and an occasional comment from the captain to his air traffic controller.

The diversionary trip was a strain on all four passengers. It was unknown whether anyone other than Mike knew of their arrival back on Florida *terra firma*.

CHAPTER SIXTEEN

"The costs that this drug war imposes upon people cannot be underestimated. Not only do we bear the costs of building and maintaining prisons, but we also bear the burdens of creating vast new classes of people who are called criminals because they have engaged in mutually agreeable exchanges with other people. Governments at all levels gobble up vast amounts of resources to pay for this drug war, and there's no end in sight."

William L. Anderson, Ph. D., U.S. academic, economist and author

1 Year and 7 Months Earlier, 9:15 AM, Friday, August 7, 1987

THE DETROIT SPECIAL

A Great Depression survivor, Mike had to be a fighter merely to feed himself. Unlike Ari's dad Murray who ended up in the Golden Gloves' ring, Mike Friedman wound up boxing in neighborhood gyms or alleyways for twenty bucks a mismatch. For two weeks, he would stretch the money so that he had enough to eat and buy a few necessities.

He boxed over and over and over and got the wind and snot beat out of him every time he faced a heavier and more athletic opponent. His skin-and-bones physical makeup and lack of muscular proportion left him at a disadvantage.

Mike really didn't care if he ever won any of those gloved or bare-knuckle fights, which he never did. Nor did he care how much of his own blood he sacrificed. Somehow, he knew that his survival instincts shone in his spilled red body fluids.

He wasn't ashamed of it at all. Quite the contrary. He wore his defeats like badges of honor and maintained his dignity every day of his life.

Mike had the inner-strength and gritty attitude of the street people of that time in America. Being resolute would be a touchstone in his life, a quality that proved to be the backbone of his existence. It was a virtue that was on full display in the summer of 1987 when Ari was subpoenaed to appear before a federal grand jury in Motown. Detroit wasn't exactly Hirsch's idea of a rock-and-roll vacation. The city had more guns than people, and Mayor Coleman Young had declared his own struggle against gang warfare.

People couldn't decide when to leave their homes and when to stay inside, frightened that weapons-wielding youth might violate the sanctity of their residences by firing at anything or anyone that moved.

Much of the crime was drug related, and the feds stepped into the free-for-all. One of Ari's clients got caught in a highly organized sweep.

Lorenzo Rossi had transported marijuana across state lines. The DEA learned that a car with a Michigan license plate, loaded with four bales of grass, was heading from Miami to Detroit. The drug agents, guns drawn, surrounded the 1984 dingy-grey Chevy Impala as it pulled into a Highland Park street space north of Detroit, snatched Rossi, and towed him and the pot off to jail.

Charged with interstate transportation of a controlled substance, he faced beaucoup years in a federal pen after the Department of Justice stepped in and implemented a "Salem Witch Hunt" conducted before an indictment factory, more commonly known as a grand jury.

Ari's client became one of the targets, but not the bullseye. The feds reserved the yellow circle for their Uncle Mikey-tipped arrow.

Friedman knew the arrestee from his marina on the Miami River, and as a good customer, lent Lorenzo fifty-thousand dollars to buy what Uncle Mikey thought was restaurant equipment.

Instead of pans to cook veal marinara, Rossi bought pot to cook up some more dough. When he spilled his garbanzos about where he had gotten the money to buy so much marijuana, Uncle Mikey immediately became the object of the feds' archery team.

Hirsch, on Lorenzo's behalf, honored the summons to appear in front of the twenty-three-member grand jury, the very panel that was questioning Rossi the same day. Hirsch waited in the marble-floored hallway outside the courtroom while his client was being grilled on the stand.

Witnesses did not get the benefit of having an attorney while testifying before a grand jury, although they could consult with counsel between questions outside the courtroom. Lorenzo was in and out of the chamber as many times as the number of questions they asked. He would have felt legally lost if he hadn't had the benefit of Ari's counsel. When the U.S. attorney finished questioning Rossi, it was Ari's turn to appear before the inquisitor.

The government's interrogator knew he wasn't going to nail Hirsch the way the Romans nailed Jesus. Not even on cross-examination. He knew his adversary had never answered a single question when brought before any number of federal grand juries.

The prosecutor purposely began to throw puffballs.

"Mr. Hirsch, can you tell us about a fifty-thousand-dollar transaction between Michael Friedman and Lorenzo Rossi?" asked the federal prosecutor.

"I hereby invoke my Fifth Amendment rights to remain silent on the grounds my answer might incriminate me."

"Mr. Hirsch, can you tell this jury how long Michael Friedman has been a client of yours?"

"I hereby invoke my Fifth Amendment rights to remain silent on the grounds my answer might incriminate me. In addition, I would like this court to honor my attorney-client privilege." Ari had lots of first-hand experience in grand jury courtrooms. He wasn't a newcomer to the system, and the judge, jury and federal prosecutor knew it, predominantly because Ari's stoicism was as noticeable as his physical presence.

"Mr. Hirsch, are you covering up documents that might prove Michael Friedman and Lorenzo Rossi conspired to move illicit drugs from Miami to Michigan? And, that the fifty- thousand dollars borrowed by Mr. Rossi was, in fact, illegally acquired by Mr. Mike Friedman via a money-laundering scheme in which he had participated with banks in The Bahamas and the Cayman Islands?"

"I hereby invoke my Fifth Amendment right to remain silent on the grounds my answers might incriminate me. Once again, I would like this court to honor my attorney-client privilege." Ari stayed cool.

The federal attorney turned toward the judge who was specially summoned to be present during the questioning.

"Your honor, I move to hold Mr. Hirsch in contempt and have him remanded into custody until he agrees to cooperate with the federal government and this panel."

Almost all prosecutors knew the background of their witnesses, and this one was no exception.

"Motion granted," the judge responded as he smacked his wooden gavel onto its sound block as if he was cracking a walnut wrapped in a two-inch-thick shell. You could have heard the slam all the way to Dearborn.

Two uniformed courtroom cops quickly bound Ari's arms behind him, handcuffed his wrists with non-slip plastic bracelets, and escorted him through a side door of the building onto West Lafayette Boulevard. They tossed him in a van and transported him about a half-mile to Clinton Street where they deposited him into a holding cell in the Wayne County jail.

This was not a new experience for Ari. He had been behind bars numerous times for the very same reason. Contempt of court.

Yes, he was in contempt. He was always in contempt of the government for subverting what he believed were constitutional guarantees as deftly as they had broken its treaties with Native Americans. Ari knew its tricks, knew its gamesmanship, knew its moves, knew its motives.

What's more, he clearly recognized that an individual citizen's rights of a writ of habeas corpus were tossed down the toilet and flushed whenever the federal government decided to do so. When it involved the War on Drugs, it was almost always.

And he knew it was always about the money. Had he been prepared to "donate" some cash to the right bureaucrats, he would have been a free man.

That was but one way to become the recipient of a get-out-of-jail-free ticket. The other was by squealing on your friends like so many of his clients had done. Sing like a songbird. Screw your buddies.

That's exactly what the government wanted.

"Turn on Uncle Mikey and tell us where he got his money and how he was dealing drugs and how he was racketeering, or we'll throw your ass in jail and let you get raped and mutilated for eighteen months."

That was the period of time the grand jury was in session.

Hirsch wouldn't bow or bend to any of it. He would have preferred spending the year-and-a-half in a Detroit slammer than pay off corrupt politicians or judges in a scheme that he knew was gratuitous government graft.

Neither would he act treacherously against Uncle Mikey. He would have given up his life before he would turn on his friend. A federal magistrate set his bail at five-hundred-thousand dollars, half-a-million bills with the face of George Washington, the same guy with the wooden teeth who led the American Revolution. Even career, hard-core criminals got lower bail amounts than that.

It was late Friday afternoon. Ari knew full well the feds perpetually threw "his kind" of attorney into the slammer on the last day of the work week. That was to assure the lawyer got a Friday-to-Monday "experience" behind bars since it was nearly impossible to make a bond payment that large during a weekend.

Before the guards gave him his orange jumpsuit, emblazoned in black on the back with WCCC, and inserted him into the general population, Ari called Sandra and used up his one call.

He reached her at home.

"Sandra, they've done it again. I'm in the Wayne County Corrections Center in Detroit for contempt and they want a half-million bond. Call Uncle Mikey and let him know. He can probably take care of it on Monday."

The next three days couldn't pass quickly enough, especially for Ari.

CHAPTER SEVENTEEN

"I would say that the war on drugs has caused as much devastation to communities around this country, particularly low-income communities, as the drugs themselves."

Rabbi Michael Feinberg, Executive Director,
Greater New York Labor-Religion Coalition

3 Days Later, 10:00 AM, Monday, August 10, 1987

THE MOTOR CITY SHOWDOWN

Even though Sandra had been through similar scenarios with Ari, she never got used to it. In a voice filled with concern, worry and resignation, she told him she'll take care of everything, hung up and immediately called Mike.

Sandra was not about to manage it solo and wanted Ari out of there as quickly as possible. She had heard too many horror stories from Ari about conditions in American jails.

General population in a Detroit lock-up was like being in actual warfare; peace treaties among prisoners were most infrequent. Not only did the inmates get their skirmish skills tested on the scummy streets but they were now behind enemy lines.

The new "recruits" had to learn to hold their ground in this theater of war. They were living in a place where even the roaches claimed their own trenches.

Throughout the longer-than-death nights, some of the "guests" who had been provided permanent accommodations really needed to be in a psych ward. They screamed as though they were being tortured.

They were.

Not physically, except by other dorm mates who went off the deep end and became abusive, but psychologically. They stayed in their cells almost 24/7. There was no occasion for a breath of fresh air, to see the sun, rain, or snow except through an out-of-reach, three-inch-by-twelve-inch window on the top of the back wall of their cells.

Ari's fingerprints and mug shot were recorded, the clothing stripped from his body and personal belongings randomly piled into a WCCC clear plastic bag. He was then cavity-checked with a flashlight stuck to the hand of a rubber-gloved guard. After donning his new brightly colored suit, a corrections officer took him from the booking room to his new living quarters.

A filthy, yellow-stained mattress on a concrete floor in a windowless room the width and length of a basketball court was Ari's new home. Because there were so many inmates, Hirsch had plenty of floor mates.

His dozens of holding-area neighbors were grumpy drug dealers, armed robbers, rapists, and murderers, not exactly the crowd he wanted to consort with on a weekend getaway package. They were every bit as frightening as the well-known cellblock "Bubbas" and head-to-toe tattooed Aryan Nation brothers.

The slug on the mattress on his immediate right had slit the throat of his girlfriend because "the bitch dissed" him by talking to another man in an inner-city juke joint while he was engaged in a crack deal.

She died, and the macho man wound up spending the next eighteen years as a "prisoner of war" but not before Ari gave his new "buddy" some valuable legal lessons for his upcoming defense. Poor bastard hadn't even spoken with a public defender. They were too busy with other cases.

Squealers were abundant among inmates, and Ari always practiced what he preached to his clients.

"Don't talk about your case to anyone inside except when your attorney visits. Not the guards. Not the prisoners. Not even the librarian. And don't ever talk on a phone, not even the visitors' phones unless you want to be recorded. When you get into the courtroom, don't take the witness stand or they'll fry you like a hushpuppy."

Trusting anyone was chancy because the government usually placed undercover agents within the jail population who had instructions to report the slightest bit of information about specific cases.

The weekend couldn't be over quickly enough for Ari. By four-thirty Monday morning, he had enough of the stench of urine, enough being verbally hassled and physically jostled by a couple of his fellow agitators, and enough of the constant insanity.

He was betting that Uncle Mikey was probably working his monetary magic to get him out.

Ari won the bet.

After receiving Sandra's call at his home in Fort Lauderdale late Friday afternoon, the first thing Mike did was call a close friend who knew a Detroit attorney. Mike called the lawyer, Aaron Holtzberg, and told him about Ari's predicament.

He asked Holtzberg to get more information on Ari's location and the date of the preliminary hearing.

"I'm flying to Detroit, Mr. Holtzberg, and I'd like to meet with you prior to the hearing," Mike said.

The attorney scheduled a meeting with Friedman at the Clerk of Court's office on Monday at 8:30 AM, the time the office opened, and would get back to him with a confirmation of the hearing time before Mike left Fort Lauderdale.

Friedman quickly called the home of the president of the bank he did business with near one of his ranches in central Florida. He asked the banker if he would open Sunday morning so that Mike could withdraw some cash. Considering Mike was his largest depositor, how could he turn him down? Mike knew it would be next to impossible to get his bankers in Miami or Fort Lauderdale to accommodate him.

"Sure, Mike. What time will you be in town?"

"9 AM."

"See you Sunday morning, my friend."

On Saturday, Friedman located his pilot and told him he needed to be at the Fort Lauderdale Executive Airport at 7:00 AM the next morning and to have the plane ready for immediate take-off.

They would be flying two-hundred-and-fifty miles to a town northwest of Orlando. At a cruising speed of two-hundred knots, the twin-engine Beechcraft 58TC could move swiftly and gracefully through the fluffy early morning clouds of the Florida sky. Forecasts offered no signs of inclement weather. Later that day, Holtzberg called Mike and told him Monday morning at ten was the time of the hearing, and that Ari was okay.

"He's minding his own business and sharing two toilets and two public showers with about a hundred other inmates," he told Friedman. Reminiscent, Mike thought, of a Soviet gulag without the frills.

Although Mike was relieved, he knew that unless everything went according to plan, the timing was going to be awfully close.

Friedman arose at 5:00 AM Sunday and after a quick cup of coffee, rambled to the local airport in plenty of time for his 7:00 AM pick-up. He was carrying a briefcase and an empty suitcase on wheels, big enough to hold a large quantity of cash. The pilot had already filed his flight plan with air traffic control and was set to go.

After a cursory pre-flight check, the plane hummed down the runway and took off for the one-and-a-half-hour flight to Mike's landing strip at one of his mid-state ranches. Once on the ground, he and the pilot jumped into Mike's Mercedes, which he had always parked next to his private hangar. The ten-minute drive to the bank put them in the parking lot at 8:55 AM, five minutes before schedule. The president was already inside. He didn't want to be late for someone who had become not only a business associate, but a good buddy.

Mike waved through the window. The banker unlocked the front door and let in the men. An hour later, Friedman left the building with his pilot rolling a suitcase stuffed with five-hundred-thousand dollars in cash.

In addition to the money, Uncle Mikey was carrying a certified statement from his banker that the marina magnate still had a balance in the small financial institution of more than $2 million.

The pilot and Mike waited out the day at Mike's rambling ranch house. They would make the flight to Detroit at 2:00 AM Monday morning leaving them enough time to make one fuel stop in Lexington, Kentucky.

They were taking no chances of walking around with that much money in a city like Detroit. It was much safer to stay where they were. Mike called Sandra and informed her of his plan to get Ari out of jail.

"Sweetheart, we're gonna bring him home sooner than you think. You can do me one big favor. Call the Detroit City Airport and rent a limo for me for tomorrow morning at seven-thirty. Tell them we need to get into the city no later than eight-thirty."

Immediately, Sandra made the call, and when Uncle Mikey arrived at the small air facility five miles northeast of the city, the limo was waiting. The pilot tied down, grabbed the baggage from the cargo compartment, wheeled it to the car and chucked it into the trunk. He joined Mikey who was already in the vehicle, puffing on his seventh cigarette of the trip and coughing like someone who had viral pneumonia.

They got lucky. Traffic was lighter than usual for a Monday morning. They arrived at the Federal Clerk of Court's office at 8:20 AM and found Holtzberg waiting outside. After the usual business amenities and introductions among the three men, the clerk arrived and opened the office.

Holtzberg informed the clerk, "Mr. Friedman is posting half-a-million-dollar bond for Mr. Aristotle Hirsch who is being held at WCCC on behalf of the federal government."

The clerk looked up the case file, and in a very business-like demeanor asked how the bond might be paid.

"In cash," Mike said. The fiftyish, hair-bunned clerk was taken aback. "In cash? We're really not equipped to deal with that much currency."

"Miss," said Holtzberg quietly but quite sternly, "my client has brought legal U.S. tender, and it is mandated by law that you accept it.

Please take out your counting machine and process the cash. If you'd like to check it for counterfeiting, be my guest. But make it fast. We have a preliminary hearing at nine-forty-five this morning, and we have little time left."

Holtzberg purposely fudged the hearing time by fifteen minutes to hurry the process and not waste time.

After counting the funds and spot-checking for phony bills, the clerk immediately called the U.S. attorney's office and advised them, "Mr. Hirsch's bond has been paid in full." When the news spread throughout the building, every U.S. attorney within hearing range got as furious as a wounded bull gashed by *picadors*.

They had but one choice. File the papers and let Ari out of jail. But Hirsch still had to face a judge at the preliminary hearing.

At 10:00 AM, not only was the preliminary hearing held but an evidentiary inquiry as well. The federal prosecutors insisted upon it so the court could determine whether the half-million dollars Mike Friedman had posted was tainted drug money, which would then be ruled unacceptable as a bond payment.

They wanted Ari, who was now dressed in his rumpled business suit and sitting at the defense table, back behind bars until he squealed like a hungry, restless piglet.

They felt duped, taken for a ride by "those drug-connected criminals who have now absolutely gone beyond the limit."

Uncle Mikey was the first one called to testify. Now quite fragile, Mikey slowly tottered to the witness stand breathing hard and hardly breathing because of his nicotine addiction that had negatively affected his lungs.

The first question was fired at him immediately after being sworn in.

"What was the source of the five-hundred-thousand dollars in cash you deposited with the clerk of court, Mr. Friedman?"

It was a direct question from the same prosecutor who was responsible for getting Ari cast into the brig. But the man in the black robe was not the same judge who sent Ari to a weekend in the joint. He was a recently appointed adjudicator who looked at the evidence closely and fell on the side of the law, not on what was convenient for the U.S. attorney.

"It came from one of my trust accounts set up by Mr. Hirsch, your honor. He is the successor trustee of that account."

The judge looked at Mikey who at seventy-one years old seemed a decade older. Dressed in faded and threadbare Dickies farmer's overalls, soiled and scuffed work boots, and a grease-stained chambray work shirt he bought at a Family Dollar store, Mikey looked like he had played a leading role in the Beverly Hillbillies. Needless to say, the judge doubted his veracity. At the same time, he felt badly because of the witness' frail and disheveled appearance.

"Mr. Friedman, do you have a copy of the bank statements for that trust account to prove you have legal access to that sum of money?"

"Certainly, your honor. They're in my briefcase on that table." Mike pointed to the defense table where Holtzberg and Ari were sitting. "Bailiff, please bring the case to Mr. Friedman."

Uncle Mikey slowly opened the old-fashioned, beaten-up leather bag that looked like it was bought in a flea market somewhere in Appalachia decades before. His hands were tremulous as he pulled out a bunch of helter-skelter papers.

He told the judge the pile contained the last three months of bank statements for the trust and a certified letter from his central Florida banker dated the previous day. It demonstrated he had more than $2 million still in his account.

Friedman handed the papers to the bailiff who in turn gave them to the judge. The jurist shuffled through the documents, quickly organized them, and found the certified banker's letter and the three monthly statements. The judge handed them to the U.S. attorney who studied them to determine if there were any mistakes.

He asked the prosecutor if he noticed any errors. The attorney quickly shook his head back and forth while grinding his teeth in anger.

"Counselor, can you please state your opinion for the record," the judge demanded.

"Not that I can see right away, your honor, but---"

"No 'buts' counselor," came words from the bench.

The judge glanced at Uncle Mikey. "The certified letter and statements seem to be in order, Mr. Friedman, but is it your common practice to keep more than $2.4 million in your bank account and carry around your bank statements and certified letters?"

"Yes, your honor."

"Why?"

"For special occasions like this, your honor, when I know I might be asked where I get my money from. I honestly don't want there to be any questions regarding money on which I've paid taxes. If you like, I can send the court my income tax returns for the last five years."

"I appreciate that, Mr. Friedman. One more question. With all this legal money in a checking account, why did you bring five-hundred-thousand dollars in cash to post a bond?"

"I didn't think the federal government would take my check, your honor, so I brought cash in the event I needed it."

The judge glowered at the prosecutor then quickly signed a piece of paper.

"Case dismissed without prejudice," ordered the judge, then darted his eyes at the prosecutor. "Counselor, the next time you want to bring this serious an issue against anyone before this court, you better have more evidence."

From that day on, the U.S. government never bothered Ari again on any case brought against Uncle Mikey. In fact, they dropped every suit against Friedman. His low-key-but- dramatic courtroom role was enough to have the feds convinced they could never lay a hand on him. For the rest of his life, they never did.

Uncle Mikey, Ari and the pilot left the courtroom, immediately waved down a cab and took the short ride back to the airport. The three got into the Beechcraft and headed back to Florida. None of them ever stepped foot in Detroit again.

The court took almost a year to send back the five-hundred thousand to Mike Friedman, but he really didn't give too much thought to it, considering he had millions stashed away in safe deposit boxes in other accounts in the states and offshore. Holtzberg sent Uncle Mikey a bill for five-thousand dollars, which he promptly paid, only this time by check. The Detroit attorney had been a big help and Mike Friedman thought it was well worth the expenditure.

Over the next two decades, Ari not only looked after Mike's business affairs, but his personal care. Both Ari and Sandra, who had themselves entered a permanent commitment in 1989 while under federal protection, were at Uncle Mikey's bedside when, in 1999, he closed his eyes for the last time.

CHAPTER EIGHTEEN

"We pour almost endless resources roughly $50 billion every year into catching, trying and incarcerating people who primarily harm themselves. This insane War on Drugs damages communities and drains crucial resources from the police, courts, and prisons. These resources could be better used to combat serious street and corporate crime."

Ralph Nader, American author, attorney, political activist, and U.S. Presidential candidate

21 Years and 9 Months Later - 8:01 AM, Tuesday, July 8, 2008

JOINT TASK FORCE MEETING: THE INTRODUCTIONS

"This way, gentlemen," said one of the two armed guards from the DOJ who had been assigned to escort E.F. and Buggy into the courtroom, no easy feat for either of the old-timers. And it wasn't easy on Hutton's feet since his ankles were giving way even with the cane he was leaning on and the spongy footwear softening his steps.

Buggelshofer, always the complainer, was breathing harder than a terminal emphysema patient.

Without a word, the pair stared at the jury box, which by now was almost filled. The men seated were all wearing dark suits, starched white shirts and conservative ties. Black-laced, freshly buffed shoes, no loafers here, were mandatory for all of them.

They were mostly in their late forties and fifties and looked like uniformed executives with government-issued haircuts.

The lone forty-five-year-old woman showed up in a tidy black business outfit and two-inch heels that matched her black shoulder bag. She was well-suited for this newly formed Task Force.

The two old-timers knew the people occupying ten of the twelve swivel seats typified feds from different agencies, all threaded alike except for the one female. Sort of made Hutton's grey suit and plain blue tie, and Buggy's solid brown sports coat, tan pants, and yellow paisley neckwear, look fashionably anachronistic. But what did they care? They weren't Brooks Brothers window mannequins, and frankly didn't give a whit about how they dressed.

They were there for the fifty-thousand-plus Big Payoff and would have more than enough dough to buy some new clothes after they got their first installment.

By now, they had placed their sunglasses in their jackets inside pockets, and with hats in hand, made their way to the jury box. Seat #11 had a small white sign with letters spelling out "R.F. Buggelshofer, U.S. Marshal Service," and #12 was set aside for "E.F. Hutton, FBI." It made for a happy courtship. Both eased their butts onto the wooden, leathered-backed chairs.

They couldn't help but notice that the impeccable, cherry-paneled courtroom was unlike any other built by cities, counties, or the federal government. This was more than a court of law; this was a masterpiece of detailed design and an inner sanctum for a privileged few.

Prosecutors and defense attorneys sat at a hand-carved table with ornate mahogany legs. Matching spindles held up the horizontal bar that separated public attendees from court officers. The ceiling-mounted chandeliers were handmade by European craftsmen, shining the only light in the elegant, windowless room. Framed photos of past and present Presidents and Supreme Court justices lined the walls. An American flag and the Justice Department seal embroidered on another banner stood guard behind the judge's bench, all overseen by the Great Seal of the United States hanging on the wall.

"Shit," said Hutton to himself, "another waste of government money. All sizzle and no steak."

There were two more men sitting in front of the jury box, also mostly dressed in the uniform of the day. One arose from his seat and announced in an almost military inflection, "Good morning. My name is John Rosselfellar and I am Chief of the Tax Section of the DOJ. I would appreciate it if all of you would stand up and introduce yourselves and tell your colleagues your position. Can we please start with number one?"

"Bill Patterson, Chief of Operations, Department of Homeland Security."

"Richard Johnston, Special Agent of the International Financial Division, Central Intelligence."

"James Whitfield, Director of the Southeast Region of the Drug Enforcement Agency."

"These aren't typical feds," Hutton thought, "They're too high level. Maybe this really is about Ari!"

"Commissioner Wilson Brown, the IRS."

"Wayne Underman, Chief of the IRS Tax Evasion office."

"Jesus, what the fuck have I gotten myself into?" Buggy asked himself.

"Commissioner Bonnie Watts, U.S. Customs."

"Wilfred Smitherman, Head of the National Security Agency."

"Joseph Ianucci, Deputy Assistant to the Secretary of State."

"George Rappaport, Chief of Internet Technology, National Drug Intelligence Center."

At this point, Hutton and Buggelshofer knew without a doubt this was turning out to be the most important case they had ever been involved with, one with international repercussions with more hidden curves than a Grand Prix racing course. No way was this a minor domestic issue.

"Stanislaw Wazinski, head of witness protection for the U.S. Marshal Service."

"Heard his name but never met him before," Buggelshofer confided in himself as he stood to speak.

"Robert Fenwick Buggelshofer, but you can call me 'Buggy' like everyone else does. I'm a retiree from the U.S. Federal Marshal Service."

Everyone but Hutton glared at Buggy as if he was.

"You're no longer retired, Marshal Buggelshofer. You'll be serving on this important Presidential Task Force along with all the other gentlemen and the lady sitting in this courtroom," said Rosselfellar. "This case is unlike any you've ever encountered and now is no time to be telling anyone you're retired. Next please."

"Elwood Frank Hutton, but I guess I can't say I'm a retired FBI agent, so I'll merely say I've been called back to full-time duty."

Rosselfellar let Hutton's introduction pass without comment because he could sense it would only be a waste of words. Besides, he understood the importance of having the two old-timers on the team and didn't want to blow what Hutton would unravel in short order.

Except for E.F. and Buggy, some of them had interacted on other matters over the years and were recognizable, as was the next person to be introduced.

"I want all of you to meet Addison Hamilton," Rosselfellar said as he pointed to the man in the chair sitting next to him, "Chief of Staff to the President."

Everyone in the courtroom recognized Hamilton. His picture had been plastered on TV, the Internet, daily newspapers, and newsmagazines for at least five years. Throughout the District and the nation, everyone knew that Hamilton was the closest man to the President and was Chief Operating Officer of the White House.

He politely raised his arm halfway and held up his right index finger to the group but didn't utter a word. He was letting Rosselfellar do the talking until the appropriate moment. The DOJ Tax Chief leaned over to a heavy-duty leather attaché case sitting on the prosecutor's table. The double-keyed portfolio had one-half pair of silver-plated, high-tensile-strength handcuffs fastened to its two handles. The other half had been locked securely around his left wrist until he entered the courtroom. Rosselfellar was taking no chances while walking with it in public. He snapped it open and removed a pile of fourteen manila file folders, then walked over to each of the "jurors" and handed them one. He gave the next to the last one to Hamilton and kept the fourteenth for himself. All were identical.

"For the record, this meeting is being videotaped and recorded. Mr. Hamilton will make electronic records available to the President and communicate to him exactly what transpires in this courtroom. In addition, the President has requested that all video and audio communications surrounding this case be temporarily stored in the National Archives until they become a permanent part of his future Presidential Library.

"The President has also asked for twice-daily updates on this highest-of-priority investigation. Further, this case involves the German Republic, the nation-state of Liechtenstein and an inactive member of WitSec."

Buggy poked E.F. in the ribs with his elbow so hard that Hutton spun halfway around in his chair and almost fell off. All Rosselfellar had to do now was to articulate Ari's name and his thoughts would be validated.

"Aristotle E. Hirsch is the man---"

"I told you it was about Ari!" Hutton interrupted, loud enough for a pedestrian on Pennsylvania Avenue to hear. "I knew it, I knew it, I just knew it!"

"Hutton, please lower your voice or we're all going to need hearing aids from your screeching," Rosselfellar demanded. "This meeting has to be conducted with respectability and you will not disrupt what we're about to discuss. Got it?"

"Sorry, chief, but I had this gut feeling that---"

"No one cares what your gut feeling was. Eruptions like that will not be tolerated!"

The sparring reflected the internecine feuding among almost all departments and agencies in the U.S. government. Turf wars were more common than nematodes squabbling with each other about which one would eat the greenest spot on the lawn.

"Let me take it from here," said Hamilton, as he urged Rosselfellar to take his seat and keep his cool while he outlined the scenario. He slowly lifted his medium-framed, jogger-like physique out of his chair.

Hamilton looked several inches taller than six feet because he was wearing fat-heeled midnight-colored snakeskin cowboy boots, the kind that had stayed on his feet since his boyhood days in Texas where he was a childhood friend of the man who would become President of the United States.

A well-respected former litigator with a Houston-based law firm, Hamilton was about to turn fifty-eight, but his full head of no-grey-strands-of-straight-black hair made him appear barely fifty. He had made his name in Texas politics by giving large sums of money to his party of choice.

His biggest problem was that his ego was so big it graduated law school a year ahead of him.

"The President has asked me to assemble this Task Force and to bring all of you current regarding one of the biggest international financial scandals in history, one which has direct links to gigantic amounts of drug trafficking.

"Some of you are keenly cognizant of the situation now taking place with the Liechtenstein Global Trust Bank of Liechtenstein, also known as LGT.

"I'm sure all of you are aware that tiny country has been a haven for those who want to avoid, and more importantly, evade-paying federal income and estate taxes on significant amounts of income by hiding assets in what they think is a safe place.

"In fact, based on credible evidence and government analysis, we believe U.S. citizens have hidden funds that amount to billions of dollars in lost tax revenues due the United States.

"These tax cheats are not only from the U.S. but from most industrialized countries around the globe plus a few third-world nations. Germany, Italy, Great Britain, France, Canada, Australia, New Zealand, Russia, Denmark, Panama, Sweden, Norway, and Greece are also involved, and all their taxing authorities are screaming for the names of their tax evaders.

"But the LGT Bank, which advertises itself as a financial institution that 'handles financial matters discreetly, as do all the banks chartered in Liechtenstein and other tax havens claim, is no longer a secure hiding place for people who want to cheat their governments.

"Several years ago, a computer whiz and bank officer at LGT headquarters in the capital city of Vaduz, stole and sold a single CD to German officials. On that disc are the names of giant financial institutions and foreign nationals, including Germans, Brits, and Americans, who have participated in this large-scale chicanery. Members of Liechtenstein's royal family, who owns the bank, are enormously embarrassed about the theft.

"But instead of cooperating, they're continuing their public outcries of improper seduction of their employees, harassment by foreign governments and being put into the position of what they call 'financial genocide'."

Buggy's hand shot up as he interrupted Hamilton.

"When are we gonna talk about Ari Hirsch?"

"Please, Mr. Buggelshofer, we'll get to him in due time. Would you mind holding your questions until I finish?"

"Certainly, but please call me Buggy like everyone else does."

Hamilton made believe he didn't hear the comment.

"As I was saying, the bank's disgruntled employee, one Franz Dieter Schnabel, was approached surreptitiously by the German intelligence agency, *Bundesnachrichtendienst*, also known as the BND. The agency sent a twenty-six-year-old, large-breasted Aryan blonde to Liechtenstein on a mission to unearth the names of German nationals and financial institutions with camouflaged funds in the Principality.

"She met Schnabel in the bank, gave him the name of the hotel where she was staying in Zurich, and asked him to spend the evening with her. Shortly thereafter, the undercover agent took Schnabel undercover. In bed.

"The spy pumped him for information and Schnabel got sucker punched. The sex-for-disc was a barter deal he couldn't refuse when it involved someone who looked like Claudia Schiffer and screwed like a power drill. He promised her the compact disc with names, dates and information that clearly spelled out how the money flowed from

Switzerland, Germany, Austria, and several other countries into the LGT Bank.

"Deutschemarks, francs, dollars, pounds, Euros, and other currencies were and are being continually deposited into the bank via individuals, transnational corporations and phony foundations.

"In deutschemarks alone, we're talking about an equivalent of $150 billion that have escaped taxation.

"The German spy told Schnabel that in exchange for the CD, the German finance minister would pay him five million Euros, today worth approximately $7.8 million U.S. So, Schnabel didn't come cheap.

"In exchange for his cooperation, he was also offered a slot in *Aussergerichtlicher Zeugenschutz*, Germany's version of WitSec. He was provided with false identification papers and phony passports so he could squirrel himself away whenever and wherever he wanted.

"We don't yet know if he was able to get his hands on a second disc. German authorities think Schnabel might have an additional CD loaded with confidential information, increasing the stake by billions of Euros, British pounds and U.S. dollars in unpaid taxes.

"As an aside, the reason you haven't been provided with legal pads and pens is because a CD and DVD of this briefing will be made available to all of you. We'll be embedding them with the highest of security protocols, coding guidelines, and .NET framework cryptography created and established by the IT Division of the Department of Homeland Security.

"We will provide you with source codes to detect possible vulnerabilities. At no time should any of you attempt to listen to or watch these discs unless you are completely alone in a room without windows or bugs."

"What the fuck is he talking about?" Hutton asked himself. "I barely know how to send an e-mail."

Hamilton pressed on.

"Presently, there are widespread investigations going on in a number of the tax-affected countries, including Germany, Great Britain and the United States. Not only from Schnabel's information but from other sources as well.

"Currently, there's a Schnabel copycat responsible for even more details flowing from Liechtenstein to the United States. A Senate subcommittee is presently investigating UBS Bank of Switzerland. One of its dissatisfied technology engineers is blowing the whistle on Americans having numbered accounts in Switzerland and the bank's branch in Liechtenstein.

"Overseas tax havens have already cost our nation hundreds of billions in lost revenues and some European financial institutions are in danger of losing their rights to do business in the United States. We think we can prove several of these banks have committed material crimes, including money laundering and racketeering.

"In addition, we're beginning to see some of the fallout in other countries. For instance, Australia's second wealthiest individual, Mr. Stewart Finch, is being probed for having funneled money into LGT, along with many other influential financial icons from almost everywhere. So, you can see how vast these difficulties have become."

One of the IRS's representatives at the meeting, Wayne Underman, had been thinking to himself, "Does anyone in this courtroom besides me know that U.S. banks are holding $10 trillion in secret accounts bearing the names of foreign nationals and corporations, making the United States one of the biggest tax havens on the planet? We don't release names or numbers. Why should Liechtenstein or other foreign countries do it for the U.S.? Isn't that a bit disingenuous and somewhat hypocritical?"

The Commissioner would have never said that aloud, but he certainly knew the inner workings of his own agency and American enterprise involving money.

Hamilton asserted, "As a result of the information furnished by Schnabel, former Deutsche Post boss, Klaus Rheingans, has been the first to be arrested, charged and incarcerated for tax evasion in Germany.

"SWAT teams batted down the front door of his house and found damning evidence. And there are dozens of inquests going on as we speak in Munich, Frankfurt, Hamburg, and Stuttgart.

"This is going to be a collapsing house of cards as countries begin to unearth and intensify their chases for tax evaders in Liechtenstein, Switzerland, and closer to home, The Bahamas and the Cayman Islands."

E.F. interrupted Hamilton and asked, "Can we take a break so I can take some medication?"

"Request denied. Mr. Rosselfellar, please pour Mr. Hutton some water from the pitcher on the table because we have no time to waste," Hamilton invoked. "Please, Mr. Hutton. Stay focused so we can get through this meeting without further interruption."

"Screw him," Hutton mused to himself. "I'm not about to risk my health for this stuffy Harvard lawyer with his fancy boots. When is he gonna get to Ari?"

Rosselfellar handed E.F. a glass of water and Hutton swallowed a five-milligram Xanax he "borrowed" from Buggy.

"Leading German politicians have condemned Rheingan's behavior and have actively engaged in politicizing and capitalizing on his downfall," Hamilton continued. "They've been calling for wider-scale inquiries because this infamous tax scandal has tarnished the image of any number of publicly elected officials.

"Even the head of the German government has admitted that the news is almost as big as the fall of the Berlin Wall and the Mossad kidnapping of Nazi SS fugitive Adolf Eichmann from the streets of Buenos Aires in 1960.

"Chancellor Gretchen Mitsch has stated that her nation's economic leaders have a significant responsibility for their behavior."

"Zey neet to konduct zemselves in a vay dat iss soshully and ekonomikally reshponsibull," Mitsch had said on German TV only a few months prior to the meeting. "Zees citicens ahr suppost to be role mottles for ower kountry, and I do not at all unterstant zis kint of excessive guh-reed. Ve do not vant to see ower ekonomy kollapse because of zis kint of illegal money movement."

Hamilton continued. "The President and I are aware that Mitsch and other in-the-loop, sophisticated Germans know the possibilities and probabilities of routine deposits being made by Deutsche nationals and companies in hidden accounts in the Principality of Liechtenstein and neighboring Switzerland. Perhaps even that a great deal of it comes from money-laundering operations involved in the drug trade.

"Governments all over the globe have intelligence indicating thousands of individuals and companies are taking advantage of Liechtenstein's low tax rates and privacy laws.

"Mitsch also knows she has to clamp down on these illegal transactions as quickly and as tight-fistedly as she can before the opposition parties make *wienerschnitzel* of her Christian Democratic Union.

"In addition, the Chancellor has received word the additional disc that may be in Schnabel's possession contains infinitely more data of covert accounts in the names of German, British and U.S. nationals in other foreign countries.

"What's more, the grapevine has it there might be even more CDs in the hands of other snitches. She desperately wants her political machine to get them in its grasp as quickly as possible."

According to Hamilton, Schnabel had gotten into legal trouble in 2003 when, without authorization or knowledge on the part of LGT brass, he transferred funds to a bank in Spain on behalf of several LGT clients.

"That was not only a clear violation of the royal family's policy but a criminal act," Hamilton continued. "He had invested a large sum of money in a real estate transaction and had made himself a partner in the deal. He opened additional accounts for other customers of LGT in the same bank and was receiving 'royalties' from King Juan Carlos' financial hierarchy.

"Schnabel has also violated the laws of Germany by helping that country's citizens establish covert bank accounts in Liechtenstein."

Hamilton's statements were not nebulous. He was positive about the facts he was laying out.

"His Swiss attorney negotiated an immunity plea with German tax authorities. When that occurred, no one at LGT had any idea of Schnabel's involvement with either the bank transactions in Spain or German authorities.

"By the time LGT officials found out about his activities via cables and e-mails from the Spanish bank's headquarters in Madrid, Schnabel had already resigned his position and fled the country.

"It was too late to catch him. Liechtenstein had issued warrants for his arrest, but no one is sending Schnabel back to Liechtenstein. Certainly not the Germans who desperately need his information.

"He had already digitized virtually every LGT Bank record in existence, taken copious amounts of hand-written notes from journals kept in coded in coded vaults, and squeezed off enough photographs with a high-tech digital camera loaded with enough gigabytes to host every document within sight.

"Undeniably, he had obtained all the cryptography to the walk-in vaults.

"In addition to Germany, *Herr* Schnabel has been trying to hawk the disc, or discs, to other foreign governments. The son-of-a-bitch thought he could cut a deal with the Blair administration in Great Britain, but the Brits insisted on pre-conditions before they would release the first shilling.

"The government would accept the data and pay Schnabel his multimillion-pound asking price but only after they received the taxes due from convicted cheats.

The Minister of Her Majesty's Revenues and Customs was not willing to risk the esteem of those who might turn out to be some of the Prime Minister's political supporters. Especially without giving them a chance to tell their stories to British officials or make amends for any wrongdoing. So, to date, no deals by the UK have been made with Schnabel."

What Hamilton failed to mention was that the Revenue and Customs Minister was already bracing for a crisis. His office had lost CDs containing twenty million names and addresses of British households because of a breach in security. If there were any deals made, it would require the highest level of confidentiality by the UK.

"This is by no means the end of the dispute," Hamilton said firmly as he paced back and forth with is arms crossed on his chest. "In fact, we're at the very beginning of our involvement. Chancellor Mitsch has personally asked the President to make a solid commitment in helping Germany in this untenable situation.

"The Chief is aware the Liechtenstein royal family is stonewalling the process and ducking the scrutiny. We're also determined that the

German government has a plea agreement with Schnabel that contains a specific condition. It's one which has become a major hurdle stopping the Mitsch administration from proceeding with many additional tax fraud cases.

"It will necessitate the cooperation of Aristotle Hirsch, a demand made by Schnabel which he will not concede. He's as rigid as a nightstick in his position.

"Agents Hutton and Buggelshofer have been reactivated from retirement to make contact with Mr. Hirsch and convince him by any means possible to assist in overcoming the obstacle."

This was exactly what Buggy and E.F. wanted to hear. Another adventure with the Renaissance Man.

As he quickened his back-and-forth gait in front of the jury box, Hamilton intensified the decibel level of his voice and began speaking quite harshly. He was conspicuously letting everyone in the courtroom know this case was even more important than perhaps what had been going through the minds of his audience of agencies.

He no longer spoke in diplomatic and accommodating tones. Hamilton was far too passionate about this situation and his anger became noticeable.

"Do not underestimate the pressing matters of this case or the effects of Ari Hirsch's participation," he emphasized. *"Mr. Hirsch holds the key to the vault and right now, he's the only one who can unlock it. Without him, everyone's paralyzed.*

"Neither should we discount the significance of Schnabel. He is as devious and as cunning as Rasputin, and as insightful as a Euclidian mathematician.

"The man speaks five languages fluently, has technological skills matching the best of our computer scientists, and he remains cloaked in secrecy. There's a high probability he has more identities than someone with multiple personality disorder."

Hamilton then dropped a bomb.

"We know those sides of Schnabel because he has also been in touch with the IRS. I believe Mr. Brown can attest to that." The Chief of Staff looked directly at Wilson Brown and every head in the room turned toward the Commissioner for his reaction.

Brown uttered his agreement, "That's correct," while Underman appeared bewildered. He knew the U.S. Senate was conducting an investigation of a Swiss bank but he was never notified about LGT.

"How could he have possibly not told me?" Underman couldn't help but question himself about his boss having coveted that information.

"I wonder what else he's not saying," he pondered, instinctively knowing that if Brown was holding back, it must be a monstrous predicament, one closely tied to the political and foreign relations policies of the United States.

"Once Schnabel was successful with the Germans, his lawyer, through back channels, contacted us and a number of other tax authorities in other countries attempting to sell what he stole," added Hamilton.

"We've already begun our negotiations with him, but that one last strand of loose thread needs to be pushed through the eye of the needle and sewn up. We must get Hirsch to meet with Schnabel."

No one else at the meeting, including Rosselfellar, knew about any discussions involving the U.S. government and Schnabel or his attorney.

"Both the American and German administrations believe," Hamilton continued, "no matter where he goes, no matter how many hiding spots he has selected, no matter how many masks he wears, his life is still in danger.

"If Schnabel disappears, Germany, the U.S. and perhaps other countries will not get their hands on the material they need to pursue their tax cases.

"The German accord with Herr Schnabel includes that one extremely difficult provision and it's up to us to get it satisfied. The stipulation presents a stumbling block which we cannot trip over," Hamilton said in a most poignant way.

"Schnabel will not release any more info to anyone unless he has an ironclad commitment of a personal meeting, in total privacy-no bugs, no hidden cameras, no hidden mikes, no leapfrogging with Mr. Hirsch.

"In addition, Schnabel is refusing to further validate the reliability of the disc in German courts. That will further stymie the prosecutions of other tax cheats who have been identified. He also believes that if he releases any more evidence names, dates, account amounts, or any other info former Mossad agents might find him and take him out.

Permanently.

"According to Schnabel's debriefing with German authorities, Hirsch had established accounts for an array of clients using methods that even the financial institution considered ingenious. He had created blind trusts and Liechtenstein foundations without listing any beneficiaries in the records.

"Therefore, funds being held by the bank would not be traceable to any of those clients since Hirsch has yet to disclose the names of the inheritors.

"Cleverly, he pre-paid all fees, expenses and Liechtenstein taxes on each account for a period of twenty-five years. There are still five years to go on Hirsch's standing instructions." Hamilton then added, "He told bank officers in 1988 he would provide them with the names of beneficiaries for the foundations and trust accounts he had established and would certify them upon his return at a later date.

"Mr. Hirsch never went back to Liechtenstein to add the names of the beneficiaries so the accounts were never documented or brought up to date. It was at approximately that same time he entered WitSec and never had the opportunity to return to Liechtenstein soil.

"Without a doubt that's true. He's been under constant scrutiny by the IRS, DEA, CIA and the NDIC. Daily. For years.

"In an act of stunning creativity, he left the fingerprints of both hands-on file at the bank knowing he would one day be the sole legal assignor of ownership interests in every account.

"He did that because that would make him the only one on Planet Earth who could withdraw the funds, bullion or coins or whatever else was in the accounts.

"We believe his legal position would be that he was holding title to those assets in trust for third parties.

"Upon revisiting the bank, he could then exercise his rights to withdraw the hard assets in the bank's vaults simply by getting the bank to verify his fingerprints. Bank managers could match them with those he imprinted more than twenty years ago."

Ari Hirsch had made an incredibly bright move that could only be affected by someone much more inventive than LGT, the IRS, CIA, FBI, DEA, or any other three- or four-lettered enforcement agency.

Hamilton and the rest of the Task Force were only now realizing the reason Ari left fingerprints of both hands. What if by "accidental" means one of them got cut off? Hutton and Buggelshofer never knew that Ari had access to LGT accounts. Something else they never knew was that Ari also had private conduits that led directly to former members of the Mossad.

"It has become apparent that Mr. Hirsch, over a period of ten years, insidiously guided gigantic sums of cash, precious metals and gold coins to the LGT Bank," Hamilton declared. "They were placed in huge safe deposit boxes in the safest safes in any safe tax haven.

"Further, we believe those deposits amounting to more than $25 million U.S. were deposited into the numbered accounts by Mossad agents working on behalf of Mr. Hirsch and his clients in the mid 1980s."

That information was readily available to Schnabel, the insider. Even now that he was self-concealed, he knew that not only was the cash still in place, but the value of the gold and platinum bullion and coins had skyrocketed in value. In the past two decades, they were approaching a worth of at least two-hundred times the initial sum.

Schnabel knew precisely how the system worked. LGT established trusts – wasn't Trust the bank's last name? – foundations, and other types of accounts so that foreign nationals could transfer assets such as cash, stocks, bonds, titles to real estate, even expensive artwork, but not directly into LGT.

Instead, the bank created special purpose vehicles such as bank accounts or shadow companies not registered in Liechtenstein but in other foreign countries around the world.

LGT could then transfer a client's assets out of the U.S. through a "clean" country like Canada and not raise a single eyebrow of IRS officials. From Canada, the "goods" could move with ease through countries with weak or non-existing compliance laws and finally land in Liechtenstein.

However, Schnabel wasn't about to squeal to any authorities of any nation about the details of those accounts until he fled Liechtenstein.

Before he bolted and spilled the information, Israeli agents decided to leave him an unclouded and quite specific message. It was in the form of a bloody human ear stuffed into one of four deposit bags, each filled with twenty-five pounds of gold coins delivered by an Israeli "messenger."

No typed or written note was necessary. Schnabel understood without having to read a word: "Don't divulge anything about any of these accounts or we will relentlessly hunt you down like an animal, the same way we pursue terrorists, and neutralize you faster than you can say shalom aleichem, farewell you rat, and peace be upon you. You won't know you're dead until your brains fall out of your skull!"

Schnabel quietly and assuredly told Uzzi the "emissary" that the cloaked accounts Ari created would remain so.

Uzzi, "my strength" in Hebrew, also referred to the internationally known and widely used Uzi submachine gun, designed, and manufactured in Israel and carried by armies, militias, and gangs on every continent.

Uzzi responded monotonically, "My chaver, my friend, do not disappoint me or my associates."

Salty globules of sweat glistened on Schnabel's forehead and rolled down his clammy cheeks. His legs got weaker than a fifty-cent cup of coffee. His hands shook as if he had a severe case of Parkinson's, and his heart started beating as loud as a timpani drum.

"We don't know the specific reason why Schnabel wants to meet with Mr. Hirsch," explained Hamilton, "but the Chief wants this done. Now. Not tomorrow. Not next week. Now!

"The Germans know where Schnabel is, but we need to get a hold of Hirsch. The next to last thing we want is to leave the Germans with a dead stoolie on their hands.

"The last thing we want is to have Hirsch walk into the LGT Bank and leave Liechtenstein with millions in cash and other treasure.

"It is the President's intent, as well as mine, to secure as much of the tax money as we can if any of those accounts are in the names of American citizens. Prosecution to the full extent of the law is inevitable for these rapacious bastards.

"That means Marshal Buggelshofer and Agent Hutton are going to begin this very day to locate Hirsch, and by the time this meeting is complete, all of you will have your assignments. They're quite comprehensive and have the complete blessing of the President of the United States."

Hamilton followed the sweep of the second hand on his family heirloom Hamilton watch. After a few seconds, he said, "I believe a fifteen-minute break is in order to allow all of you to digest and discuss this among yourselves. When you return to your seats, I would appreciate as much input as you can possibly give, and I will be happy to entertain any questions you might have.

"It appears the future in this matter is in the hands and fingertips of Ari Hirsch. And that, my compatriots, should be taken quite literally."

CHAPTER NINETEEN

"I believe it is long past time to end the War on Drugs. That's not because I approve of drug use or have any desire to encourage it. But this particular war has already gone on longer than the ones in Korea, Vietnam, Afghanistan and Iraq, put together, with no end in sight and far less to show for it."

Burt Prelutsky, American newspaper and magazine columnist, TV writer, author

21 Minutes Later - 9:47 AM, Tuesday, July 8, 2008

JOINT TASK FORCE MEETING-COURTROOM CHAOS

Within minutes of the attendees returning to the courtroom, hell reigned.

The devil didn't know Hamilton had called the Commander-in-Chief during the respite and told him everything was going "on course."

Now, it was time for the interrogation of the Chief of Staff by the hand-picked Task Force.

"Mr. Hamilton. How could you possibly think that Ari Hirsch is going to cooperate with the federal government after what he's been through?"

Buggy's question was more than rhetorical.

"The government, including the agencies represented in this courtroom, screwed him over and over unmercifully. Now we want his commitment to help us with a notable international issue, one that will affect the future of our relations with Germany and who knows how many other countries. Have you any idea what you'll be asking of this man?"

Buggy wasn't so buggy after all. It now appeared as though he had used a double string of mental floss that very morning. He was clear-headed and cogent and began to defend what he thought was an affront to the intelligence of everyone gathered in the room.

Neither did he want to drag Ari back into the donnybrook, principally because his former WitSec enlistee had always treated him with total respect, and he didn't want to see Hirsch go through any more trouble.

"You'll be asking him," Hamilton fired back. "If you're thinking of walking away from your commitment to this Task Force, think again."

"I didn't say that so stop the dictatorial methods," Buggy argued. "I've been in similar situations more times than you have hairs on your ass. So don't get testy with me! Hutton and I know Ari better than anyone else in this room, so you'll need my full cooperation and his as well!"

Hamilton's eyes flashed toward Hutton who was bobbing his head and ratifying what Buggelshofer had just espoused.

The marshal's vocal cords and lower lip began to shake, and his eyes bulged as he tried to convince Hamilton to be realistic and more moderate. He couldn't believe Hamilton had once served as a U.S. Undersecretary of State considering his insensitive approach to solving what could be a colossal diplomatic nightmare.

"That's why the both of you are here. I apologize for the firmness in my voice, but this case has potentially immense complications," said Hamilton in a more conciliatory way.

He knew he had stepped across the boundary with the two veterans, and he didn't want them to bolt. This was a Presidential matter and he better not screw it up.

"Now, would both of you be kind enough to call Mr. Hirsch?" Hamilton pointed to the specially installed high-tech Polycom conference speakerphone sitting in the middle of the defense table and connected to a tape and CD recorder. The state-of-the-art instrument had enough amplification and extension speakers to accommodate a twenty-plus-person conversation.

"The equipment has been thoroughly security-checked and cannot be hacked into or tapped. Mr. Rosselfellar, with Mr. Rappaport's help, has made certain all incoming and outgoing calls remain completely protected. When Mr. Hirsch answers, tell him he doesn't have to be concerned about what he says, and make certain you communicate the importance of the situation.

"Our best strategy is to get an immediate idea of how receptive he is to a meeting with Schnabel. After we make that determination, we can decide what our next move will be."

"Buggy," Hamilton asked, "you do have Hirsch's phone number, don't you?"

Buggelshofer put his hand into his inside coat pocket and pulled out his Nokia.

"I believe I have it stored in my cell phone. Can I turn it on so I can get Hirsch's number?"

"Go ahead," said Rosselfellar.

"That's too impulsive a move right now," said the IRS Commissioner. "Hirsch will definitely know he's being recorded. From the stories I've heard about him, he leaves nothing to the imagination. He'll have it figured out before we even dial his number."

"The reality is that he might agree to meet with Schnabel which would satisfy the administration, but Hirsch is likely not to go along with it unless there's some kind of quid pro quo," said Wazinski, the head of WitSec.

"Remember, he still has some outstanding personal grievances with the government that he wants to resolve."

"Like what?" asked the DEA's Whitfield.

"He's still not over the fact that we kept him active much longer than he needed to be," Wazinski said. "I've read Hirsch's file over and over and I have it practically memorized. The client who wanted Mr. Hirsch rubbed out, this Dino Morelli. He asked for federal protection himself because he crooned like a canary on some of his drug associates in front of a grand jury a few days after Hirsch went into protective custody.

"So, the threat to Hirsch's life only lasted two weeks. He could have resumed a normal life had he known Morelli went into WitSec so quickly.

"He didn't unearth that until more than three years later, and it only added to his unshakeable distaste for us."

"How'd that happen?" asked Hamilton.

"Just a normal miscommunication between agencies," Wazinski responded.

"If we allow Hirsch and Schnabel to meet privately, we're gonna get screwed. I'm convinced they'll split the money, the coins, and whatever other ill-gotten gains there are in LGT. They're liable to go into hiding and we'll never see a dime," Underman said.

"The IRS will strongly object," he continued, "if we allow either man to get his hands on that fortune without collecting the taxes due, which will likely be in the millions. Certainly, we will be compliant with the President's wishes, but we cannot allow that kind of money to slip away."

"I understand your concern, Mr. Underman," Rosselfellar conceded, "and we will consider that as things unfold. However, we have yet to determine the contents of the safe deposit boxes in LGT.

"The Germans already have Schnabel under twenty-four-hour guard. Besides, the accommodation we're making to Schnabel on behalf of the German authorities will not infringe on our ability to collect any taxes due the U.S. Treasury. You can rest assured of that."

Whitfield got on his feet with the carriage of a commandant.

"I can tell all of you that the Drug Enforcement Agency is on record, here and now, as strongly opposing any meeting between Hirsch and Schnabel.

"I know Hirsch's modus operandi. He's as elusive and as evasive as anyone we've come up against. Like Casper the Friendly Ghost, except

Hirsch isn't so transparent. We've had him under constant observation for thirty-five years. I've participated in his ongoing investigation, and I can assure you this man is not to be trusted.

"I've researched Hirsch for decades," screamed Whitfield, "including reviewing the reports submitted by Marshal Buggelshofer and Agent Hutton. Both failed to note clandestine meetings between Hirsch and at least two men suspected of being agents of the Mossad. These men are guilty of large-scale international money laundering of every currency imaginable, and we have evidence the assets in question were involved with illegal drug trafficking within our borders.

"As such, we're informing all agencies inside and outside this courtroom that the DEA has rightful ownership to some of those funds.

"To protect our interests, we will file a federal claim which will include recovery of accumulated costs our agency has incurred during its lengthy, ongoing investigation. We're also going to request a reasonable amount of money from any excess funds recovered by this Task Force."

Hutton knew about the double-dealing on the part of the U.S. government, particularly by the DEA, and he was angry.

As a middle-aged FBI agent in 1983, he had attended the first International Drug Enforcement Conference, IDEC, in Panama as the global drug war cranked its engines. By the time the U.S. engineered the confab, Hutton had become aware that governments began sharing more than mere statistics and ways to combat narco traffic.

They all scampered to get their slices of the money pie from illegal drug smuggling. By 2008, the annual gathering had grown from eleven Latin American nations plus the U.S. to almost one hundred countries ministering to and observing each other in the name of fighting illicit drug activity.

The textbook for those conferences could have been "Money for Dummies." All those drug profits with no place to go. Why not keep it and create profit centers? A perfect plan for imperfect people who paid more attention to creating economic empires by sequestering the money and putting it in their pockets than they did in helping their countries' commoners live decent lives.

Every member of the Task Force knew the ironic results of a quarter-century of these nationally sponsored drug carnivals.

A staggering increase in illegal drug manufacturing. Record-breaking narcotics smuggling and incarcerations. Higher profits than the Dow Jones thirty blue-chip stocks combined, split among nations who adhered to these profitable pursuits. More money stashed in esoteric places than ever before. Corruption and payoffs in the public sector on a scale that surpassed many countries' gross domestic product statistics.

And everyone in the FISA courtroom knew that U.S. taxpayers were footing the bill for the IDEC conferences.

"How could they hold that kickoff conference in Panama?" Hutton asked himself that question. He knew that was the same country ruled by military dictator Manuel Noriega, a CIA operative for three decades. The same Noriega who was convicted in 1992 and sentenced in the United States for trafficking cocaine, racketeering, and money laundering, all at the urging of the DEA.

Since Whitfield was the head of the Southeast Region for the agency, he knew everything practically firsthand. He was aware it was the U.S. government that claimed Noriega was a double agent.

It was learned Noriega had refused to cooperate with Marine Lt. Col. Oliver North of Iran-Contra infamy to supply arms to the Nicaraguan rebels fighting their nation's Sandinista government. North, accused of participating in the organizing and transporting of cocaine and marijuana from various places in Central and South America and then into the United States, allegedly used the sales proceeds as a means of funding the Contras.

The DEA's Whitfield and Buggelshofer knew all that dirt, as did the CIA which had offered its private "air force" to assist North. Hutton and key FBI officials were aware of it as well. Wazinski had the inside story, including the fact that Hirsch had represented Noriega's personal pilot, a U.S. citizen who secretly transferred money worldwide for the pockmarked-face El Jefe, Panama's strongman. Fearing for his life and that of his family, the pilot entered WitSec after Hirsch filed ten years of delinquent income tax returns on monies earned from moving Noriega's assets.

The aviator's testimony led to the recovery of tens of millions of dollars which were then split among the U.S. and Panamanian governments and the pilot who snitched! The head of WitSec also had knowledge about how the DEA got drug merchants placed under witness protection and allowed them to work under cover, pay no income taxes on profits, and receive open-ended expense accounts. According to Wazinski, the agency had boasted about a number of prodigious drug nabs from Hirsch's clients. They were then employed to set up bigger drug dealers with written and confidential consent of the DEA. That was a move that notably helped increase the magnitude of the agency.

The history of the DEA was well-known ever since the time it had planted its agency roots during Prohibition by pinching moonshiners. Certainly, every member of the Task Force knew that. However, the agency faced extinction unless some sort of transformation took place.

Hence, the DEA was established to control the flow of illegal drugs into the U.S.

More money. More taxes. More greed. More corruption.

"Whitfield." Hutton looked straight into his bloodshot eyes. "I'm sure you remember the $207 million confiscation set up by two of Hirsch's clients on behalf of your agency, or have you conveniently forgotten you guys set up illegal drug operations? Let me repeat that, Whitfield.

"A whopping $207 million! Do the names Bobby and Timmy Smith ring a bell?"

Hutton started shaking his finger at Whitfield and was getting himself worked up once again, so much so that he started trembling and his throat dried. He took a sip of water from his plastic bottle of Dasani and stopped for a few seconds before speaking again.

"Whitfield, you know those two clients of Ari's are probably still cooperating with you and the CIA. How dare you point your finger at the Marshals and the FBI for not doing their jobs when your agencies set up illegal drug operations?

"That's right, illegal! The government has absolutely no right to put people in the drug business at the risk of people's lives and the abridgement of the U.S. Constitution."

Ari had taught Hutton well and turned him into a keen observer.

"You've allowed traffickers to continue to operate at the expense of the federal treasury," Hutton added.

"You permitted Hirsch's clients to enter WitSec after he prepared addenda to the standard agreements that required the DEA to pay them reward money.

"Yes, I even know they used whatever means were necessary to set up successful stings and seizures and you do, too! If you claim it's our fault for not keeping an eye on Hirsch twenty years ago, you're a few bricks short of a chimney!

"I'm completely aware that the State Department was, and probably still is, privately helping in the drug war by hiding money in its budgets and earmarking it for countries that assist in intercepting illegal narcotics and arresting smugglers and dealers. I could go on and on, but I think I've said enough."

Hutton finally rested his vocal cords.

Rosselfellar inhaled deeply for fear he might lose patience. He couldn't believe agencies were blaming each other and wrangling about money before they even had an opportunity to find out if there was any. The system, he knew, was so damn broken.

"Did the DEA ever share its WitSec surveillance reports on Hirsch with other security agencies even though he was under the protective custody of the FBI and the Marshal Service?" Rosselfellar asked Whitfield.

"Well, yeah, we might have." Whitfield replied.

Hamilton felt like he had to bite a ball bearing to keep him from going into a wild rage.

"We had to supply other agencies with information," Whitfield continued. We thought Hirsch might be setting up some big scores while he was in hiding. We could never nail him."

"Didn't you realize you were putting that man's life in danger by sharing that info?" asked Hamilton. "The purpose of putting him in WitSec was to protect his life, wasn't it?"

"That wasn't up to the DEA. That responsibility was left to the Marshals and the FBI."

Don't say anything else, Whitfield, or you might regret these admissions.

"Does your agency have any proof of those cloak-and-dagger meetings with the presumed Mossad agents?" asked Rosselfellar.

"Yes. We have an electronic intercept recorded in the late 1980s indicating Hirsch met with an Israeli with the street name of Newnew in Sturgis, South Dakota."

"You've got to be jesting!" Rosselfellar replied in an almost astonished tone. "Rappaport, have you ever come across that name before?"

"Sturgis or Newnew?"

"Newnew."

"Doesn't sound familiar. Our databases include some of the most arcane surnames and code names in virtually every language on Earth. I've seen them all, but that sounds too contrived, and I don't recognize it. You did say Newnew, didn't you?"

"Yes. As in N-u-n-u."

"Oh, I thought you meant N-e-w-n-e-w. That shines a different light on the name."

Not only was George Rappaport a computer genius, but he was also a linguist and etymologist who understood the most obscure origin of words. That knowledge often came in handy with the National Drug Intelligence Center.

"There's a Yiddish word 'n-u' which loosely means 'so?' or 'well?' which makes the connection to an Israeli a clear possibility. I've never seen or heard it used as a proper name. We have to assume he travels under a series of phony passports because that would fit a pattern we've seen before."

"If you had this intelligence twenty years ago, Whitfield, why didn't you arrest him?" Rosselfellar asked.

"On what charges? We had nothing to link him with any illegal activities. Only rumors. There simply wasn't enough to go on."

"What were the rumors?"

"First, Nunu was a free-lance enforcer and worked for the Mossad on a contract basis. Second, he allegedly moved money into Liechtenstein and Switzerland for Hirsch. Third, his extreme violence was legendary.

"Supposedly, he cut off the testicles of a PLO terrorist and put them in the camel jockey's mouth while he was still alive, then put a live round between his eyes and another through an ear. Our records indicate he was a veteran of the 1967 Six-Day War and considered a military hero by the Israelis.

"Although we've never been able to confirm it, we believe he got killed seventeen years ago while working covertly for the CIA in Desert Storm."

"I cannot confirm or deny that as factual." Johnston, the CIA's representative at the meeting, wanted to clarify the agency's position if Nunu's involvement ever surfaced. Right or wrong, he had to protect the agency since it had received an oral shellacking from government gurus and military officers who prosecuted the 1991 Iraq operation. The allied commander of the Gulf War, U.S. Army General Norman Schwarzkopf, wrote years later, "The CIA was the only agency to dissent. On the evening of the ground war, it was still telling the President that we were grossly exaggerating the damage inflicted on the Iraqis. If we'd waited to convince the CIA, we'd still be in Saudi Arabia."

"What about the National Security Agency, Smitherman? Did you ever hear chatter about Nunu?" A full-court press was on.

Smitherman answered Rosselfellar's question with remarkable clarity.

"The NSA has files on virtually every American citizen living in the states and abroad, in addition to subversive groups and crime cells. We continually mine and monitor every byte of data we get our hands and eyes on, including electronic, telephonic, digital, and satellite communications.

"We deploy personnel to listen, photograph and compile data. You're being more than naïve if you don't recognize that. Mr. Rosselfellar, because the NSA had a debriefing about this meeting yesterday with several of your own Justice Department investigators, you already know we don't have anything on the name Nunu."

Rosselfellar, the top dog in the DOJ's tax section, hadn't a clue there was a meeting between the NSA and DOJ the day prior because none of the participants had filed a report.

"Steady," he said to himself, "before this gathering implodes."

"Five-minute break. I need to attend to an important matter. Keep your seats." Rosselfellar left the court, walked into the men's room, and took a mega-dose of tranquilizers.

He knew he would need them before initiating any more conversations about private meetings held without him.

CHAPTER TWENTY

"As America's drug war continues to expand, so does collateral damage such as the black-market violence that accompanies prohibition. And so does the government violence that comes with militarized policing. Meanwhile, civil liberties are eroded further and further. It is legitimate to want your kids and neighborhoods free of the damage drugs often do, but it is equally legitimate to ask if the way the War on Drugs is being fought is worth the damage being done to our constitutional liberties."

Mike Krause, Director, Justice Policy Initiative

21 Minutes Later–9:47 AM, Tuesday, July 8, 2008

JOINT TASK FORCE MEETING: THE DUDU DUDE

"What was the net result of yesterday's private caucus, Mr. Smitherman?" That was Rosselfellar's first question upon his return to the courtroom.

"We told your people we have files on a Dudu – D-u-d-u – who's originally from Morocco but immigrated to Israel a month before the Six-Day War in 1967. Supposedly, this Dudu character also has ties to the Mossad. We've lost any sign of him since the Hezbollah incursion.

"However, we heard he's dug himself underground somewhere near Haifa like a frightened gopher. Can't find him."

"We had him on our radar years ago." Bonnie Watts, the twenty-two-year veteran and head of the U.S. Customs Service knew of Dudu during her time in the late 80s when she was a border agent at the crossing between Sweetgrass, Montana, and Coutts, Alberta, Canada.

"There were serious tabs being kept on this Dudu dude because of a heads-up we received from the Royal Canadian Mounted Police. It had him under drug surveillance for a couple of years in and around Calgary and Banff. But we never learned anything that would have led us to believe he had drugs on his person or in his car. Believe me we checked several times. Rappaport's agency always picked up Dudu's trail as he headed south on I-15 to Helena, then west to Missoula."

"That's true," said Rappaport. Even though he hadn't been with the intelligence agency when Dudu was around, he had the facts memorized. "It was mandatory. We knew through our intelligence sources around the country he was a perilous risk. The entire Upper Plains, especially Montana, was and still is vulnerable to heavy drug activity."

The NDIC was also responsible for assessing threat levels among the large number of native people living in Montana and about twenty other states. Conducting interviews in and around reservations became routine. They were done to root out info about the manufacturing and trafficking of illegal narcotics. Arrests were not only common, but they also occurred daily.

"Those featherheads were into hallucinogenic drugs more than they were into drinking firewater," Whitfield said. "The Indians in Texas even shipped their peyote to the Seminoles in Florida. Add grass and cocaine to that mix and you get some of the wildest bunches of powwows you ever saw."

"This is not the South of the 1950s, Mr. Whitfield. 'Featherheads,' 'Indians,' and 'firewater' are not words we use in any kind of a setting, let alone a Department of Justice courtroom. That kind of speech is unacceptable." Flames shooting from Rosselfellar's ears seemed almost to appear.

"Sorry I used that jargon, but facts are facts," Whitfield responded as though he thought he was on solid ground.

"When's the last time you knew of Dudu's whereabouts?" Rosselfellar was trying to zero in on something - anything that might lead to a solid connection to Hirsch's activities. He wanted to get past the slurs.

"According to our current records, the last time he was seen was in 1990 by the Office of Drug Control Policy," Rappaport said.

"We know he met Hirsch at the Missoula airport on an incoming flight from Miami. Passed a package to him and sat around the lounge. Took the next flight back to Florida. The contents of the package were never known, but it was believed to be an illegal substance, probably pot."

The NSA and the DEA, according to Smitherman and Whitfield, both thought it was something much more sinister than marijuana.

"It was our opinion that Dudu was passing messages, and perhaps some illegal substance, to a third party, probably someone who Hirsch knew and was working for him," said Whitfield. Even though Hirsch and Sandra had been in protective custody and under close surveillance, they had carte blanche to wander throughout the Upper Plains and Great Northwest on their own.

The Marshals and the FBI couldn't have possibly followed them twenty-four hours a day and neither could they spot every move they made or record every conversation they had. There were times they had deep suspicions but nothing concrete ever surfaced.

Johnston was next. "We got photographs of Hirsch handing small pieces of folded paper to Dudu at the airport, but we couldn't figure out what they were. We had no legal grounds to arrest either man, but we certainly wanted to bring them in for questioning.

"The chief said no. We didn't need any lawsuits for violating their civil rights. Kind of like what Whitfield did with his mouth a minute ago.

"From my familiarity with Hirsch and Dudu, I'd bet the store the message transfers concerned large amounts of money tucked away in Swiss and Liechtenstein bank accounts." Johnston thought he had it perfectly diagrammed.

"He knew as much about the ins-and-outs of money laundering as well as anyone in the U.S. government. I can almost guarantee those messages were not about drugs. They simply had to be about deposits of assets into those foreign accounts. We know a lot more than you might think. We've even traced Hirsch's travels back and forth to Liechtenstein and Switzerland on at least two occasions, even before he went into witness protection.

"We have the travel vouchers, customs and immigration reports, his old passport with visa stamps from both countries, and hotel receipts for those trips. We also know he had a personal relationship with the prince in Vaduz."

Patterson of Homeland Security concurred. "We further checked into immigration and customs records and can avow for what Mr. Johnston stated. That validates our theory that the written communications passed from Hirsch to Dudu had something to do with asset transfers. But who knows? He might also have been trafficking in drugs as well."

Rosselfellar had heard about enough. Time was vital and he didn't want to squander it by having discussions about ancient history that would prove and accomplish nothing.

By now, they had expected another update from Hamilton. In addition, waiting in typical Teutonic patience across the pond, was Chancellor Mitsch panting for information. The stiff line from the corner of her lips angling down to the edges of her chin had made the stumpy politician appear as though her muzzle was stuck in a permanent frown. Especially after learning about the Schnabel saga.

Although her jowls were slightly less saggy than those of an English bulldog, her baggy-blue eyes uncovered a slight sparkle that betrayed her real feelings about this case. Moreover, she wanted the deal done without delay before the scandal got even bigger.

Rosselfellar's unease showed as he continued speaking.

"The more I hear the details about Hirsch and the more I read in his dossier, the more I'm learning that he went about his own business for more than three years. Meanwhile, none of your agencies has a fucking thing we can possibly use as leverage to make him collaborate. Excuse the language, Ms. Watts."

"I've heard the word before. Get on with it." The customs lady was acquainted with the vernacular of pop culture. She was pushing forty-six and didn't care for Rosselfellar or his characterization of Mitsch. But she didn't mind the four-letter word.

Really, she didn't.

"I don't think I'm needed here right now," said Ianucci from State. "I know we're indispensable to this effort, but right now I have much more critical matters to deal with, including a couple of Middle East uncertainties that arose yesterday."

"Fuckin' wop weasel. Indispensable? He's probably a grease ball button man for his godfather."

Wazinski, in fact, actually said that, but quietly enough so that the Deputy Assistant to the Secretary of State didn't hear.

The WitSec head had dealt with so many Italian goons in the program, he didn't care for anyone whose last name ended in "i" except for himself and his Polish ancestors.

As he lifted his derriere to depart the courtroom, Ianucci exhibited his what-the-fuck-is-going-on swagger position and delivered a mini-speech.

"We've been here for two-and-a-half hours, and nobody has even begun to create a strategy. Until you do, I'm not willing to participate in what I believe to be a dumber-than-dirt meeting. I'm not going to risk my good name by affiliating myself with a cross-section of government bunglers."

"You have crossed the diplomatic line, Mr. Ianucci, and are betraying a public trust," Rosselfellar shot back after the ambush. "There's the door. Don't let the knob get stuck in your ass on your way out. And if I hear that you've said one word about this meeting to anyone, I will personally get the DOJ to hold you in contempt!"

Hamilton was hotter than two foxes fornicating in a forest fire.

Seconds later, Ianucci shepherded himself through the double doors and scooted out in a fury. There was no alternate for the newly emptied jury seat nor was there a missing doorknob.

"Now, where were we?" Rosselfellar tried to compose himself and fend off any more hostility. Keep it focused or it would self-destruct.

Hamilton would have to explain the debacle to the President. Uh-uh. No way would he do that and risk the wrath of *Numero Uno*.

"You were talking about Hirsch vagabonding around Montana like Moses wandered the desert." Righteously indignant was a politically correct way of saying Buggelshofer was now severely scornful of what he perceived to be unjust behavior.

He was three-quarters-of-a-century old and thought that at this age he had, by default, the license to criticize anybody and anything wherever and whenever he wanted. The hell with the money and the capriciousness occurring here. Buggy was pissed. He went into a soliloquy illustrating he had more lucidity in that courtroom than he had in all his years of active duty.

"Listen and listen well. All of you. E.F. and I spent three years of our lives with Hirsch. Did it ever occur to you to talk to us before now? No-o-o-o-o! Of course not! You probably don't like associating with old-timers because we probably know more than you do and make you look like amateurs, which you are.

"You're thinking about pleasing the head of Naziland, cogitating about whether Hirsch and the drug trade go hand in hand. Of course, he was involved with drug traffickers! He represented the vanguard of that industry. He helped get dozens of them into WitSec, and I'm betting he's still in touch with some of them.

"So, what the hell does all that mean? Big deal if Hirsch met with Nunu and Dudu and even someone named Fufu if there even was someone by the name of Fufu! What does that prove? Absolutely nothing!

"He didn't need to go to Missoula for drugs, so let's get off that kick about what was in the package. Yes, Hirsch did smoke some pot, but so what? So do tens of millions of other Americans. Isn't it about time we stopped spending money on the stupidity of Prohibition?

"Yeah, I can hear what you're saying to yourselves right now. 'Buggy is not only buggy but a traitor and a doper'. Let me make this perfectly clear. If Hirsch wanted to get a 'happy cigarette,' 'hash,' 'haybutt' or any of the hundreds of words potheads substitute for marijuana, he and Sandra could've hopped in their Jeep and gone to Sturgis. Yes, Sturgis, South

Dakota, was less than twenty minutes from where they lived. As if some of you didn't know.

"I have to believe that everyone in this courtroom, plus the asshole from State who left, has heard of Sturgis. Every August since 1938, almost every motorcycle club in the world invades that town the way the Vikings raided England. More than half-a-million of them. Almost as many as the entire population of South Dakota. "Social bikers and criminal bikers. From doctors to accountants to some of the worst gangsters in the United States. If you like riding two-wheelers, you go to Sturgis.

"Those motorized maniacs even pulled off a robbery at a federal credit union that netted more than twenty grand because of a federal fuck-up. Right in the middle of the day while we were watching! No, it wasn't the MDs and bean counters but the professional lawbreakers.

"Nobody could do a thing because we had to stay with Hirsch and protect him at all costs. We couldn't chase the bastards after they went zooming off on their bikes onto the back roads of the Black Hills' wilderness. There were other feds disguised in biker clothing, but they were too busy taking their spy pictures of potheads even to notice what was happening.

"Those thieves got away with armed robbery and terrorized everyone inside. We couldn't find them - even with more than a hundred undercover feds within several blocks of the stick-up. Now was that any way to run a government operation?

"From the Bandidos to the Black Pistons, Outlaws, Hell's Angels, Pagans, and the Vagos, those gangbangers loved Hirsch because he knew how to make a sweetheart deal for the leaders of the packs. He represented a couple of those badasses who sometime later got into WitSec with Ari's help.

"Yes, they were hoodies, but they still needed legal representation. Hirsch got a few to plead guilty for not filing income tax returns. He got the IRS to reduce the charges to misdemeanors and they served no jail time.

"The sitting judge ordered them to join the Christian Bikers Association, and each had to do one-thousand hours of community service. They wound up giving all their assets to the revenue department, except for their motorcycles. They began going to church and unmistakably proved Ari's belief in redemption was dead right.

They went from being cutthroats to converts.

"They knew they owed their emancipation and rediscovered lives to Hirsch. Anytime he needed a favor, even if it wasn't at the annual bikers' rally, he knew somewhere in Sturgis someone would help. Everyone knew Ari. I mean everyone, including the mayor, the innkeepers, shopkeepers, the wait staffs in the restaurants, the local constables, the town's attorneys, doctors, even the undercover agents."

Unconsciously, Buggelshofer was now beginning to refer to Hirsch by his first name indicating their relationship was far more than federal Marshal and federal witness.

"Now that I've said my bit, let's get past this drug and money-grabbing crap and move on to how we're going to help solve the real puzzle facing the President and Mitsch the bitch." A rare hush infused the courtroom. Its temporary inhabitants became as quiet as motionless butterflies feasting on flowers. Everyone sat in sweet-and-welcome silence and ruminated about Buggelshofer's short, well-intentioned, and well-intoned oratory. They knew he was right. Way deep down, they all knew he was right, particularly about Hirsch's stubbornness to ensure everyone was legally protected.

"It's time for a lunch break." Rosselfellar interrupted the uncomfortable quiet and asked his minions to stay in the courtroom.

He walked to the entrance, opened the door halfway, and asked one of the guards to bring in lunch his secretary had arranged.

There would be one leftover ham sandwich and potato chips because of Ianucci bolting from the meeting. Buggy and E.F. wolfed down the extra pig-meat-on-rye as though they hadn't eaten in a month. It was a bit more pork delivered by the U.S. government and paid for by the taxpayers.

Hamilton walked into the judge's chambers, turned on his mobile phone and dialed the classified number to the Oval Office.

"Mr. President, I apologize but once again I have nothing significant to report. I hope we'll be able to make progress this afternoon and institute an action plan. We're working on it as hard as we can, and I won't disappoint you."

He paused for about ten seconds, frustrated that the boss was speaking in rather a strong pitch.

"Thank you for your confidence, Mr. President. I'll be back to you in a couple of hours." Hamilton put down the phone and thought how great it would be to go find an empty beach somewhere in the Caribbean, settle himself on the warm sand, and light up a big fat joint of "yellow sunshine."

CHAPTER TWENTY-ONE

"The fight against drug trafficking is a wildfire that threatens to consume those fundamental rights of the individual deliberately enshrined in our Constitution."

Juan Burciaga, Chief Judge, U.S. District Court of New Mexico

One Hour Later-1:15 PM, Tuesday, July 8, 2008

JOINT TASK FORCE MEETING-BEFORE THE CALL

Buggelshofer may have had his say a bit more than an hour prior, but E.F. Hutton hadn't. Before this meeting would continue, the FBI retiree demanded time. He didn't give Rosselfellar or Hamilton enough leeway even to open their mouths. Neither was everyone sitting when Hutton began his fluid testimony.

"This is for the record. Perhaps I should have mentioned these things before the break. By the way," he said, looking at Rosselfellar, "thanks for the extra half sandwich."

"You're welcome, E.F. Keep talking."

"I don't think any of you appreciate the full scope of Ari's affiliations, connections, movements. We're talking about big-time associations few people know about. Radical ones that made no sense to me but as you begin to age you become a bit more incisive and understand what makes people revolve.

"I'm not here to give you lessons on life. I'm here to give you the benefit of the facts so that maybe you'll figure out who Ari Hirsch really is and what he's capable of doing.

"One of the philosophies of the bureau was to always create a situational analysis with as much background material as possible before acting impulsively. So, allow me to give you some history on Ari Hirsch.

"Some of you are too young to remember the Wounded Knee incident back in seventy-three at the Pine Ridge Reservation in southwest South Dakota. You may have heard of it, but you weren't there. Buggy and I were.

"Damn reservation was the poorest one in the country. The government didn't care about any Native Americans who ever lived there, including Crazy Horse. Two of my bureau buddies were killed and a Marshal was paralyzed during that Wounded Knee stand-off.

"Two years later, we lost two more men in the Pine Ridge Shootout. We extradited a Sioux, Leonard Peltier, who had escaped to Canada. We tried and convicted him for the murders, and he landed in the federal pen at Lewisburg. "There was always doubt in a lot of minds, including mine, as to whether he was guilty. We tried two of his tribesmen for the same crime and found them not guilty even before Peltier's extradition back to the states.

"The evidence against him was as flimsy as a cheap negligee. His penalty was two life terms, and he's still sitting in that Pennsylvania slammer.

"So, you know what Ari does? Takes a hundred grand from the profits he made on his Deadwood deal and turns it over to Peltier's legal defense fund! Cash! Every time he went out to that reservation, he donated always in cash to the Sioux Nation. He thought the trial was political garbage.

"I'll tell you what I learned when he donated that outrageous sum. Hirsch has more allies than the United States government. Why? Because so many people believe he's always doing the right thing. Maybe the government never agreed with him, but the people he helped sure did."

He looked at Rappaport from NDIC and asked, "What's that word in Hebrew for doing something good?"

"Mitzvah," Rappaport said.

"That's a hard word for me to remember but one we shouldn't forget."

The retiree got a bit melancholy knowing he had spent a lifetime thinking he was tracking down the bad guys when some of those "bad guys" turned out to be not as "bad" as he had once been led to believe.

"Hirsch always thought he was doing good deeds. He probably still believes that. Those 'mitzvies' he used to call them."

"Mitzvahs," said Rappaport. "It's pronounced mitzvahs."

"Mitzvahs or mitzvies. It doesn't matter. He earned the respect from the best of us and the worst of us, but not the government. When it came to taking care of people, Hirsch was the first one to take a step forward. He didn't really have to like the people. He merely had to believe that what he was doing was the right thing.

"Like he did with those Monkey Wrenchers out west. Arizona, Colorado, Utah, Washington, Oregon. Those eco-terrorists did everything they could to blow up roads, homes, dams, and everything else they could destroy in the name of stopping what they said was the 'bastardization' of the land.

"Some of those saboteurs were even growing acres and acres of marijuana on public lands and in forests they were trying to protect. Those crazies broke the RICO statutes. No question they were involved in some serious crimes in their attempts to save the planet. "We called 'em The Monkey Wrench Gang because they adopted the philosophies of a book by the same name written by some ecology freak.

"They might as well have called themselves the 'Multibombers' because as a group they acted like the 'Unabomber.' Some of these so-called educated environmental misfits to this day make the pronouncement that there's no compromise in defense of the Earth.

Those assholes even plant explosives in trees to maim and kill loggers just to prove their point. "But there was Ari again. Saved a couple of their skins big time. Hirsch got one of them into WitSec because he gave up a couple of his tree-hugging friends in a plea deal. Those guys conspired to blow up a chemical plant. They probably would have if their tell-all buddy hadn't betrayed them. They'd have taken him out as well."

"WitSec? We're protecting radical environmentalists in WitSec?"

Rosselfellar couldn't believe what he was hearing.

"Have you been hiding in an overgrown onion field?" Wazinski was always quick to deride what he thought was a churlish question.

Hutton interrupted. "Ari wanted to protect all of 'em and he probably still would. So don't think for a second, he's not capable even at the age of sixty-eight to be as clear-headed and as legally astute as he was at forty-eight. The only thing you're gonna pull on him is his pecker. Sorry, Ms. Watts."

"No apology necessary."

"Throughout the years, the bureau has tried to predict every one of Hirsch's moves. No matter how many times we tried profiling him, we could never figure him out. We brought in experts from Quantico and from every think-tank in DC, but to no avail.

"He's singular. There's no precedent and no template to follow. And there are no delineators. So, the best thing for everyone in this room to do is pay attention to Buggelshofer's and my experiences with him."

What Hutton hadn't told them yet was Hirsch's ability to adapt and avoid detection. Ari and Sandra had taken to living like they never had. They camped, they hiked, they rode horses. They illegally crossed the U.S.-Canadian border as easily as easily as Mexicans traversed the Rio Grande.

With Sandra's north-of-the-border relatives spread across the provinces, it was easy for them to keep in contact with family and perhaps get a little pot to boot. When Hutton mentioned this aspect of their lives under witness protection, Rosselfellar quickly responded.

"I don't really give a damn about Hirsch smoking some marijuana or where he got it from. For all I care he could have had a few grass patches growing in his backyard.

"What really concerns me is his talent for going undetected like a cat burglar. How do we know that if he agrees to meet with Schnabel that Hirsch won't fly to Europe and make his way to those Liechtenstein vaults?"

"We don't know," said Hutton. "You can be assured of that. As much as we want Hirsch's cooperation, it's going to be an uphill battle the whole way."

Hutton was through talking. At least until the call from the President to Hamilton and Buggelshofer's call to Ari.

CHAPTER TWENTY-TWO

"A first-time drug offender will get a ten-year mandatory minimum without chance of parole in the federal system. That's a long goddamn time. And there's no out. You're looking at an office that has an over 90 percent conviction rate. And if you're convicted, you spend ten years, and there's no more parole in the federal system."

Jonathan Turley, U.S. Constitutional scholar, law professor and television commentator

15 Minutes Later-1:30 PM, Tuesday, July 8, 2008

JOINT TASK FORCE MEETING-TWO CALLS LATER

"The President does not want to linger another minute. The pressure he's getting from Mitsch and her ministers is getting unbearable." Hamilton needed to move the meeting into high gear, which meant the call to Hirsch had to happen quickly.

"The German Chancellor is saying that the United States cannot justify its lack of action which might undermine the economic well-being of an ally," Hamilton said. He actually believed Mitsch was attempting political exploitation.

"Tell the Chancellor I think she's full of spoiled sauerkraut," snapped Smitherman. "We've protected those swine long enough. German citizens are the culprits, not us. They're the ones who hid the money in shielded accounts so why do we have to be put on the grill?"

The rest of his colleagues wanted to give him a standing ovation but took the clap out of their applause because of the conservative courtroom setting. They also appreciated his not cursing in front of Bonnie Watts.

"That bitch has no business pressuring us. Forgive me, Ms. Watts."

"For heaven's sake, quit trying to vindicate yourself for cussing already and move ahead with the important matters. Call Hirsch and screw Mitsch. And Mr. Hamilton, the next time you call the Oval Office tell the occupant we're going to get this fucking case resolved."

Watts was as anxious to cure the headache as the rest of the feds in the courtroom, and eager to let everybody know she was one of the guys.

"Can't do that, Ms. Watts, but thanks for the suggestion," replied Hamilton.

"There's something else many of you already know," said Homeland Security's Patterson. "We've had Hirsch and Sandra under twenty-four-hour surveillance for the past six years. Prior to that the NSA, DEA, Customs – every department represented in this courtroom – have cooperated in observing their every move.

"Car tracking devices, GPS, night vision goggles, wireless hidden cameras, computer monitoring, fiber optic inspection scopes, audio intercepts – we've used everything possible to keep tabs on them. Even rummaged through their trash at least fifty times. Rest assured there have been no lapses in security and no travel outside of the continental United States on the part of either of them."

Buggelshofer added, "Although decades have passed, every fed in Florida and many in the district knew that Hirsch was one of a small list of attorneys who major drug smugglers would seek out for advice.

"Hirsch taught them how to pay their income taxes, manage their international finances and make sweet deals with the government. We suspect he and Sandra know they've been watched for a very long time.

But as far as we can tell, they've moved on and are living under new identities."

"Make the phone call, Buggy, make the call." Hamilton wanted to rev up the meeting.

Once again, Buggelshofer reached in his pocket for his cell phone to look up Ari's number. Stalling further was not an option. Everyone's arguments were played out. The important thing now was to speak to Hirsch so at least the President would know there was some momentum.

"How is it that Hirsch hasn't gotten to the LGT vaults already? Because Schnabel says so? How do we know he's telling the truth when he's already been proven to be a thief and a calculated liar?" asked Underman from the IRS.

"We don't know for certain," said Patterson, "but it's highly unlikely. If Schnabel knew Hirsch had already raided the safe deposit boxes, there would be no reason for him to want the meeting. The only thing I can come up with is that he wants to smooth-talk him into a share of the money. Hirsch will have him stuck like a fuckin' duck in a dry pond if he tries that."

By now, Rosselfellar was angrier than a rampaging Rambo. "Will everyone now please shut up? This is turning out to be the mother of all government cluster-fucks! You people are like a colony of E. coli infecting each other. Let's get to the phone call. Forget all this supposition and move on. Buggelshofer, dial the goddamn number."

Rosselfellar leaned over and pressed the voice-activation toggle on the speakerphone. "All you need to do is call out the number and it will connect."

"I'm not gonna repeat it aloud. This number is unpublished. I don't want anyone in this room to think I don't trust them." Buggy knew he couldn't trust anybody in the courtroom with anything. "But that would break a confidence with Hirsch, and I'm not gonna do that."

"Well, then, get over here and dial it," demanded Rosselfellar, trying his best to hasten the pace. Buggelshofer, who forgot the feds had Ari's number for years, got up from his jury seat, took a step down to the courtroom floor, and walked over to the phone. He push-buttoned the number and let it ring.

"You don't have to scream. Speak in a normal voice and it'll be fine." Rosselfellar didn't want everyone in the District to hear what was about to take place.

"Hello. Ari Hirsch speaking."

"Ari, it's Buggy from the Marshal Service."

"Hey, Buggy. Long time no speak. It's been almost a year. Where have you been and what are you doing? No need to really answer right now since I know you're calling me from the District."

"What are you, psychic? How'd you know that?"

"The area code, Buggy. Your phone is programmed 'private caller' but my decoder pops it on the screener. Hey, I didn't mean to say 'pops' to make you sound old. Good to hear from you. Have you spoken to Hutton lately?"

No way was Hirsch going to say anything that could be misconstrued and used against him later.

"He's here with me now, Ari. We're on speakerphone with some folks at Justice. Before we begin our conversation, I need to let you know this call is authorized and sanctioned by the White House."

The click of the speakerphone and the dial tone that followed stunned everyone in the courtroom. Yes, without another word, Hirsch purposely disconnected the call. The White House? What could Buggy possibly be calling about concerning the President and me? Are recruits so hard to find that they brought back two 75-year-old retirees? How dumb do they think I am? Buggelshofer's mouth is in gear, but his brain is in neutral.

Hirsch knew it was a set-up, a ruse, a way of getting him pliable enough to help with something the government wanted. What he wanted to say was, "Tell one of the feds to get on a plane and come down to meet me in a private setting. No wires. No bugs. No surveillance. Those bastards."

Puzzled as he was, it wasn't enough for Ari to stay on the phone and talk. That's the way it would be at least until he came up with a plan.

"Who the hell does he think he is?" Hamilton asked as he jumped to his feet, stiffened his body, and felt his blood pressure reach the near-stroke point. As he paced back and forth in front of the jury box, it was demonstrable he didn't give a thought about how he appeared to anyone.

"Call him back and tell him we're not going to take any of his horseshit! You tell that scumbag he's not only going to cause constant harassment of his family and friends, but that he's hindering a Presidential transition team and a major Task Force operation. Any charges we can slap on him, we will!"

Although the November elections were months away, the contenders were well ahead of the results. They were making swift decisions about whom their cabinet members and key staff appointees might be.

Hamilton, as Chief of Staff, had to make sure everything went as unwrinkled as a nylon American flag, now and during the passing of the Presidential baton.

"Hold it, Hamilton! If you threaten Hirsch in this courtroom again, so help me Jesus I will walk out of this room the same way Ianucci did! Wanna shoot yourself in the foot and have Mitsch on yours and the President's ass? Go right ahead.

"Now if you'll quit being a damn fool, I'll dial his number again. Believe me I'll get him to assist us but let me steer it from here. If not, I trot." Buggelshofer was in no mood for political pursuits.

Hamilton said nothing. He was too nervous, too embarrassed, too frustrated. All he could do was mumble the words, "Go ahead."

Once again, Rosselfellar turned on the speakerphone and Buggy punched the numbers. The phone rang endlessly then stopped.

"Are you there, Ari?" Buggy heard nothing but noiselessness and a tension punctured only by the quiet hiss of the speaker. Would there be a breakthrough? Would Hirsch relent and answer the question? Did he have the chutzpah to turn down the President of the United States?

The courtroom was as silent as an extinction chamber seconds before the needle was inserted into the arm of a death-row inmate on killing night.

As the feds held their breath, they suddenly heard a dial tone. Again. A loud one. Their stomachs churned then tumbled. Hutton leaned forward in his seat, placed his elbows on his knees, and placed his hands over his face.

Did anyone really think Hirsch was going to answer and speak to anyone calling from the 202-area code? If they did, they were half a bubble off plumb.

No, Ari wasn't there. It was apparent he picked up the phone and hung up a few moments later given they all heard another loud and clear dial tone. He wasn't going to answer a second time while government agents were listening to him, recording him, pestering him, prodding him. He knew better. Time to ponder and discern how he was going to treat the next call was what Hirsch needed most. How, he thought, could he protect himself without landing in the slammer?

One slip of the tongue and he'd be in front of a federal judge within hours, defending whatever charges they could create even if they weren't legitimate.

The situation, Ari thought, was almost equal to that of the East German Stasi or the Romanian Securitate. Public denunciation and humiliation by ultranationalists against those in disagreement with the government were customary. Monitoring and breaking into homes and offices were commonplace.

Self-preservation was Hirsch's objective during and after his law career. He feverishly protected himself and his clients because he knew what the outcome had often been. He had studied and analyzed the legal structures of repressive regimes when the Iron Curtain was still open on the world stage.

Monitoring all incoming and outgoing voice and electronic communications was the daily cycle. Bugging telephones and intercepting wire transmissions. Placing microphones in public and private buildings. Nearly all conversations were listened to by the government apparatus.

Autocrats and informants ran the system. If they thought "traitors" were undermining the state, ghastly prison conditions or liquidation were the answers. "Enemies of the state" were routinely beaten, denied medical attention, had their mail taken away, not to mention their dignity. Removing family members from their jobs and assailing their human rights were routine. They, too, knew they could soon be behind bars if they took a single liberty of nay-saying the established order.

Those kinds of events somehow didn't seem too foreign to Ari and many of his clients. Or even thousands of others who were the victims of trumped-up charges.

Other than automatic executions, Hirsch always questioned if the government of the United States of America acted much differently. By all standards, if the feds wanted to pin the tail on your donkey-ass, they did. They conveniently adopted all-encompassing laws, including conspiracy, to make it easier to arrest people.

That was the way the Nazis did it. They enacted the Nuremburg Laws and made it legal to discriminate against millions of their fellow citizens. Laws became the tools du jour, the devices that made it perfectly acceptable to annihilate millions. In the United States, criminal conspiracy and obstruction of justice were two of the favorite legal weapons. Ari knew that all too well. The U.S. government always had the leverage. Always.

Hirsch wasn't going to make it easy this time. He had three-and-a-half decades of daily intrusion into his professional and personal life. Jailed. Beleaguered. Harried. Hounded. Provoked.

They never relented. The feds were like dingoes feasting on a kangaroo kill. Ari had repeatedly seen government vultures rip the flesh from the helpless and the hopeless. Unlike cornered rats, there was no way to fight back successfully. Once the feds wanted to prosecute, they began by intimidation, then worked their way up to hounding, heckling, plaguing, tormenting, badgering, and finally stuffing you away in some forbidden place.

Whether you were in WitSec or one of the secluded cells in a basement of a federal courthouse, they had you until you cooperated and told them what they wanted to know. If you didn't, you paid a heavy price.

Like the one paid by Susan McDougal in the Whitewater real estate scandal during the William Jefferson Clinton presidency in the 90s. After refusing to answer questions in front of a grand jury, she was locked in jail for almost two years, including eight months in solitary confinement.

It might have been a famous story in American history, but it wasn't the finest hour for American jurisprudence.

Ari followed the case closely. He had been outraged by the proceedings because he had a number of clients who had suffered similar consequences. No evidence and no proof of committing a crime yet being jailed anyway. "I feared being accused of perjury if I told the grand jury the truth," said McDougal. She became the subject of the American government's time-tested prosecutorial practice of "diesel hauling,"; schlepping defendants frequently around the country and locking them in different jails to make it difficult for them to be in contact with their lawyers and case files.

They shackled her legs and wrists, chained them together then transported her from Arkansas to Los Angeles to Oklahoma City and back to Arkansas.

Friends questioned Ari about the charges. He could only tell them what the government "set-up" was: obstruction of an agency proceeding, making false statements to federal investigators, and civil and criminal contempt of court.

Without a shred of evidence, the woman suffered her sentence in silence. Finally pardoned at the end of Clinton's second term in office, McDougal served every day of her imposed prison time.

"Even serial killer Ted Bundy got better legal treatment than that," remarked one of Hirsch's lawyer friends."

"True," Hirsch had contended. "But then look what they did to Bill Clinton. Was he treated any better?"

The entire country knew Kenneth Starr wanted to put President Clinton into impeachment status by getting someone to testify against him.

"If they did that to the world's most powerful individual," Hirsch asserted, "they could easily stick it to me and everyone else they wanted. That Starr Chamber was a stain on the Constitution."

The thought of what happened to McDougal and Clinton was enough motivation for Hirsch to remain silent when his phone rang the second time.

With the disappearance of his voice, almost every agent in the courtroom went one step short of psycho. Haywire. Loony. Frantic. Daffy. Each was delirious and had something sparkling and profound to say.

"The President is going to have a shit fit," Hamilton said. "Now what the hell are we supposed to do? I can't call him without a successful outcome. What are you going to do about this?" he asked Rosselfellar.

"Me? What do you mean me? I'm in the tax division of Justice. I can't nab him on any creatively devised tax charge. Don't bug me about it, Hamilton. You're the one who wants this done so you can kiss the administration's collective ass! "I hate the son-of-a-bitch, but I can't charge him with a thing and without legal ammunition, my hands are tied. What do you want me to do? Charge him with real estate speculation?"

"Hang another charge on the prick! What about conspiracy?" asked Smitherman, a lawyer himself who knew how to lock up anyone under the guise of 'national security.'

"Who did he conspire with? His wife? His kids? His unidentified friends? How're you gonna prove that stupid charge?" asked Buggy.

"We're not, damn it. All we need to do is charge him and arrest him. Let him rot in a fucking cell until he decides to help us." Watts finally proved she was one of the guys. "I'll make a firm promise we'll get him on obstruction. He knows it, too. So don't even think twice about trying to get him to play ball. We can strike him out more times than the Babe whiffed."

Rappaport was a big baseball fan. He grew up in the Bronx attending Yankees' games in "The House That Ruth Built" and couldn't help sliding in those lines. Patterson of Homeland Security hadn't said much. Until now. He was apoplectic. "For the rest of his life, we'll never leave Hirsch alone. If he steps near an airport, he's going down. Every TSA employee will be on the lookout for him, his wife, his kids, and his grandkids!

"We're not going to let him or any member of his family out of the country or take a flight even within the contiguous forty-eight. They'll all be on no-fly lists. If there is anything our department can do to haunt them, we'll do it. Tell him that! We'll pry him loose with whatever it takes."

If the feds thought Hirsch was as sharp as a set of Ginsu Knives, they were going to make sure his blades were blunted even though they wanted him castrated.

CHAPTER TWENTY-THREE

"Yes, I'm saying that we might as well legalize the junk. Put taxes on it, license the distributors, establish age limits and treat it like hooch. If someone wants to sniff away their nose or addle their brain, so be it. They're doing it now, anyway, and at least we'd be rid of the gun battles, the corruption, and the wasted money and effort trying to save the brains and noses of those who don't want them saved."

Mike Royko, Pulitzer Prize-winning syndicated columnist and best-selling author

2 Hour and 55 Minutes Later - 4:25 PM, Tuesday, July 8, 2008

JOINT TASK FORCE MEETING - THIRD TIME'S A CHARM

Fruitful result or not, Hamilton knew he had to call the President once again. As soon as the half-hour conversation was finished, he walked into the courtroom. In a clarion appeal he told everyone that unless they got a hold of Hirsch and he conceded to a meeting with Schnabel, there would be absolutely no rest for any of them. They were there for the stretch.

"President's orders."

They already knew that. All of them. No one was able to argue the point. Reaching Hirsch had to happen immediately, or they'd all be in the courtroom till midnight or after.

Physically and mentally spent, the one thing they all had in common was a desire to go home. They certainly didn't want to have to spend the night in a District hotel and get up early the next morning to continue psychological warfare.

No one was going anywhere until the President gave his blessing.

"Buggelshofer, if you and Hutton can't get Hirsch to answer the phone, you might as well be prepared to stay here until you do. Whatever creative talents you have for getting Hirsch to speak to us, use them. If you don't, it's going to be quite an ordeal," sniped Hamilton.

The group expected that kind of comment as Hamilton's voice began to take on an off keynote of strain.

"We're going to have to keep trying until Hirsch decides to speak to us," offered Brown. "Eventually, we'll break him. He has to talk because he knows what his silence will precipitate." In his daily life as head of the IRS, Brown was a hardliner. His department used threats and every other devious action to extract any information they could from people whether they cooperated or not. Throwing people in the slammer was not a big deal to Brown or to most people who worked for the Revenue Service.

Buggy," barked Rosselfellar, "get back to the phone and call that ball breaker!" "

For the third time, Buggelshofer, who by now felt like life in a nursing facility would have been a better alternative to his present situation, walked to the phone even more reluctantly than before and pressed "redial."

"Leave a message." Beep.

That was it. A three-word command in a male voice followed by a tone that bewildered everyone. Buggy was so stupefied that he blathered incoherently. "Huh? Who is this? What?"

Rosselfellar pressed the "off" button and terminated the call.

"Where the hell did that come from? I thought he'd at least answer, even if he didn't say anything," bemoaned Rosselfellar.

"Try Hirsch again and tell him to call our speakerphone number," Smitherman said. Becoming bigwig of the National Security Agency meant the former top-level security analyst at least had some well-founded thoughts.

He knew the meaning of clever. "He may be signaling a clue that he wants to talk to us, but that he wants to control the conversation. Trust me on this one."

"Leave a message." Beep.

Same number, same voice, same message.

Different response from the feds.

"Ari, it's Buggy again. Please call me at – what's the number here?"

Rosselfellar yelled, "202-555-1971." Buggelshofer had forgotten to ask for the number prior to the call.

"This guy's a few shingles short of a roof," thought Wazinski.

"And please do it as quickly as possible," added Buggy. "There's an international crisis involved. Thank you, Ari."

At least Rappaport had the presence of mind to activate the CD recorder. He wanted to be ready for any contingency.

"If Hirsch calls back, does anyone want to add anything to the conversation that we haven't already discussed?" As Rosselfellar recharged his meeting battery, he anticipated there would be some comments, but none was forthcoming.

What he didn't anticipate was the reappearance of Ianucci. The entry door to the courtroom swung open and in walked the man from State.

"What are you doing here?" Rosselfellar demanded an answer.

"Well, perhaps I misjudged the need for my participation. Don't for a minute think I made an error in judgment by walking out this morning. I'm still quite convinced you haven't done a thing to move this case forward.

"In addition, it seems the Middle East concerns were not as much of a crunch as I thought. I was able to assuage all sides engaged in the controversy."

They all knew he was lying like a kid who'd played hooky from school and went to the movies. Political babble was easy to recognize. The Secretary of State, they found out later, had threatened to have him deployed to Kabul unless he went back to the FISA courtroom and tried to loosen the rope around the government's neck. Ianucci was running on scared and the panicked look he wore on his face was proof enough.

In deference to the Schnabel mission, Rosselfellar told Ianucci to take the previously occupied jury seat that still held the sign referencing his name. "I'll do that Rosselfellar but keep this thing moving before I leave it behind me, only next time I won't come back. This is incompetence at its worst."

"Fuckin' dago," Wazinski mouthed, once again not loud enough for anyone to hear. He had more than enough experience with his vocabulary several years before when one of his African American colleagues decked him after he called him "Brillo-head."

He learned to keep his voice down to an acceptable dulcet volume after a conscious right hook knocked him unconscious.

The waiting was nerve-racking and painfully tense. Would Ari call? If he did, what would he say? If he agreed to help the feds, what demands would he make? If he didn't call, what would be their fallback position? Was he fool enough to think the government wouldn't get him? Indict him? Pummel him in court? Throw him behind bars? The big hand on each of their wristwatches and large courtroom clock indicated that twenty-one minutes had passed since Buggelshofer called Hirsch. Each of the succeeding seconds was making the scene more taut, more strained. Suddenly, the phone rang. Everyone was still as though a photographer was about to take a group picture. Rosselfellar pressed the button so everyone could hear.

"This is Ari Hirsch. Please do not talk or I will hang up. I will, indeed, cooperate with the government but only after you meet certain criteria, including legal assurances. No changes. No negotiating away my rights. No breaking commitments. As soon as a single letter is changed, the deal is off. As soon as I sense betrayal, the deal goes sour. As soon as I feel the federal government is not keeping its word, the deal disappears.

"I want everyone who's in the room right now" – Ari hadn't the vaguest idea who or where they were, only that Buggy and Hutton were somewhere with colleagues – "to agree to send me daily transcripts of all of our telephone conversations, audio and video intercepts, and all documents pertinent to this case. I want all those papers signed and notarized by the transcriber with appropriate certifications of correctness.

"In addition, ship all of the documents via overnight federal courier directly to my home.

"I still have assets that were tied up during my time in WitSec. I have never been fully compensated for those unlaundered funds. A check in the amount of fifty-two-thousand-seven-hundred-seventy-seven dollars needs to be drawn by the U.S. Treasury made out to my covert name and sent to me along with the documents.

"I'm now sixty-eight and don't know how much longer I'll be around. No money? No honey.

"Our agreement will provide that any failure to comply in full with its terms and conditions shall constitute a complete and irrevocable breach of our understanding, and as such, will be considered an act of bad faith and prosecutorial misconduct on the part of everyone in the room you're in, the United States government, and the agencies participating in this case.

"In addition, I want a complete list of names and titles of everyone who is listening to or recording this conversation.

"Further, if you default on any of these promises, requests or demands, a civil rights lawsuit for recovery can and will be filed and admitted into a federal court in the county where I reside and cannot be objected to under any grounds presently contained in any federal criminal or civil code of procedure.

"As part of the agreement, all parties accused of wrongful conduct under its covenants will be jointly and severally liable for their conduct in violation hereof and agree to waive any and all governmental and sovereign immunity defenses in the event of subsequent civil rights litigation filed by me."

The heads of everyone on the Task Force were spinning faster than a record-breaking Frisbee toss.

"Is that it Ari?" Buggy was getting crankier by the second and began licking his parched lips.

"No, it's not. In addition to the above and by the way, since you're recording all this communication, I want it properly prepared in written form with appropriate signatures, certifications, and authorizations, and tell your superiors the following: for me to speak with any or all designated persons regarding our understanding, I am demanding a grant of full and complete national and international immunity.

"That includes criminal and civil charges for all acts that may unfold directly or indirectly from this conversation, and any events, which may have occurred before this conversation with federal agents or representatives-or any other conversations or events which might follow this conversation."

Buggy butted in. "Ari, you're going a bit too fast for us. Would you mind holding for a minute?"

"Make it fast, Buggy. I have an appointment in ten minutes."

Rappaport hit the "mute" switch while Hamilton screamed, "This is the biggest prick I've ever encountered! The bastard belongs in a federal pen."

"He's already been in more than a few visiting clients," Hutton injected.

"The other times he was locked up the government couldn't keep him for very long. Hirsch always, but always, came up with a legal loophole to get himself out. I can guarantee you he knows what iron bars are all about." Hamilton's heart raced as though he had just run a marathon, and he started to flex his jawbones not aware his ears were wiggling. His fists clenched shut almost as hard as he gnashed his teeth. The only thing he could think of was to slap the crap out of his nemesis. Time was of the essence and Hamilton knew he was losing it.

As Rappaport turned on the speakerphone again, Buggy asked, "Are there any other contingencies, Ari?" Everyone was praying there weren't. Except Ari.

"Yes. I want all the immunity agreements signed by the President and Attorney-General of the United States. I want the Chief Justice of the Supreme Court, as well as the head of the Department of Justice, to sign them as well. I also want the leaders of those countries which may be involved and affected in this investigation to sign and certify similar immunity waivers. No signatures, no deal.

"Once you've completed your work, overnight the original and one photocopy of all of the documents to me. Also, send the content of all documentation to my BlackBerry – you already have that number – and a completed copy of everything to my attorney, Jordan O'Banion.

"As soon as I receive and review all of the exercised documents, we can do business. Until then, gentlemen, I have nothing else to say."

Another click and another dial tone that seemed louder than the previous ones.

Hirsch didn't even have a plan. How could he? He had zero knowledge about the investigation or even if it was an investigation. He had no notion that he would soon have a meeting with the one person who single-handedly could collapse individual financial empires and politically destroy regimes. He was beginning to internalize and personalize the position he was in.

How was my government going to take back all the years of abuse my wife, my family, my friends, and my clients have suffered because of the endless War on Drugs? When will my government stop invalidating sections of the U.S. Constitution?

The only thing he knew for sure was the feds had all of his and his attorney's contact information from decades of spying on him and Sandra. They also had twenty-year-old WitSec records.

While Ari was pondering what would happen, Hamilton was playing it out in his own mind.

Even if the President agrees to all these outrageous demands, how in the world are we going to get the drafts of what he wants without going through pure hell? Which agency is going to supervise all of this? Who has bottom-line responsibility? How long will it take to get all this accomplished? Will Hirsch agree to the meeting with Schnabel? How can we end the War on Drugs?

The questions were endless and there were no quick answers. The one thing Hamilton knew for sure: there was no way the government would stop the drug war. "Jesus," Hamilton snorted, "we're even more fucked up than before! My apology, Ms. Watts."

CHAPTER TWENTY-FOUR

"The War on Drugs is wrong, both tactically and morally. It assumes that people are too stupid, too reckless, and too irresponsible to decide whether and under what conditions to consume drugs. The War on Drugs is morally bankrupt."

Larry Elder, Attorney, author, and conservative/libertarian radio and television personality

1 Hour and 35 Minutes Later - 6:00 PM, Tuesday, July 8, 2008

JOINT TASK FORCE MEETING - PREPARATION H

"I didn't realize Preparation H was your ointment of choice, Hamilton." What a way to end a phone call with the fabled resident of the White House.

"Mr. President, I'm sorry but I don't understand."

"The 'H' is for Hirsch, Hamilton. You're preparing to let him squeeze out of a tube and grease your ass! Don't you know what he's attempting to do? If you let him control the situation, we'll never get this done and I need it done today! No more stalling! No more excuses! You need to accomplish the assignment!"

"Mr. President, we're doing everything we possibly can to get everything done in a timely manner." In all the years he had known him, Hamilton never heard the boss talk that way. Not even when he was governor.

Normally, he had been moderate in expression and quite accommodating but now he was acting completely out of character; almost irrationally perhaps because he didn't grasp the enormity of the complicated process.

Could have been he was under too much strain. But Hamilton wasn't prepared to yield. Neither did he want to give the Commander-in-Chief legal and logistics lessons.

"I'll call you in your private quarters tonight. It might be quite late before I have all the answers. Thank you for your time." He had taken enough Presidential abuse by now and politely dropped the phone into its reservoir. He hurriedly and worriedly walked back into the courtroom and announced to the group that not only would they be eating take-in Chinese food but needed to prepare their noodles for an all-nighter.

Ianucci called himself an "asshole" for coming back. Buggy passed out Xanax to anybody who wanted one. Other than Buggelshofer himself, E.F. was the only one who indulged. Watts told herself she'd rather be back at a border crossing in the Bitterroot Mountain range in Montana. It was bittersweet for the IRS and DEA guys since they wanted to go home but also wanted to protect their agencies' financial interests.

And Wazinski speculated, "Hirsch is a kike."

The rest of the Task Force grumbled about having to stay, but believed it was the right thing to do for the country. They knew the President was in a grievous mess, and recognized they were the linchpins in averting a serious scandal.

"Let's have another quick break so we can contact our families," Rappaport suggested. Rosselfellar yielded. Other than Buggy, each pulled out a cell phone from a pocket, purse or belt clip and reported to their individual spouses.

Bonnie Watts dialed a number and in a muffled voice said, "Arlene, I won't be home until after midnight." That's when the rest of the boys knew what they had already suspected. She was one of the guys.

"The first thing we need to get done is a flow chart, so think systematically," said Hamilton after everyone made the necessary calls. From his experience, he knew the team had to identify tasks, who was responsible for getting them done, and when they would realistically finish them.

"I'm sure all of you are going to need help tonight and tomorrow on a number of assignments. As soon as we take another break, call your most trusted people and have them on standby. Be sure to communicate that it's a national security issue but do not give them any of the details.

"We don't want rumors spreading throughout the District, and we certainly don't want anyone in The Capitol knowing what's going on. The underground rail system connecting the House and Senate buildings will become clogged forever if they find out.

"Rappaport. Set up a computer template and start entering the data. Get someone in the National Security Intelligence Center to transcribe, sign and notarize today's phone conversations with Hirsch. Make sure to find any audio or video intercepts of Hirsch or anyone connected with him. Record them on CDs and DVDs. If they're archived it shouldn't take long to accomplish.

"Smitherman, you can help in getting this done in tandem with Rappaport. Start digging out the information as quickly as possible.

"Rosselfellar, your department will write the grant of immunity and cooperation agreement. Make sure it's an omnibus one. Shield Hirsch from any crimes he might have committed-even those you think he might have committed. Include any possible illegalities relating to this case. I'll review it upon completion.

"In addition, you'll be responsible for getting the signature of the Chief Justice. I don't care if you have to wake him in the middle of the night. Get it! And it better be bona fide. I don't need any of this backfiring on us.

"Commissioner Brown, get someone in your office to cut a check for fifty-two-thousand-seven-hundred-seventy-seven dollars made out to Brian Goodman. And make sure it's not a penny less.

"Watts, once we have all the necessary materials in our hand including the check, you'll coordinate the delivery to Hirsch and his lawyer.

Call your department now and assign two persons to be ready for a travel alert within thirty minutes.

"They'll be heading for Broward County, Florida, so be certain you have all necessary clearances at all airports. Make sure your personnel have access to the Federal Aviation Interactive Reporting System web site to put an F-16 on readiness status.

"Ianucci, get a hold of the Secretary of State so she can contact Chancellor Mitsch to let her know it's mandatory that she grants immunity to Hirsch like she gave Schnabel.

"If she doesn't agree to it, there are standing orders from the White House to tell her she's hit a brick wall. Make that the Berlin Wall. If necessary, tell Mitsch that Hirsch has never stepped foot on German soil, nor will he.

"By the way, Ianucci, don't even think about walking out again.

"I'll personally take care of the President and ask him to get the necessary signatures from the Attorney-General.

"Hutton, call Hirsch again immediately," Hamilton said. "Under no circumstances can we negotiate with him. He knows he has the advantage, and we have no time left.

"If he still doesn't answer the phone, leave him a message. Tell him everything – and I mean everything – is occurring at warp speed. Get his number from Buggelshofer." Instead of talking into the speakerphone, Hutton picked up the receiver. He dialed Hirsch's number. 'Leave a message.' Beep.

"Ari, this is E.F. I'm giving you my word as an intermediary for the government we will enact everything you've requested. On behalf of the President, Chief of Staff Addison Hamilton has approved all conditions and will meet any additional demands he considers reasonable. You have my solemn word on that.

"All we want is your cooperation. We're not going to ask you to do anything illegal, immoral or that might put you at personal risk. You have to take my word on this, Ari.

"Without going into lots of detail, we're asking you to select a time and place for a meeting between you and Franz Schnabel, the ex-banker and technology guy from Liechtenstein. I'm sure you remember him. He's involved in an international swindle and the Germans have him on lockdown.

"The only way he'll continue to speak to authorities, including the Germans and us, is if you grant him a private meeting. And no, we haven't any idea why he wants to get together with you, but it must be of extreme importance.

"As soon as we let Chancellor Mitsch's office know you've consented to confer with Schnabel, they'll be flying him to Florida under extraordinarily tight security. That's most likely going to occur tomorrow between four and five in the afternoon.

"No need to call back. Pick the location and we'll know where you are. Once we determine you've left your home, that's enough of a signal to let us know you're on board." The phones and Hirsch's recording device went 'click-click' and took a rest.

Hirsch knew no matter where he went the feds were always there or would be there shortly. He was aware they knew his every move the minute he heard the words Schnabel, Liechtenstein, and Germany, he knew beyond a question of a doubt where this was heading.

Directly to the LGT Bank in Vaduz.

Hamilton paused for a moment as everyone in the courtroom began to digest the steamroller effect.

"I know that a number of you want a piece of Hirsch. That's not going to happen. At least not until we settle everything with the Germans. Hirsch holds the perfect hand right now.

"Let me inject something else." Hamilton turned to the jury box and sang out a warning.

"If Hirsch makes a single mistake or doesn't fully cooperate, his arrest will be swift. We'll hold him based on a misstatement to a federal agent and lack of good faith cooperation.

"If he acts in a conspiratorial manner in furtherance of violating a federal statute, if he interferes with this ongoing investigation, if he coerces testimony from anyone, or if he even speaks with someone who we consider a conspirator, we will consider those actions as breaking the deal. By federal law, all those charges are felonies.

"We can then slap him with obstruction of justice which would virtually guarantee that Hirsch would become a guest in a federal pen for the rest of his life."

That's what everyone in the room wanted to hear. Everyone except Buggy and E.F. The others were gloating gleefully.

Neither Buggelshofer nor Hutton would have taken on this responsibility unless it had been an issue of national security, even if their priority was the money. But they also had a sense of propriety and loyalty to Ari. Not holier-than-thou propriety and loyalty, but enough self-righteousness and sense of obligation to know they were doing the right thing even though the government was being appallingly vindictive.

Both felt morally squeezed.

Although some in the courtroom had never even met Ari Hirsch, they had learned to hate him. His distinction for being as ephemeral as an eel doused in a pail of petroleum jelly was as celebrated as New Year's Eve. Except no one was wearing a funny hat or drinking champagne.

"What about the taxes due if we recover any monies?" asked the IRS Commissioner. Rosselfellar assured him the accords with Hirsch, or any other party would not prevent the service from taxing the proceeds.

"If drug trafficking resulted in illegal profits, perhaps the government would be in a position to seize the funds and satisfy the claims made by all agencies entitled to the money," Rosselfellar added.

Hamilton hurled a surprise.

"The President has informed me that until this Task Force succeeds in securing the tax monies owed to the U.S., additional hiring and budgets are on hold for all agencies represented in this room."

Wazinski piped up. "What? This is a wholesale sellout. Pure bullshit. We have dozens of ways to get the entire story from Schnabel. By tying up our money and personnel in this political spectacle, how are my Marshals going to do their jobs?

"You're making one of the most horrendous mistakes in the history of the drug war. This is absolutely no way to continue the fight and all of you know it!"

197 / Ron Ruthfield

"This has little or nothing to do with the War on Drugs, but everything to do with tax fraud," said IRS Commissioner Brown. "What the hell have you been thinking during this meeting?"

"I know you want to grab as much as you can, Brown, but if you can't recognize that drug money is behind all of this, you must be suffering from insanity and enjoying every moment!" Wazinski was on a tear.

"The bank vaults over there may be filled with currency and gold, but where do you think those assets came from? Santa Claus? They came from international drug deals and Hirsch was involved. Why do you think he asked for complete immunity?"

Throughout the years, everyone in the cavernous chamber had heard about the deals in the 70s and 80s Hirsch had been able to cut with the DEA, DOJ, IRS, Customs, and the FBI.

"Sleaze-deals between your agencies and Hirsch are nothing new," Wazinski added. "And all of you know damn well the Marshals never once entered into that kind of agreement with anyone."

Hirsch's negotiations often took space on the front page. Many of his drug-dealing clients had never gone to jail at all. Instead, they received fines for minor tax infractions and served little time, if any. Most of the racketeers lived out their existences financially well fixed, mystifying a whole bunch of feds, especially the Marshals. To Wazinski, it was inexplicable and maddening and caused more than a few raised eyebrows.

"We've even given safe haven to fucking murderers!" Wazinski was as frosted as his agency's frozen funds. "Shit, there was one guy from the ginzo mob in Philly who spent only ten months in jail for killing seventeen people! Do you have a case of the crazies?"

Rosselfellar was not distracted from keeping his cool. For the most part, his law school and courtroom experience grounded him. He wasn't about to display how deeply provoked he was at Wazinski.

"What you're not remembering," remarked Rosselfellar, "is that Hirsch has made deals with informers who continue to work undercover to the benefit of the United States. That's right, Wazinski. Even for the Marshal Service, DEA, IRS, and FBI. This is not the time to talk about monetary seizures, how they were divided and who got away with what."

"Some of these criminals have been paid millions and millions of dollars in rewards," said Underman in noticeable union with Wazinski.

"What about the arrangements Hirsch made for Aurelio Cortez in Puerto Rico? Anybody remember that ghoulish case? That psychopath murdered one of our finest and most productive undercover agents. Shoots him three times in the head, chops him to pieces with a machete, burns his remains, buries his ashes, and lets everyone on the island know what happens to rats who work with the DEA.

"Hirsch gets him off because of a sweetheart deal! Cortez then testifies against a federal judge on the take in San Juan, goes into WitSec- and Cortez kills another agent while he's in protective custody! And you want to do this deal? For chrissakes, that killer left behind two widows and five kids!"

Whitfield thought entering into any contract with Cortez was preposterous. Not only was the Puerto Rican a vicious killer but had established shadow operations throughout the Caribbean and ran up a high fatality toll among DEA agents.

There were dozens of other deals consummated by Hirsch, including one that involved dirty cops in Chicago. They received immunity after working as part-time hit men for racketeers and who had rubbed out at least a dozen gangsters.

"Hirsch had even made a deal for one of them to secure a seven-hundred-fifty-thousand-dollar, interest-free federal loan to start a new business after escaping into WitSec," Wazinski added as his temper raged.

"He was doing his job," said Buggelshofer in defense of Hirsch, "and he did it because that's what the Constitution demands. And he didn't go into a fit of brainsick like you're doing now."

"Hey! That's enough! Set aside your individual differences and help the President comply with his assurances to the German Chancellor, no matter how much it stinks and no matter what the outcome is," Rosselfellar said firmly.

He turned to Hamilton. "We're going to need the German taxing authority and its witness protection organization to begin moving Schnabel into South Florida. Will you take care of that, Addison?"

Before Hamilton had a chance to answer, Patterson's cell phone rang to the tune of Puff, the Magic Dragon. His compatriots stayed hushed while he answered. The head of operations for Homeland Security was crafty and careful about how and what he said to the person at the other end of the phone. He also took copious notes.

After six or seven minutes, he folded the flip-phone and revealed to the group, "I called the chief of the Hirsch surveillance team during the last break to give him a heads up. "They've spotted Hirsch via satellite and he's already on the move. He's alone and on foot. He left his house twenty minutes ago, headed south and is holed up in a huge house on highway A1A along the beach in Hillsboro Mile. The FBI is attempting to secure the home's architectural plans filed with the county.

"We're also picking up some infrared readings from low altitudes indicating there are four people in the house. We know one is Hirsch and our ground camera has identified another as one of Hirsch's former drug clients.

"They ran his photo through the federal digital identification system and came up with Oliverio Navarro Ortiz, a one-time, big-time, almost-no-jail-time narcotics trafficker. He owns the house.

"We'll secure all of Terminal Four at the Fort Lauderdale/Hollywood International Airport by 8:00 AM tomorrow. As soon as we receive aircraft identification and the ETA of Schnabel's plane, we'll deploy Coast Guard helicopters and two Navy F-35B jets attached to a U.S. carrier strike group about ninety miles off the Florida coast.

"Excellent job, Whitfield." Hamilton was pleased. "Now, everyone go to work. Make certain everything's in order. No screw-ups or attempts to be covert because Hirsch will pick up on anything that's not in his best interests." And by the way, Buggelshofer and Hutton will be boarding a military flight to Florida first thing tomorrow morning. We need you down there with Hirsch. No questions now. I have to call the President."

No wonder Hamilton became Chief of Staff. He was a takeover guy who had a mind that was as compartmentalized as a fifty-foot wall of floor-to-ceiling post office boxes. Rosselfellar was a great partner. Under their aegis, the Task Force members were beginning to feel as though everything might fall into place,

Except for more money in their agencies' bank accounts.

CHAPTER TWENTY-FIVE

"The illegality of cannabis is outrageous, an impediment to full utilization of a drug which helps produce the serenity and insight, sensitivity and fellowship so desperately needed in this increasingly mad and dangerous world."

Carl Sagan, American astronomer,
physicist, and author

17 Hours Later - 4:00 PM, Wednesday, July 9, 2008

ASSEMBLY TIME

Nobody at the previous evening's frenzied federal session could have ever imagined it would last until a bit after 11:00 PM. Ianucci was the only one who had even left the DOJ building during the entire day. A fifteen-hour stretch was a bit much for Buggelshofer and Hutton. They were too enervated to drive back to Virginia Beach. Without their knowledge Rosselfellar had his administrative coordinator reserve two rooms-traveling toiletry kits included-at the Capitol Hill Suites, barely a two-minute ride.

He knew they wouldn't return home for at least another day or two, and their cars would be safe in the garages where they parked.

When Rosselfellar informed them about their arrangements he also told them to get up early and go shopping for some tropical-weight clothing.

"Put it on the expense record, along with the cost of suitcases you're going to need for your trip. You may not get back for a couple of days so buy enough.

"You'll need to be at Andrews no later than noon. Your names will be at the front gate. There'll be a car waiting so you shouldn't have any deterrents getting to the Eleventh Mission Support Group headquarters.

"From there, someone will take you aboard a C-21 attached to the Eighty-Ninth Airlift Wing for the hour-and-forty-five-minute trip to Fort Lauderdale. Once you arrive, there'll be a contingent you can't miss."

While everyone else at the meeting went home for the night – they all lived within close proximity to the District – Buggy and E.F. groaned their way to the hotel.

Heck, at least they were getting a free trip to a vacation paradise.

The others were to report to the FISA courtroom by seven-thirty the next morning.

"Look at this pile of shit we've gotten ourselves into," Hutton blustered as they stepped off the hotel elevator on the fifth floor and walked to their rooms.

"I hate Florida, the heat, the humidity, the people, and I detest this assignment. I want to say, 'screw the money' but I can't afford to. Anyway, I gotta call Annabelle and let her know. She's probably worried sick by now. Boy, is she gonna be ticked off. I'll see you at seven-thirty, Buggy."

Their eyes opened at seven. After showering and shaving, they dressed in the same clothes they had worn the day before the underarm deodorant wasn't much of a help-and met in the lobby precisely at seven-thirty. They went into the hotel's dining area where each wolfed down a toasted bagel and cream cheese, a cherry Danish, and three cups of coffee before they checked out. At five minutes past nine they arrived by cab at Filene's Basement on Fourteenth Street, typically a twelve-minute ride at the right time of day, but thirty-five in the heavy traffic that seemed even busier during the summer months because of so many tourists.

The men's department was immediately inside the main entrance. They shuffled through piles of cotton twill pants. Buggy bought a pair of tan and another in light blue, while Hutton grabbed khaki and white. Each rifled through the Tommy Bahama knockoff shirts and selected two they thought matched their slacks. It was evident to the salesclerk the two seniors must have been suffering from color blindness.

Both grabbed a three-pack of Fruit of the Loom underwear, three-for-nine-bucks private-label white socks, brown and black stretch belts, and crepe-soled deck shoes; perfect accoutrements for blending with the millions of retirees in the land of warm breezes during the annual hurricane season.

They walked into dressing rooms and put on a set of their spunky new duds then headed to the luggage department. After selecting a couple of on-sale rolling travel bags they packed their purchases, toiletries, and yesterday's clothes, and wheeled their all-black travel gear outside.

Within two minutes they bent their elderly bodies into a taxi and told the turban-topped cabbie to take them to Andrews Air Force Base a few miles southeast of DC.

The driver pulled up to the front gate, the pair disembarked, paid the driver, and walked to the sentry booth with their luggage lagging behind them. Hutton's cane thumped a half-step in front of him. They displayed their identification, were waved through, and got driven to the jet in a Humvee by an airman behind the wheel. The two-man crew welcomed them aboard the aircraft. Hutton and Buggelshofer took their seats and snapped their safety belts while their driver placed their bags in the cargo hold.

"We're expecting a few bumps after takeoff but nothing extreme, gentlemen." The captain was reassuring. "When we reach ten-thousand feet, you may use the head." The pilot and co-pilot knew these guys were old and might well have to use the facilities. Buggy and Hutton had already gone to the bathroom twice at Filene's. The three cups of dark roast they drank hadn't helped their bladder pressure.

They were already antsy about the assignment and were getting even more jumpy as they pondered the possibility that high altitudes might cause some personal leakage.

Neither had been on an airplane in years but had flown enough in their careers to know that a trip like this would be uneventful. It was, except for the frequent use of Mr. John. After three trips by Buggelshofer and four by Hutton, both were running on empty. The C-21 arrived at Terminal Four in Fort Lauderdale and parked next to the only other plane on the ground, a Lufthansa Airbus 330 adorned with the airline's orange logo painted on its blue tail. A half-dozen black Chevy SUVs with blackened windows and a twelve-member federal Marshal VIPR team side-armed with .357 Magnums and assault rifles surrounded the German aircraft.

As soon as Buggy and E.F. pulled within sight of the word Lufthansa spread across the white body of the plane and laid eyes on the federal agents, they knew Schnabel had to be aboard.

The engines were still whirring fifty yards from the gate. The captain, given strict orders to keep far from the jet-way, waited until the metal-stairs-on-wheels rolled their way to the front door by a member of the ground crew. Only then could the passengers depart.

The exit door swung open and a quartet of six-foot-plus, blonde-headed Aryan bodyguards in their late twenties and early thirties, dressed in dark suits, talc-white shirts, coal-colored ties, and black shoes bounded down the steps. One was toting a conventional carry-on. A nondescript, balding nebbish of a man who could have been mistaken for a villain in a grade B movie was sandwiched between the two "friends" in front of him and the two behind.

"Scrubby" and "toady" were the best designations for the Liechtenstein loser. Perhaps "scruffy" was even more apropos.

At a runty five-foot-five and two-hundred-twelve pounds, Schnabel was inordinately overweight, bulky enough to call obese. Morbidly. His dirty fingernails and middle-age facial pimples, along with deep-brown moles on each cheek, made him as ugly as the south end of a horse heading north.

Hiding like a hermit for several years took a physical toll on the one-time banker-turned-desperado. He no longer looked the part of a reputable businessman or technology savant.

The transformation was more than subtle. One might have mistaken him for a Hun without the trinkets. Schnabel's dark brown pants, purple-and-green plaid shirt, navy-blue sport coat, dirty Reeboks, and four-day-old beard made him look like a reject from a Salvation Army fashion boutique.

He was wearing a pair of glasses with lenses so thick that some people might have thought the scoundrel could see into the future. They magnified his squinty, blue eyes, and the bluish frames complemented his grayish skin.

His heavily wrinkled forehead made him appear qualified for Medicare. At fifty-four Schnabel was more aged than the best Swiss cheese.

The instant the guards' shoe bottoms touched the ground, a Marshal ushered the five into the closest SUV. Schnabel sat in the middle row between two of his German escorts. Another took a front-row passenger seat and the fourth sat in the back row. The driver of the vehicle sped off through a private, secure entrance to the field and stopped to wait for the other feds.

The co-pilot of the C-21 lowered the stairs. Buggelshofer hobbled out first while Hutton followed with the help of his cane. He wasn't taking any chances of tumbling down the narrow, shaky steps and landing on his creaky kneecaps.

The sweltering sun and suffocating humidity made them feel like they had arrived in purgatory.

A second SUV pulled up and the pair slid onto the center row seat. A member of the VIPR team lifted their luggage from the belly of the plane and placed them in the back of the Chevy. Only sixty seconds from the first vehicle, the driver followed its tracks and caught up outside the fenced-in area where an eight-man Broward County motorcycle escort met both SUVs.

Kind of like a funeral entourage without the hearse.

The contingent exited the airport, slipped onto 1-595 with blue-and-red lights spinning like UFOs, and headed west to the entrance curve that put them on northbound 1-95. This was a serious parade of engines. The regular civilian traffic in the two right-hand lanes veered left to make way for the high-speed procession.

The lead two-wheelers parted with the highway twelve minutes ahead at Hillsboro Boulevard, headed east and rolled over the bridge crossing the Intracoastal Waterway. They tacked right onto U.S. Highway A1A and stopped five-hundred feet ahead in front of a sprawling, suburban beachfront palace.

While waiting for the balance of the squad to catch up, the motorcycle cops sneaked a view of the empty Mars Red Mercedes SLR McLaren parked behind the eight-foot-high cinderblock, stucco, and wrought iron fence.

At four-hundred-ninety-five thousand dollars, the car was the most expensive in the seven-car stable. The vanity plate was labeled O-NO, an apparent reference to Oliverio Navarro Ortiz.

When the German guards saw the vehicle from their motherland, their faces lit up. It appeared as though their mouths began to drool. Alas, they resigned themselves to having to drive seven-year-old Volkswagens back in Deutschland.

Another four Chevy SUVs filled with federal agents were stationed on the west side of the road. Behind them was a central command and communications vehicle, a kind of White House War Room on wheels.

Inside were laptops with screens flashing wavy-green lines. The computers were manned by six agents with earphones and high-tech mikes. A head honcho was directing them to zero in on radio frequencies beaming from satellite signals.

A dozen TV monitors were actively displaying different exterior angles of the lavish home, including anyone who was in the neighborhood. The images were being beamed by hidden cameras feeding wireless images.

The conspicuous and continuous air slaps by the rotor blades of two predominantly orange-and-white U.S. Coast Guard Dolphin helicopters circling overhead were distracting. The craft had been activated for additional security and surveillance, while the Navy jet that had been ordered to stand by was circling some ninety miles offshore.

The eighty-five-hundred-square-foot, four-story oceanfront fortress was in the town of Hillsboro Beach, a spit of land between Pompano Beach to the south and Deerfield Beach to the north. The town's year-round population of eighteen-hundred swelled to three thousand during the winter months. It was easily identified by the one-hundred-thirty-six-foot-high Hillsboro Lighthouse that housed the most powerful beam on the east coast of the United States. The geography of the town was a reminder of Golden Beach where Kenny Cooper began his infamous entry into the illegal drug business.

The biggest differences were that Golden Beach was twenty-five miles south of Hillsboro Beach and had no known drug dealers among its residents. The biggest similarities were that traffic on two-lane Highway A1A began to back up for miles and the townspeople were as equally affluent. Local police courteously provided the blockades at both ends of town. At one time, Ortiz had owned an extensive stake in the narcotics trade. Originally from Colombia, he had become an American citizen as a child when his parents moved from Cali to Miami in the early 1960s.

He earned a diploma in international business from the University of Miami and put it to good use by illegally importing marijuana, cocaine, and crystal meth from throughout Latin America. Trips to Colombia to visit family and friends were frequent and mostly used for networking and establishing himself as one of the preeminent luminaries in Florida's booming drug business.

His transactions, estimated to total in the billions, ultimately forced him to bargain with the DEA. He was girding himself for more than sixty years behind bars when Hirsch stepped into his life and saved it.

Ari struck a most non-cordial deal with the feds, or at least that's what government agencies thought.

Ortiz paid the government nearly $12 million in back income taxes, forfeiture of various assets and spent six months in a minimum-security federal golf-and-tennis "resort" prison. After his release, he retired from the drug business. By that time, he had enough money to support the entire country of Djibouti for a decade. Hirsch knew the $15 million chateau included excellent sound insulation. When the house was in the design stage, Ortiz insisted upon two undetectable rooms where he could carry on conversations freely, ones without interference from electronic, microwave or digital interception.

The builders encased the pair of rooms with two sheets of half-inch layers of lead and two slabs of half-inch steel. When welded together, the third-floor rooms became impenetrable even from chemical attacks.

At the push of a button walls that were exposed to all open areas descended from the hidden slots in the ceiling within a split second. They sealed the rooms tighter than a pit bull's teeth latched to a T-bone steak. Air vents had been installed, and enough rations were on hand for at least two weeks. Each room had its own marble bathroom and shower. Satellite TV had been connected so whoever was in either room could receive news from the outside.

The commercial elevator led to a rooftop terrace from which a visitor could peer down on an indoor-outdoor swimming pool designed in the form of the state of Florida, panhandle, and all. The two whirlpools lay at the edge of the beach.

Landscaping for the entire area was adorned with more than five-hundred lush tropical trees, dense bushes, and an abundance of variegated and vibrant flowering plants.

The aviary housing a collection of multi-colored macaws, parrots, cockatiels, and hundreds of native flying feathered creatures was the largest enclosed private bird sanctuary in the state.

Ari and Oliverio had become close confidantes. They had been through a lot of tough times together and bonded through every trial, every tribulation, and every trick the government pulled. Ortiz had quickly acknowledged he would help the moment Hirsch called him a bit earlier in the day.

Hirsch's only concern now was whether the government would meet his demands. He would find out soon enough.

CHAPTER TWENTY-SIX

"Complete prohibition of all chemical mind changers can be decreed, but cannot be enforced, and tends to create more evils than it cures."

Aldous Huxley, Author of Brave New World

35 Minutes Later - 4:35 PM, Wednesday, July 9, 2008

THE REUNION

One of Ortiz's personal security guards pivoted his head while his eyes followed a bank of twelve HDTV screens receiving images by hidden, strategically placed cameras. The federal government wasn't the only entity in the area with spying equipment.

The images showed everything occurring around the seaside estate in sharp high definition. The guard noticed a single member of the federal posse attempting to get into the electronically controlled gate at the front of the house.

"Mr. Ortiz, one of them is carrying a metal briefcase and appears as though he wants access. What are your orders?"

"Buzz him in, Ricky. I'll have Manny meet him at the front door," replied Ortiz.

By the time the agent jumped the three brick steps and onto the front landing, the door was already ajar.

A troika of trained-to-kill Doberman Pinschers, individually chained to a metal brace on the side of the house, was almost within bite of the messenger. Manny, Ortiz's personal chief of staff, peered out and matter-of-factly asked what he wanted. The courier reached through the door and said, "I have a package for Ari Hirsch. Is he here?"

Manny took the briefcase and asked the visitor to step outside the gate. He locked the door behind him and took the elevator to the top floor where Hirsch was biding his time. Even though his "company" had arrived and was outside, the final documents he requested hadn't.

Ari had already received a phone call from Sandra saying the home fax had printed out "dozens of papers" and she had checked them over.

"Everything looks in order at my end.

Jordan O'Banion called me seconds ago. He said an emissary from U.S. Customs had already hand-delivered a completely filled legal carton to his office."

"Good, Sandra. Tell Jordan to call me on this same number when he phones you back. I'm opening my package now. If I spot something I'm not comfortable with, I'll let Jordan know. It should take us about the same amount of time to review everything."

Ari opened the case, finger-flipped through the mass of documents, and matched them with the information he had already received via his PDA. After a seemingly endless forty- five minutes, he wasn't totally satisfied the government had met its commitments.

The phone rang once and Hirsch answered. "This is Jordan, Ari. I haven't found a single detail not taken care of. I assume you've reached the same conclusion."

"Jordan, I'm missing the signature of the head of the DOJ. Even though the President has signed on, I'm not going through with the deal without it." Ari may have been in his late sixties, but his eyes and judgment were still twenty-twenty. O'Banion responded, "I can't believe I missed that. I'll get in touch with John Rosselfellar. He's the DOJ tax chief running the case, along with Addison Hamilton, the President's Chief of Staff.

"I'll tell Rosselfellar to draft an addendum to the existing document, get it signed, then have it faxed to Sandra and me and forwarded to your PDA. Will that be acceptable, Ari? We've come this far so we might as well get it put to bed."

Even though Hirsch was uncomfortable his instincts were always to take the advice of someone he considered one of his closest allies.

"So it is a tax investigation," Ari said to Jordan while trying to figure the unknown. "When I heard the names Schnabel and Liechtenstein I figured as much. But I didn't see any mention of Bobby and Timmy Smith. Did I miss it?"

"Not that I know of Ari. I didn't see it, either. I remember your telling me about those guys, though. What do they have to do with it?"

"I don't know, Jordan. I don't know. But somehow, they must be involved. I can't believe whatever this is about has gone all the way to the White House. Anyway, get the documents completed and we'll move ahead if you think that's the right thing to do under the circumstances.

"Tell the feds to do it as quickly as possible so we don't waste any valuable time. I don't want to stretch this thing any further than it has to go."

Neither did Ortiz. He rendered his plan to say *adios* until Ari's meeting with Schnabel had ended. Leaving the estate in Hirsch and his personal staff's hands was as safe as if he was there himself with a squad of personal assassins. He hopped into his McLaren and sped south to Miami to stay with his significant other until the coast was clear. By 6:15 PM, Hirsch's BlackBerry vibrated on the glass-top coffee table in front of him. He picked it up and found a text message with an attachment of the addendum. O'Banion left Ari word that both he and Sandra had received the faxes with signatures intact and that it was safe to proceed. What Ari didn't know was the deal was almost blown the previous day. It seems the American President and the German Chancellor had a verbal contest about the heavy cost of getting Schnabel to the states by using a Lufthansa jetliner with only five passengers and a crew of two.

"Addison, get the cheap bitch off my back. Make certain Schnabel is on time for the meeting tomorrow. I don't give a crap what you tell her." Hamilton obeyed the order.

"My goodness, Chancellor Mitsch, the President has gone out of his way to make certain this meeting takes place on your behalf." Hamilton called her as soon as he hung up with the Commander-in-Chief.

"However, I think we may have a complication. Our Department of Homeland Security has been getting some chatter about the possibility of an al-Qaeda attack by a cell whose home base is in Frankfurt.

"That might require the halting of landing rights for a number of Lufthansa flights at busy American gateways. If you can get Schnabel here by tomorrow afternoon as scheduled, there might be something the President can do to help keep those rights secured."

"I unterstant, Herr Hamilton. I vil haf it done." Mitsch knew it was a beautiful bluff but there was no way she was going to call it and perhaps crush the opportunity she might not get again. "He vil be on time, I ah-shurr you." The "cheap bitch" crumpled. At Ari's request, Manny opened the front gate and ten agents in SWAT gear swarmed in, carefully avoiding the snarky canines. They quickly surrounded the house preventing anyone from entering or leaving. Then again, there was Schnabel and his escorts, and they weren't exactly anyone.

Deep down, Hirsch and Schnabel both knew this was an auspicious moment.

Although they were born and grew up in different cultures and had limited contact with one another, they had similar experiences that explained their linkage. Both were money masters. Both were under constant government stakeout. Both had conducted business with the highest of national authorities. Both had been in hiding and called upon to decipher a major conundrum.

It was by no means a friendship but an affinity for one another reminiscent of Yin and Yang.

"After all these years, it boils down to my having trusted secrets about secret trusts," Ari confided in himself.

Even at his age he knew he was facing another crisis in his life. He felt he had little to lose if he cooperated with the investigation, especially when he had an irrevocable get-out-of-jail-free card, and comprehensive immunity accords insulating him from any negative events that might unfold.

Schnabel's guards stepped out of their vehicle with the charlatan in tow. That was the signal for Buggelshofer and Hutton to leave their SUV and walk to the house. Seven men passed through the front gate and entered the home.

Hirsch thought Schnabel's companions looked like the types who would have turned their parents into the Gestapo during World War II for sympathizing with the plight of Hitler's victims. He asked the four of them to wait outside. "Have a seat at one of the patio tables. Stroll through the gardens. Walk on the beach. Take off your clothes and take a dip in the pool. Do anything you want but please stay outside during our meeting. It may be lengthy so make yourselves comfortable," Ari requested.

One of the guards attended college in the U.S. and spoke fluent English. He translated Hirsch's comments for the other three. All of them scuttled from the house and headed back to the SUV.

Mitsch might have balked at their leaving Schnabel without German protection, but the guards knew they were outnumbered should any trouble start anyway. They felt way too vulnerable and dashed back to the SUV they arrived in. E.F. and Buggy took turns embracing Ari. Their warm feelings toward one another were on display. In Hirsch's mind, the meeting with Schnabel didn't include his two old federal pals but it was good to see them. The feeling was mutual.

"Ari, we're sorry we're a part of putting you into this position, but Buggy and I are in our final stretch. We still have a responsibility to the government. The feds didn't give us a choice. They were going to cut us off from our pensions, but they made it more than financially interesting for us to reactivate." Hutton made it clear he and Buggelshofer were running out of money and monetarily challenged, and their bankrolls at this time of their lives were a primary consideration.

Ari whispered to them to not talk about their personal finances. He knew the feds were electronically picking up the conversation as they had minutes before when Ari spoke with Sandra and O'Banion. Hirsch quickly changed the subject.

"Please don't ask me to stick my neck out so the government's hatchet squad can chop it off." That was a bold request from Ari since everyone knew the government could do anything it wanted. "Out of curiosity, where were you in the district when we spoke?"

"In the DOJ building on Pennsylvania. Hasn't changed a bit except for more expensive furniture," Buggy remarked sarcastically.

"Seventh floor?" Ari knew he didn't have to ask the question. "The FISA courtroom, am I right?" The lack of a response by Buggy and E.F. was enough to satisfy Hirsch's inquisitiveness.

Schnabel walked over to Ari. They both smiled at each other and cordially shook hands. They barely recognized one another. Their relationship seemed as though generations had passed since they had first met decades ago. They looked physically different.

That poor son-of-a-bitch. He went through a washing machine and was hung out to dry like a used towel.

They both thought the same thought.

"Herr Schnabel. It's good to see you again after all these years."

"Yes, Mr. Hirsch. I feel as though it was yesterday."

The lying bastard. He thought he could ingratiate himself.

"How nice of you to say that Herr Schnabel. I wish I could say the same. You look as though you've been to hell and back."

"Not exactly, Mr. Hirsch. Perhaps a few difficulties, but I would not characterize it as hell." Schnabel knew Ari used the right word, but he would never admit his innermost thoughts. He was too stoic, too Germanic. Buggy butted in and kiddingly said, "Ari, this is the most incredible house I've ever been in. It's a perfect spot for smuggling."

Ari smiled and responded, "Still fighting the old drug wars, Buggy?"

He was aware that Buggelshofer and Hutton probably knew exactly what this house looked like inside and out. The feds never undertook this kind of an investigation without doing their homework. Hutton jumped in with a question. "Ari, don't you think a smuggler could bring in speedboats from Bimini, beach them, unload the drugs, bring them inside, and load them into a motor home that could make its way up A1A for distribution and sale?"

It was a wry query, one which Ari knew Hutton had the answer to. The FBI agent knew exactly what had occurred along this quiet strip of Florida coastline. He wasn't exactly a newcomer in these matters.

A single load of pot, they all knew, could yield enough money to make a notable down payment on the house they were standing in. Three loads could pay it off. From the looks of Ortiz's palace, Buggy and E.F. knew that the drug war they originally signed up for was never going to be won. There was too much money at stake and too many people on the take.

"Mr. Hirsch, you have a superb home." Schnabel was aiming to please. "It is not like the grand estates of Liechtenstein, but lovely nevertheless."

That was his finest attempt at diplomacy. Nobody ever accused him of being his country's version of Thomas Jefferson. Generally speaking, Schnabel never learned the art of statecraft because his mouth was always moving.

'It's not mine, Herr Schnabel. It belongs to one of my former clients. Let me show the three of you around."

After a twenty-minute tour, they were back in the living room. The three newcomers were aghast at the décor, the architecture, the amenities, the electronic features, and the number of rooms.

"Are you sure we're not gonna be on Lifestyles of the Rich and Famous?" asked Buggy.

"I'd like to confer with Herr Schnabel now, guys." Ari completely avoided Buggy's question.

"We need the utmost privacy, as you can imagine. You can relax in the living room, watch TV, shoot billiards in the den, or lie down on a chaise lounge by the pool. Take this remote. If you need anything, push the 'call' button and Ricky will bring you anything you need. In the meantime, if you'll excuse us, we're going upstairs." E.F. and Buggy walked outside while Ari and Schnabel strolled to the elevator. They rode the lift to the third floor. As they got off, Hirsch told Schnabel to stop in his tracks.

"I'm going to have to blindfold you now, Herr Schnabel. The owner of the house doesn't want any outsiders to know where we are. Please turn around. You don't need to be afraid."

Schnabel reluctantly did as he was asked. Ari reached in his back pocket and pulled out a black denim sack large enough to put over

Schnabel's head. Hirsch led him into a wide hallway on both sides of which were bookcases that took up every inch of wall space.

The indiscernible entrances to the unexposed rooms were at the opposite ends of each. Ari took a digital card from his pocket, swiped it across an invisible bar code on a volume of The Pit and the Pendulum, and a section at the far end of one of the bookcases automatically swung open.

Once inside, Hirsch switched on the lights as the door closed behind them as securely as the main hatch on a NASA space shuttle. Schnabel's headgear was removed, and he fluttered his eyes to get used to the light.

Inside the outside communications' vehicle there was nothing but cursing when Hirsch secured the room. Now, both men were undetectable. The feds wireless audio feeds had been totally interrupted. The only thing they heard was the informal conversations among the other occupants of the estate. Except for Buggy and E.F.

They immediately fell asleep. on the poolside lounges.

Schnabel and Hirsch's conference would begin in a few minutes. In the meantime, the American and German administrations would have to wait as patiently as they could.

There were no other prerogatives.

CHAPTER TWENTY-SEVEN

"Prohibition was introduced as a fraud...it comes to serve the devil. It comes to regulate by law our appetites and our daily lives. It comes to tear down liberty and built-up fanaticism, hypocrisy, and intolerance. It comes to confiscate by legislative decree the property of many of our fellow citizens. It comes to send spites, detectives, and informers into our homes."

Robert Q. Mills, Nineteenth century U.S. Congressman, U.S. Senator, Confederate Army colonel

5 Minutes Later - 5:10 PM, Wednesday, July 9, 2008

THE ROOM WITH NO VIEW

"Care for some wine, Herr Schnabel?"

"Maybe you have a little German Schnapps?"

Ari stepped behind the bar and opened the doors to the fully stocked liquor cabinet. "Yes, we have some German Schnapps. Cherry. Is that okay?"

"Yes, Herr Hirsch. Cherry is my favorite."

Ari knew that every closet and cubbyhole in the Ortiz home had every imaginable alcoholic beverage. Schnabel's selection was no exception.

After pouring the Schnapps for Schnabel and a Pepsi for himself, Ari set the drinks on the coffee table coasters and both men sat opposite each other in puffy-cushioned lounge chairs.

"Let's get started, Franz. You know I was never one for wasting much time. Tell me why you're here and what you need from me. Something tells me you're in trouble. Otherwise, you wouldn't be in Florida surrounded by what looks like the entire Liechtenstein security service."

"Those men are not from Liechtenstein, Mr. Hirsch. They are from Germany. I am indeed in trouble. Big trouble. But I fear you too are in terrible difficulties as well."

"Please, Franz. Cut the 'Herr Hirsch' and 'Mr. Hirsch' crap. You've known me a long time, long enough to call me by my first name. Leave the formalities for the prince and the rest of the royals. Now explain to me what kind of problems I have. You need to tell me why we're meeting, and I need the truth. If I don't get it, you'll make it impossible for me to help you.

"When I practiced law, I insisted that my clients never lie. If they withheld or distorted information and I found out later, it made it impossible to represent them properly. I'm expecting total honesty from you."

"Ari, *bitte*. Another Schnapps if you don't mind." Schnabel had gulped his first like it was his last. "*Danke*, thanks. I need to loosen up a bit, yah?"

"Yes, Franz. Relax. I know we're in the tropics but let's make believe we're on the ski slopes at St. Moritz." Hirsch was trying his best to keep the meeting running unruffled and not get Schnabel upset or off track.

"Ah, yes Ari. St. Moritz. And the parties. Who can forget those wonderful parties with those *schöne frauleins*, those beautiful girls? Those days were the best. I remember them well."

"Zurich, too. Do you remember the time we were, shall we say, stoned? We made love to those two Austrian princesses on the funicular?"

Schnabel's face broke into a big smile as he visually recalled the Polybahn railway that connected the center of Zurich with the Dolder

Grande, the five-star hotel where he and Hirsch had done business and partied together on a couple of occasions.

"It was a good thing there were no other passengers, yah Ari? I can still smell the joyous bouquet of her perfume as she sat on my lap facing me, her legs straddled over mine while she pumped up and down on my penis. I do not know how we managed on such a narrow tram. And you in the back doing the same thing with your own royal piece of ass." By now, Schnabel was laughing aloud.

He could always get the LGT Bank to spring for the romps because, as he had told the royal family, "We need to solidify our depositor-banker relationships."

In fact, the affiliation between LGT and Hirsch's ancestry began half a century before Ari was even born. In the 1890s, Ari's Austrian maternal grandmother and matriarch of that branch of the clan, Lena Einshtein, had done business with the prince's grandfather. That was enough of a lineal connection for the bank to accept Ari as one of its clients. There was geographical linkage as well since the Liechtenstein family of Austria had acquired the fiefdom of Vaduz in 1699, thereby making the mountainous nation-state a hereditary constitutional monarchy.

"Ari, one more Schnapps, please."

"Okay, Franz, but this is the last one. Enough paying homage to our memories. By the way, they weren't Austrian princesses. They were German hookers paid for by my clients."

"No-o-o-o! Really, Ari?" Schnabel was almost in shock at learning the truth. "I told the managing director of the bank the money he gave me was for our entertainment. What did you do with the francs I gave you those times?"

"I gave them back to the bank," Ari answered. "The memorable festivities were one way I was also able to solidify my depositor-banker relationship with you and LGT." Hirsch had always made certain he would stay on the plus side of the Liechtenstein royal ledger particularly because his trustworthiness was at stake. Losing his good name, he knew, would destroy his global banking relationships.

One way of protecting it was refusing to allow the leverage he built come under attack by representatives of the banks with which he dealt. Letting them pay for prostitutes and parties were a no-no.

"Well, one thing I know for certain," Schnabel said with absolute authority. "I owe you my life. I will never forget how you saved it in St. Moritz during the most terrible whiteout ski conditions I have ever seen. We were not in the best of shape that day *mein freund*.

"With all of the drugs and alcohol we consumed the night before with the ladies, we did not have clear heads skiing at seventeen-hundred meters.

"I have nightmares until this day thinking for sure I was going to die on that mountain. If you had not kept us moving in the proper direction in that storm, both of us would have perished.

"I panicked and you were the one with the cool head. I pray you still have that same skill because I think you and I both are going to need it. Yah, Ari, both of us are going to need your sense of balance to how do you say it? – 'negotiate' these very messy circumstances."

"We're not young men anymore, Franz. We need to use our energy and ability efficiently and effectively. Don't worry about my stress under fire. I haven't lost it. However, I must know everything that's led to this meeting. And no more Schnapps right now."

By this time, Schnabel had finished his third and was well on his way to Tipsyville.

"Let me say that my conscience is clear, Ari."

"Franz, a clear conscience is usually the sign of a bad memory."

"Yah, okay Ari. I understand. First, let me apologize in advance for any troubles I have caused you. That was not my intent.

"As you know, I always honored your request never to call you, never to send you documents, never to communicate with you except through an intermediary. I respected the arrangement, but it is now all unfolding in a very negative manner."

"Apology accepted. Let's move this conversation fast forward, Franz." Ari was getting edgy waiting for the reason Schnabel wanted this meeting.

"Yah, Ari. Now I will tell you. A few years ago, I got into terrible trouble with LGT and with Spanish authorities. I became the lead investor in a real estate deal, a thirty-six-hole golf resort and development near Torremolinos on the Costa del Sol. I was such a *dumpkopf*! I wish you had been around to forewarn me. I think you never lost your fundamental understanding of what makes a good deal good and a bad deal bad. You understood government crooks and unscrupulous bankers. I never did. So, I borrowed some of the bank's financial resources, you might say, inappropriately."

"You mean you stole it." Ari's statement turned into a question. "How much was involved?"

"About $2.5 million U.S. The timing could not have been worse for a real estate deal, and then the pressure Spain put on me was unbearable. I quickly had to cover my tax bills from the Spanish government. I do not know how they found out about where my investment money came from, but they threatened to expose me, put me on trial and lock me up. "I thought $2.5 million would satisfy the debt, but it wasn't enough. Those corrupt conquistadores wanted another million! Ari, they took $2.5 million and still wanted more!"

"Franz, that's almost always the way governments conduct themselves. You should have known better." Hirsch was matter of fact.

"Of course, Ari, of course. Believe me, I tried every way I knew to get them off my back, but it was *nicht gut*. No good whatsoever. It was worse than being on the mountain in St. Moritz during that *schneesturm*. It was the worst storm I had ever seen other than when I took the money from the bank and other investors.

"I thought I would be able to sell the property quickly and make immense profits for every investor. When the economy went *kaput*, I did everything to *shtoppsmefromflippin'*!"

"What's that?" questioned Ari.

"*Shtoppsmefromflippin'*. Or as you say in America, 'stops me from flipping. You know, Ari, flipping out. I was nearly out of my mind with worry. They indicted me on ten counts of financial crimes. The legal system in Madrid found me guilty in absentia."

It was rather perceptible that Schnabel was getting more spooked by the second as he slipped in and out of his native German tongue and spit out a little Latin as well.

"They took the $2.5 million and tried to throw me into the bullring. They wanted to *setzen mein hammel*, stick my ass in a Spanish jail. I did everything to raise the additional million dollars to make these charges go away, but those *schweinhunds shtupped me*." Ari knew the word "shtupped" was Yiddish and German slang for "fucked." He had first heard the word as a youth when one of his parents' friends used it to describe what a business associate had done to him.

"The prince – that pretentious putz – he wanted me to stand trial for the theft of the money. What a fool. The whole royal family is a bunch of fools! How could they bring me into a criminal court without letting the world know their money was no longer safe in Liechtenstein?

"Stupid. Ach, they were stupid. Didn't they realize I could tell anybody who would listen about whose money was in LGT and from where it originated? Did they think I was as stupid as them?

"My old comrade, you and I both know the illegality and exploitation of all of it. We know there was, and still is, so much laundered money from drug trafficking in LGT and other financial institutions. The washing continues until this very day.

"We know what the game is all about. Do these money zealots masquerading as legitimate businessmen think they are the only ones who know what is going on?

"They are nothing more than drug profiteers. They conspire with governments, including your own, Ari. The amounts of money are so immense that these so-called financiers now control a large percentage of global money movement.

"But I do not have to tell you all of this. You already know and have seen it with your own eyes. You have much field experience, yah?"

Hirsch nodded his head. Yes, he was familiar with global manipulation in transporting funds, and no one had to remind him about the part that illegal drugs played. If educational institutions had offered degrees in International Narcotics Trafficking, Hirsch would have earned his Ph.D. years before. "My legal counsel in Zurich made a deal for me that I could not turn down, Ari. He knew the authorities in my own country wanted to silence me. I had little choice but to secure computer discs from LGT."

"You mean you stole those as well as the money?" This time, Ari was asking. Now he knew there were indeed stolen CDs filled with secrets. Hirsch wasn't about to press Schnabel about their status. He wasn't going to let this snake slither out of his hands by asking probative questions that might rattle him.

"When you put it that way, Ari, you make me sound like a bad person. An *erpresser*, a blackmailer. I had seen so many others commit illegal financial acts at the very highest levels and get away with it. I could no longer sit by without *schnitzeling* a little for myself."

Perhaps Schnabel should have taken some courses in business ethics.

"Sounds like you took a big bite out of the bratwurst, Franz."

"Maybe so but I was hungry. Those two discs provided a perfect recipe for me staying out of the Spanish *zuchthaus* – what you call the 'big house." They include the names of many, many Deutschlanders, Englishmen, Americans, including bankers, government tyrants, and wealthy businesspeople.

"All of them have had assets in LGT for many years. Tax swindlers and cheats! In addition, they got away with it for so long. They were arrogant enough to think it would be tax-free money forever. No more undisclosed accounts for them, Ari. No more at all."

So, there were two discs, Ari thought to himself.

"The information I have includes how all of the money went from country to country to country. I am talking about hundreds of billions of U.S. dollars, deutschemarks, francs, all associated with thousands and thousands of names. Yah, Ari. That is a lot of *gelt* and a lot of people.

"You know, Ari, I am a humble man. I always worked very hard to feed my family, *spiel mit mein kinder*, and enjoy my life. However, I needed to make more francs and I could not convince my employer to give me a substantial wage increase.

"Yah, Ari. They forgot how important I was to their operation and to the well-being of Liechtenstein. Now they remember but it has taken a very large toll on me, my motherland and on many people in other countries. The veil of banking secrecy is being lifted almost everywhere and there will be many consequences for many depositors.

I hope they do not blame me for all of this mess."

"I wouldn't worry about that, Franz. There's plenty of blame to go around the equator several times."

Ari could easily detect the bitterness, the sadness, the woefulness. Schnabel was so angry at the system that he could no longer live inside or outside of it. He reckoned he was his own hero but didn't recognize his own frailties, and he was sorely lacking remorse and a sense of responsibility for what he had done.

"*Danke*, Ari, *danke*. Let me finish what I was saying. We have much more to talk about. My lawyer in Zurich got in touch with the German authorities who offered to put me in their witness protection program, like yours in the United States. You know about that, yah, Ari?"

"Yes, I've heard of it, Franz."

"The final requirement of my settlement with the Germans was to have this private meeting with you. Without it, I refuse to testify in a German court to validate the information on the disc in their possession. They still need my testimony. That gives me great leverage, but it is only temporary."

"Leverage is a good thing, Schnabel, as long as you don't press down too hard," Hirsch said.

"Then you know exactly what I am saying. I sold the Germans one of the discs, but only with data about the Germans involved in tax evasion.

"I transferred the information about the Americans and the British to the second disc and erased those names from the first one. The Germans provided me with false identification papers and phony passports so I can hide.

"Before I disappear, I want you to know what happened to the foundations and trusts that your Liechtenstein lawyer created with the LGT Bank.

"Ari, neither your government nor the Germans know the legal owners of the foundations and trusts established by you. The original files verify that your fingerprints are on the assignment of ownership documents for all of them. I know that for sure. Yes, Ari, you are the sole designee."

"Why did you come to me, Franz? Why me? You didn't come all the way here just to tell me about my fingerprints and that you had a couple of compact discs. What's in it for you?" Hirsch's skepticism was an acquired skill. He had years of being able to sharpen it.

"Several things, Ari. First, my life is in danger and so are the lives of *mein frau und zwei kinder*, my wife and two children. They have been in hiding since I fled the country, but I have not seen or heard from them in many months. Not even through intermediaries. I would like you to find them and contact them to tell them I am okay. I know they are somewhere in Switzerland.

"Second, you were always a *gut freund*. You treated me with great respect. Maybe giving you this information will help pay you back for all the good times we had. Perhaps you can become a wealthy man with this information I am giving you. If anything happens to me, you might be able to take care of my wife and children. At least get them a little money.

"Finally, I remember your circle of associates. I know they might come looking for me. Those kinds of people could find me and my family. I do not want to be running from them for the rest of my life. Perhaps you can contact them on my behalf and get me out of this predicament."

"Franz, how about another Schnapps?" Even though he had earlier declared 'last call, Hirsch purposely offered another. Schnabel was getting more skittish by the second. "This will be the last one for the day so enjoy it while I do some thinking for the both of us. This will require some atypical and thoughtful moves, but right now, I need to do a mental jeopardy assessment of your situation.

"My initial thought is that it appears as though you're a slice of toasted pumpernickel in a big jam."

CHAPTER TWENTY-EIGHT

"One of the problems that the marijuana reform movement consistently faces is that everyone wants to talk about what marijuana does, but no one ever wants to look at what marijuana prohibition does. Marijuana never kicks down your door in the middle of the night. Marijuana never locks up sick and dying people. Marijuana does not suppress medical research. Marijuana does not peek in bedroom windows. Even if one takes every reefer madness allegation of the prohibitionists at face value, marijuana prohibition has done far more harm to far more people than marijuana ever could."

Richard Cowan, Former head of National Organization for the Reform of Marijuana Laws (NORML)

1 Hour and 30 Minutes Later–7:15 PM, Wednesday, July 9, 2008

CODE BLUE

While Schnabel sat in his self-induced, torturous misery listening to a Schumann piano concerto on a CD Ari had inserted into the stereo, he became as clucky as an overweight turkey the day before Thanksgiving.

The music did not soothe the savage beast.

Hirsch left the room, secured his European "friend" inside, rode the elevator to the top floor, and stepped onto the rooftop terrace. He put on sunglasses and an oversized straw hat so he couldn't be identified by photographers even with zoom lenses.

The sun was beginning to disappear and left streaky hues of red, yellow, and orange in its descent through wispy clouds. It was a perfect time for Ari to get lost in his own consciousness, even though the sounds of the choppers' engines and vibrating blades interrupted the quietude.

He was disciplined enough to tune out the noise and think - really think-until he arrived at what more than likely would turn out to be valid answers to critical questions. This is when logic became Ari's strongest accomplice.

He didn't want to meet with me to find his family or because I'm a nice guy. He knows the Germans will look after him. They have one of the best witness protection programs in existence, making it unlikely anyone will assassinate him. He wants me to get him out of this pickle so he can get his hands on as much money as possible. He wants what he thinks is his share of the money from the vaults. He wants me to pay him for the information if the assets are put in my name. It's always about the damn money. He's still a stinking skunk!

When the teeth of his brain gears engaged, Hirsch went back to the room where Schnabel was engrossed in shaking like a sheet on a clothesline in a thirty-mile-an-hour wind. "Schnabel, let me give you some legal insight. My fingerprints may be on file at LGT, and it appears I'm the current legal owner, but I am not the beneficial owner. I haven't spoken or communicated with the beneficial owners or their heirs in more than twenty years for reasons I cannot divulge."

Ari wasn't about to tell the fraudster he had been in the Federal Witness Protection Program and had been forced to retire from his law and accounting practice.

"Right now," Hirsch continued, "I need your cooperation to prove their ownership. I had a sacred trust with those people. They were my clients. There's unfinished business I must finalize on their behalf, but I cannot reveal the details under any circumstances, even if it's two decades old.

"Once that's accomplished, I feel certain they will handsomely reward both of us. As of now they may think their assets have been frozen because of all the investigations. I'm sure compensation for your efforts will be fair and come quickly. That should satisfy your continuing need for finances."

Hirsch was attaching the carrot to the stick.

"Are you sure you have not testified in any of the German cases either in court or at depositions?"

"No, Ari. I already told you that." Schnabel was already feeling quite good about his possible "inheritance" of even more money.

"I needed to hear it again. I don't want any part of my plan to backfire. This may well be a way for you to negate and renegotiate your contract."

"Are you delirious? Ari, I think you have lost your *kopf!* I have told them I would testify as soon as this meeting is over. I will wind up in a German *klinker* for sure, or under the ground. This is *verboten!* I cannot break this personal accord. I gave my word."

Ari knew trusting Schnabel with his "word" was like trusting Charles Ponzi with your life's savings.

"Stop the dreck, the shit! Every government manipulator you've dealt with broke their words and where has that gotten you? Scared and alone and in a room you can't even leave. The only person you can trust right now is me, the same way you did on that mountain.

"Here's my analysis, Franz. Whether you want to believe it is up to you. I'm convinced the Germans are pursuing only some of the individuals on the disc, not all of them. They don't have the time or the resources to go after everyone. There are too many people involved.

"They don't want you. They want to bury their political enemies. It's all about control and the money. Don't you get it yet? The German administration is using you for its own ambitions. They have an agenda, and it doesn't include the welfare of Franz Schnabel. You're just a tool to achieve their real goals."

"Maybe or maybe not, Ari. But the American government is using you as well. They might even know about your involvement with LGT. I am sure they do not have sufficient evidence to prove you are the legal owner of what may be in those accounts or the safe deposit boxes. But if they find out, they will force you to reveal the contents."

"Don't worry about me. The government has granted me complete immunity. Whether they know or don't know really is of no concern." Although this was an accurate declaration, Ari knew the feds could and might void their deal if and whenever they wished.

"The bank has records of visits by your old associates," revealed Schnabel. "All of the entries had to be correct so each time there was a deposit made a bank officer took note. There is some clear evidence – I actually saw photographs – of your business partners dumping large amounts of platinum and gold into the main vault. The metals, in trust for all these years, have remained in the bank, at least up until the time I left."

"Did you blab to the Germans about this?"

"What is blab?"

"*Shprechen. Shpillin der beaners!* Tell them. Did you, Franz? Did you tell the Germans about my connection to the gold and platinum?"

"Yah, Ari, it was all part of the information I had when I was debriefed."

"Man, what a schmuck!" Ari thought as he tried to figure out a way to get hold of the other disc his "guest" had. "He didn't have to tell them that! That information wasn't on the German disc, only the one with American and British names! So now I must wrestle that second disc away from Schnabel!"

"Do you have any idea how much the gold and platinum are worth?"

Damn right he knows. That's why he wanted this meeting in Florida.

"I suspect there are profits from their potential sale far exceeding their worth when they were deposited many years ago," declared Schnabel. "Some entered the vaults as early as 1974. I know these dates because I have seen all the records. I estimate their worth now to be between $200 million and $300 million U.S."

"Schnabel, how much did the Germans pay you?"

"About $7.8 million U.S. The British government is also interested in the intelligence and the disc because they contain similar details about some of their citizens. They will give me millions more, I am sure, but only after they collect the taxes due on the deposits.

"My lawyer also has been in touch with U.S. authorities. Yes, Ari, your own government wants their portion of the taxes, too. And the disc."

This con artist robs millions from LGT, Spain, takes even more millions from the Germans, and is negotiating for additional millions with other governments. Now he wants even more from the trusts and foundations. Scare him as much as you can, the greedy bastard.

"What good is the money when you might be dead tomorrow?"

"What do you mean, 'dead tomorrow?' That is a simple joke, I am sure, yah, Ari?"

"No, it's not even close to being funny. Even with twenty-four-hour protection, you will not be safe. You, my dear Schnabel, are a walking corpse."

"What are you talking about? I am giving the Germans as much as they need to prosecute those who are guilty. Who would kill me, other than the people whose names they already have? Other nations' authorities do not even know about me."

"Of course, they know about you, Franz! Don't you think all these countries transfer the dirt to each other? What do you think those annual international drug conferences are all about? They're a networking system, a clearing house to uncover hidden financial instruments throughout the world. They don't care who they take down—they want their money, and they'll do whatever it takes to get it."

You would too, you little prick.

"One thing you must absolutely pay attention to, Schnabel. German intelligence has hundreds of former East German Stasi agents from the days of the Cold War. Hardened Communists and murderers who would eliminate you as quickly as turning off a light.

"Like magicians, they can make you evaporate and not leave a trace. Stasi headquarters was in East Berlin. After the wall came down the leftover killers remained in Berlin. Now, those gunmen are a significant part of the despotic investigative apparatus.

"Do not underestimate what they may do to you. Do you really think they're going to allow you to keep all that money?

"Expendability is a key word in the vocabulary of countries that have witness protection programs, Franz. Once they're through with you they will either cut your throat and take the money or cut you loose and turn you over to someone else who will cut your throat. The Germans don't operate any differently than the British or the Americans."

Schnabel was getting sick to his stomach, and the sweet Schnapps didn't help. He unequivocally knew the IRS, DEA, the Germans, the Russians, and other worldwide eavesdropping agencies had the LGT Bank under surveillance 24/7.

None of those countries was going to allow its nationals to evade taxation under any conditions. Neither would they allow illicit drug monies to remain stashed in a foreign bank. They could use those precious resources themselves to bulge their budgets and maybe even take a little off the top for themselves.

"You are making me very, very nervous, Ari. Very, very fearful. Is the threat a reality?"

"I've represented dozens of people who have gone into witness security, Franz. Once you've outlived your usefulness, the protection disappears and so do the witnesses.

"There's even more to make you apprehensive. Do you remember my friends who partied with us in Switzerland? Nunu and Dudu?"

"Yes, of course I remember them."

"Do you remember Rami and Uzzi?"

"Them, too. Yes, I remember all of them. Nunu frightened me the last time he came to the bank. There was a bloody human ear mixed in with platinum bullion in one of the deposit bags. Did you know that Ari? I have not seen any of them in the past twenty years, around the same time I last saw you. I had to dispose of the ear by throwing it into the bank's industrial shredder."

None had ever revealed his true identity to Schnabel. The only thing he knew was that the men were from Israel and had dropped off "surprise packages" to him at the bank from time to time.

"They were all elite commandos in the Israeli army, Franz. All four of them went on to become Mossad enforcers responsible for the permanent removal of key terrorist cells, and not only in the Middle East. Their network was like a giant spider web and still is.

"They probably know you're already in the hands of *Bundesnachrichtendienst* and I can tell you those guys hate the Germans and their intelligence agency almost as much as they despise Arab terrorists."

Ari didn't want to scare Schnabel too much for fear of him taking some rather drastic action. Like suicide. He wanted to let him know this was much more serious than the former banker might imagine.

Hirsch didn't mention any of the gory details about his Israeli friends. Like the time Nunu liquidated an eight-member PLO terror cell when one of them lit a candle – it was a rigged fuse – on a birthday cake for Chairman Arafat.

The flour-based explosive sent each one of the octets to meet his seventy-two virgins. And it wasn't even a cherry bomb! Arafat was in the next room and escaped injury. These guerilla demolitions were common practice for the Israelis; they implemented methods employed only by the most sophisticated spy agencies.

Schnabel's gaudy shirt was now drenched with secretions from his sweat glands.

"Ari, can you protect me? I would not want any trouble with any of them or your clients. You know I would never say a thing, don't you? I gave no information about them to anyone."

"But the Germans have the disc, don't they?" asked Hirsch. "If the Americans, British and Israelis know they have it, does that give you any hint about the trouble you're in? I don't care if there are no American or British names on it.

"Reality and perception are totally different, Franz. If there's even a hint those secrets are in German hands, it won't be just the Americans and the British who come after you." Hirsch purposely did not answer Schnabel's protection question.

"Ari, nothing can be proved against them! There is no information about them on that disc. You know Franz Schnabel is a man of integrity and would never reveal any of the information. Never!"

Integrity? Schnabel and integrity were polar opposites.

"You might know that, and I might know that, but they don't know that. Franz, I'm afraid you've overdosed on a handful of bad judgment pills."

"I'll be back in a few minutes." Ari said after a slight pause in the conversation. Hirsch lifted himself from the chair and once again left the room, making sure to swipe the digital card to lock in Schnabel.

He made his way downstairs to the pool deck and found E.F. and Buggy on chaise lounges, each sipping a margarita and eating tortilla chips with tangy salsa, courtesy of the Ortiz pantry and refrigerator.

Ari leaned over and whispered, "I need both of you to get something done for me. Quickly."

"Can we finish our drinks?" asked Buggy. "No. You're now an ad hoc committee of two, so keep your voices down. Put the booze away and listen. Get over to my house and ask Sandra to give you the Code Blue file.

She'll know exactly what you're talking about.

"Bring it back to me as quickly as possible. Make sure you don't lose it or screw it up. You know where the house is. Get going. I can't trust anyone else."

"Why don't you call her and have her bring it over?" asked Buggy. "It'll take less time."

"Because I can't call her. There's no safe phone here and the communications crew in the van outside will pick up a cell phone or landline conversation, as I'm sure they did when Sandra called a while ago. Here's my address. Just do it!"

If there were a Museum of Modern Dimwits, these two would have been co-curators. It was evident Buggy had an IQ that equaled room temperature and the booze didn't help them retrieve lost brain cells.

A piece of paper with Ari's address and directions passed from Ari to E.F. who quickly put it into a pocket.

The pair walked outside and headed up the walkway past three members of the at-ready SWAT team and the attack Dobermans. By that time, they had calmed down but were still hungry enough to munch on a human leg or meaty forearm.

A buzzer went off and the two feds walked through the front gate. Hutton immediately placed a call to Rosselfellar to let him know they were going to retrieve "some sort of confidential file to bring to Hirsch."

"Go ahead, but before you deliver it to him inspect the contents and let me know what they are. Not only does Justice want to know, but the DEA and IRS as well."

"Will do." Hutton's two-word reply was half-hearted because he knew Ari probably had some sort of protective device on the package, and he really didn't want to tamper with Ari's privacy.

Buggy and E.F. walked across the street to one of the communications vehicles, knocked on a window then flashed their badges as the side door slid open.

"We need you to call security at the north end of town to let us through." Hutton spoke with appropriate authority.

The two walked over to the SUV they arrived in and asked the driver to step out and let them have the vehicle. Buggy got behind the wheel and turned south along the coastal highway.

"Where the hell are you going?" asked E.F. "You're supposed to be heading north."

"Isn't this north?"

"No, Marco Polo. Don't you see the ocean on your left?"

"I think you're right about the left."

Buggy made a quick U-turn and took the two-and-a-half-minute drive north to the Hirsch residence after successfully weaving through the three horizontally placed squad cars fending off a long stream of vehicles trying to make their way south.

Peering through the corner of a curtain covering an upstairs window, Sandra saw Buggelshofer and Hutton pull into the driveway and make their way to the front door. By the time they reached it, she was halfway down the steps and got there before the second half of the bell-ring gonged.

She opened the door and hugged the men while trying to avoid the smell of liquor on their breaths. Sandra remembered how both had been so kind and compassionate during their days on the run, and she was quite fond of them.

In fact, Buggy and E.F. were the ones responsible for getting her clandestinely back to South Florida after being in WitSec for a month. She needed to oversee the packing of clothes and other necessities from their condo.

They never left her side, and she was grateful they were such kind souls. Through their contacts in the Justice Department, Buggy and E.F. kept the couple constantly informed if there had been any known threats to Ari and Sandra's existence.

"My, my, my. It's terrific to see you guys again," Sandra said. She invited the two inside. "I don't mean to rush you, but is Ari all right?"

"Sandra, he's fine and you look as beautiful as ever. He asked us to come over and bring him back the Code Blue file. Said you'd know what he was talking about."

"Sure. Can I fix you a cold drink while you're waiting? Orange juice? Diet Coke?"

"No thanks, Sandra. We've already had enough cold drinks for the day."

As if Sandra didn't already know. It smelled like the two could have been taste testers for Jose Cuervo. What Sandra didn't know was each had already consumed three margaritas and was working on fourths.

"Ari says he's really in a hurry," Hutton said quickly. "We'll wait here in the hallway."

"Give me a minute or two and I'll get you the file."

Sandra headed back upstairs to the office then closed and locked the door. She opened a large closet, lifted the back edge of a rug, and accessed a concealed, practically indestructible, deep-set, fifteen-cubic-foot floor safe.

Inside was the ten-inch-by-fourteen-inch-by-two-inch file which was made of non-tear thick polyethylene. The lock on it required a specially made key, one of only two that originally came with the file and were mechanically impossible to duplicate except by the manufacturer.

Sandra returned to E.F. and Buggy, handed them the portfolio and kissed each on the cheek. "Drive safely and tell Ari I'm fine. I'll be right here if anyone needs me again." Sandra hadn't been this startled since she learned she was going into WitSec more than twenty years ago.

She had no idea there were unsettled matters that might haunt her and Ari. As soon as he had received the first series of calls from the feds, he quietly advised Sandra that he couldn't relate anything to her about what was about to unfold. That would have unquestionably put her at legal risk.

Had she known any of the information, Sandra could have been indicted by the Department of Justice for aiding, abetting, and acting in concert to violate various federal statutes. This time, being in the dark was much less scary than being in the sunlight, although what was occurring left her feeling troubled and vulnerable.

The two old feds smiled, thanked Sandra, and headed back in the direction of the Ortiz house. Buggy pulled over to the side of the road once the vehicle was out of Sandra's sight.

Neither knew what was contained in their newly acquired package but noticed it was almost impossible to open without damaging it.

They knew if they screwed with the lock Ari would certainly call off the deal and might even sue them and every department represented on the Task Force for violating his civil rights. He could have also claimed illegal search and seizure. At their ages, they weren't taking any chances since the government would probably make them pay for their own defenses.

"Rosselfellar. This is Hutton. There's no way to get into this goddamn file. It's impenetrable and if Ari sees we attempted to mess with it, he'll call off the deal. I'm telling you, we gotta get it in his hands and see what happens from there."

"What do you mean 'it's impenetrable'? Can't you slice it open and reseal it?"

"If you saw the package, you'd know there's no possible way to do that without detection."

What they thought was that the assignment to get the file safely into Ari's hands were much more crucial than another couple of swallows of Mexican liquor or becoming homeless and broke because of a lawsuit.

"That motherfucker!" snorted Rosselfellar loudly enough for the two old-timers to hear. He hung up the phone in a huff. Buggy murmured to E.F., "Rosselfellar ought to keep his mother off the streets."

CHAPTER TWENTY-NINE

"We did not view marijuana as a significant health problem as it was not...Nobody dies from marijuana. Marijuana smoking, in fact, if one wants to be honest, is a source of pleasure and amusement to countless millions of people in America, and it continues to be that way."

Dr. Peter Bourne, Physician, author, anthropologist, decorated war hero, former U.S. Presidential health adviser, and Assistant Secretary-General of the U.N.

20 Minutes Later - 7:35 PM, Wednesday, July 9, 2008

SPECIAL DELIVERY

Ari was waiting downstairs when the file arrived. Hutton speedily turned it over. Instead of taking the elevator, he ran up the steps two at a time, a tough task for a sixty-eight-year-old. He went straight to the secure room where he found Schnabel contemplating life and expiration.

Hirsch locked the door behind him, pulled a small key from a false compartment in the heel of his shoe, and easily opened the portfolio while his visitor remained lost in his own thoughts of death.

Buggy and E.F. assumed their prostrate positions on the chaise lounges, staying awake long enough to finish their margaritas.

"With your help, maybe I could somehow get out of here and go to Latin America, Ari. I know there are lots of German nationals living there. Maybe even get to Paraguay or Argentina, yah Ari? I speak their language and can hide quite easily."

"No, Schnabel. That's not a choice. There are substitutes for the people who are and will be looking for you. Besides, your wife and family are looking for you, or did you forget that?"

Carefully, Hirsch took out the contents and laid them in a single stack on the coffee table. It was a chunky bunch of eight-by-ten color photographs resting face up. No captions, just photos. Ari had committed to memory the names of the people and places depicted on the glossy paper.

"Franz, I need your full attention. I want to know if you've ever seen any of these people. Look at them and tell me if you recognize anyone as a client of the LGT Bank or anyone you ever dealt with while you were still employed there."

At a cadenced pace, Schnabel began to go through them one at a time, turning each one over as he licked his index finger to separate and turn them. His face flushed each time he looked at a new image. They were a mixture of close-up head shots and groups of two to five people meeting in different geographic locations.

"Yes, Ari, I recognize all of them" Schnabel admitted after looking at dozens of images. They were clients of the bank for as long as I worked there. Most of them dealt with LGT for decades."

"Do you know how they made their money?"

"They were businessmen, yah Ari, mostly from Israel, Russia, Bulgaria, and Italy, no?" Schnabel couldn't make up his mind whether to ask for an affirmative or negative answer.

"Nobody at the bank, not even the royal family, cared about how they earned their money. Only that they made large deposits very often. Did they do something wrong?"

"Enlightenment is the least of your troubles," warned Ari. "It doesn't matter what they've done wrong. In their eyes it's what you've done wrong,

Franz. You are now in the middle of a minefield walking across the Golan Heights.

"These photos are men who are Russian KGB agents and members of the most notorious Italian Mafia families. They're all surrogates for some of the most powerful people on earth, including the Red Mafiya."

The dark and dismal characters were in sharp contrast to the richly colored photos. The Alps of Switzerland in winter. The Caribbean's Cayman Islands and British Virgin Islands.

Tax havens like The Bahamas, Luxembourg, the picturesque Channel Islands and the Isle of Man, Bermuda, and Dubai. All served as landscape scenery for the photographers.

"I must warn you, Franz, that some of the Russians have been hit men for the Putin regime. I'm sure you're aware of the recent rash of polonium, plutonium and other toxic poisonings that killed or maimed several anti-Putin leaders. The fatal drugs that you can't see, smell or taste and can be discharged effortlessly and effectively even by the tip of an umbrella?"

"Who is not aware of those murders?" snapped Schnabel as his eyes lit up like three-way bulbs.

"Moments ago, you looked at photos of their killers going in and out of LGT. If they dig up the records of their bosses' business fortunes, and political careers are in trouble because of a con artist who testified for the Germans-or anyone else-they will take considerable action against you.

"Schnabel, you know it's not only the politicians but the oligarchs they represent. Whatever Boris Yeltsin began, they continue. They have a stranglehold on anything they touch. "The new global financial empires, the military-industrial complex, the drug business, the sex trade in dozens of countries, the energy industry these henchmen run those operations.

"The list of names is so long it reads like a Pasternak novel. Viktorovich, Chemezov, Borisov, Patrushev, Petrovich, Ivanovich, Luzinky – these men are the power behind the power, and they'll stop at nothing – do you hear me Franz? Nothing!

"They'll snuff out your life as though you were a subterranean termite, a bug, an inconsequential insect. They'll torture you, then cut off your genitals and strap a rat in a jar around your stomach till it gnaws you from the outside-in until your intestines spill out of your abdomen.

"And then they'll stick a tag on your toe so that you can be identified.

These people run everything in Russia. They're involved at every level of the establishment. From the Duma to tourism, from security to transportation, from manufacturing to exporting, from retail operations to hospital operations. Everything.

"You will perish if you testify, and you might even if you don't. They don't even trust one another, let alone you.

"In the unlikely event you're fortunate enough to escape the Russian killing machine, the Italian Mafia will hold you accountable with your life, Schnabel. They kill at will and no life is sacred. Not your wife, not your kids.

"They no longer operate only in Sicily, the mainland of Italy and the United States. Today, they're streamlined. They use the Internet for communications and have confederations of muscle and mayhem and money throughout Europe, the Middle East, and the Far East. They're everywhere including this very neighborhood."

Never did Franz Dieter Schnabel realize the extent of this madness and manipulation. Never did he believe how a Liechtensteiner could ever become part of this insidiousness. Never was he more contrite for what he had done.

Contrite, hell. The thieving turncoat got stung in a streak of bad luck, which manifested itself by Schnabel's praying for his life like a soldier who finds a god in a foxhole. He had the distinct feeling this was the end of days for him, the dolt. Damn if he wouldn't have done the same thing had he had the same opportunity. Only next time he'd make sure he escaped permanently and without detection.

"How did you get such pictures, Ari?"

"Let's just say some photographer friends of mine used innovative techniques and were highly skilled."

Hirsch was speaking about his contractors, his one-time Mossad stand-ins who were quite inventive. Before and after they made deposits in LGT, they stationed themselves inside a van with dark-shaded windows and clicked off hundreds of photos with high-speed film and Nikon cameras with long lenses.

This was years prior to digital imagery. Nevertheless, they captured many Kodak moments. After midnight, when the streets of Vaduz were void of people, they would mount cameras atop telephone poles that electronically swiveled and operated from the blacked-out vehicle.

Twenty-four hours later, after a full day of snapping thousands of exposures, the shooting stopped, and cameras dismantled.

They also were able to take extensive video in a similar manner, but Hirsch was holding the tapes for another time. To exhibit his complete inventory to Schnabel or anyone else wouldn't make sense. He never knew when he might have to employ their usage to an even greater advantage.

As independent contractors, the agents first made the photos available to Hirsch to assure him the deposits of his clients' assets were not monitored by U.S. authorities. Being entrepreneurs, they shopped the "market" and resold them to the highest bidders, including Israel's Mossad. The U.S. Central Intelligence Agency also bought them on occasion, as did Interpol which needed the images of the Russians who were KGB professionals and mobsters.

Typically, the DEA offered the most money because the agency had the most money and didn't pay much attention to the large expenditures. Agents tossed around money balls as quickly as Nolan Ryan pitched fastballs.

Neither did they share their photographic purchases with any other governmental agencies. Internal warfare prevented that type of exposure.

Hirsch withheld mentioning his female associate, "The Comedian," aptly named because of her infectious laugh, sense of humor and practical jokes. Like the time she sold video to an Iraqi spy that contained nothing except Iranian cartoons with voiceovers in Farsi.

Her real name was Geela, Hebrew for eternal joy. As a veteran of the Israel Defense Forces and former employee of the Mossad, she was legendary. Geela always wore slacks, which gave her the ability to strap her Model F Beretta onto one of her long, sleek, Sports Illustrated-bathing-suit-issue legs. She used her weapon – the pistol, not her legs – more than a few times, including those when she took dead aim and expunged more than a few former Nazis and Arab terrorists.

About the same height as a five-and-a-half-foot, short-range missile, she had the body of an athlete, a face like Miss Universe, long hair as black as a Hasidic coat, a love for her country that compensated for her hardness, and a hatred for anyone who despised her people.

She was also a close friend of Dudu and Nunu.

With her ravishing looks and olive skin she certainly didn't need any Bronze-Tone that gave away her being a native-born sabra, "The Comedian" always worked in the background.

Ordinarily, she traveled to Vaduz a few days before making any deposits or withdrawals.

She would manage to place discreetly three or four wireless, remote-controlled miniature video cameras on a rooftop or in a tree across the street from the bank to secure images of whoever entered and left.

The high-tech sector of Israeli business provided these types of operations with the latest and best spying technology.

Geela captured LGT's clients stooped over carrying large suitcases and attaché cases, and upon leaving the bank there was a noticeable difference. No one's body was arched from the weight because the cases were empty, a dead giveaway of live money being deposited in the financial institution.

Once the video was in the hands of the Israeli secret service, they identified the KGB agents and further confirmed their status via Russian press reports and their own ground intelligence.

Ari continued his one-way conversation with Schnabel. "The others are Mafia 'godfathers' with many cohorts in Germany and Switzerland. When news of your testimony appears in the media, expect a contract on your life. You will then have vast networks of the most formidable international criminals chasing you.

"In fact, there may already be a contract on your life, Franz."

These pictures would come in handy someday, Hirsch thought, and that day had arrived.

Ari wanted to show Schnabel several more photos. They were images of more than a dozen secret agents vacationing with Putin when the Russian leader was head of the Committee for State Security, the KGB.

Yes, Yeltsin had changed its acronym to FSB in the mid 90s in his attempt to change public perception, but everyone still knew the agency operated as it had in the old days. Like a band of party-sponsored murderers. A Mossad agent had snapped the detailed photo at Lake Komsomolskoye near St. Petersburg, one of three bodies of water in the Soviet Union with the same name commemorating the youth wing of the Communist Party.

"They're all friends, Franz. They've been banking in Liechtenstein and Switzerland for many years. Now they have control of a group of Russian companies worth more than $1.5 trillion U.S. That's 't' as in tycoons. They're still gangsters so don't let their wealth fool you.

"Your cover hasn't been blown, Franz, because you never had it in the first place. You cannot testify under any circumstances."

Tears of fear were beginning to stream down Schnabel's cheeks as though he had been chopping a bushel of onions. His face turned from the tint of tomatoes to the color of cauliflower. He was pitiful, and as petrified as a thousand-year-old tree in eastern Arizona.

Hirsch distracted his attention. "Look at the television screen, Franz."

With a click of the remote, the sixty-inch LCD screen split into twelve separate images, each of them displaying three-hundred-sixty-degree, high-resolution images of the home's exterior. It was a specially designed video monitoring system.

Equipped with night-vision and infrared scanning capabilities, it covered all entry and exit points of the mansion and all areas within one-half mile of the residence.

"Schnabel, we're surrounded."

In one of the frames, there was the pair of Coast Guard helicopters fitted with heat sensors for imaging, and extra fuel tanks for longer missions. They were whirling in circles like vultures tracking their prey.

"The press choppers are close but at slightly higher altitudes. With the town's only road barricaded and all the tumult, I can assure you that every national news network, like CNN, FOX, and ABC are up there looking for their next pound of flesh. Next thing you know, we'll see Geraldo trying to sneak in to get an exclusive."

Schnabel was speechless. There he was. A sniveling extortionist multimillionaire whistle-blower on a free trip to Florida who was too terrified to even stroll on the beach and was now genuflecting, praying that his life would be spared.

When he heard the name "Geraldo" he guessed it was someone from the Spanish press corps keeping watch on Schnabel for henchman on the Iberian Peninsula.

"Franz, you probably thought you'd be able to meet with me and get me to add to the money you've already received and stolen. And then, you'd probably go into hiding. That's not going to happen. You've created too many problems for too many people. You now have too many enemies."

Ari pointed to the TV and said emphatically, "Look at all of these images. Police cars, federal Marshals, FBI agents, unmarked Chevy Sports Utility Vehicles, a communications center, German security, a special weapons and tactics team, attack dogs.

"But notice these others."

As Ari isolated and magnified a single screen, Schnabel stood to get closer to the TV.

"Look at the faces of the people in the back. The man in the red baseball cap and jeans. The blonde-haired guy in the green shorts and yellow golf shirt sitting on the bicycle. The young woman in the straw hat wearing a white sleeveless blouse and white shorts.

"Do they appear familiar to you? Do some of them look like the same faces I showed you in the photos? Could your good German 'friends' have turned on you already?

"There's no way out, my friend, no way out. This could be the last day of your life."

For Schnabel, Judgment Day was here.

CHAPTER THIRTY

"I think that marijuana should not only be legal, I think it should be a cottage industry. It would be wonderful for the state of Maine. There's some pretty good homegrown dope. I'm sure it would be even better if you could grow it with fertilizers and have greenhouses."

Stephen King, American author, screenwriter, columnist, musician, actor, producer, and director

---

1 Hour and 35 Minutes Later - 9:10 PM, Wednesday, July 9, 2008

THE PIZZA PARTY

Although Schnabel was in the middle of a tropical heat wave, his brain was as frozen as the Arctic tundra.

He couldn't process what he was hearing and worse, the combination of the long-distance travel, Schnapps and stress made him succumb to fainting and hallucinating. It was as though every thought he ever had become one complicated mass of mush. He was going crazy right in front of Hirsch's eyes.

"Damnit, Schnabel, you can't go on an unconscious journey! Get your butt up and moving!" Ari became unglued. He walked over to the wet bar, filled a large tumbler with tap water, poured it over the "dead man's" head, then tried to put him on his feet.

Schnabel was too heavy a load and landed back on his behind in the plush chair as he flailed his arms and draped them on the chair wings.

Hirsch hit the emergency switch on the intercom. "Manny, get up here as quickly as possible and bring some smelling salts from the medicine cabinet in the bathroom off the kitchen."

In less than a minute, Manny was inside the panic room holding the open container of ammonium carbonate under Schnabel's bulbous nose trying to trigger an inhaling reflex. After breathing in the fumes several times, the "patient" was aroused enough to awaken, although somewhat in a fuzzy daze.

He fell back into a state of semi-consciousness and slumped over in his chair, his head hanging over one side.

Manny picked him up by his lapels and suddenly slapped Schnabel across his face twice with the open palm and back of his right hand and placed him back in the seat.

He took a cold, wet washcloth, and wiped it along his forehead, eyes and cheeks. Schnabel slowly opened his eyes and asked, "*Was fällt dir denn eigentlich ein?* What's the big idea?"

He felt the sting of the strikes on both cheeks and felt the welts with his fingers. "Compose yourself," Ari said. "You've been out cold. You're under severe pressure you visibly can't handle. You'll be okay once you loosen up and the alcohol wears off."

"Manny, we haven't eaten all day," Hirsch said as his stomach lamented being on empty. "Can you make a pot of coffee and order a large pizza?"

"No problem, Ari."

Schnabel then added, "Yes, coffee and pizza would be good. I am sorry. You have made me jumpier than a broken cuckoo clock. There is only so much a man can take. Please. You will help me, yah Ari?"

"Yes, I'll help you Franz, but you have to follow my explicit instructions. There's no room for any mistakes, and the condition you're in doesn't help. Let's wait until after you get some coffee in you before I explain the plan."

Let him sweat it out for a few more minutes. Just make small talk until Manny gets back. Schnabel won't be aware of anything now anyway.

Several minutes later, Manny returned with a pot of coffee, cream, and a selection of sweeteners. It didn't take more than another sixty seconds for Schnabel to drink his first cup, then a second and third after which he perked up at least enough to indulge in conversation.

After Manny once again left the room, Ari said cryptically, "When you pick your enemies and your friends, Schnabel, pick them carefully. You never know when your choices will come back to either plague you or sustain you."

"What do you mean, Ari?"

"Your life is now in my hands and don't presume anything else. If you think I don't know what you've attempted to pull, think again. Yes, I will try to get you out of this with your life, but little else.

"Now that I've made myself abundantly clear, you have to commit yourself to full and total concurrence. If you step over the line even a millimeter, you will not be able to erase the outcome. Do we understand each other, Schnabel?"

Ari didn't have to spell it out. He knew that Schnabel knew what he was implying.

"Yah, Ari, of course we do. You make me feel very guilty."

He flies six-thousand miles at the expense of the German government to shake down Hirsch and if he could, the U.S. government, and he feels guilty?

He immediately poured his fourth cup of Arabica and took exactly three gulps to finish it. Now almost fully awake, Schnabel finally admitted to himself he didn't know beans about how sagacious his new adversary was.

At the same time, he felt a palpable sense of relief knowing that Hirsch was one of the few people who could extricate him from this self-imposed dilemma.

It was momentous for Schnabel, as was the decision by Ari to keep him breathing. He knew that perpetuating the hustle was useless. It would only earn him a headstone above an empty hole since he would have probably ended up at the bottom of a deep lake or in a can of dog food for Schnauzers.

"I need to go to the toilet. Excuse me, *bitte*." Saying please in German had a mundane sound, especially when spoken by Schnabel.

"Leave the door open. I want to make sure you're okay." Ari was taking no chances. He didn't want to wind up with having to take care of a case of bloodied wrists, a clear possibility that would wind up with massive local and federal investigations.

"And I want to hear the *flushingosplashin*."

"Yah, Ari. I know you are joking with me, but do not worry. I will not do anything to harm myself." Schnabel went about his private business and came back, partially unzipped.

"I didn't hear you turn on the sink water. Go back and wash your hands. The food's here."

Manny was in the room holding a large pizza pie box from Prestipino's Italian Palace. He placed it in the middle of the coffee table, laid some napkins down and left without saying a word.

Ari walked to the bar and poured a pair of club sodas. The Schnapps for Schnabel dried up as quickly as a rain-soaked polyester umbrella. No alcohol for him. Not even a Miller Lite. The meeting had to take on a different air, one that would lead to untangling the snags that beset the two men.

After finishing six of the eight cheesy pizza slices and consuming half their bubbly beverages, Ari took the lead.

"We need expert legal help, Franz, the best we can find. There are many complications ahead, including pivotal negotiations with several different entities. The lawyer we need must have broad knowledge of the American and European Union legal systems and a complete grasp of Napoleonic civil and criminal codes. It would be best if he or she was fluent in English, German and Spanish.

"Above everything, he must have the highest standing and unsurpassed reputation within the most respected courts on both sides of the Atlantic."

Hirsch knew a person with those credentials would be almost impossible to identify, let alone locate. But with the stakes being bigger than big, he needed that kind of legal arsenal.

The Germans were demanding Schnabel's testimony or would demand their money be returned. The first disc was already in their hands so that was no longer an issue on the table.

Spain wanted its million dollars or the extradition of Schnabel.

The United States and Great Britain were clamoring for the disc with the names of Americans and Brits who were hiding money in Liechtenstein.

But the only person who knew the whereabouts of that second CD was Schnabel.

Liechtenstein's LGT Bank would insist on getting the money stolen by Schnabel, and the royal family wanted the fugitive back in the Principality to mete out punishment. How could they let him skate when he might embarrass the entire country by further divulging the names of depositors?

In addition, Hirsch had some unfinished business regarding the identity of his old clients who had assets in trusts, foundations, vaults, and safe deposit boxes in LGT. Those assets needed ongoing protection.

The Russian "bears" and KGB functionaries had to be convinced that nothing would leak to the media and international monitors to further diminish the image of the "new democratic order," or interfere with their long-standing confidential banking relationships with LGT.

Other spy and criminal organizations needed guarantees as well. In addition, Hirsch wanted to doubly ensure his and Sandra's safety against prosecution and legal harm from any of the damaged or undamaged parties, if there were any.

"There is a broad framework of problems Schnabel, but something has occurred to me. I think I know the person, the one attorney I've met who might be able to handle this intricate pattern of difficult situations. Do you recall the lawyer I retained in Vaduz to establish the foundations and trusts?"

"Certainly, I remember. You are speaking of Baron Julius ben Mendel Rudfeld, yah Ari?"

"Yes, that was his name. A remarkably brilliant man as I recall."

"He is the most well-known attorney in Liechtenstein and a personal friend of the royal family," Schnabel said, "but we cannot hire a lawyer from Vaduz! He will turn me in, and I will be jailed! Get one from Switzerland! I am not a wanted man there."

"He's not going to turn you into the authorities or the royal household. I told you to leave everything in my hands," Ari said. "I believe the Baron can probably mediate agreements among all the aggrieved parties."

Schnabel knew that Baron Rudfeld had worked on some of the largest civil and criminal cases on the European continent and had been chief legal counsel to the President of the European Commission and consultant to the World Court.

But Hirsch hadn't spoken or heard about him in twenty years and didn't realize the Baron had established himself in international circles.

The Baron, he knew, was a prodigious linguist and handily conducted conversations simultaneously with several different people speaking different languages, including Russian.

Except for members of the royal family, he was the most famous citizen of Liechtenstein and certainly one of the most admired for his cultural and philanthropic endeavors. At seventy-six, he was still physically active and continued his unparalleled and distinguished legal career from his estate in Galprin outside the capital city.

"Some of my associates called him the 'Alan Dershowitz' of Europe," Ari disclosed. "My dealings with Baron Rudfeld were outstanding. As I recollect, he came from a lineage of great legal minds. Nobility, I think."

"Noble yes. Nobility no." Schnabel responded as though he was quite familiar with the renowned Baron and his descendants. In fact, he was.

"Liechtenstein has less than thirty-five-thousand citizens, and practically all of them know about Herr Rudfeld, or I should say Baron Rudfeld. I knew of him in my youth and for most of my adult life; not that we were close friends, mind you."

"Yeah, like I thought a baron would be your best buddy," thought Ari.

"I had many pleasant days at LGT with this man, Ari."

Clearly, this wasn't one of those "pleasant days"' and neither would it be a "pleasant day" the next time he saw the Baron.

"We did many transactions together and on a number of occasions he took me *essen*, for lunch."

You probably never even left the tip, you money-grubbing Midas.

"This honorary title of Baron was bestowed upon him by the Liechtenstein bloodline almost forty years ago for his accomplishments and devotion to his native country. Yes, he was born in the northern mountains of the Principality near the medieval town of Mauren close to the Austrian border.

"His father, too, was a lawyer but as a Jew, it was very difficult for him to practice. He earned meager wages by accepting cases that were quite unimportant. Small disputes between family members and the like. But he was a very intelligent and kind gentleman."

"Then why would you be afraid to deal with the Baron?" asked Hirsch. "He's not going to turn you over to the police, so why are you so fearful?"

Hirsch interrupted himself. "Never mind answering that, Franz. Right now, you're afraid of your own shadow. Continue."

"The Baron's wife, Rosa, passed away about fifteen years ago. I believe breast cancer took her life. Fortunately, he had two very intelligent and devoted sons who both became physicians. When I fled Liechtenstein, one had been practicing in Jerusalem and the other in New York City.

"I knew his parents and two older sisters. They are all gone. They survived the Holocaust by fleeing Salzburg. If a family had not hidden them in Mauren they would have ended up in a death camp. You may not know this, Ari, but Liechtenstein like Switzerland was neutral."

Switzerland neutral? Is that why the Swiss still pay reparations for their complicity with the Third Reich after sending Jews back to their deaths by turning them away at the border when they had a red "J" stamped on their passports? And stealing all of their assets? Go back to your history books, Schnabel. Austria had been the ancestral home of the

Rudfelds, according to Schnabel, until the expulsion of Jews from Vienna in the seventeenth century.

Since his days at the University of Zurich, Schnabel had become an amateur devotee of genealogy and had traced historical records and family trees on some of the most prominent citizens of Liechtenstein.

During semester breaks and vacations, he had been employed as an historical archivist for the Principality.

He told Ari the Baron's descendants trekked to the Pale of Settlement, an area in imperial Russia, and took refuge in the towns of Slavuta and Zaslav a few hundred kilometers west of Kiev in present-day Ukraine. Another one-hundred-eight years passed before Jews could return to Austrian society.

The small Rudfeld clan, Schnabel reported, returned to Austria and to a life of significantly more freedom.

"I haven't been in touch with the Baron in a number of years, Franz. How can we get a hold of him? I'll need his phone and fax numbers."

"Yah, Ari. I can make a few calls and get them. It should not be a problem, but you must make sure he will not hand me over to the police or the royal family."

"Get over it, Franz. Don't worry about things until you have to."

Ari knew the feds closely audited telephones, something he wanted to avoid. Neither did he want signals intercepted by anyone who might be involved in this international imbroglio.

By now, the media had already descended onto the tense scene and attempted to uncover what they suspected was a monumental story. Some reporters had seen the federal vehicles, but none could get through the police barricades.

Television sets around the world were telecasting the story from satellite newsfeeds. Some of the newshounds were already complaining about the "lack of cooperation on the art of the security personnel."

Suddenly, Manny entered the room and whispered something to Ari who immediately grabbed the remote control and tuned in to CNN.

"It appears as though there's big trouble in little Hillsboro Beach, an upscale community along the southeast coast of Florida. Late this afternoon, federal agents and

SWAT teams sealed off this small strip of oceanfront highway you see behind me. Authorities have surrounded the estate of the infamous former drug smuggler Oliverio Navarro Ortiz, at one time one of the most wanted men in the Western Hemisphere. Traffic is piled up both north and south of this heavily traveled road, Highway A-1-A, and police have not yet set up alternate routes for drivers to get to their destinations. As you can hear, there are Coast Guard helicopters circling overhead and witnesses have told us the whirlybirds have been here for a number of hours. It appears there's some kind of a standoff and we are awaiting further details. There is no official comment about these unfolding events and police are not permitting journalists to proceed to the actual scene. There are rumors that two federal agents left the mansion a couple of hours ago and returned a short time later. An anonymous police source told this reporter that officials have done a door-to-door canvas of every residence in the entire town and occupants have been told to stay in their homes. This could be a very dangerous situation. Back to you, Samantha."

"Thank you, Zack, for that up-to-the-minute report. CNN will continue to update our viewers with any fast-breaking developments in what could be a very explosive story. And now back to Larry King Live..."

"Franz, I've changed my mind. I'm going downstairs. Manny, please stay here with Herr Schnabel. I'll be in Mr. Ortiz's office for a while. Be patient, Schnabel, be patient. And be prepared to spend your millions to get your life back."

On his way out, Ari grabbed the photos, inserted them into the Code Blue file and took the case with him. He would need to add additional documents before sunrise and there was no time to lose.

CHAPTER THIRTY-ONE

"Marijuana in its natural form is one of the safest therapeutically active substances known to man."

Francis Young, Former administrative law judge, U.S. Drug Enforcement Agency.

8 Hours Later - 6:30 AM, Thursday, July 10, 2008

ENTER THE BARON

Hirsch spent the next seven-and-a-half hours sitting in front of a computer screen. He listened to the shuffling of single sheets of paper as they glided out of the laser printer. Baron Rudfeld needed the instructions quickly. Ari knew he would comprehend exactly what to expedite.

In no way was Ari going to expose his messages to the feds, which is why he used Ortiz's office computer and printed but one copy. He knew the National Security Intelligence Center hacked into hard drives to access and download stored Internet files.

The NSIC didn't have a clue that Ari would not log onto the worldwide web and would only use Microsoft Word to accomplish his goals.

Besides, Ortiz's IBM was encrypted and security-checked daily, making it almost impossible to crack.

Hell, thought Ari, if the Code Blue file worked once to convey instructions, it would work again.

Might as well use the old guys as my messenger service. They have nothing better to do.

After Ari had completed his computer thumping, he went upstairs to the crisis quarters where Schnabel once again had fallen asleep in the comfort of the cushy chair, while Manny tuned into Univision to watch Sabado Gigante. During the commercials, he glanced at the sports section of El Diario.

"Franz, it's time again. I'm about to send a fax to Herr Rudfeld and I need you to read it."

"Huh? What is this? What does it say?" Schnabel's brain, enveloped in thick fog, couldn't quite think. "Let me gather my wits, yah, Ari?"

"Go right ahead, Franz. Gather your wits and gather your memory of where your money is. You're going to have to give up the $7.8 million to pay the Spanish government, the Germans, LGT, and legal fees.

"You're going to rescind your pledge with the Germans to testify to the facts and withdraw from its *Aussergerichtlicher Zeugenschutz*. That goddamn program is run by former Stasi operatives, Communists and Nazis and supported by drug profiteering.

"Schnabel, there's no way out except to make restitution to the injured parties. Each step of the way will cost money galore. It will take all you have, but there's no other way out." Yes, Franz Schnabel was going to be nearly broke and financially ruined, but it was a lot better than being the leading star in a snuff film. He hesitated, but then read the fax. He handed it back to Ari with a defeated look on his face.

Hirsch walked outside to E.F. who had shared poolside lifeguard duty with Buggelshofer the entire night.

Both had fallen asleep on the padded lounges shortly after midnight when the copters were ordered to return to the Tactical Law Enforcement

Team South at the Opa-locka Air Station, an eighteen-minute flight from the Ortiz compound. Overhead surveillance was no longer needed.

"E.F., wake up," Ari said in a hushed voice. "I need your help again." It seemed like Hirsch was playing Mr. Sandman for everyone inside and outside the house.

Squinting from the early morning light, E.F. said, "What? What the hell are you waking me for? I was sleeping. Can't it wait?" Buggelshofer continued his loud snoring and was undisturbed.

"I need you to return the file to Sandra. Go. You'll be back in no time."

"Okay, okay. At least let me go brush my teeth."

"There's a couple of new toothbrushes and paste in one of the drawers in the guest bathroom drawer." Ari didn't want Hutton to lose any time.

E.F. washed his face, brushed his choppers, left the grounds, and again called Rosselfellar. The DOJ exec went schizo after Hutton told him what he was in the midst of doing.

"That dirt bag is using the same fucking package? Sweet Jesus, Hutton, can't you get it open? Can't you just take the damn thing and not deliver it?"

"Sorry but that's impossible, Rosselfellar. Believe me, I would if I could. If I don't get it to Sandra, you might as well close this entire exercise. Remember, we have cooperation commitments to live up to."

Without waiting for a response, Hutton hung up. He delivered the package to the Hirsch household – the only difference between his driving and Buggy's was that E.F. drove in the correct direction – rang the bell and awakened Sandra.

The instant she saw the file in Hutton's hand, Sandra knew it had to be important. Very important.

After E.F. departed, she ran upstairs and retrieved her file key taped on the bottom of the fireproof floor safe that had been covered with a sheet of removable steel. She opened the lock and slid out the photos and removed a pile of paper. On top was the following:

Sandra...

Please follow these directions carefully:
1. Take these documents to Jordan O'Banion's office. He should be there by 8:00 AM. MAKE SURE YOU'RE NOT FOLLOWED.
2. Do not call him. I don't want anyone intercepting and/or recording any conversations.
3. Ask Jordan to get the telephone number for Baron Julius ben Mendel Rudfeld. The Baron is still located in Vaduz.
4. Jordan must call him, get his fax number and inform the Baron he will be receiving a facsimile from me. I've enclosed the draft for Jordan's review.
5. Tell Jordan I would appreciate the Baron responding with faxes directly to Jordan's office.
6. Once Jordan receives the Baron's responses, he needs to call you to pick them up and put them back in the Code Blue file.
7. Once they're locked in the file, call E.F. or Buggy and have either or both pick up the file and deliver it to me at Oliverio's house. You should have both of their cell phone numbers in the safe.
8. Burn this document after you've memorized it, and don't show it to anybody.
9. I've been in a meeting with Franz Schnabel from Liechtenstein and things are getting complicated. I asked Schnabel to get me the Baron's phone and fax numbers, but he's frightened and useless.

Don't worry about me. I'm fine. Just a bit tired. Miss you.

Ari

Although the papers contained privileged information, Hirsch was always skittish about the all-encompassing charges of criminal conspiracy and obstruction of justice. The law was supposed to provide attorneys and their clients with unassailable communication, but that legal canon had been continually distorted and often squashed at the whim and will of the U.S. government.

Jordan O'Banion knew that as well. That was one of the reasons he was careful in reviewing the documents Ari had prepared, the ones that Sandra had brought to his office a few minutes before eight.

Instead of taking the short route to O'Banion's, Sandra performed a series of left and right turns every three or four blocks, making sure no one was on her tail. Too risky. She had plenty of practice making those same multi-directional moves while hiding in WitSec.

Once she was assured no one had followed her, she safely delivered the file directly to Jordan.

As soon as he was satisfied, they met his interpretation of the privilege evidentiary rule based on the Fourteenth Amendment to the Constitution, he picked up his Martindale International Lawyers Directory, retrieved the number of the Liechtenstein office of Baron Julius ben Mendel Rudfeld, and dialed.

"*Guten tag!*" O'Banion expected that German greeting by whoever answered. It was the Baron's secretary.

"*Guten tag*. Baron Rudfeld, *bitte*." O'Banion knew a few words of rudimentary German.

"*Wie heißen Sie?*"

"Jordan O'Banion from the United States."

After a long pause, a deep voice asserted, "This is Baron Rudfeld. May I help you?"

"Baron Rudfeld. This is Jordan O'Banion from Florida. You may remember speaking with me some years ago on behalf of Ari Hirsch. You were responsible for establishing some business entities for Mr. Hirsch in Liechtenstein.

"You might recall I was his legal counsel in Florida. In fact, I still am, and I'm calling to let you know that your services are needed once again. I hope I've called at a convenient time."

"My goodness, Herr O'Banion. It is wonderful to hear your voice again. Certainly, I remember speaking with you. And how is Ari? Both of you were quite accomplished attorneys and it was always a delight working with you."

"Ari's in a bit of a spot, Baron Rudfeld, and he needs your help. Rather than have me personally convey all of the extenuating circumstances by telephone I would like to send a comprehensive facsimile to your office. Would that be okay?"

"Most certainly. You know, at my age I am very selective about whom I represent, and this is an unexpected pleasure. Let me give you the facsimile number.

"I will review the documents and get back with you as soon as I accomplish my due diligence. Let me see what you have, and I will contact you as soon as possible. Does that work for you, Mr. O'Banion?"

"Yes, Baron Rudfeld. That would be fine. However, there is a great sense of urgency about this particular situation, and we need to proceed expeditiously.

"I also want to inform you there are pressing issues with Franz Dieter Schnabel, one of your countrymen who used to work at LGT. He will also need your legal services."

"I understand. May I call you Jordan?"

"But of course." Jordan was flattered that a man of the Baron's stature would call him by his first name.

"Yes, I am familiar with some of the problems Herr Schnabel is dealing with. I will do my best to discern whether I can be of help to him. I have heard many rumors and innuendoes but until I see and balance the facts of the legal issues for myself, I cannot determine if representation for Herr Schnabel will be possible. We shall see after I receive your facsimile."

"Thank you, Baron Rudfeld. You'll be receiving it shortly."

The two lawyers exchanged fax numbers and ended their pleasantries. Jordan knew the Baron was going to have to make a speedy decision.

Hutton had made his way back to the Ortiz residence before Sandra had even left the house to transfer the Code Blue file. E.F. had forgotten that Rosselfellar was on his way to the 7:30 AM meeting in the FISA courtroom with the bulk of the team from the day before.

To say Rosselfellar had been in touch with the command center in Hillsboro Beach was more than an understatement. Throughout the evening and wee hours of the morning he had been updated every twenty minutes by the operations chief on the ground. The news was sparse and speculative. No one, in fact, knew what was going on between Hirsch and Schnabel. All news reports were vague.

That's exactly what Hamilton twice told the President during the same time span. It didn't quite satisfy the Chief. "You're helping to destroy my international legacy, Addison, and this is something I will not forget.

"If you cannot bring resolution to the central issues of this case, the Germans will finally defeat an American president, and I don't want that as part of the record in my Presidential library - if it ever gets built.

"That would be a crushing blow to the continuity of our influence over that country since our victory in World War II. It will also diminish our standing among many other nations."

The Chief of State was quacking like a lame duck, which of course, he was. But his ego was the fuel in his engine and the cylinders were beginning to sputter. In six months, his second term was expiring. He was afraid his spot in history would be smudged.

This case might be one helluva great way to end his administration's tenure with a flourish of positive accomplishment. Lord knows he needed it after almost eight years of a plethora of failures which cast global doubt on America's ability to continue to lead the free world.

"Mr. President. Rosselfellar is keeping close tabs on the situation. All of us are doing everything possible to keep this under wraps. The Germans need to be told the situation will be under control very soon and I will personally make sure that's accomplished. This is not conjecture but an objective overview based on current facts.

"If the meeting between Schnabel and Hirsch has broken down, I can assure you, Mr. President, Schnabel would already be on his way back to Berlin to go into hiding. That is not the case.

"At this juncture, we must let it play out until we can gather additional intelligence. What's more, not really knowing what issues are being talked about at this two-man conference leaves us at a distinct disadvantage."

"Addison, you're one of the only domestic allies I have left and I'm depending upon you like never before. Don't let me down the way Congress and some of my closest supporters and appointees have," urged the President. "Continue to keep me abreast of all activities, and don't be concerned about the hour.

"This could well be my swan song and no matter how hard we all have to work to get this situation on sound ground, we must do it successfully."

At last, the President had divulged the truth. This wasn't so much about recovering the tax money and helping the Germans, but a deeply intense and personal vanity-driven challenge.

Sure, the IRS and DEA demanded financial payback but neither agency would negate what the President believed was his worthy place in history.

The hell with the Germans, Herr Schnabel and others who might be caught in this web of deceit, the kind that would forever put a plague on their one-time good names. As long as it didn't defame the President, all was acceptable.

Since no one with any knowledge of governmental framework had a clue about what was about to unfold, there would be many revelations. They would somehow find their way to daily newspapers, tabloids that lived on the flip side of good journalistic endeavor, the Internet, and radio and television newscasts.

At about the same time the Task Force members filed into the Department of Justice Building, O'Banion was preparing to fax the documents to Baron Rudfeld.

The only ones who knew what the papers contained were Ari, Sandra and Jordan. In short order, the Baron himself would know of Ari's master plan, one that would involve vast amounts of money the U.S. government might never get its hands on.

It was enough the United States had already been trying to ferret out taxable funds in Switzerland. Now, the feds were knocking on the door of the royal family of Liechtenstein, not to mention attempting to break down the banking secrecy laws of other countries.

The questions about Liechtenstein were plentiful and perplexing.

Would the Baron intercede on behalf of Ari? Would the erudite gentleman of the law protect the privacy of Liechtenstein banking authorities? How much longer can the small Principality of Liechtenstein stand up to an onslaught from industrialized nations chasing their citizens for unpaid income taxes?

It wouldn't be long before those and other questions would be answered.

CHAPTER THIRTY-TWO

"Stop wasting jail space on prostitutes, drug users and other victimless criminals. Even if we find it morally acceptable to imprison these people for choices they make regarding their bodies, we must realize that we simply cannot afford to continue clogging the court system and the prison system with these harmless criminals."

Edward B. Wagner, Administrative law judge, U.S. Securities and Exchange Commission

2 Hours Later - 10:00 AM, Thursday, July 10, 2008

THE FACTS FAX

Jordan O'Banion placed the papers face down in a tray, dialed the overseas number, pressed the "send" button, and waited for the fax machine to eat the documents and cough them up at the other end.

PRIVILEGED COMMUNICATION-FACSIMILE

TO: The Honorable Baron Julius ben Mendel Rudfeld, Esq.
FROM: Aristotle E. Hirsch, Esq.
INFO: Jordan O'Banion, Esq.
SUBJ: Miscellaneous Requests
DATE: 10 July 2008

Dear Baron Rudfeld: Thank you for speaking with my attorney, Jordan O'Banion, and for agreeing to represent me. I anticipate you will also attempt to help a fellow Liechtensteiner, Herr Franz Dieter Schnabel.
Please note the following legal action steps that need to be executed on our behalf by your firm:

1. I am requesting a motion be filed under the laws of Liechtenstein requesting the Court of Justice in Vaduz take jurisdiction of all assets of the Estates of Bobby Smith and Timmy Smith presently situated in the jurisdiction of the Principality. At the hearing, Aristotle E. Hirsch, Esq., will furnish credible information and testimony clearly demonstrating that substantial assets exist in LGT Bank in Vaduz which belong to these Estates and/or Mr. Hirsch as the legal title owner.

2. I am also requesting that a motion be prepared to solicit a hearing under Liechtenstein probate statutes regarding the determination of presumptive deaths of Bobby Smith and Timmy Smith provided under the laws of Liechtenstein Presumptive Death Statutes which, as I understand, require a ten-year period of continuous disappearance from the Jurisdiction.

3. Please petition the Court of Justice to issue an order allowing the Executor of the Estates, Mr. Aristotle E. Hirsch, Esq., to enter the safe deposit boxes and inventory the contents of same in the names of the Estates of Bobby Smith and Timmy Smith at LGT Bank in Vaduz. To avoid any controversy, please provide that all U.S. government authorities shall be permitted to be present at the inventory of the safe deposit boxes but prior to such action shall be required to show the Court appropriate identification and U.S. government authorization.

4. I would like your firm to obtain a routine, unchallenged order appointing Aristotle E. Hirsch, Esq., as Personal Representative of these Estates pursuant to the certified copies of the Last Wills and Testaments of each decedent now in the possession of Baron Julius ben Mendel Rudfeld, Esq. Please assure the Court that a diligent search will be made to locate the original Last Wills and Testaments of the decedents and will be presented to the Court upon receipt.
5. At the earliest possible time, I would like you to meet with the Prince of Liechtenstein and negotiate a safe passage agreement for Herr Franz Dieter Schnabel, a citizen of Liechtenstein. I am requesting that Schnabel be able to legally enter and exit the Jurisdiction of Liechtenstein. He should not have to risk apprehension or arrest for prior violations of Liechtenstein bank secrecy laws, or any criminal charges that may be pending.
6. In addition, as an agent and intermediary between Baron Julius ben Mendel Rudfeld and the aforementioned Herr Franz Dieter Schnabel, I am requesting that Baron Rudfeld consider representing Herr Schnabel's open legal case and any outstanding arrest warrants and litigation in Spain. Further, in representing Herr Schnabel, you will need to negotiate a settlement between Herr Schnabel and Spanish authorities regarding the aforementioned legal case. 1 will personally guarantee payment to the Spanish government of $1 million to bring about a resolution of all legal disputes. All settlements must be acceptable to the royal family of Liechtenstein and made within the framework of Spanish and Liechtenstein laws.
7. Please obtain the appropriate paperwork from the Liechtenstein government and proceed to the Court of Justice to secure a proper court order to allow limited testimony by Herr Schnabel in the probate and anticipated Estate litigation of Bobby Smith and Timmy Smith.
8. All necessary official security protection needs to be provided by the Principality of Liechtenstein to Herr Schnabel for his travel to Liechtenstein and his appearances before the Court of Justice. It is Herr Schnabel's present intent to remain in Liechtenstein, his native

country, as a permanent resident and full citizenship rights must be afforded him.
9. Herr Schnabel's ability to travel and continuing obligations toward Aristotle E. Hirsch, plus Herr Schnabel's incomplete work at LGT Bank, should be made part of any plea arrangement between Herr Schnabel and a Liechtenstein Court of Competent Jurisdiction and should be an essential prerequisite prior to Herr Schnabel's being legally obligated to testify in any Jurisdiction, including Germany. This request needs to be addressed with and approved by German authorities and properly certified paperwork must be issued by the German government. There may be considerable resistance from Chancellor Mitsch to alter an existing agreement with Herr Schnabel. To that end, I am requesting that Chancellor Mitsch be told that various secret service agencies from several countries are inextricably involved. Further, this Schnabel matter will most certainly bring into question the banking activities of certain Russian oligarchs and KGB agents. This could well threaten the oil and gas supply agreements between those countries inasmuch as the companies supplying those commodities to Germany are run by Russian nationals who want all of their activities in Liechtenstein to remain within the confines of the Principality. If the Germans pressure LGT Bank and/or any other Liechtenstein authority(ies), all names, including those of the Russians, will be revealed as a matter of necessity. Officials of Germany's witness protection program, *Aussergerichtlicher Zeugenschutz*, have given Herr Schnabel a permanent berth. However, he has decided not to participate any longer and wishes to return to Liechtenstein. His wife and two children are living somewhere in Switzerland. They, too, would like to return to the Principality and be reunited as a family.
10. Additionally, German authorities need to be informed there is continual chatter among security agencies. Certain Bulgarian nationals with accounts at LGT Bank have threatened to travel to Munich, Frankfurt, Berlin, Bonn, Hamburg, and several other large cities in Germany to create a wave of terror that will cause the German people more trouble than previously experienced under

Russian hegemony over East Germany. Please remind German officials the excessive killings and corruption in Sofia, Varna and other Bulgarian cities are completely out of control. If Chancellor Mitsch helps destroy the integrity of the Liechtenstein banking system, the top organized crime figures in Bulgaria will create more havoc than the Third Reich. Emphasize that the European Convention of Human Rights, which Germany has signed and agreed to, would exempt the Bulgarians from its Jurisdiction. Further, there are also Israeli citizens who are depositors at LGT Bank, and as such have strong connections with former Mossad agents. Should any of those depositors' names be divulged because of German interference, there may be severe penalties.

In terms of financial considerations, please be advised the budget for all legal matters, including remuneration to all governmental entities, is $7.5 million U.S. I will supplement any additional legal fees from my stipend due me as the Personal Representative of the Estates of Bobby Smith and Timmy Smith. From our past relationship I'm sure you know that all fees due your firm will be paid via a transfer of funds directly to your bank.

If you have any questions regarding any of the above, I look forward to discussing them with you. We appreciate your speedy action on the above and I will communicate all developments as they occur.

Signed **Aristotle Einshtein Hirsch, Esq.**
Aristotle Einshtein Hirsch

This facsimile is strictly confidential and intended solely for the person or organization to who it is addressed. It may contain privileged and confidential information and may be subject to the attorney-client privilege or other confidentiality protections. Insofar as that the content relates to official business the content will be confidential and the proprietary. information of the sender. This information is private and protected by law. Any use, copying, retention,

or disclosure by any person other than the intended recipient or the intended recipient's designees is strictly prohibited. If you are not the intended recipient, you must not copy, distribute, or take any action in reliance on it. If you have received this facsimile in error, please notify us as soon as possible. The sender does not accept any liability or responsibility for any interception, corruption, destruction, loss, late arrival, or incompleteness of or tampering or interference with any of the information contained in this facsimile or for its incorrect delivery or non-delivery for whatsoever reason or for its effect on any electronic device of the recipient. If verification of this facsimile is required, please request an original version and we will forward it via airmail.

No sooner had O'Banion secured the successful transmission page from his fax machine than three armed men bolted into the attorney's office and seized the documents.

O'Banion didn't even have the opportunity to have the pages photocopied, let alone secured in a locked file.

The DEA had multiple ways of tracking communications, and although the department couldn't determine what the pages O'Banion transmitted said, a communications satellite in a geostationary orbit easily picked up the fax machine's signal and translated the document.

If the comsat hadn't done the job, the DEA was prepared to barge into O'Banion's office anyway. Sandra had been tracked by satellite photo navigational digital electronics. No matter what route she had taken to the office, she was spotted from the air. Indeed, they shadowed her as sure as they had followed Ari to Ortiz's house.

The feds hung out in a forty-thousand-square-foot windowless building enclosed by a razor-wire fence on Northwest Twenty-First Avenue between Sunrise and Oakland Park Boulevards in Fort Lauderdale, only a few blocks west of I-95.

There were three dead giveaways that it was a federal command center. In the parking lot were more black SUVs with tinted windows than the combined total of the five largest Chevy dealerships in the nation. The antennae and satellite dishes on the roof gave the structure the appearance of being an espionage fortress. And it was the perfect location to zip onto a major north-south artery and reach anywhere in South Florida quickly.

It wasn't merely a home for the DEA. It also housed agents representing the NDIC, CIA, NSA, U.S. Customs, and the U.S. Marshal Service.

The cold-looking building, with high-intensity spotlights and shrieking alarm systems, also gave them an inconspicuous place to monitor illegal activities for the southeastern U.S., Mexico, the Caribbean, and Central and South America.

It gave them all a super spot to keep track of all sorts of people who the government deemed "undesirables." Sandra and Ari fit the government's profile. O'Banion didn't. The moment the feds received the satellite information, the trio of drug enforcement agents hightailed it to O'Banion's office and barged in quickly, similar to the way they'd made drug busts.

"Great job, Jordan, great job," one of the agents said. "Now I know why your nickname is the 'Florida Flipper'."

It turned out that O'Banion wasn't just another fish in the sea.

CHAPTER THIRTY-THREE

"The War on Drugs is a price support system for terrorists and drug pushers. It turns ordinary, cheap plants like marijuana and poppies into fantastically lucrative black-market products. Without the War on Drugs, the financial engine that fuels terrorist organizations would sputter to a halt."

Ron Crickenberger, Former Libertarian Party Political Director

1 Hour Later - 11:00 AM, Thursday, July 10, 2008

THE SMITH COURTSHIP

O'Banion was more than a garden-variety informant. He cultivated relationships like a farmer fertilizes vegetables. For more than twenty-five years, he represented clients connected to the drug trade and the federal government, which enabled him to harvest a crop load of money from each side of the plowed field.

There were drug dealers he represented who he knew could not only fill his bank account but his ceramic weed bong.

When the feds caught him with two pounds of grass in 1983, instead of arresting him for a felony they told him they would pay him to "cooperate with us." Neither would they turn him into the Florida Bar for disciplinary action. It was a deal he couldn't turn down. He got away with his little flimflam until some two months after turning over to the feds the fax he sent to the Baron. His body was found at a muddy canal between Alligator Alley west of Fort Lauderdale and Naples on the southwest coast of the Florida peninsula.

The bottom of the name of the east-west road implied, large chunks of his corpse were chomped off by what police described as "at least one six-foot reptile, presumably an alligator." His 2009 Porsche Carrera also took a dive into the swampy abyss, but automobile parts were not digestible by the local inhabitants.

The bullet wound in the back of his head, located a quarter mile from O'Banion's body, suggested it wasn't an accident. Investigators said it was more than likely a hit by the Dixie Mafia, a loosely organized group of traveling criminals whose motto was, "Thou shalt not snitch to the cops." From its base of operations in Biloxi, Mississippi, members from the Gulf of Mexico to Appalachia fanned out across the Southeast and conducted very nasty business enterprises.

Customarily, its members were ex-cons and provided a variety of services, including murder-for-hire, robbery, drug trafficking, and selling weapons illegally.

A nine-millimeter was their slug of choice and that's exactly what was found lodged in O'Banion's scalp. Investigators determined the trigger was pulled at close range.

The dead attorney had been feeding the DEA dirt on the Dixie Mafia's importing of cocaine from Mexico and Caribbean islands in exchange for money. The gang members found out.

Information had been passed along to O'Banion by an informant who knew that some of the Dixie boys ran an antique business in nearby Dania, a town south of Fort Lauderdale known for its jai alai fronton and variety of stores selling vintage artifacts and relics.

One of those retail operations was run by the notorious group. It was an easy way to fence stolen goods and wash drug money. When the store got raided by the feds and several Dixie Mafia members wound up in a not-so-old-timey jail, the evidence pointed to O'Banion being the blabbermouth.

So much for tattletales. So much for deceptive attorneys.

By now, Rosselfellar and Hamilton reviewed all the elements of the fax sent to them by one of the feds at O'Banion's. The rest of the Task Force sans Buggy and E.F. had been in the FISA courtroom for three-and-a-half hours waiting for some news of the meeting between Schnabel and Hirsch.

Whitfield already had some of the information. As head of the DEA for the Southeast, he was immediately called on his cell phone by one of his agents who summarized the fax info while still in O'Banion's office. Whitfield remained closemouthed. He didn't want to alert any of the others about the Smith "brothers."

It would turn out to be an epic embarrassment for him and the department, and he knew it. Unfolding the facts was something he simply wasn't ready to do.

Rosselfellar was.

"We've made significant progress. We now have intelligence that links Hirsch and Schnabel to a Baron Julius ben Mendel Rudfeld, an attorney in Liechtenstein. The report also outlines the legal status of Schnabel in various countries. We've studied the information and we're ready to proceed.

"Hirsch is attempting to locate the assets of a Bobby Smith and a Timmy Smith in Liechtenstein. Any of you ever heard of those two?"

Ten arms and ten hands shot into the air almost in unison.

"All of you know them?"

"Every federal law enforcement agency has files on those bastards," said Patterson, operations chief for Homeland Security. "Even the DOJ. You probably don't know about them because every file's been buried since you came to Justice."

"What do you mean 'buried'?"

"Those files are now sealed and labeled Sensitive Compartmented Information. It'll probably take an act of Congress to get 'em here." Patterson had been down this road before.

"Get a warrant to open them and put a rush on it," Hamilton ordered. In the thirty years since its inception, the Federal Intelligence Security Court, formed because of FISA, had morphed from a seven-judge panel into an eleven-judge chamber in charge of secret, non-public legal proceedings.

"Virtually impossible! We can petition for a warrant, but no judge is going to grant one," Rosselfellar replied. "Not when they're marked SCI. You'll be chasing rainbows, Addison, and we don't have time to appeal to the Court of Review for a warrant or a pot of gold.

"If all of you know about the Smiths, let's hear some background before this gets more out of hand than it already is. Hirsch has already begun a legal onslaught unlike most of us has ever experienced. With the Smiths involved, this is going to be more convoluted, and will create more judicial bedlam than Enron and the Exxon Valdez together." Rosselfellar scowled at Wazinski, but the WitSec director simply stared at his own shoes while losing a great deal of his bravado. He knew he was being eyeballed but refused to make visual contact.

"Were they in WitSec, Wazinski?"

No response.

"Can't you hear, Wazinski? Were the Smiths ever in witness protection?"

"At one time, they were. I'm a bit foggy about the details because it was decades ago."

Foggy? He was as sure they were in WitSec just as sure as he had seen Smith Brothers Cough Drops in the drugstore. He never missed a good chance to keep his mouth shut.

"We haven't heard anything about them for years. For all we know, they could be dead. Once they left the program, we lost them. I heard they had made some kind of red-letter arrangements with Johnston and Whitfield's agencies before they joined."

Rosselfellar's eyes focused on Johnston. "What did the CIA have to do with them? What kind of deal did you make?"

"I didn't make any kind of deal with 'em, dammit! Maybe some of my predecessors did but I didn't! Not on my watch! Listen, we've made deals with thousands of guys during various stages of the drug war, but I had nothing to do with the Smiths."

Actually, the Smith brothers didn't even exist. At least not on paper since neither had ever found his birth certificate. They weren't even blood brothers. The pacts the feds made with them went beyond the boundaries of comprehension and believability. It was one of the craziest courtships in the history of the CIA. The multiple arrangements were so bizarre one would think the parties met at the intersection of Insanity Street and Bonkers Boulevard, both familiar locales to the Smiths.

The "brothers" were formally uneducated but summa cum laude graduates of SSU, Street Smart University. Both took classes offered to runaway teen-agers by the night dwellers in the Midwest metropolises of Chicago, where Bobby came from, and St. Louis, Timmy's town. Each majored in Social and Economic Survival and minored in Shrewdness. Their best friends and teachers were male and female hookers, pimps, junkies, alcoholics, homeless souls, and general mendicants of their respective communities.

Their backgrounds were startlingly similar. The difference in their ages was a negligible eight months. Both were abandoned - a nicer way of saying dumped-by their parents at orphanages at the age of four. In their teen years, each escaped state-run shelters and opted to become homeless waifs.

They knew neither their real last names nor where they were born. Smith, they thought, was as good a name as any so they borrowed and used it for the rest of their lives. After multiple arrests for drug possession, petty larcenies, breaking and entering, battery, and vagrancy, both landed in juvenile detention centers where social workers, guards and administrators were getting tired of seeing their faces.

Describing them as "juvenile delinquents" sounded much more decent than they were. Scrappy characters, they were always up to their eyeballs in serious trouble, and as mean as the inhabitants and conditions in seedy alleys and homeless shelters had made them. As youth, "juvie" felt more like home than the orphanage. As eighteen-year-old men, they ran out of choices of whether to be bad or good.

"Join the Army or you're going to be put behind bars faster than you can hum Sing-Sing," roared one judge at Bobby in Chicago. Timmy was given the same option by another member of the judiciary in St. Louis.

Both elected to stay out of penitentiaries. They took advantage of the courts' good graces and headed to South Carolina's Fort Jackson for basic training where the two met as recruits in the same platoon. They quickly became known as the Smith "brothers" but not simply because of their surname.

They didn't exactly share a common coat of arms, but they looked like brothers. Despite their nasty street lives, they were in excellent physical condition and were an inch apart in height; Bobby at six-foot-one was the taller of the two. Each had steel-blue eyes draped with long lashes, sandy-blonde military-length hair, slightly protruding ears, and yellowish teeth because of their cigarette smoking.

The Army embraced them, and although the barracks they lived in weren't furnished by advertisers in Architectural Digest, they were grateful for finally having a place to call home.

After boot camp, they volunteered to go one state north to Fort Bragg where they trained in the same Special Operations unit. "What the hell," they agreed, "we're in the U.S. Army so we might as well be warriors."

They became experts in almost everything military. Rifles, machine guns, explosives, artillery. They learned how to pilot helicopters and multi-engine aircraft. They became snipers and survivalists – hell, they were naturals at surviving – so they thrived, although at times they violated the rules.

Nevertheless, they always accomplished their many missions, dangerous or otherwise.

The first assignment after Special Ops included an all-expense-paid trip to Vietnam. The late 1960s was perfect timing for the Smiths to become soldiers. Men like them were desperately needed. Not only did they now have a place to hang their hats, but they belonged to a tribe of kindred spirits, some of whom had histories similar to their own and who guarded each other's backs while combing the dense jungles for Viet Cong.

And using the best dope in the universe. Thai sticks, dipped joints, Cambodian red, and every hue of hash oil, heroin and hooter-nothing got better than that for those who made their living by killing and who needed psychological breaks to avoid mental breakdowns.

They jumped in and out of "Hueys" holding a machine gun. They sprayed rounds at anything they saw move and took incoming fire from automatic weapons. They lobbed grenades and fired stinger missiles. They airlifted their buddies to safety and turned them over to medical teams so they might see their loved ones again.

And they watched people perish daily.

These were activities few could emotionally endure, but almost anything was acceptable and respectable in what they were told was the fight for America's freedom. Bobby and Timmy also saved the lives of many of their wounded Army chums. They risked their own lives to evacuate them by helicopter after they were shot down or wounded in ground fighting.

In return, they would have done virtually anything for the "brothers" and often did when the aircraft the Smiths were flying got hit by enemy missiles or friendly fire. When their tours of duty ended, the Smiths and some Army buddies were hired by the CIA, more widely known as the "The Company." Their engagements included wildly unsafe and secret assignments in Laos and Cambodia where contacts to get illegal drugs were made as easily as talking to a local cop.

Notwithstanding facts to the contrary, the U.S. government simply denied being involved militarily in those two countries contiguous to Vietnam. Sort of like the same way the forty-second President of the United States said, "I did not have sexual relations with that woman."

Central Intelligence had been sanctified by successive White House administrations to conduct "unknown" armed conflicts and use soldiers-of-fortune like the Smiths to implement them. They made airdrops of guns, ammo, radios, food, generators – anything needed by America's private army of U.S. soldiers and allies.

Contract fighting paid well, above all if you were experienced and knew the terrain and the enemy's habits. It also provided extreme highs from adrenalin rushes and the best quality drugs money could buy.

Nothing frightened the Smiths. Not even being shot down in their choppers any number of times and being rescued by other Special Ops contractors. They simply couldn't get enough action.

Both had multiple bullets enter their bodies from enemy fire causing five-to-twelve-inch scars stitched across their stomachs, chests, backs, and legs. But their battle missions paled in comparison to their drug missions. Once the CIA took control of the two-hundred-seventeen-square-mile, opium-producing Golden Triangle in Southeast Asia, Bobby, and Timmy began to dabble in narco trading.

Early one morning, armed with two Vietnamese women he had partied with the night before still in his Saigon bed and hungry for more sexual fantasies, Timmy received a call on his satellite phone from his CIA field director.

"Timbo, I need you on a critical run tonight."

"Can't this wait until tomorrow? I haven't had a day off in almost three months. I have some personal business to attend to."

"Yeah, like getting your dick sucked in a ménage trois, only with youI hear it's a ménage à blah." Any kind of a wise crack from a field director was rare. "You're going tonight you cock hound. Be at the airport by six-thirty."

"Where am I going?"

"You're flying the triangle. Vientiane, Bangkok, Rangoon. When you're done, head back to Saigon."

"What am I carrying?"

"CHH. You'll have your instructions waiting for you as usual. Call me on the way back."

"Flying in these severe thunderstorms ain't exactly like a kids' airplane ride in a traveling carnie."

"That's why the company pays you so well. Take one of the de Havilands. I'll have it loaded by the time you get there." He was referring to the twin-engine, short-takeoff-and-landing aircraft manufactured in Canada which had plenty of cargo space. Pilots were high on the plane some literally because they could maneuver with great flexibility.

"That's a roger. Will do." He hung up the phone and said, "Come on girls, I'm ready for another round." He clicked off the phone, laid on his back, and smiled as his Asian delights took turns giving him a double dose of fellatio, or in more common terms, a two-tongued blowjob.

From the initials CHH, Timmy automatically knew he would be carrying cash, hash and heroin to Laos, Thailand, and Burma. As he laid on his back enjoying the joint licks, he said aloud, "Cash for the Martinellis, Hash for the King of Siam, and Heroin to some members of the People's Assembly."

Through hearsay, insinuation, and even first-hand knowledge at times, almost every pilot employed by "The Company" knew precisely who their shipments were going to. They also had knowledge of the CIA taking some of the cash and using it to get pay increases, fatter expense accounts, and newer and better equipment and never having to report its budget to anyone.

The only two years Central Intelligence ever released those figures publicly, in fact, were in 1997 and 1998, long after the Smiths were active or had even been seen.

At the prodding of their compatriots who finally made it home from the harsh and angry primeval forests of Vietnam, the Smiths began their serious "pharmacology" careers. Word filtered back from the States that many of their friends sorely missed Thai sticks and other cannabis products that could only be found in Southeast Asia. They were quite inexpensive compared with prices in the U.S.

Being bonded in battle with those back-home buddies meant loyalty and friendship.

So, they started a side business of shipping pot in airtight, sealed packages tucked inside body bags. No bodies, just drugs. The bags were constantly being shipped to specific stateside cities for "burial." Sometimes they'd stuff a casket as well. Via satellite phone, Bobby or Timmy would call the ex-GI who ordered the weed.

Then, one of the Smiths would speak with a Special Ops sidekick and inform him that his former platoon buddy, "Lance Corporal Dewey Ferguson," would be at the airport morgue at "seven in the morning."

The recipient would appear at either a military air base or a CIA air facility. The Ops contractor located the bag or casket tagged with the false ID and turned it over to the buyer. Most of the end users were generally depressed and out of work since many companies wouldn't even consider hiring a Vietnam vet.

Securing the money for the shipment was simple. The "brothers" opened bank accounts in Hong Kong via an intermediary bank in Bangkok. They hired attorneys in regions of the States as collection agents who Bobby and Timmy knew were engaged in underground work for the CIA.

Upon receipt, the legal eagles took their cut and wired the rest to the Smiths' secret account in the former British Crown Colony.

They were making so much money they could have afforded custom-made, fashionable camouflage outfits for every day of the year.

Word about drug shipments to America's veterans spread like hot lava from an active volcano sliding down the side of a steep mountain. Orders were coming in faster than they could be filled and reached the point where the two fully understood the concept of supply and demand like business moguls.

They established an operation in Laos where they paid locals to bag, bundle, weigh and transport the marijuana through jungles, and ultimately into the body bags and coffins. In the states, the Smiths created a network of field agents who worked the airports and conveyed by hand the drug shipment to the buyer. They, like the lawyers, took their piece and sent the rest to the bank in Hong Kong. But the consignment cargo came to a standstill when a Cambodian coffin-stuffer got stoned and crammed the packages of drugs into a bag with a dead soldier. When the body was transported to the funeral home, the undertaker and grieving survivors were astonished and outraged when they found the hash stash.

They immediately contacted the appropriate military authorities who tightened security at all morgues at all shipping points in Southeast Asian countries where Americans were fighting.

At about the same time, Bobby and Timmy heard rumors that the CIA was zealously creating alliances with innumerable organized crime families.

Rumor had it "The Company" was transporting prodigious amounts of heroin into the United States from labs their operatives had set up in Laos. The heavy-duty drug was converted into money that was paid to toughs, arms manufacturers and dealers, bankers, military personnel, politicians, and narcotics kingpins.

The rumblings didn't last too long. Only until some well-respected researchers and documentarians shoveled deeply into the hole the U.S. government dug for itself and exposed the facts.

CHAPTER THIRTY-FOUR

"American involvement had gone far beyond coincidental complicity; embassies had covered up involvement by client governments, CIA contract airlines had carried opium, and individual CIA agents had winked at the opium traffic. As an indirect consequence of American involvement in the Golden Triangle until 1972, opium production steadily increased...Southeast Asia's Golden Triangle grew 70 percent of the world's illicit opium, supplied an estimated 30 percent of America's heroin, and was capable of supplying the United States with unlimited quantities of heroin for generations to come."

Alfred W. McCoy, Ph.D., American author, professor and Southeast Asia historian

36 Years Earlier-1972

DOCUMENTED HISTORY AND THE HIRSCH CONNECTION

Some of the gossip turned out to be factual and was eventually documented in a number of books, including The Politics of Heroin in Southeast Asia, an acclaimed study written in 1972 by historian <u>Alfred W. McCoy.</u>

He alleged the CIA helped facilitate the delivery of opium and heroin by collaborating with drug cartels in Southeast Asia.

A professor of History at the University of Wisconsin-Madison, McCoy held a Ph.D. in Southeast Asian History from Yale University, and his research was considered cutting edge.

As a thirty-two-year-old attorney, Hirsch had read the publication repeatedly. It was difficult not only for him but for most people to understand the enormity of America's activity in the drug trade.

In his work, McCoy stated, "In most cases, the CIA's role involved various forms of complicity, tolerance or studied ignorance about the trade, not any direct culpability in the actual trafficking...the CIA did not handle heroin, but it did provide its drug-lord allies with transport, arms, and political protection. In sum, the CIA's role in the Southeast Asian heroin trade involved indirect complicity rather than direct culpability."

It was widely known that organized crime, including the Sicilian, Corsican, and American Mafia, had infiltrated the drug trade in Southeast Asia in the 1940s.

Well into the 1970s, names like Meyer Lansky, "Lucky" Luciano and Santo Trafficante popped up in conversations among journalists, CIA operatives, high-ranking military personnel, politicians, and lawyers, including Hirsch.

Neither was it hush-hush that the South Vietnamese government had been corrupted by drugs and money. Trafficante, the syndicate boss in Tampa, ran the Marseilles or "French Connection" in Cuba during the 1950s. In 1968 he visited Saigon to meet with members of the Nguyen Van Thieu administration and Corsican Mafia leaders.

The outcome of that meeting, Hirsch learned from McCoy's well-documented book, was a significant increase in the production of heroin, much of it provided by the Hmong people of Laos, thousands of whom provided a covert army for the CIA.

The Hmong's manufacture of heroin finally became so ingrained that its centuries-old rice-planting-and-harvesting culture became almost extinct.

After 1970, Asian heroin began turning up in the U.S. Drug lords with CIA and Mafia contacts released large amounts of heroin and cocaine in stages as reflected in the soaring drug supplies on the North American continent. The withdrawal of American troops from Vietnam in the early 1970s was out of the question. It would have been met with extreme disdain by the U.S. government because the administration would have had to admit military and political defeat.

More importantly, the amounts of money being made were so unthinkable that forces on the top rung of the government ladder wanted to stay in Southeast Asia at any cost. They included the CIA, Pentagon officials and their military and industrial confederates. The bottom line for the agency was 10 percent of the gross and untold amounts for the rest of the feds and their friends.

Plus, continuing the war gave Central Intelligence the ability to fill bigger baskets of loot with hundreds of millions in financial reserves to help solidify their relationships with criminal enterprises.

The money the mobsters and federal agencies made was laundered and deposited in foreign banks which the U.S. government couldn't or didn't even want to touch. Neither could it stop the resources from being invested on Wall Street and in mainstream businesses.

Like the nice little CIA enterprise called Air America.

Not the left-leaning, nationwide radio station but the start-up airline built from U.S. government financial resources. Ari thought it was almost a certainty some of the proceeds from drug sales helped get Air America's engines running. Air America was evolutionary. Its predecessor, Civil Air Transport, was bought by the CIA under a heavy cloak of secrecy in 1950.

In the middle of 1970, its zenith, the airline paid some three-hundred pilots, expert mechanics, and ground personnel to operate a fleet of more than eighty aircraft, including fixed-wing planes and the latest in sophisticated choppers.

It advertised itself as the "Anything, Anywhere, Anytime, Professionally" civilian airline. Some might have thought it was in competition with some of the world's best passenger and cargo transporters.

Well, it was if the shipments were contraband, rife with spies, cash, saboteurs, drug enforcement agents, special ops personnel, and politicians.

And because South Florida was beginning to become the nation's portal for importing drugs, Hirsch paid attention to the details of global drug trafficking, including Southeast Asia.

Miami International Airport had become a thriving hub for international trade with shipments going and coming from around the world. Its growth was exponential. Hirsch suspected a lot of that increase in air traffic was due to drug shipments.

Cambodia, Burma, Thailand, and Laos were the destination countries where Bobby and Timmy Smith and their fellow Air America pilots helped in logistical support for Asian allies of the U.S. Each time they flew, they took more chances than Siegfried and Roy. Heavy enemy fire. Daunting mountainous geography. Disorganized flight charts. Flying in extreme heat and monsoons.

Which is why Air America pilots could expect to earn four times more than the average civilian or military aviator. Hazardous duty compensation was mandatory, and the Smith boys earned every dollar. Indeed, both were among the last of "The Company's" aviators to airlift South Vietnamese and American civilians from Saigon in 1975.

By the time the war ended, Bobby and Timmy had learned more ins and outs of importing and exporting narcotics than most enforcement agents. They experienced it from every angle imaginable, which gave them a distinct leg up on their competitors, including agencies within the U.S. government. It was time for Bobby and Timmy to do something quite special. Instead of opening a boutique drug business, they felt the necessity to employ their Big Bang theory: the bigger the business the bigger the bucks the bigger the bang.

They settled into a two-bedroom flat in the charmingly seductive Riverside area of Bangkok, continued their contract work with Air America, and once again created a lucrative partnership.

After a number of meetings with several drug contacts the "brothers" bought a sixteen-year-old, seaworthy, ocean-crossing, handy-size freighter capable of housing twenty-thousand long tons.

Shipping containers were located and purchased at deep-discounted prices in ports along the coasts of Cambodia and Laos. *A cargo vessel including its crew! Heavy metal boxes aboard! Hell, they had enough money to buy an entire fleet and sell drugs worldwide!*

They filled the seagoing bins with a variety of packaged pot and paid a drug captain an enormous sum of bucks to sail directly to the port of Los Angeles.

The customs and clearance documents were marked "Top Secret" and the shipment was waived through without inspection after some cash and hash changed hands. Local civil servants wanted their fair share, too.

A couple of phone calls from Thailand to their Army friends in the states began a domino effect.

The containers were picked up and transported by flatbed trains, trailers, and trucks to different parts of the United States, then sold and distributed by a highly efficient marketing structure the Smiths had established. Body bags and coffins were the perfect hiding places. Dead men don't talk.

Tens of millions of tax-free dollars went into the credit column of their Hong Kong ledger, and they never looked back. They were set for life.

That was until they felt obligated and squeezed to score more on behalf of their battlefield pals.

As long as they were part of Special Ops working for the CIA, they moved around with ease. From Kansas City to Karachi, Miami to Medellin, Boston to Bangkok, Pittsburgh to Paraguay.

The two best friends had more connections than a telephone trunk line and were involved in drug trafficking on four continents.

The Smiths replicated the Bangkok-to-LA cruise on the high seas twice before the CIA transferred them to Panama where they continued their contract work. They flew south into Colombia and points north for almost a year. They got the lay of the Latin landscape and made it their business to make the acquaintance of politically powerful heads of the drug cartels and their government sponsors.

Knowledge of logistics and downstream distribution became keenly important. Bobby and Timmy could pinpoint where the drug labs were in the jungles and forests of Colombia as well as in Southeast Asia. They knew when to ship and when to keep a low profile. They knew who to bribe and who to stay away from.

Yes, they were at the peak of their professions.

Then, word of potential financial disaster struck. While in Panama, Bobby got a call from an attorney representing the bank in Hong Kong with news that the IRS was insisting upon cooperation by bankers on assets held in the names of American citizens.

"How much will it take to keep it quiet, Mr. Wong?"

"We cannot take that kind of chance for under $25 million U.S."

"Don't get me wrong, Mr. Wong in Hong Kong. The bank's been fair but that's going to practically wipe us out!"

"Do not be funny, Mr. Smith. Unless you agree to the $25 million, I am afraid we will have no choice but to give the IRS anything it needs."

They knew they were being blackmailed. Bobby took the next Air America flight to Hong Kong, contacted a friendly high-level bank employee, and promised him a substantial "reward" if he would wire transfer their funds to an account they had established in the Cayman Islands.

Luckily, the bank had not yet frozen the funds. It was simpler than a People Magazine crossword puzzle and at a deeply discounted price of $1 million U.S. When the bank president found out what had happened, he became steamier than an overcooked bowl of wonton soup. Bobby left town rather quickly, but now there was a warrant out for him and Timmy. The Chinese would have to wait in line and behind many others who were chasing them.

With the money gods on their side, they prepared a new caper to make even more. They flew to Laos, bought another cargo ship, then looked up and hooked up with old acquaintances who would buy additional product.

This time, they decided to go along on the journey. They took the vessel across the Pacific, through the Panama Canal, and finally reached the Port of New Orleans.

Vietnam buddies were waiting in speedboats offshore. They took turns racing to the freighter, unloading their piece of the potpie and leaving behind canvas bags filled with cash as payment. There was so much grass aboard it took two full days and nights to run out.

After returning to Panama, they flew the cash to an intermediary on Grand Cayman Island where it was dispatched into their tax-free accounts.

The Smiths knew that Panama's military dictator, Manuel Noriega who was later convicted in absentia by France of murder, human rights abuses, and money laundering, could have taken it all. Too risky.

He ruled the nation with an iron fist and took every opportunity to stuff tens of millions of dollars in his pockets at will. The generalissimo eventually wound up in a U.S. federal prison after being found guilty of cocaine trafficking, money laundering and racketeering.

The message to banana republic dictators was, "Don't fuck with the feds." Apparently, Noriega was too much of a renegade. He paid the piper for his public indiscretions. Bobby and Timmy always kept up their guard while stationed in Panama. They knew to trust and believe no one even though they were familiar with almost everyone involved in the drug business. As a result, it was less difficult for them to be forewarned about an impending problem compared with the uninitiated.

The Smiths kept working for "The Company" and flew with spotless credentials furnished by the U.S. State Department, which via its foreign embassies concealed CIA operatives.

The "brothers" breezed in and out of military bases in Texas, Florida, Illinois, California, New York, and Massachusetts. Each airport was left with large amounts of drugs illegally flown into the country on flights cleared by Special Operations employees. Some were more than happy to share in the spoils. Soon, they took some time off from their Panamanian activities to make their longest vessel voyage ever. This time, their freighter journeyed from Laos to Boston. They didn't exactly heave tealeaves into the harbor, but another leafy agricultural product that could be smoked, not dunked and drunk. That voyage should have made it into the Guinness Book of World Records in the Longest Drug-Run category.

Narcotics suppliers, buyers, middlemen, human assets from Central Intelligence, and a far-reaching network of government and civilian gangsters weren't the only contacts with whom they hooked up.

There were those fabulous-bodied, party-animal hookers. They genuinely fell in love with two they had met on a trip from Central America to South Florida. Debbie, a calculating thousand-dollar-a-night beauty, knew how to invest her money and how to please Bobby sexually.

It wasn't long before Debbie and her best friend, Lana, unearthed Bobby and Timmy's actual business enterprise, and Lana latched onto Timmy's love stick.

Debbie had invested her prostitution money wisely. Her holdings included a diversified investment portfolio, including real estate. She wasn't about to blow her fortune and possibly her liberty by not filing income taxes. That led to her developing a solid relationship with a competent tax attorney.

When she learned the "brothers" had never filed income tax returns with the money they raked in, she encouraged them to make an appointment with him as soon as possible. What the hell did these streetwise guys know about paying the government its share?

Besides giving them the name and number of her lawyer, Debbie gave them some excellent advice. She told them they would get into big-time trouble if they didn't fork over some of their earnings to the IRS.

Trouble? The brothers Smith already were being chased by the FBI, Hong Kong police, U.S. Customs, Interpol, the IRS, Britain's MI5 counterintelligence and security agency - all while the madcap duo worked for the CIA. They had more problems than the Big Three U.S. automakers in 2009.

As money continued to pour in, they finally called Debbie's attorney during one of their visits to South Florida.

"Hirsch and Hirsch. How may I help you?"

"I'd like to make an appointment to see Ari Hirsch as soon as possible." Bobby was the lead man on this assignment.

"May I have your name, please?"

"Bobby Smith. Please tell Mr. Hirsch I'm a friend of Debbie. I believe he'll know who I'm talking about." So did Hirsch's receptionist.

"Hold, please," she said.

After thirty or so seconds, "Will Monday at two be okay?"

"That's perfect. My brother Timmy and I will be there. Thanks."

During the next several months, Ari, with the help of Baron Rudfeld, established trusts and foundations in their names in Liechtenstein and filed voluntary-but-delinquent income tax returns with the IRS and paid the agency millions of dollars on behalf of the Smiths.

He also wrote last wills and testaments for both and, since there were no known relatives, Ari was named personal representative and trustee for each. And oh yes, Hirsch and the Smiths participated in some amazing and memorable social endeavors.

CHAPTER THIRTY-FIVE

"If the words life, liberty, and the pursuit of happiness don't include the right to experiment with your own consciousness, then the Declaration of Independence isn't worth the piece of hemp it was written on."

Terence McKenna, American writer, philosopher, psychonaut, and ethnobotanist

36 Years Later-11:20 AM, Thursday, July 10, 2008

THE DUDES

"With the word 'intelligence' in its name, how could Central Intelligence be so fucking stupid?"

Those were exactly the words John Rosselfellar used to communicate to the Task Force his humble opinion, but he directed his irascibility and his sardonic question toward Johnston. White, foamy spittle started spraying from Rosselfellar's lips.

"The Smiths made Jesse and Frank James appear as though they were stealing piggy banks from kids! And you put them in WitSec?" Rosselfellar was in a state of disbelief.

"It wasn't only my agency to make that determination. The DEA also thought it was the best thing to do under the circumstances," Johnston said, defending the CIA's decision to go along with the mandate. He was certain Whitfield would support him.

"That's the way it went down, Rosselfellar," said Whitfield, confirming Johnston's words.

"What kind of a deal did your agencies make?" Rosselfellar threw out the question for everybody since they all knew about the infamous Smiths.

"We busted them like a weather balloon at Miami International's cargo area," asserted Watts, the head of Customs.

"We'd been tailing them in Panama for two years. We had surveillance on 'em when they picked up a load in Jamaica. They were piloting their own 727. But who knew the CIA was using them covertly to set up other drug dealers? Customs was never informed, and we nabbed them by accident."

"How could a blunder like that occur?" asked Rosselfellar as he creased his forehead.

"Because no one told us, that's how," Watts responded. We assumed the Smiths were high-level, dirty smugglers. What else were we supposed to think?"

The story was so noteworthy it was made part of the agency's training program. A perfect case study, U.S. Customs officials called it. The Smiths were captured with more than six-thousand pounds of marijuana and one-thousand kilos of cocaine. The drugs and plane had a combined retail value of $64 million, including the $20 million appraisal price on the 727.

After considerable time, the aircraft was secretly sold by Customs to the CIA, which paid $22 million or 10 percent above fair market value.

"The money from the plane sale was distributed to Customs and other participating agencies," Watts revealed, although hesitantly.

Rosselfellar was astounded. "Are you telling me you auctioned off the aircraft and the CIA bought it back? And then you split up the proceeds as though they were profits resulting from a successful business venture?" "That's correct. That's the way it worked. Until that time, it was the biggest sting operation we'd ever put together in the Southeast. The Smiths got bitten by an informant we nabbed with coke stuffed up his ass in a condom playing tourist on Avianca." Watts knew all the details. She was part of the Customs unit that helped set up the wallop. Before it was all over, the singing canary was put into a WitSec birdcage.

The publicity that followed was international. In the U.S., front-page banner headlines heralded the "continuing success of the War on Drugs," as did TV stations across the nation. Bonita "Bonnie" Watts was awarded with a Presidential medal and became U.S. Customs' Agent of the Year. The CIA used one of her photos as a dartboard. Internally, members of the agency were as embarrassed and humiliated as they had ever been.

The public never realized the collar was against two of Central Intelligence's covert operatives. Unfortunately for the CIA, other government agencies did. The foul-up largely occurred because of the lack of inter-agency information sharing.

Within three hours of being caught, Timmy called Ari Hirsch.

"Ari, Bobby and I are at FCI in Dade County. Can you come down and get us out?"

"Shit, Timmy, what did you guys do now?"

"We got captured when we landed at---"

"Never mind, Timmy, don't talk. Say nothing. Not even a syllable. And don't speak to anyone until I get there. No one." Ari hung up without warning.

"Sure, Ari, sure." Timmy was talking to dead air.

Hirsch left his office immediately and sped to the Federal Correctional Institution in the southwest part of the county. He was familiar with the one-hour drive, having taken it any number of times to visit many of his clients who had been locked up at that facility. Arrestees were there either as full-time prisoners or had been charged with federal crimes.

Ari could have found the place by smell.

After a two-hour meeting with Bobby and Timmy, Ari knew what he had to accomplish. Within three days of being caught, the "brothers" were released.

"The Smiths cashed in one of their get-out-of-jail-free cards after Hirsch spoke to their DC handlers," said Watts. "Customs netted $2 million on the plane sale and the $44 million worth of drugs went up in smoke. But Jesus, Rosselfellar, we made a hell of a score and a damn good swap!"

It was the money again. The goddamn money.

"Who did they turn on?" asked Rosselfellar.

"No one," answered Watts.

"No one? Now I know you're putting me on. Why were they in witness protection?"

"Listen, when the Smiths went to Panama from their Air America work in Southeast Asia, they had brigades from all over the map looking for them," Johnston said. "Witness protection was part of the negotiations we worked out with Hirsch when he filed their delinquent income tax returns.

"The Smiths knew too much and Central Intelligence couldn't let them get taken out by anybody who thought the duo might betray them. There was always a chance the Smiths might spill their guts to us, but they never did. We couldn't take a chance of them being arrested and winding up beyond our jurisdiction, either."

Johnston then began to lay out the patches for a story quilt and started sewing them together.

Because the Smiths knew so much about where the bodies were buried in the CIA's drug-trafficking, money-hauling, and arms-smuggling operations, they were cloistered away like Trappist monks soon after the Miami Airport episode.

No, not in a cell. Not even close. After the Big Bust, their new home became an oceanfront condo along A1A in Hillsboro Beach.

The same highway that took Kenny Cooper down the path to pot profits. The same spot where former drug lord Oliverio Navarro Ortiz lived. And on the very same road where Debbie and Lana dwelled as "significant other" bi-sexual partners and pre-eminent call girls.

Indeed, they were locally famous for screwing a number of men and frolicking with some of the women in the building housing Bobby and Timmy.

The crash pad was also a floor below where two of Hirsch's other clients resided and ran their drug-running businesses. It was a sublime location to watch the "pharmacy" boats heading ashore with the help of the Hillsboro Lighthouse and a powerful pair of night-vision binoculars. The CIA-owned apartment occupied by Bobby and Timmy had been used as a safe house at one time by Special Ops. Now, it was being used by the Smiths who were once again flying for Air America and making mysterious flights back and forth to Nicaragua during the infamous Iran-Contra affair.

"That was their punishment for being bad boys?" thought Hamilton. "Maybe we should have put dunce caps on them and stuck them in a corner for a couple of hours or grounded them for a couple of weeks."

It was but several months after the Miami Airport incident, so the CIA made sure they were accompanied by federal Marshals to perform their civic duty.

However, another member of "The Company" found out the Smiths had become rogues. He told the feds Bobby and Timmy had executed more than a dozen private drugs deals without ever leaving their seventh-floor abode.

"They had the audacity not to share the profits with their buddies," the snitch told them.

This was the second time the Smiths got nailed. The CIA arranged for Bobby and Timmy to stay out of the slammer by getting them to snitch on several drug runners, which led to a rash of raids and major seizures executed by the DEA. Bobby and Timmy had lived up to their part of the bargain, and as a result, they went straight back to the condo under federal protection and straight into the arms, and between the legs, of Debbie and Lana.

That was until the DEA caught the "brothers" in an encore performance. They had taken their cue, chalked it up and snookered themselves into a side pocket for the third straight rack-up.

They had robbed the dough from the cookie jar during another series of inside drug transactions and kept the money, thereby crossing their sanctioned limitations.

Strike three.

"You guys simply never learn your lesson, do you?" asked their handler in a way he knew he wouldn't get an answer. "We granted you every privilege, made unusual accommodations, gave you vats of money over and over and over again - and you're still not satisfied!

"You're misfits, repeat offenders, violators of the government's beneficence! This time you're both doing hard time, maximum security, got it chumps?"

Not so fast Sir Speedy. Back to the slammer? Absolutely.

But the power elite at the Federal Bureau of Prisons refused to place Bobby and Timmy in a conventional facility.

Now they were in WitSec and as protected witnesses, putting them in a mainstream lock-up would have been sentencing them to death. Fellow witness security inmates would have quickly learned of the Smiths' propensity to squeal.

WitSec jailbirds were, for the most part, notorious, hard-core criminals, including mass murderers, hit men and other social incorrigibles. They were housed in well-guarded, nearly impenetrable, and obscure cellblocks next to a regular lock-up. Their confinement was so secret that when attorneys and kinfolk came to see their clients and relatives, the visitors had black hoods slipped over their heads to ensure they would not find out where they and the prisoners were.

The bureau wasn't about to have bloodstains on its badges if the Smiths had been killed on the inside by one of their nasty-ass residents or an outsider. The guys were charged with tax evasion, a white-collar crime that required the authorities to put them in a minimum-security facility.

But there weren't any of those facilities for WitSec prisoners.

Hirsch insisted that the brothers be in an inviolable environment, one where they could complete their fifteen-month sentences safely. The plea deal Ari negotiated was clear. Bobby and Timmy had to be placed in a minimum-security venue available only to WitSec enrollees.

Accompanied by four Marshals, the pair of sociable scalawags was escorted to new digs.

The Brothers Smith became cowboys-on-the-run at a dude ranch. Yes, it was the same kind of place where horses and hay and stables and bunk beds and chuck wagons were the institutional fixtures. Where everybody wore ten-gallon Stetsons and leather boots with spinning rowels on the back of their spurs. Where everybody yearned to be given a home where the buffalo roam and the skies were not clouded all day. The government-qualified stockade was twenty-two miles from the nearest Montana highway, and fifty-five miles from Knowhere, a place where three-hundred-thirty-seven decent folks knew a stranger before he even entered the town limits.

Where the only cop in the hamlet had been notified by the Marshals to report any "foreigners" who may come through town with "no visible means of support, not even a jockstrap."

Because there were no phones at the Lonely Rider Ranch and the federally funded owner had but one key to his burgundy Ford F-150 pickup, it was highly unlikely another drug deal could be implemented by the pair. None was. Except for the over-the-counter aspirin and multi-vitamins that always arrived at the main house by mail or the delivery man from Knowhere.

As the Smiths' attorney-of-record Ari was granted visiting rights if he was accompanied by a federal Marshal. On three occasions he flew to Kalispell, the closest big city in Montana, to make sure the Smiths were safe.

Each time, he was met at the airport and chauffeured by a U.S. Marshal in a government vehicle directly to the two dudes,

Once the two men completed their sentences, they were experienced enough to be broncobusters and rodeo clowns. "Hopalong" Bobby and "Cisco" Timmy didn't exactly want to be yodeling "Get Along Little Dogies" while riding on "Topper" and "Diablo" along the Oregon Trail. They had been sober and sexless for more than three-hundred days and didn't miss either one iota.

Sure, exactly like an orchestra conductor wouldn't miss his first violinist.

"Give up that kind of life and fun for feeding fucking foals and a fried omelet every morning?" Timmy asked Bobby. "Screw this cowboy crap and let's get back to work."

"Bobby. If I have to sweep up one more scuttle of horseshit, I might as well turn my life over to Jesus."

"You mean you'd switch from horseshit to bullshit?"

They both chuckled, almost shouted "yippee-i-a-o-k" as their U.S. Marshal picked them up from the front stoop of the bunkhouse and delivered them directly to the airport in Kalispell. Their welcoming committee included a representative from the Central Intelligence Agency.

"We have more work for you guys. Kick the shit off your boots. We're heading to Florida." This was the best news Bobby and Timmy had received in more than a year. Their hiding-out time in Montana hadn't been the bang-up High Holidays they had expected.

Freedom to the Smiths meant being where the action was, not on some dusty, backwater parcel of land where the only weapons were pellet guns and branding irons. "Gimme an AK-47 or an Uzi to sleep with, not some piss-ant pea shooter," Bobby had muttered to Timmy one night from one bunk over. "We can't even get hold of a Ruger in this place."

The negotiations for the next deal between the Smiths and Central Intelligence included the DEA as well and were finalized before they boarded the CIA-owned DC-9 headed for Miami. Once again, these were heady and risky times for the Smiths, especially because they were going deep undercover on behalf of the feds.

One grand bust at Chicago's O'Hare Airport, another on a freighter flush with Colombian cocaine heading for the Port of Miami, and a third in a major American metropolitan city's police department they had infiltrated turned into the largest paydays of their lives.

They divvied up the proceeds with the CIA and continued their operations.

"We sent them down to Peru to get info on the biggest nab in American history. The Shining Path might have gotten them," said Johnston. "They disappeared like a cobweb in a hurricane. We never heard from them again."

"Weren't they still in WitSec?" asked Rosselfellar.

"They were," Wazinski confirmed, "but those buttholes were uncontrollable."

"Where was their damn cover?" Rosselfellar asked.

"Cover? They didn't want cover. Those guys worked alone. They wanted their independence. So, we gave them a little too much leash. So what? For all I care, they're dead and gone."

Wazinski again was displaying his venomous streak.

"The two of them represented the worst criminal element in the country. They fed every junkie – even kids – in every major city with whatever the hell they wanted. Where was their goddamn cover? Looking the other way so we could finally get rid of them, that's where they were.

"I'm glad we left them alone in Lima. Alternatively, they'd have spent the next decade doing more and more damage to the United States.

"The rest of you may not give a shit, but I do! We need to get rid of that kind of vermin from our midst. Those nothings made us look like morons, like canisters of swill, and I was fucking happy they got wasted!"

"Mr. Wazinski, do you have any idea what you just said?" The query came directly from Hamilton. "Do you realize the implications of your statements? Don't you even remember this meeting is being recorded?"

The courtroom fell into a thirty-second silence until it was broken by Rosselfellar.

"Chief of Staff Hamilton needs to call the President now. Be back here in thirty minutes. Except for you, Wazinski. Stay in the courtroom. We have something to discuss," Rosselfellar said in a low, oily voice as he turned off the audio and video recorders.

CHAPTER THIRTY-SIX

"I favor free trade in drugs for the same reason the Founding Fathers favored free trade in ideas: in a free society it is none of the government's business what ideas a man puts into his mind; likewise, it should be none of its business what drugs he puts into his body."

Dr. Thomas S. Szasz, American psychiatrist, academic and author

45 Minutes Later - 12:05 PM, Thursday, July 10, 2008

SAY GOOD-BYE TO THE POLISH GUY

"I've informed the President about Hirsch's attempts to secure the services of an attorney in Liechtenstein," said Hamilton as everyone settled into what would turn out to be a very lengthy session.

"He's more than a bit concerned and wants us to throw everything we can at him to stop that from happening. I believe the President is going to be disappointed. There's nothing we can possibly do to stop Hirsch short of arresting him and that's not going to occur."

All of them were already in their seats when Hamilton walked in a couple of minutes after they were scheduled to return.

Except for Wazinski.

"One of our operatives," Hamilton said in a reference to O'Banion, "has been in touch with Baron Julius ben Mendel Rudfeld, a noted lawyer and prominent figure in international circles. I've personally met him twice. The first time at the University of Texas Law School a number of years ago. He gave an impressive lecture on public international law and its impact on American and European jurisprudence systems."

"Just the subject I want to hear about," IRS Commissioner Wilson Brown whispered to himself. "Doesn't this stiff neck know the only thing I care about is getting our hands on the money?"

"I also encountered him at a meeting of the European Union," continued Hamilton.

"Judging from the people who surrounded and knew him, he's a potent legal force we might have to deal with if he accepts the case. He'd be a formidable foe. We hope to know quite soon, perhaps even by the end of the day, whether he'll represent Hirsch.

"I've made copies of a fax Hirsch sent to Baron Rudfeld that we were able to get our hands on. Follow along and I'll condense the major points. Nobody questioned how Hamilton got his hands on the document.

"Hirsch wants the Baron to solicit the Liechtenstein justice department to grant a motion that would give jurisdiction of the Smiths' estates directly to the court in Vaduz."

"What estates? We don't even know if those guys are dead or alive." The NSA's Smitherman was perplexed. "They might surface tomorrow."

Hamilton added, "True, but they haven't been heard from in twenty years and there's no court that I know of that won't grant an initial hearing on the case. The situation is even more complicated. Hirsch is also asking the court to declare him the legal owner."

"Hirsch? The legal owner? How could he be the legal owner of their assets, particularly if it's dirty money?" asked the CIA's Johnston.

"You're another genius heard from, eh, Johnston? Central Intelligence and its group of damn idiots let those two make almost as much money as Oprah Winfrey! And now you're questioning the ownership?

"Never mind. Don't answer that question. I'm afraid of another dumb comment coming out of your mouth." Hamilton was staggered by Johnston's lack of mental clarity.

"Our source further notified us that Hirsch is requesting the court to determine if the Smiths can be presumed dead. Plainly, Liechtenstein requires evidence that the men haven't been there for ten consecutive years. They probably haven't. It's going to take a lot of work to prove they were. I think we'd come up empty-handed."

"Mr. Hamilton, puh-leeze! We can Photoshop a picture of the brothers and place them on a street in Vaduz, then timestamp it February 2008. Present it to the court and the problem's solved."

That suggestion from Underman from the IRS's tax evasion office went beyond the line of lunacy.

"Now isn't that simple! Why didn't I think of that?" Rosselfellar asked like he was responding to someone who thought asphalt was rectum trouble.

"You must be a quart low on brain oil, Underman! That's fraud! It might even be criminal fraud! That's illegal and that's not how we operate!"

"We don't?" Underman asked. "Then why were the Smiths part of a covert military operation run by Central Intelligence?"

"You little prick!" shouted the CIA's Johnston. "The only thing you revenue guys do is walk around with adding machines and sit on your asses counting money in air-conditioned offices!"

"Stop this goddamn in-fighting! Right this second!" Rosselfellar could not have been more serious or appalled. "Both of you might wind up like Wazinski!"

The group knew Wazinski stayed in the courtroom when the last break was called, but nobody saw him leave the building. Strange that he wasn't in the courtroom, they thought.

Perhaps he went to the bathroom or got called away.

In reality, Wazinski was shown the way out of the building after Rosselfellar threw him off the Task Force.

The head of WitSec was directed to the emergency stairway exit, walked the seven floors to the lobby, and exited. He quick-stepped back to his office a couple of blocks away, typed a letter of resignation and printed it out of his Hewlett-Packard.

Handing it personally to an administrative assistant of the head of the U.S. Marshal Service was inordinately difficult for Wazinski to do emotionally, but he had no choice.

"If you don't resign your post, I'll bring you up on conspiracy charges," Rosselfellar had told him during their private conversation. The DOJ attorney's demeanor was that of a military commander. He pulled no punches with someone he believed was a detriment to government service.

"Conspiracy? Conspiracy to do what?"

"To get rid of the Smiths."

"What the hell are you talking about? I had nothing to do with their disappearance, you lying son-of-a-bitch. And how the hell would you prove it even if it was true." Wazinski spoke with his usual arrogance.

"Everything you've mentioned in this courtroom these past two days has been recorded," Rosselfellar said. "Do you really believe I can't bring you up on conspiracy charges? Do you really believe the EEOC won't hear about your racism? Do you really believe you're going to walk away from this unscathed?

"I don't give a good goddamn whether or not you're head of WitSec. You are not going to meddle with me and the Department of Justice, and you're certainly not going to poison this carefully selected Task Force. Neither will you continue to denigrate certain members nor the work that they're doing. You're through."

Wazinski wasn't leaving without a final statement. "You're a disingenuous asshole, Rosselfellar, considering Hamilton guaranteed that Hirsch would spend the rest of his life in federal pen based on illegitimate charges! So don't preach to me about poisoning the Task Force."

But Rosselfellar had Wazinski cold. It didn't matter what Hamilton had said.

The WitSec chief's only way out was to agree to relinquish his position or he would be summarily dismissed and perhaps tried in a court of law. Yes, he was one of the few who got fired from a high-level civil service position, but there were legitimate grounds for dismissal.

When Wazinski arrived home, he told his wife he resigned because of "internal squabbles, and I can't take any more of it." He committed himself to looking for another job in the private sector since it would have been nearly impossible to gain employment in any civil service position. Asking for a reference from his boss would have been next to useless.

"Where's Wazinski?" asked Patterson of Homeland Security. "Is he okay?"

"Yes, he's fine. However, he's decided to leave the assignment because he felt he was no longer needed and couldn't make any significant contribution." Rosselfellar thought that was enough of a politically correct answer for the moment.

Buggelshofer and Hutton were on the case anyway, and he felt they both knew much more about Hirsch and the Smiths than Wazinski. He came to an immediate decision. There would be no need to replace the malcontent.

The rest of the members would find out much later the reason for the schism between Wazinski and Rosselfellar. But now there was much more work to do.

CHAPTER THIRTY-SEVEN

"In the 1960s, people took acid to make the world weird. Now the world is weird, and people take Prozac to make it normal."

Author unknown

15 Minutes Later - 12:20 PM, Thursday, July 10, 2008

STRATEGIC DEVELOPMENT

"We envision another considerable problem. Hirsch will be asking the Liechtenstein court to allow him to inventory the Smiths' safe deposit boxes."

Rosselfellar sounded deeply concerned.

"As we previously noted, there's probably bullion as well as gold coins secured in those boxes. There might also be large amounts of cash in foreign denominations. If the court permits Hirsch to dig into those boxes, he's liable to walk off with everything."

"Hirsch may not even be able to get over the first hindrance, which would make the rest of the requests impotent and moot." As Deputy Assistant to the Secretary of State, Ianucci knew legal machinations well considering he had graduated number one in his class at Princeton University Law School and had earned an MBA in International Finance.

"You're quite correct, Ianucci, but don't disregard the potency of Baron Rudfeld. He's much more than another mediocre attorney," Rosselfellar asserted.

"He's on a first-name basis with every member of the royal family and his connections in the Liechtenstein Court of Justice are as tight as a thirty-six-inch bra on Dolly Parton." Rosselfellar stared down at the fax to make sure he covered all the points.

"Any of you aware that the Smiths had last wills and testaments?" Rosselfellar let about ten seconds pass and didn't see or hear anyone coming forth with an answer.

"I take it the answer is 'no' which means we have even more of a mystery on our hands. Hirsch claims he's going to attempt to locate the originals of those two documents, if there are any, and hand them over to the court.

"He says copies are being held by the Baron and wants him to get the justices to appoint Hirsch the personal representative of both estates."

"Maybe the Baron has the copies and the originals," offered Brown.

"I can't believe he would since Hirsch was the attorney-of-record. Perhaps Hirsch has them hidden," guessed Smitherman. "If he does, we might be able to find them in his house. We'll need a warrant."

"Can't do that. We'd be breaking our own written stipulations with Hirsch, and we'll wind up with zero," said Rosselfellar, "and so will the Germans. We're at a dead-end on this one. The originals will only appear once they're in Hirsch and Rudfeld's hands. Don't bet on getting them beforehand."

"Will the Liechtenstein court turn over personal representation to Hirsch if they can't find the originals?" asked Watts.

"Good question," responded Rosselfellar. "The court can and might rule to accept certified copies. In that case Hirsch could wind up as personal representative and executor. We can't depend on anything right now which is why we need a fallback position."

"It seems to me we need legal counsel in Liechtenstein ourselves." Ianucci made an excellent point. "The sooner the better or we're going to lose before the skirmish begins. There's too much at stake."

Hamilton, Rosselfellar and the rest of the Task Force now were in perfect harmony.

"We'll begin work on securing a Liechtenstein attorney as soon as we're through with today's meeting. Ianucci, can you do a search?" Hamilton asked.

"I'll call our embassy in Bern, secure a few names, and begin making contact immediately. It's an absolute must that we find a highly proficient legal adversary." Ianucci was now getting into the mix quite easily.

Hamilton continued. "Hirsch has asked Rudfeld to meet with the prince and plead his case for Schnabel's safe return to Liechtenstein. He also wants immunity for Schnabel for all past crimes he may have committed. Hirsch is asking for permission for Schnabel and his brood to be able to live in Liechtenstein as permanent residents with full citizenship status."

"What about Schnabel's compact with the Germans?" Patterson, like the others, was trying to cover the basic questions.

"We have no idea how the Germans will react until I call Chancellor Mitsch," answered Hamilton. "It's too early to do that. We need to arrive at some definitive decisions about how to proceed with each of the points our intelligence has provided us."

Hamilton damn well knew the Germans would sic their vicious pack-dogs on the President's inner staff if they didn't get Schnabel back on German soil. They had already paid Schnabel $7.8 million and weren't about to let that slide.

Neither would they allow their "hostage" to renege on his oath to testify about the credibility of the disc.

"You should also know Hirsch has asked the Baron to inform Chancellor Mitsch about the severe consequences – including assassinations and terror attacks – if Germany is the cause of exposing other LGT depositors' names," Hamilton added. "We don't know if she would be willing to take the chance of allowing terrorists and assassins from several countries create the kind of carnage and bloodshed those bastards can inflict.

"As for Schnabel's problems with Spain, Hirsch wants the Baron to represent him in unresolved criminal and civil cases there as well. Hirsch is even willing to personally guarantee the money that Schnabel owes the Spanish government.

"Where in the hell is he going to get that sum-and why?" Rosselfellar asked.

"He's probably banking on the bank," said Ianucci. "There has to be a ton of money in LGT that Hirsch thinks he can get his hands on and keep."

He added, "It's clear Hirsch needs Schnabel to testify about something on his behalf."

"Exactly. That's another one of his requests," said Rosselfellar. "He wants the court to let Schnabel testify about the Smiths' estates."

"Which is another ploy to get the money," added Ianucci.

"Right again," said Hamilton. "But here's the kicker. Hirsch wants the Baron to make sure any plea arrangement Liechtenstein makes with Schnabel is in place before that crook is forced to testify in any other country.

"That means they're going to have to get Germany and Spain's approvals before Schnabel says the first word. It also means we'll never be able to extradite Schnabel and get him into court in the U.S. if he's granted immunity by Liechtenstein." "If the Liechtenstein judges deny the initial motion of granting jurisdiction of the Smiths' estates to its own Court of Justice, all the rest falls into place for us." Ianucci knew his business well.

"We can claim the assets belong to the American government and the court will be forced, based upon international law, to turn over whatever is found in the deposit boxes to the U.S. Treasury. Each agency can then lay claim to its proportionate share of the estates.

"If we hire the finest local counsel we can locate, we can and will defeat Hirsch, the Baron, Schnabel, and Liechtenstein itself.

"We have an opportunity to set international precedence. It would give us enough political clout to force banking authorities and the royals to turn over the names of American citizens and the amounts of concealed money in Liechtenstein.

"It will also have a rippling effect by sending a clear message to other nations that have permitted numbered bank accounts for decades.

"Not only will we be able to get the taxes owed, but interest and penalties to boot. We will then bring legal actions and criminal investigations against those individuals who have opened accounts under the names of shell companies, foundations, trusts, or charities."

And continue the system of organized, government-sanctioned robbery.

CHAPTER THIRTY-EIGHT

"IT'S THE MONEY, STUPID. After 35 years as a police officer in three of the country's largest cities, that is my message to the righteous politicians who obstinately proclaim that a War on Drugs will lead to a drug-free America. About $500 worth of heroin or cocaine in a source country will bring in as much as $100,000 on the streets of an American city. All the cops, armies, prisons, and executions in the world can't impede a market with that kind of tax-free profit margin. It is the illegality that permits the obscene markup, enriching drug traffickers, distributors, dealers, crooked cops, lawyers, judges, politicians, bankers, businessmen."

Joseph McNamara, Ph.D., Former police chief Kansas City, Missouri, and San Jose, California, author and researcher

1 Hour and 10 Minutes Later - 1:30 PM, Thursday, July 10, 2008

TAKING CARE OF BUSINESS

The Task Force members were on a high. They thought their healthy financial appetites might be satisfied. Down to the last one, they believed this was the beginning of a major fiscal victory for each of their agencies and the U.S. government.

They finished their lunches of sweet and sour pork, fried rice, beef lo mein, and shrimp with lobster sauce. The food had been dropped off in traditional take-out boxes at the DOJ building. Ding Ho was the Chinaman of choice, and his restaurant was but five minutes from the meeting.

Rosselfellar was getting Gung Ho about something more than the food "All of you. When you get home tonight, start packing for an extended overseas stay," he said with authority. Don't forget to bring warm clothes. Even in the summer, it gets pretty damn cold in that part of Europe.

"We have some things that need taking care of immediately. But before any of you undertake any assignments, we're scheduled to meet back here at 6:00 PM sharp.

"Ianucci, get on the phone to our embassy in Bern and speak to the legal attaché. We need that attorney quickly." Rosselfellar thought that time might be running way too short.

"Even if the Baron doesn't take on the case, Hirsch will make sure a tough and aggressive attorney does. Let's not take any chances."

"Will do." Ianucci knew there had to be someone in the diplomatic office who knew a Swiss or Liechtenstein lawyer who could coordinate exceptionally complex cases, someone who could wade through and quickly comprehend all the complicated information.

He or she would have to be able to create a sophisticated legal strategy and be intimately familiar with Liechtenstein, European and international law, as well as their jurisdictional structures. Ianucci scurried out of the courtroom to get to his office quickly. He knew the time difference between DC and Bern wasn't conducive to reaching anyone at the embassy except an operator. Nevertheless, he had to give it his best shot.

There was so much at stake that budget wasn't a consideration. Not even for the hotel accommodations.

"Watts, speak to your department's travel desk and arrange for individual rooms at the Baur au Lac Hotel in Zurich," ordered Rosselfellar. "Rent a large van or minibus at either Hertz or Avis. Make sure they provide a driver for thirteen of us. For everyone's information it's an hour's drive from the hotel to Vaduz."

Rosselfellar had stayed at the five-star luxury and ghastly expensive hotel on two other occasions. He knew its location was close to the financial district of the wealthiest city in Europe. It was in an area that would be convenient if he had to withdraw funds from a secret Department of Justice account to pay for any contingency that might occur.

"Is there anyone who doesn't have a valid passport?" Rosselfellar knew Ianucci and Hamilton didn't need them because of their diplomatic status, but the rest of them did. No one uttered a negative.

"Fine. Please make sure you carry them on your person, along with your official agency credentials.

"All of you. Please inform your individual deputies and aides to prepare dossiers on whatever information they can find on Bobby and Timmy Smith. We'll need everything they can get their hands on. Tell them to have it prepared within twenty-four hours.

"Johnston, call the deputy on duty at the Marshal's office and give him a heads up. Tell him you're faxing him a list of agencies.

"Ask him to send a couple of his men to pick up the documents the agencies are preparing and deliver them to me. Make sure they keep them under lock and key until the papers arrive at the DOJ." Johnston departed to get the list together.

Rosselfellar continued to spout orders. "Get the schedule for the next military hop to Zurich, Patterson. There should be something leaving within the next forty-eight hours. All of us need to be on the same flight. If you have a problem, tell them it's at the order of POTUS."

"I'll tell the President immediately," Hamilton said. "In addition, I'll call Mitsch even if I have to wake her up and give her an overview. She may not like it, but she's going to have to live with it." Hamilton left the courtroom and went back to the White House. This time he could tell the President directly what was happening and call Mitsch in the privacy of his own office.

If Hamilton needed the President to run interference with the German Chancellor, the Chief of State would be right down the hall in the

White House's West Wing. Patterson ran to his office and asked one of his administrators to call the Air Mobility Command at Andrews. "Get the schedule for all one-way military flights to Zurich for the next forty-eight hours. We need thirteen spots. Make sure you tell them it's on orders from the President's Chief of Staff and me. If they need to bump some people, so be it." "Rappaport," continued Rosselfellar, "you're going to have to figure out a way to get everything recorded in Liechtenstein. That will include meetings with the attorney we select and in the Court of Justice. Even though we'll request transcripts they might take too long to get in our hands. We'll need to act faster than usual."

"Sir, I'm sure we'd be breaking international and Liechtenstein laws if we electronically document in the courtroom. Are you sure you want to take that chance?" asked Rappaport.

"Rappaport, turn off the recorders." The NDIC Internet Technology Chief shut them down."

Rosselfellar uttered, "We're only breaking the law if they catch us. Anyway, if we can get the court reporter to transcribe them overnight, we won't have to secretly record anything."

"I'll figure out a way." Rappaport replied with reluctance. He would do no such thing, especially in a foreign country.

"I forgot the equipment" would be a likely and convenient excuse if Rosselfellar asked him. Landing in a European jail during his civil service employment was not what Rappaport had signed up for.

"Everybody has their assignments. Get to them and come back at six o'clock with complete updates." Rosselfellar concluded.

As soon as the meeting broke, Rosselfellar's cell phone rang. On the other end was a DEA agent from Florida telling him O'Banion had gotten a call from Liechtenstein.

"The Baron's on board," the agent said. "He's accepted the assignment. You can be pretty well assured we're going to begin receiving notice of litigation from the Liechtenstein government very quickly."

"The Baron is known for moving swiftly and deftly, according to O'Banion. He's most likely already proceeding with great speed preparing motions and calling everyone who needs to be contacted."

"That would include some close acquaintances in the Court of Justice in Vaduz. He's also tapping into alliances from Madrid to Moscow, Berlin to Bulgaria, and Tel Aviv to Thailand."

That's not what Rosselfellar wanted to hear.

CHAPTER THIRTY-NINE

"Marijuana gives rise to insanity-not in its users but in the policies directed against it. A nation that sentences the possessor of a single joint to life imprisonment without parole but sets a murderer free after perhaps six years, is in the grips of a deep psychosis."

Eric Schlosser, American journalist and award-winning author

4 Hours and 30 Minutes Later-6:00 PM, Thursday, July 10, 2008

THE UPDATE

At almost the same time the Task Force had filed back into the DOJ courtroom, word got back to Ari that the Baron would be representing him and Schnabel in Liechtenstein. It came as no surprise. Hirsch knew the Baron was a man of great principle and incisive enough to read between the lines of the fax. Unmistakably, Baron Rudfeld thought it was a winnable case but certainly one fraught with problems. He also believed in redemption and knew Schnabel deserved at least a chance to recapture some of his lost honor by making restitution for his improper conduct.

It took less than five minutes for O'Banion to call Sandra with the news about the Baron heading the legal team. Even less time to send the affirmation of the Baron's involvement directly to Hirsch's PDA.

Although Ari was pleased, he knew the task would be somewhat like climbing the steps of the Statue of Liberty on crutches while tugging Schnabel behind him by his collar. mansion and watched the feds leave as quickly as they had arrived.

By now, Hirsch and Schnabel were in the living room of the Ortiz No more noisy choppers. No more carbon-color SUVs. No more SWAT team. No more communications vehicles. No more ominous threats. No more barricades along A1A. Even the media muggers had taken leave, but without a story. No government spokesperson would reveal a word about why there was such a show of force. And no one else knew anything about it except for Schnabel and Hirsch. Rosselfellar called Buggy and told him to stay put in Florida with E.F. until they heard back from someone in Washington. He also told him about the Baron agreeing to take the case.

"Who? A baron? Who is he?"

"Baron Julius ben Mendel Rudfeld. He's a lawyer from Liechtenstein. You'll be hearing a lot more about him."

"Never heard of him. How 'bout an attorney for our side?"

"We're working on that right now, Buggy. Stay put until you hear back."

The three Dobermans were still tied outside the Ortiz estate even though Rosselfellar called from DC to call off the dogs. The government already had the information it needed and was proceeding with all due speed.

The Task Force assumed Hirsch and Schnabel would be making plans to fly to Zurich, the closest major city to Vaduz, Liechtenstein, on the Lufthansa jet still waiting at the Fort Lauderdale airport.

In the FISA courtroom, Rosselfellar was listening to the members' reports as quickly as they could detail them.

"We've secured an excellent attorney," announced Ianucci while running his right index finger across a sheet of paper, his eyes focused on the content.

"He meets all of our criteria and is ready to respond quickly. I had his curriculum vitae and background faxed to me. The man's name is Reinhold von Stülpnagel. Comes from a long line of German peerage.

"Looks like after one of his uncles became involved in the Nazi occupation of France in June 1942, the rest of the family members distanced themselves. After the war, they moved to Zurich where von Stülpnagel was born in 1955.

"He's impressive. Law school at Oxford and a Ph.D. from the London School of Economics. Reads, speaks, and writes four languages. Knows the inner workings of the Swiss and Liechtenstein banking systems. Was an Executive Vice President of Tax Analysis for UBS and an economic consultant to Switzerland's Federal Banking Commission."

Ianucci put the paper down and lifted his head to speak to the group.

"In the courtroom, he's acknowledged as being persuasive and smoother than the water of Lake Geneva in the summertime. The pros in our Bern embassy, including the ambassador, say he has one of the best legal minds in the country.

"I've already sent him a briefing on the matter as well as the fax from Hirsch to the Baron. Von Stülpnagel is expecting our arrival in Zurich within the next forty-eight hours, depending on our flight schedule. By the way, he's had a series of legal disputes with the Baron and knows what to expect.

"The President is quite pleased with the selection and so am I. We couldn't be in better hands."

"How did the President find out?" asked Hamilton, seemingly pleased and displeased.

"I had the Secretary of State call him directly." Ianucci responded.

"From now on, any information given to the President relating to this case must come from me. Does everyone understand that?" Hamilton was playing strongman and rightly so. Ianucci stepped beyond his political boundaries. He received a mild "congratulations" from Rosselfellar for tracking down such a "legal heavyweight" but no one else said a word. They didn't like that protocol had been broken by Ianucci on such a highly sensitive issue.

"I was able to secure thirteen seats on an Air Force C-17 on its way from Dover Air Force Base in Delaware to Tbilisi, Georgia," Patterson reported. "It's making an out-of-the-way stop at Andrews to accommodate us tomorrow at 0900 hours. We'll make one refuel stop in Shannon. Then on to Zurich."

Patterson was thankful, considering Switzerland's political position precluded military planes from landing on its soil and breaking its self-imposed status of neutrality. Since the plane was not bound for a U.S. base in Iraq or Afghanistan but was loaded with medical equipment and food for war-ravaged Tbilisi, Swiss authorities granted landing rights.

"A C-17?" questioned Johnston. "That's like flying in a frigid echo chamber! And on seats along the bulkhead no less! We're going to feel like forty miles of bad road and be half- deaf and whole-daffy when we arrive! Couldn't you find anything else? Like Swissair?"

Ever since Johnston had made it to the top tier of the CIA he traveled overseas extensively. He was addicted to flying first-class on a commercial airline or military jet outfitted for high-ranking government officials.

"That's the only flight we could find on such short notice. Unless you'd rather take a hot-air balloon!" Patterson shot back.

Watts was afraid to mention what was coming next. She had no choice.

"Gentlemen, don't be alarmed but there are no rooms at the Baur au Lac. In fact, there are no hotel rooms within a hundred kilometers of Zurich because the World Psychiatric Association is having its annual congress there.

"Nothing in Vaduz, either. I've made arrangements for us to stay at a youth hostel about ten minutes from downtown Zurich."

"What? A youth hostel? With raggedy-ass backpackers and junkies? You expect the White House Chief of Staff to stay in a place like that? What about a hotel in Bern?"

"Nope. That's a hundred kilometers from Zurich and everything's booked."

"Goddamn it, I'm not staying in a hostel! It's a hostile environment!" Hamilton was having a public tantrum while several others followed suit.

"Why not get us a big tent and set it up in the middle of town?"

"Where can we steal our food?"

"Some damn expense account we're on!"

"You might as well have us sleep under an overpass!"

"I wonder how many shrinks will be staying in the same joint!"

Watts was more than a bit perturbed about their attitudes but was smart enough not to respond to the remarks. It would have only elicited more grumbling.

What she didn't mention was that she even had to pull strings to get those reservations, especially since they were made without a definite departure date.

Neither did she tell them they'd be staying in four-bed dorm rooms for thirty-eight bucks a night per person. Upper and lower wooden bunk beds. Multi-colored, speckled vinyl floors. Public showers and toilets. Coin-operated washing machines and dryers. Cocktail bar. Breakfast, linens, elevator, and security lockers included. Plus, a small meeting room.

If nothing else, Watts was pragmatic.

"Oh, I almost forgot," she added. "Hertz and Avis have zero vehicles available. We tried every imaginable alternative, but the head docs rented them all.

"I called our embassy. One of the administrative assistants there has a friend in Zurich who owns a private jitney service. She's going to call him with our ETA and he'll be there to meet us." Thank goodness nobody complained about that part of Watts' assignment.

"All of the background files on the Smiths will be downstairs by seven-thirty tonight," said Johnston. "They'll be totally secure."

"I'll pick them up," said Rosselfellar, "and take them with me to Andrews. I'll review them on the flight over."

"What about Mitsch?"

"I met with the President in the Oval Office a couple of hours ago and told him Chancellor Mitsch is becoming an itch. I updated him on everything to that point. He recognizes we have our own imminent problems.

"The Commander-in-Chief asked me to resolve the dilemma with Germany by telling Mitsch the United States has bigger fish to fry right now. I've already spoken with the Chancellor and delivered an ultimatum in the presence of the President."

Hamilton seemed eager to let everybody know he told Mitsch that she either backs off Germany's agreements with Schnabel or the United States will be forced to expose some of her administration's top appointments and elected public servants.

"We have intelligence, Chancellor Mitsch, indicating that at least two dozen members of the Bundestag and five members of the Bundesrat have hidden assets in Switzerland, The Bahamas and several other so-called safe tax havens.

"We have also identified certain German cabinet-level ministers, as well as judges in your *Bundesverfassungsgericht*, who engage in 'private banking' matters. I doubt that the German people would like to find out in *Der Spiegel*, on the Internet, or *Deutsche Welle* television, the names of judges in your Constitutional Court who may be evading their own tax laws.

"Furthermore, you already have the disc and other information from Herr Schnabel so the $7.8 million U.S. that Germany paid him may not be returned."

"But ve do not haf propper autentikation, you *dummes huhn*!"

"This conversation is over, Chancellor Mitsch. I will not allow you to call me a 'stupid chicken.' You have lost all credibility with me and the President of the United States. *Auf Wiedersehen.*"

Hamilton didn't bother to wait for a response. He left Mitsch clucking as he gently put down the receiver.

As for Schnabel's problems with Spain, Hamilton was planning to put pressure on them as well. When he couldn't reach anyone in the Madrid bureaucracy because "everyone was taking their siesta" he called the Spanish embassy in the district.

"*Hola. No está aquí. Es hora de siesta.*"

The entire embassy was taking a break. It was siesta time there, too.

"I'll take care of that problem later. Right now, we need to concentrate on getting to Zurich."

"What about Hutton and Buggelshofer?" asked Watts.

"I almost forgot." Rosselfellar was on brain overload. "I've already spoken with E.F. I don't want to waste any time getting him and Buggelshofer back to Washington in time for our flight. I told him to keep close to Hirsch and Schnabel and find out what they were planning.

"They most likely want to get to the Baron's quickly. What they don't realize is that Mitsch has probably already informed the chief operating officer of the airline to keep the plane on the ground if Hirsch and Schnabel are aboard the Lufthansa. "That will certainly slow them down and perhaps cause them to miss the initial hearing. Besides, there's no room at the inn, remember? They're not going to have any place to stay."

Poor Rosselfellar. He could not have been more wrong. It wasn't Hamilton who was a "stupid chicken." It was Rosselfellar.

CHAPTER FORTY

"The War on Drugs is a huge and wasteful drain on resources, and we're finding more and more alliances with fiscally conservative Republicans who say we need to think more critically about how we spend our money in this area. We have an issue that is mobilizing for people who care about social justice and racial justice. Things are not going to change in Congress, they are not going to change in Washington, until things first change at the ground level in the states and the communities."

Ethan A. Nadelmann, Executive Director, Drug Policy Alliance

Same Time - 6:00 PM, Thursday, July 10, 2008

MEANWHILE, BACK AT THE MANSION

The McLaren came screeching into the driveway of the beachfront estate. Ortiz was behind the wheel. Quickly, he opened the door, slid onto his white-loafered feet, ran inside his own home, and found Hirsch and company sitting in the living room.

There was Schnabel, his four guards, Buggy, E.F. and Ari. Manny and Ricky were in the kitchen grabbing a quick dinner. Ortiz wasted no time.

"Ari, I need to speak with you right now. Alone."

"Please, Oliverio. Can you wait a moment? I'm in the middle of something important."

"No, amigo, I can't. We need to talk immediately!"

"Okay, okay," Ari said in a weary voice as he rose from his chair and turned toward Schnabel. "I want you to tell your German brigade to get ready for a trip to Zurich. Tell them to call the Lufthansa pilot. We must get to the Baron as soon as we can. And I mean fast."

Ortiz grabbed Hirsch firmly by the arm and led him into the adjacent office.

"Ari, tell Schnabel to hold up. There'll be no need to take Lufthansa."

"What the hell are you talking about? I've got to get to Liechtenstein with Schnabel and the two feds, Oliverio. This case is about to break wide open, and I'm deeply involved. You already know the feds are on it, and it's a giant one.

"Hundred-dollar bills are beginning to fall off the money tree and I need to get over there. The Germans, Spaniards, Americans, Russians, Italians, Bulgarians, Israelis – they're all involved, and I need to stop the information flow because some of them might go on a killing spree if there's a leak.

"This case is as twisted as a corkscrew, and I have to make it straight. You know the government's been hammering me for years and I don't want to give them any more chances.

"They've granted me immunity, but we both know they can throw me in the cooler in an instant. Obstruction, conspiracy, lack of good faith and cooperation-whatever the hell charges they want to make up.

"My life's been settled for a long time and now they're at my throat again. Plus, I have some unfinished business in Vaduz."

"Ari, I know all that, and I know about the case as well."

"What are you talking about? How could you possibly know about the case?"

"I used to listen attentively to your stories when we first met years ago, and I never forgot about the antics of Bobby and Timmy Smith. Neither did I forget the name Baron Julius ben Mendel Rudfeld and the role he played in helping you in Liechtenstein with their last wills and testaments, foundations, trusts, safe deposit boxes.

"I remember all of it, Ari, including what you did for me in Liechtenstein as well.

"But if you think the feds are the only ones attempting every way possible to overhear what's going in my home, think again. Ari, as disappointed as you might be, I bug my own home.

"Yes, I have monitoring and recording devices hidden in every room and on the outside of the house that pick up every sound. You probably didn't know but Manny and Ricky have the skills of electronics engineers.

"While I was at Sonia's last night and today, I was able to listen to your conversations by dialing into a private audio frequency.

"Let me tell you something else, Ari. Like Bobby and Timmy, I did a lot of business with the CIA, and I still have friends on the inside who from time to time do me favors. Like Richard Johnston. He's still on my payroll and he's kept me informed every step of the way.

"You've saved my life several times, and now it's payback time. If you board the Lufthansa flight, you're as good as dead. Mitsch has been put on notice by the feds. No money, no Schnabel, no information.

"If her people get their hands on you, you're going to disappear without a trial. At least the Nazis stood trial in a Nuremberg courtroom. No trial for you or Schnabel. They want their deutschmarks back and they want those names corroborated because they want the tax money."

Ari was standing there astonished. He was dumbstruck, confused, incredulous, and astounded that Ortiz knew everything, or at least more than Hirsch did.

"What else do you know that I don't?" asked Ari.

"Only that I spoke with a friend of Baron Rudfeld a few hours ago and told him of the complications with the Germans."

"You what? How the hell did you do that?"

"I have an old banking acquaintance in Vaduz. I called him. He's very tight with the Baron. He told me about an initial motion regarding the Smiths' estate status had already been filed, and that a court date has been set for the day after tomorrow at 10:00 AM. He needs you to be there without delay.

"The Baron has already sent a Gulfstream G550 from Atlanta to fly you and Schnabel to Switzerland. It will be landing at Fort Lauderdale Executive in a little while. I'll take a run over there and hold the aircraft.

It'll give you time to go home and pack."

Hirsch knew Gulfstream manufactured some of the most efficient planes in the skies. The G550 had a range of more than sixty-seven-hundred miles and could fly the forty-nine-hundred miles to Zurich non-stop. It cruised at forty-one-thousand feet at a speed of more than five-hundred-miles-an-hour, making it about a nine-and-a-half-hour flight.

With thirteen passenger seats and a crew of two, Ari knew he could easily bring Schnabel, E.F. and Buggy.

But the more he thought about it, the worse the idea sounded. Buggelshofer and Hutton were working for the feds, and they were now opponents. Granted, they had created friendships among each other but now wasn't a good time to be cozy. If the government needed the pair of old feds in Liechtenstein, let Rosselfellar find a way of getting them there. The Baron wasn't running a travel agency for seniors, especially on a plane that cost seventeen-hundred dollars an hour.

"Ari, the Baron said he'll have a limousine waiting for you in Zurich, and that you and Schnabel will be staying at his place for the duration of the trial."

"Oliverio, you have no idea how much I appreciate what you've done."

"If I hadn't, I wouldn't have been able to live with myself. I owe you *mucho*."

Ortiz left for the airport as Hirsch walked into the living room.

"Herr Schnabel, please tell your bodyguards to find their way back to the airport and go home. If they're unwilling to listen to what I tell them, then have them call their security chief in Germany to get clearance to leave.

"If they're unwilling to do that, tell them they're going to be arrested by the FBI for kidnapping."

Schnabel obeyed and the guards took off like Messerschmitts on a bombing run.

"Sorry, Buggy. Sorry, E.F. Schnabel and I are leaving now and you're going to have to vacate the premises. I don't think Mr. Ortiz is going to allow you to stay here any longer. I would suggest you go back to the airport with the bodyguards and head back to Washington. The game here is over."

"Ari, where are we going?" Schnabel asked in a panic.

"To rob a bank, Franz. To rob a bank."

CHAPTER FORTY-ONE

"I have learned a great deal about the current War on Drugs and have experienced an awakening with respect to public policy and sanctioning practices in our criminal-justice system. After four decades of effort, a trillion dollars spent, and too many deaths fighting the war, the result is racial disparity in the application of the law, nonviolent offenders incarcerated when it isn't necessary-and none of the drug war's goals have been met. Illegal drugs are in greater supply, more potent, and less expensive than ever. It is a failed policy and should be considered a national crisis demanding immediate reform."

Richard Van Wickler, Superintendent, Department of Corrections, Cheshire County, New Hampshire

3 Hours Later - 9:00 PM, Thursday, July 10, 2008

ALL ABOARD

As the Baron had promised Ortiz, the Gulfstream was waiting for the arrival of Ari Hirsch and Franz Dieter Schnabel at one of the six full-service fixed-based operations at Fort Lauderdale Executive.

On his way to the airport, Ortiz had called Sandra to pick up Ari and Schnabel at his home. He told her about the travel plans, and within five minutes, she steered her 4WD Range Rover into Ortiz's driveway and beeped the horn twice to alert her would-be passengers.

The three of them drove to the Hirsch household. Ari showered and packed a week's worth of clothes, including a couple of sweaters. He jammed some files, his passport and Dell laptop into his ostrich-skin briefcase, grabbed his tan Land's End quilted down jacket and inserted a pair of gloves into its pockets.

Ari hated the cold. It reminded him of his and Sandra's years in the shivery Upper Plains while they were in active witness protection.

For Schnabel, it was case closed. Literally. He hadn't opened his suitcase since he had been on his one-day Florida retreat. Never changed a stitch of clothing or lathered his body with a bar of soap. The hairs on his face were one day older and almost as long as the ones protruding from his nostrils. Neither did he have much to say.

"This guy's a bit creepy, Ari." Sandra couldn't stop whispering missives about the fugitive. "He's so damn grimy looking, and he has halitosis and body odor! How are you going to be able to stand being in a plane with him for so many hours?" Robbery and extortion were Schnabel's strong suits, not personal hygiene.

"I'll stick him in the last passenger seat at the rear of the plane. I offered him a shower and he didn't want it. I can't make him brush his teeth. If I lived through WitSec, I could live through this, too."

"I want you to be careful, Ari. You never know what the feds might do to the both of you if the court rules against them."

"We both know they can do anything they want no matter how the court rules, Sandra. I'll be fine. Let's go. The plane's waiting." Ari was rattling a bit himself.

On the way to Fort Lauderdale Executive, Hirsch asked Schnabel if he had a valid passport. "Yah, Ari, Yah. I have two. One from Germany and one from Liechtenstein. Which one should I use?"

"The one from Liechtenstein. You'll get through customs and immigration a lot easier. The Germans may have told the Swiss to be on the lookout for you and that you might be carrying a German passport. You could be whizzed away before we even get to Liechtenstein."

"You have me very nervous again, Ari. Please do not say things like that. I might be up the whole night during the entire flight from sheer fright." Schnabel was shaking like he had Mad-Cow disease.

"Oh, quit being a wuss!" Sandra couldn't hold it in.

"Madame, what is 'wuss'?"

"Forget it, Herr Schnabel. I thought it was a German word for sissy."

They arrived at the airport at 9:00 PM. and found Ortiz standing next to the Gulfstream.

Twenty-five minutes later they were cleared for take-off. The six-hour difference in flight time would put them in Zurich at 11:30 AM. They would probably arrive at the Baron's estate in time for lunch, although Ari wasn't certain Schnabel would be allowed at the table unless and until he bathed.

"I'll call you on your cell phone when I arrive, sweetheart. Try not to be apprehensive. I'll keep you posted about everything. I don't care if the feds are still doing surveillance on you and the house. They won't find out anything they don't already know. Besides, remember that I have immunity."

"Ari! You know those bastards can do anything they want, and they will! Protect your back." They hugged, kissed, and said their informal "see ya" and "love ya" to each other. Ortiz and Hirsch shook hands. "Much luck, mi amigo. You know how to reach me if you need to."

"Thanks, Oliverio. Keep in touch with Sandra. She'll know exactly what's happening. It's great having a friend like you."

Schnabel simply was quaking in place on the tarmac like someone who had been sentenced to death by guillotine. As far as he was concerned, his future was completely pre-determined by Divine Providence, and that his life might be over by a falling blade across his neck, leaving his head in a basket.

He couldn't even conceive that he might be luckier than he thought, most notably with Hirsch and the Baron by his side.

Captain Kirk Sawyer and Co-captain Nora Colquitt welcomed the two aboard as their bags were put into the cargo hold by an airport attendant. The crew closed the door, completed their operational checks, barreled down the runway and headed toward the moonless sky. Within thirty seconds, they pressed the "wheels-up" control, tucked their wings into the belly of the plane and headed toward the Atlantic Ocean. After having been awake for so many hours, Ari fell asleep within fifteen minutes of take-off. He briefly awakened a few hours later to grab an egg salad sandwich and orange juice the crew had brought aboard, then nodded off again.

Schnabel's prediction came true. Not about losing his head; only that he was awake the entire flight to Zurich. He managed to gorge himself on three bologna and American cheese sandwiches, two packages of potato chips, another of pretzels, and four aluminum-foiled bags of peanuts.

He also consumed four cups of dark-roasted coffee. The belches were louder than the plane's engines.

When he asked if there was Schnapps on board, Co-captain Nora sarcastically asked, "Any particular flavor, Adolf?"

"Cherry, please," Schnabel responded, "and my name is Franz."

"Drink another cup of coffee, Fritzie. The Schnapps cabinet is closed."

It was a good thing for Ari and the crew there was a bathroom on board.

CHAPTER FORTY-TWO

"After twenty years on the bench I have concluded that federal drug laws are a disaster. It is time to get the government out of drug enforcement." –

Whitman Knapp, U.S. District Court Judge and head of New York City's 1970 Knapp Commission exposing police corruption.

Same Time - 9:00 PM, Thursday, July 10, 2008

TO HELL AND BACK

While Hirsch and Schnabel were jetting toward Zurich, Buggelshofer and Hutton were boarding a one-way Delta flight to Reagan National. By now, the old-timers felt like they had been in a bruiser of a boxing battle and had lost every round. The cranky-and-crabby twins were disgusted, haggard, wasted, debilitated.

Earlier, they had barely managed to stop the SUV with the four German bodyguards as it pulled away from Ortiz's home. If they hadn't, they would have had to call a taxi or hitchhiked to get to the airport.

During the ride, Buggy reached Rosselfellar at home, cell phone to cell phone.

"This is Buggelshofer. We're fucked, Mr. Justice Department. Just plain fucked!"

"For chrissakes, what the hell are you talking about?"

"Your fed driver who brought us to the Ortiz house from the airport took off with our luggage when you wound down the siege! We don't have a stitch of clothing except what we're wearing!

"Besides, we can't get on any flight with our weapons. TSA will have us cuffed as soon as we walk through the metal detector!"

"Calm down, Buggy. You sound like you're going to have a heart attack. Who's in the car with you?"

"E.F., the four Hamburgers, and their driver."

"Be careful of what you say! We've cut off Chancellor Mitsch. I'll explain it tomorrow when I see you. Don't say anything else. You've already said too much."

"How the hell did I know? If my aorta doesn't give out before I reach the airport, it'll be a miracle. And if I don't make it, it'll be on your head!"

"You're worrying too much. I'll locate the guy who took your bags and have him bring them to the airport. Be outside on the upper level outside the Delta counter. He's probably at our South Florida command center and only a few minutes away. If he's not, I'll have someone else bring them. I'm sure they're still in the SUV.

"I'll also call Patterson from Homeland Security and have him get both of you cleared with your handguns. You won't even have to go through electronic inspection. Do you have your passports and government ID?"

"Yeah, we got 'em."

"Good. When you get back to DC, go right to the Capitol Hill Suites. I'll reserve a couple of rooms for you. You're going to need a good night's sleep but be up early. We're leaving Andrews shortly after 9:00 AM to Zurich. Meet us at the front gate."

"Zurich? Who says we're going to Zurich?"

"The entire Task Force is going, you included."

"Have you completely lost your marbles?"

"No, Buggy, but if you don't want to lose your bonus, you and E.F. are coming with us," Rosselfellar said.

"On a C-17? Hutton and I will never make it. Not on that transporter. We'll be totally deaf by the time we land. Besides, that plane must be on its last wheels."

"No more, Buggelshofer," insisted Rosselfellar. "We don't have time for your moaning and griping. Make sure you're both there on time. The first motion is going to be heard in two days. Everyone must be prepared, including you.

"We've hired local counsel. Reinhold von Stülpnagel's his name. He's already been briefed about the motions being filed by Ari's attorney. Our guy will be as primed as anybody and will debrief all of us. Except for Wazinski."

"What do you mean except for Wazinski? He knows as much as anyone about the Smiths and the background of everything that's going on. Who's taking his place?"

"You are, Buggy, you are. You and Hutton, actually. You'll be representing the Marshal Service and Hutton the FBI."

"We can't replace Wazinski! We may have been drafted to help, but that's even a questionable move since Ari threw us out of Ortiz's house."

"Threw you out?"

"He said Ortiz wouldn't allow us to stay there any longer. How the hell were we going to argue with him? Hirsch and Schnabel were leaving, and he told us to evacuate the house.

And by the way, it's not only a house – it's a fucking palace."

"Shit, Buggy. If he was leaving with Schnabel, they might have found some way to get to Zurich ahead of us. They may already be on their way. I might have to get Patterson to do an immediate investigation of all departing flight manifests from South Florida to Zurich. I'm also going to call Bern and have our CIA operation locate where they're staying in Zurich."

"Don't waste your time," said Buggy. "If they're on the way, there's nothing we can do to stop them. What are they really gaining except a little more time with their attorney?

What's his name again?"

"Baron Julius ben Mendel Rudfeld. You'll learn much more about him on the flight to Zurich. And remember, you and Hutton are probably going to have to testify at the hearing which begins at 10:00 AM the day after tomorrow."

"About what?"

"Hirsch and the Smith brothers."

"What am I gonna tell the court about Hirsch? And I thought the Smiths were dead."

"You're going to help us destroy Hirsch's credibility. You and Hutton are going to talk about your WitSec days, the deals he pulled behind our backs, the conniving he did, the deviant clients he represented. As for the Smiths, we don't know for certain they're dead.

"They haven't been heard from in twenty years, but that doesn't mean they're not alive. The two of them vanished about the same time you and Hutton retired."

"Hey, we never laid eyes on those guys! What are you implying?"

"I didn't mean to imply anything, Buggy. Forget that I even said it. I'm bringing a load of background material on those two and-"

"Hold on for a second. We're at the airport." Buggy told the driver to let them off at the Delta departure terminal. He and Hutton slammed two of the car doors and stepped onto the sidewalk.

"Okay, we're outside the Delta terminal. Get our suitcases, will ya? We need our clothes. Now what were you saying?"

"Only that I'm bringing a box load of files with me about the Smiths so you can familiarize yourself with both of them. I don't need to bring anything on Hirsch since the two of you know more about him than anyone else in any government agency."

"E.F. and I both know the Smiths did a lot of deals with Central Intelligence, and with Ari's help they beat most of their charges. How's the court in Liechtenstein gonna react to that?" questioned Buggy.

"We're not going to tell them," said the DOJ.

"I'll tell you even before we get on the plane tonight, Rosselfellar. Neither one of us is going to commit perjury for anybody!" Buggy was perturbed. "I don't give a shit what the court asks and neither does Hutton. We're not gonna wind up in a Liechtenstein prison! How could the

Department of Justice have the balls to even think about asking us to do that?" "We have to protect our national interests at all costs, Buggelshofer. The administration doesn't care what it takes - we have to utilize every necessary precaution. And we want our goddamn tax monies. Am I clear?"

"As clear as a fogged-in airport on a rainy day!"

"Both of you are on the government's payroll. Don't forget that Buggelshofer. Remember your pensions. If you break the oath you took when you first signed on with the Marshal Service and Hutton with the Bureau, drastic actions will be taken. I can assure you of that."

Irritated more than ever, Buggelshofer flipped the phone shut, shared Rosselfellar's side of the conversation with E.F., and waited impatiently for the luggage. They made it through security with the help of Patterson's intervention, waited for their 9:27 PM flight to DC and fell asleep until the boarding announcement.

E.F. leaned heavily on his cane to lift himself out of the vinyl seat, which was still trying to hold onto his moist shirt and pants. Buggy took a Xanax and snoozed his way back to Washington.

Both men knew it would be near impossible to get out of traveling to Switzerland.

Unless they wanted to live in poverty.

CHAPTER FORTY-THREE

"Where's the federal 'Drug War' when we really need it? They'll throw you in jail for smoking a joint, but you can get Ritalin for a two-year-old from a doctor. What a horrible joke!"

Jim Hightower, Syndicated columnist, national radio commentator, activist, and author

11 Hours and 30 Minutes Later - 9:00 AM, Friday, July 11, 2008

THE FLYING FEDS

All members of the Task Force were on time for their flight aboard the C-17 Globemaster III. Too bad the plane wasn't.

"We've been delayed two hours," said Patterson who moments before had received the information from the flight control officer at Andrews.

"The commander of the 436th Airlift Wing out of Dover radioed to let us know the cargo hadn't been loaded because the medical equipment hadn't arrived until a few minutes ago. It's going to take a while to get it on board.

"He assured me the aircraft will be here by eleven. Sorry, but that's the best we're going to get."

Patterson was angry, but nothing compared to the rest of them.

"How the hell are we going to reach the guy in Zurich who's picking us up?" asked Watts.

"Hey, you made the arrangements. Don't you have his number?" queried Ianucci.

"I forgot to put it in my briefcase." Watts immediately dialed her office to get the phone number of the embassy. By nine-thirty she reached the administrative assistant and had her reschedule the pick-up for two hours later than the original time.

"Mission accomplished," Watts said. Somehow, all the feds thought that was a familiar phrase.

"How can she be so incompetent and still be in her position?" Whitfield whispered to Rappaport.

"It's called affirmative inaction."

"We could have slept another couple of hours. God knows we need the rest." Smitherman usually didn't complain. The NSA chief was accustomed to eighteen-hour days and long-winded sessions with executive and legislative members of the government. But this case was taking its toll on everyone.

"It's sweltering out here," said Underman as he sat on the top of his suitcase and wiped the perspiration off his face.

The men had taken off their suit jackets, loosened their ties and rolled up their sleeves.

Except for Underman's IRS boss, Wilson Brown. He was wearing a tight-fitting, unstarched, short-sleeve shirt. His belly was so rotund three buttons were hanging by single threads and were about to fall off.

"Let's go inside and get out of this heat! It's already ninety-three degrees and it's supposed to hit ninety-nine by noon." Rosselfellar also wanted to take the time to examine and consult with the others about the Smith files prior to getting on the plane.

He knew it would be a noisy ride and trying to converse aloft would be akin to moving his lips without any words coming out. Nobody, particularly Buggy and E.F., would have heard a word.

Leaving their luggage outside, they walked inside and headed to seats in the waiting area. Each brandished a briefcase. After almost two hours discussing the upcoming legal contest, the giant plane lumbered to within sight of the operations facility.

Its wingspan of one-hundred-seventy-feet-nine-inches was a mere three feet less than its length. Thirteen sets of eyes bulged out of their sockets as the craft came closer. They had never seen a cargo plane this mammoth. Not even the CIA's Johnston who had been on more types of aircraft than test pilot and Brigadier General Chuck Yeager.

Each of its four engines was rated for almost forty-one-thousand pounds of thrust and could take off and land on a three-thousand-foot runway. Cruising at five-hundred-mph got it to where it needed to be quickly. It carried a crew of three, including a pilot, co-pilot, and loadmaster.

No flight attendants on this baby. It was self-serving the whole way.

It could carry more than one-hundred troops and almost one-hundred-seventy-one thousand pounds of cargo.

Awesome stats for an awesome motorized bird.

The only thing the plane was loaded with were OSHA-approved corrugated cartons stamped with a gigantic "USA" in bold red on their sides and on top. No one could tell what was in them. For all anyone knew, the boxes could have been loaded with illegal drugs, bags of cash, hand grenades, or nukes.

They entered the gaping, rear-end cavity via the same platform that was hinged to the body of the plane and angled to the ground. It was a gentle slope up; it would be a not-so- gentle journey.

"How do they expect us to sit in these goddamn seats?"

Ianucci wasn't the only one complaining. When the baker's dozen looked at the thinly padded, non-adjustable, black Naugahyde, fold-down seats fastened to the bulkheads, twelve of them wanted to smack Patterson.

"You don't know crap about planes, Patterson. If you did, you would have gotten one that had actual seats. Next time – and there won't be a next time – don't play like you're Sky King or Buck Rogers." Hamilton was infuriated. Is this the way the President's Chief of Staff should travel?

"Can we at least get a parachute and a cup of coffee on this beast? How 'bout a window so we can see where we're going?" Rappaport was in rare form even though he was in the business of questioning everything. His high-tech job with the National Drug Intelligence Center had given him great training.

"There's no place to even put our valises. What are we supposed to do-hold them in our laps?" Watts was even rankled.

"Do we have to take a military flight back as well? If it's anything like this, I'll jump out over the Alps and kill myself." Was that a threat from Whitfield?

What none of them realized was that the folks in the cockpit had been listening to everyone's squawking over the speaker system.

"Welcome aboard. This is Air Force Captain Brent Jenkins. Lieutenant Garrett Emerson and I are happy you selected our C-17 to get you to your destination.

"We're scheduled to arrive at Shannon Airport in Dublin for refueling at 2300 hours Ireland time, after which we will continue our flight to Vladivostok, Siberia, where we will be delighted to drop you off to visit a real old-fashioned Soviet gulag for a couple of years.

"Please buckle your seatbelts for take-off. If you don't know how to use one, you shouldn't be on this plane. Also note we will be shutting the lights for the entire flight. Have fun in the dark, flyboys."

"Does this guy think he's funny?" Johnston asked Rosselfellar. "We had Air America pilots like him. They all got paddled."

"So will you if you don't stop acting like a spoiled child," said Smitherman.

The loadmaster electronically lifted the ramp into its closed position. Captain Jenkins rolled the C-17 toward the runway and within five minutes the flying-tube-with-wings thundered toward the hot sun scalding the nation's capital.

Within thirty minutes, it reached its cruising altitude of forty-five-thousand feet.

"I'm freezing my gonads off in here." It was a man's voice. "I wish I was sweating again. And turn on the fuckin' lights, Captain Marvel!"

CHAPTER FORTY-FOUR

"The 4th Amendment and the personal rights it secures have a long history. At the very core stands the right of a man to retreat into his own home and there be free from unreasonable governmental intrusion."

Potter Stewart, U.S. Supreme Court Associate Justice (1958-81)

26 Hours and 30 Minutes Later - 11:30 AM (Switzerland Time), Saturday, July 12, 2008

ARRIVAL TIME

The Gulfstream made a butter-smooth, three-point landing as it touched down on a runway of Zurich-Kloten Airport within three minutes of its ETA.

It rolled its way to Jet Aviation's FBO executive terminal and came to a clean stop. Captain Kirk and Co-captain Nora bid the passengers farewell with handshakes and smiles while an air facility attendant unloaded the bags.

Hirsch easily deplaned and waited for Schnabel to reach the ground. Even with rubber-soled sneakers, he was so bleary-eyed and tired he tripped on the last step. Ari caught him by an arm to keep the swindler from injuring himself.

They cleared customs and passport control without the slightest problem, and gaited to the front of the building where they observed a spotless black Mercedes limousine that looked like the Swiss Federal Chancellor's personal conveyance.

"I presume you are Herren Hirsch and Schnabel?" The chauffeur of the vehicle, a tallish man whose hair was covered with a puffy, blue-twill cap accessorized with a shiny brim, was standing under the canopy of the entrance. His English was impeccable as were his midnight-blue blazer, contrasting grey slacks, long-sleeved heavily starched white shirt, and dark blue tie monogrammed in red with a logo of a rampart lion.

"That's correct. I'm Herr Hirsch." Ari was direct. He wasn't in the mood to engage in much conversation. He had a lot to think about.

"*Bitte*, thank you." The fiftyish driver rolled both suitcases to the vehicle, opened the trunk via remote control, and placed the bags in the empty compartment. Hirsch held onto his briefcase; he wasn't going to let that out of his sight.

"Excuse me, Ari."

"Yes, Franz."

"I noticed the Liechtenstein Vaterland newspaper inside the terminal. I have not read one in several years. Do you mind if I go back in and buy a copy?"

"Sure, Franz, but make it quick. Do you have francs?"

"I have deutschemarks. They will accept those. I will be right back."

By the time Schnabel returned, the chauffeur had already pulled the car to the terminal entrance. He opened the passenger door as the pair slid into the back seat.

"*Bitte*, my name is Helmut. If you need anything at all, please call me on the intercom by pressing the button on your arm rest. If you are thirsty, please help yourself to a beverage of your choice in the bar located behind the wood panel next to Herr Hirsch."

"We shall be at Baron Rudfeld's estate in a little more than an hour and twenty minutes."

Helmut closed the door, got into his seat, and mashed a button on the front console, which raised a thick piece of glass separating the driver's area from the rest of the interior of the double-stretch limo. He dashed out the terminal parking lot onto the ramp of highway A51. After negotiating several right-and left-hand turns, he connected onto the A3 toll road in a southeasterly direction. A few kilometers south of Sargans, they looped onto A13 and headed north toward Vaduz.

"I very much miss the beauty of my country, Ari. The mountains, the rivers, the countryside – it is like Shangri-La. I forgot how imposing and exquisite it is."

"Franz, I'm not interested in the fact that you left this all behind. Quit romanticizing and read your paper until we get to the Baron's."

Sulking Schnabel was so busy looking at the scenery, he hadn't even opened the paper. When he did, he screamed so loud that even Helmut heard him. *"Ari...you will not believe this. Das is nicht gut, nicht gut, nicht gut. <u>Ach du lieber Gatz!</u>"*

"Will you please speak English! That's not a question – that's an order. What the hell are you so excited about?"

"Ari, this is not good, not good at all! Look at this! Just look! Oh, my God!"

"I can't read a word of it Schnabel so tell me why you're so flustered, dammit!"

"Look at this headline on the front page, Ari. It is about our court appearance on Monday. Shush! Let me read it and I will explain it to you. Please. Before I faint."

Schnabel "The Diva" read the article quickly and once again began to secrete bubbles of perspiration.

"This news is about me and you and the Baron and the American government and a Swiss attorney by the name of Reinhold von Stülpnagel.

"The story is written by the newspaper's investigative journalist acting under Liechtenstein's Public Information laws. He found court documents listing the various motions Baron Rudfeld will be making on our behalf. There is additional information from sources he has in Vaduz and Switzerland.

"It gets worse. This information leaked yesterday, and many citizens of Liechtenstein are planning to demonstrate in front of the Court of Justice on Monday! They have formed a group called *Nicht Auf Ihr Leben*, or NAIL. In English, it means "not on your life," Ari. They do not want any country to destroy Liechtenstein's financial system, and this case will test its endurance.

"The report says this case might become Liechtenstein's version of 9/11. I know this sounds crazy to you because no one will be killed, except perhaps me, and there will probably be no physical damage.

"But it is potentially devastating to the country's infrastructure and its ability to remain financially stable. We have no military, but the citizens are calling for every Liechtensteiner to bring whatever armaments they have to the steps of the courthouse."

What's this "we" crap? Ari thought. You're practically a traitor to your country and now you're injecting yourself back into full-blown citizenship? Schnabel's got more nerve than a spinal cord.

Ari opened the door to the bar, pulled out a bottle of Cherry Schnapps and poured it into the biggest glass stowed in the pigeonhole.

"Drink this, Franz. It'll calm you down."

Schnabel guzzled it and handed the tumbler to Ari who quickly poured another. That, too, was gone before Ari could screw the cap back on the bottle.

"If German or Spanish spies see this article, Ari, they will come looking for me for sure. I am not even certain if I am safe from Liechtenstein authorities. There are still warrants for my arrest and the prince is out to get me."

"I'm sure the Baron has taken care of the Liechtenstein problem and may have already negotiated on your behalf with Germany and Spain. We'll find out in a little while.

"In the meantime, if you don't stop grumbling, I'm going to throw you out of the car and underneath the wheels!"

Helmut drove a bit north of Vaduz and exited at Gamprin. He followed the road a few kilometers to the entrance of Baron Julius ben Mendel's estate of eighty-nine hectares, the equivalent of two-hundred-twenty acres.

This was not only an estate. Other than the royal family's real estate holdings, this one parcel made the Baron the second largest landowner in the Principality.

The gate was always manned by two armed guards. The Baron could not afford to take chances. He was on the enemies' lists of several foreign organizations, including terrorist groups with home bases in the Middle East. A perpetual target, he took all the necessary precautions to keep from getting assassinated.

The Mercedes rode along a paved road that passed between two rows of manicured, flowering hedges, and the manor house came into full view.

Ari and Schnabel saw this was no ordinary home. In fact, it wasn't a home at all. It was a thirty-four-room schloss – a castle built from quarry stone in the middle of the eighteenth century-in the center of the forested property, making surrounding views spectacular.

One could almost hear The Hills are Alive with the Sound of Music except the von Trapps lived in Salzburg, a city in Austria to the east of Liechtenstein.

"Holy crap," Ari said a bit out of context. "This place has a moat and a drawbridge. Talk about being in a safe haven. You don't have to worry about a thing, Franz. You'll definitely be okay here for the weekend." Helmut hit an electronic device on the dashboard and the drawbridge slowly came down between the two entrance towers and across the circular ten-foot-deep canal surrounding the castle. The limo wheeled across as the steel drawbridge lifted itself into its up-and-locked position to ensure security.

Poised in the courtyard framed by colorful, flowering bushes of all varieties was the Baron Julius ben Mendel Rudfeld waiting to greet his guests and clients. He, too, was wearing a rampart lion, but this one was embroidered in red on the chest of his tan suede horseback riding jacket.

The lion was identical to the one displayed on the tie of Helmut the chauffeur. It was also the same design painted on the entrance guardhouse. After all, it was the mark and family crest of the Baron.

"Ari, Franz, it is so good to see both of you again. Please. Come in, come in and make yourselves at home. Helmut will bring in your bags.

You will be quite safe here, no doubt." The three men disappeared behind a pair of hand-carved, twenty-five-feet-tall arched mahogany doors embellished and braced with art nouveau wrought iron latches. Luther the butler followed them in.

The grand foyer of the castle was dazzling. Curved wooden stairways with matching chiseled walnut balustrades on the two sidewalls gracefully swept upward to the second level giving the entry room a sense of symmetry. The walls were decorated with artwork by several Dutch masters, as well as famous Flemish and German artisans. All the oil paintings were surrounded in rich, gilt-edged frames.

On the back wall was a twenty-foot-wide by twelve-foot-high medieval tapestry hung with loops slid over a solid brass rod capped on each end with filigreed finials. Directly above the exquisite, hand-knotted, predominantly red Persian carpet dangled a shimmering, lead-crystal, and hand-etched art-glass chandelier hanging from a fifty-five-foot gold chain attached to the domed ceiling. The floor of harmonious colors of slate squares was from the original floor laid more than two-and-a-half centuries prior.

"Luther, we'll be in the library. Please bring our guests some refreshments."

The dark-coated manservant, one of three in the castle, disappeared into the kitchen.

The Baron, Hirsch and Schnabel walked to their right and into a large, oak-paneled room that had more than two-thousand books, including a complete law library, stacked from floor to ceiling. A sliding ladder attached to a rail that ran along each section enabled one to reach any publication on any shelf. Three enormous chandeliers festooned with the finest Austrian crystal hung from the ceiling. There were two large baroque-style couches facing one another in the middle of the room, separated by a granite-topped coffee table. Brass sconces gave off even more light, making the commodious area glow with warmth. The travertine marble façade surrounding the fireplace at the far end of the library had been imported from Italy and lent even more elegance to this most remarkable space. A few minutes later Luther shuffled in with tea, coffee, a variety of fresh fruits, crackers, and several kinds of gourmet cheese.

"We have much to discuss, gentlemen. My staff and I have been quite busy since I received your facsimile, Ari. I believe we have made significant progress, and I would like to bring you up to date.

"But first, the both of you are probably quite hungry after such a long journey. Please, have something to drink and eat and let's get comfortable."

Comfortable? There was no place on earth as comfy as the Baron's castle.

"Thank you, Baron Rudfeld," Ari said. "This is going to be quite an experience for all of us." Hirsch was sitting on the same couch with Schnabel.

Ari was looking at the baron who was occupying one of the four sets of cushions on the opposite lounge. He couldn't help but notice that same look of determination the Baron had twenty years prior, and that his fate was in his hands.

Ari gently nudged Schnabel and whispered, "Don't you dare ask for any more Cherry Schnapps."

The Baron and Ari spent the next thirty minutes or so engaged in small talk and sipped tea. That's the way Europeans were. More social even when problems were extreme. The conversation covered a wide variety of subjects, none of which had anything to do with the upcoming hearing. Schnabel stuffed his mouth with Gruyere, Emmenthal, half a wheel of Appenzeller, one shiny red apple, and a couple of dozen home-baked wafers.

"Baron Rudfeld, I'd like to begin the rundown of what has transpired since you began working on the case," suggested Hirsch.

"By all means, Ari. However, prior to that, I'll have Luther take you to your rooms. Please unpack and if you like, there are private baths in each suite. I will await your return." Hirsch was thinking, "Schnabel, you better bathe this time and not stink up the *schloss*."

CHAPTER FORTY-FIVE

"The goal of legalizing drugs is to bring them under effective legal control. If it were legal to produce and distribute drugs, legitimate businessmen would enter the business. There would be less need for violence and corruption since the industry would have access to the courts. And, instead of absorbing tax dollars as targets of expensive enforcement efforts, the drug sellers might begin to pay taxes. So, legalization might well solve the organized crime aspects of the drug trafficking problem. On average, drug use under legalization might not be as destructive to users and to society as under the current prohibition, because drugs would be less expensive, purer, and more conveniently available."

National Institute of Justice, Research, development, and evaluation agency of the U.S. Department of Justice

45 Minutes Later-2:15 PM (Liechtenstein Time), Saturday, July 12, 2008

INFORMATION PLEASE

Hirsch and Schnabel reappeared in the library after bathing and changing clothes – yes, Franz cleaned up but was still wearing his mucky-looking Reeboks – and found the Baron sitting at a table with a pile of manila folders.

They sat down in brick-red, leather-tufted chairs across from their patrician attorney.

"Gentlemen, I beg your indulgence. Your trip has been long and arduous, I know, but I do not want to waste time because we have much to accomplish. Let me report what I have done thus far on your behalf. Please let me know if you have any questions as we move along.

"First, as requested, I have filed a motion with the Court of Justice to begin the probate process for the estates of the Smiths. What both of you may not be aware of is that the law in Liechtenstein currently states if a will has been signed before a Liechtenstein notary public, it is automatically accepted by the court as a true and verified copy of the original last will and testament.

"The bottom line, as you say in America, Ari, is that even if we cannot find the original wills there will be no delay in probating them. The conformed copies in my possession are completely acceptable.

"I'm sure this will come as no shock to the U.S. administration. Herr Reinhold von Stülpnagel, the Zurich attorney representing the United States, has thorough knowledge of the laws of Liechtenstein. He has received via the American embassy the court papers with the motions I have filed.

"In return, he has filed claims on behalf of the U.S. government and a number of its agencies. Some of those claims allege the Smiths' wills are fraudulent. However, his motions do not contain any specifics of his accusation."

Von Stülpnagel had worked quickly.

Within twenty-four hours of being contacted and contracted by the American embassy, he had completed his homework by recording with the Court of Justice the proper motions in response to the Baron's. He, too, had friends in the Principality with influence and power.

"Second, I have asked the court to issue an order to accept tentatively the last wills and testaments of Bobby and Timmy Smith for probate and permit us time while we search for the originals. They should still be in the safe deposit boxes in the LGT Bank unless either or both were removed by the Smiths themselves. We shall find out when we take the inventory of the assets.

"Third, upon legal acceptance of the last wills and testaments the court will begin the probate process and assume jurisdictions for all assets of the estates located in Liechtenstein.

"That is, if there are any assets. I do not wish to presume anything at this time. None of us has seen the Smiths in decades and we cannot prove they have anything at all in LGT Bank.

"We know the trusts and foundations which we created in early 1988 must be legally transferred into their names by you, Ari. We will then ask the court to reverse the process. You will testify you were the witness to the signing of the last wills and testaments."

"Baron, I apologize for not mentioning this to you in my original fax," Ari offered as he searched his memory. "As you may recall, I left my fingerprints and palm prints on file with the bank more than twenty years ago so I could access the vault on behalf of the Smiths.

"Unfortunately, the assignments of the foundations and trusts to them were only partially completed.

"I left off their names thinking I would soon be back at LGT to take care of it. I never returned to Liechtenstein until now because of many personal predicaments and being spied on by agencies of the U.S. government.

"I wanted to put all of this in my past and not have them endlessly tugging at me.

"As a result, the Smiths never actually had legal ownership. I would like to transfer the title before we go into court on Monday. I don't want the judge to wrongfully presume I was seeking to obtain any of the estates' assets for my personal gain."

"This is not a problem, Ari, and quite frankly I anticipated this. I have a simple solution which will be accomplished by this affidavit I have prepared for you to sign that merely states what you have just told me. I will enter it with the court clerk prior to the hearing."

The Baron turned the newly prepared document toward Hirsch so he could read and sign it. After a quick review, Ari penned his name. He handed the finalized papers to the Baron and said, "Certain names which may arise at the legal proceedings, Baron Rudfeld, are Nunu and Dudu. Both were clients and friends of mine.

"At one time they disclosed to me they had done significant subcontract work for Bobby and Timmy Smith. I had introduced the Smiths to the two Israelis in Florida. Their relationship among each other leads me to believe there may well be significant assets in LGT. I recall we prepaid the fees on those entities twenty-five years in advance and that was in 1988.

"Schnabel can testify he personally saw Nunu and Dudu visit the bank on a number of occasions to make deposits into the Smiths' foundations, trusts and safe deposit boxes. My only involvement was having them meet one another." "It will be impossible for Franz to testify, Ari. I will get to that in a moment. However, it is clear," said the Baron as he pulled a document from one of the folders, "that upon the presumption of death of the Smiths, any and all assets would revert to you as the legal titleholder and trustee based upon the terms and conditions of the trusts.

"Here is the way the clause reads in both wills. I know you have not seen them in many years and have probably forgotten what they state."

"In the event that I fail to contact in writing, either Baron Julius ben Mendel Rudfeld, of Liechtenstein, Herr Aristotle Einshtein Hirsch, of the U.S.A., or, any bank officer at the LGT Bank, in Liechtenstein for a continuous ten-year period, then, and in that event, I direct the Probate Court of Justice, in Vaduz, to legally presume my death by violent causes and process the probate of my estate to carry out my last wishes and desires."

"I haven't heard from them in more than two decades. At least that is my understanding." The Baron was virtually certain the Smiths had disappeared as had been suggested.

"No one has. We will have to wait until Monday to see if anyone comes forward with clear evidence and sworn testimony declaring that one or both putative decedents has been seen in Liechtenstein during the past decade.

"I feel there should be little dispute over the demise of the Smiths, thereby supporting our claim of ownership of their estates."

The immunity agreements Hirsch insisted upon were right on the money. He could have and probably would have been charged with a variety of crimes had those accords not been signed.

"I have also filed a motion to have you named executor, Ari, but the U.S. government will most likely raise some argument against allowing that. We'll have to address that matter as it arises.

"As for the safe deposit boxes, procedurally we must have a representative of the Liechtenstein court in the vault of the LGT Bank while the inventory of the contents is taking place. It is virtually assured the court will allow the safe deposit boxes to be opened. If they find anything illegal in the contents the motion will be reversed immediately.

"In that eventuality, it might take many years to obtain any of the assets. I'm not saying this to concern you but merely to have you prepared."

Hirsch wondered to himself. Did anyone have access to the boxes during the past twenty years? Could someone have gotten into them other than me? It couldn't have been Schnabel because he would have stolen everything and escaped Liechtenstein with his family and never would have surfaced. Were the original last wills and testaments still there? Without them, we might have a problem.

"Herr Schnabel." The Baron looked directly at the convicted felon. "As of now, I'm afraid you will not be able to testify in court on Monday since you are technically a fugitive from Liechtenstein justice. No judge in the Principality will permit your appearance on the stand."

"Are you sure that will not be possible?" asked Schnabel.

"I am getting to that point, Herr Schnabel. Please be patient."

Patience? Schnabel? That was like asking a nymphomaniac to give up sex.

"Franz, I have good and not-so-good news for you, *mein freund*. The prince has already granted you safe passage and has allowed you to return to your home country. He knows you are here, as does the head of the National Police and his entire force.

"You will be able to remain in Liechtenstein as a citizen and not endure any negative consequences of your actions. But you must cooperate in these estate proceedings and allow me to make appropriate restitution to Spanish and German authorities.

"By that I mean you will not be put on trial even though you broke many laws, including criminal codes. If we can locate your wife and daughters, they will be allowed to return as well."

"Will the authorities put all of this in writing?" Schnabel was looking for a security blanket.

Put it in writing? Have you lost your mental capacity! You're lucky you're alive!

"No, Herr Schnabel. The authorities will not put it on paper. You will have to trust them to live up to their commitment precisely the way they expected you to live up to yours, which unfortunately, you did not do.

"If you prefer, I will tell them you have not accepted the terms. They will probably sentence you to at least five years in prison. I am sure you are aware, Herr Schnabel, that anyone in the Principality who receives a sentence of more than two years is incarcerated in an Austrian penitentiary."

The Baron was testing the level of Schnabel's aptitude.

"Please, Baron Rudfeld. I will accept the conditions unconditionally. I did not want to mislead you into thinking I must have a signed document." A closed mouth gathers no foot!

"Good. Then we shall discuss some other contingencies. You will not be permitted to leave the jurisdiction of Liechtenstein except to go to Switzerland. The money you – shall we say, withdrew? – from LGT will have to be repaid in full.

"One more Liechtenstein item. You will never be allowed to work in the financial industry again. You may find employment in a technology position, but you will not have access to any kind of personal or financial information.

"Regarding you're not being able to testify, Liechtenstein legal statutes dictate it will not be possible. That is non-negotiable. I hope that answers your earlier question.

"Spain has no interest in extraditing you, Franz. One of my staff attorneys went to law school in Madrid and has many friends within that nation's legal system. He has arranged for you to pay back five-hundred-thousand of the $1 million fine in full settlement.

"The embassy in Switzerland will deliver a document corroborating legal satisfaction of the debt as soon as you agree to pay them back. Once they receive the monies, they will also grant you clemency. I have consented to wire them the payment as soon as I have clear funds from you in my trust account.

"Please do not spoil my professional status by disappointing me, Herr Schnabel. I have worked very hard for many years helping the people of Europe, and especially Liechtenstein, become financially stable.

"If you will pardon me for paying myself a compliment, I am held in rather high esteem for my persuading much of the continent to enact forward-thinking legislation within the framework of modern law. That is one legacy I do not want to destroy."

"My goodness, Baron. I would not do anything to harm your standing at all. Not at all. You have my word as a gentleman on that. I cannot thank you enough for accepting me as a client."

Schnabel was lying through his teeth. He got his butt saved by a savvy, sophisticated, world-class barrister who knew how to work his lifetime contacts to the satisfaction of his clients, but Schnabel was...well, a pimp.

"Now the German problem. I have spoken with Deutschland authorities and worked out an arrangement. I informed them you cannot and will not testify against clients of the LGT Bank since they have already collected tens of millions of deutschemarks of back taxes from the information you have given them.

"To complete the matter, I have promised the German Minister of Finance and Minister of Justice, both personal acquaintances of mine, that we will return to them a total of $3.5 million U.S. In exchange, the Germans will consider the matter closed and drop all potential criminal proceedings against you."

"Did you say $3.5 million?" Schnabel's outer skin was now a shade of purple. "They have already collected twenty times that much from the disc I supplied them! How could you agree to that, Baron? They should have given me even more reward money for what I turned over! This will make me a poor man."

"It's significantly better to be a poor man than it is to be a dead man without anyone at your funeral to mourn your cold, smelly body," the Baron responded calmly.

"Franz, a brain is a wonderful thing to possess, but only if you use it. Now would be a good time to engage yours."

Unlike Schnabel, the Baron Rudfeld was left unruffled. "May I continue, or do you think you might be better served by retaining other counsel?"

"No, I did not mean it that way Baron," responded the money-hustler. "It was not my intention to quarrel with you. It would not be a good decision on my part to find another attorney. Please continue. Please."

Quit begging you wretched kvetch!

"Thank you, Franz. I would encourage you not to interrupt me during this important discussion," urged the Baron as he momentarily paused.

"Chancellor Mitsch has been informed about the potential dangers throughout her nation by foreign security agencies should the information her government possesses fall into the wrong hands.

"The Chancellor is a prudent lady. I can assure you it will be now kept confidential. She knows well which of those organizations can do the most destruction across Germany and is quite unwilling to take a politically damaging position.

"The same goes for you, Herr Schnabel. Should you decide to make public any of the information, you will put yourself in grave danger and will experience a whip-stinging backlash.

"You do not want to dismantle the financial well-being of not only Liechtenstein, but that of certain individuals and groups who will forever look to destroy you. But I think you already know that.

"If you break the slightest part of any accord we have mediated on your behalf, I am afraid all of what we have finalized will be reversed and you will stand trial in Liechtenstein's civil and criminal courts. I believe you should avoid that at all costs.

"The prince will also sever the agreements among Liechtenstein and the other injured governments and will provide them with approved extradition papers for your return to those sovereignties.

"Speaking of costs, I am urging you to speak to whoever has your money, Herr Schnabel, and have them immediately wire $7.5 million U.S. to my escrow fund so that I can distribute the money to the appropriate parties.

"Of course, part of that will also be my fee. I am afraid you will not have much money left, but at least you will have your autonomy and can be reunited with your *frau und kinder*.

"Please take this," the Baron said as he lifted an engraved business card decorated with his coat of arms from a holder on his desk and handed it to Schnabel.

"The wiring information and my account number are printed on this card. I would appreciate your executing this first thing Monday morning. You may use the library telephone to call whomever you need to complete the transaction.

"Now you know your punishments, Franz Dieter Schnabel. They are more than fair, and I believe go beyond the scope of being equitable.

"Putting you in prison would not benefit anyone, but do not provoke the temperament of any of our authorities, or those of any other country."

Leaning across the desk and getting within a couple of inches of Schnabel's protrusive nose, the Baron said in a soft voice, "Herr Schnabel. You have continuing obligations to many people. Do not tempt fate because right now fate is your enemy. It would be wise to have as many friends on your side as possible. Do I make myself understood?"

"Yah, Baron Rudfeld. It is perfectly clear to me now that you have explained it in detail. Thank you."

Thank you? You meant to say "fuck you" didn't you Schnabel? You'll never lose your transparency, and everyone knows it, including the Baron.

"Oh, I almost forgot. One last detail, Herr Schnabel." Ari and Franz thought the Baron was through.

"The second disc, Schnabel. We want the second disc. Where is it?"

"What? How did you know about the second disc?" Schnabel asked. The Baron's question terrified Schnabel and baffled Ari.

How did the Baron know about it? Neither man could determine how he had found out. Yes, Schnabel had told Ari about the second disc when he was in Florida, but Ari never discussed it with Baron Rudfeld.

The Baron answered. "Aristotle, one of the most poignant of the Greek philosophers and the namesake of Ari, Herr Schnabel, once said that 'the antidote to fifty enemies is one friend.' Do you understand, Franz? I need but one friend to tell me things that my enemies will not. I would like to think I do not have fifty enemies, but in this particular case, the only thing I needed was simply one friend.

"Now, I will ask you only once again. Where is the disc?"

"I don't have it! I left it in Germany in the apartment where I was hiding!"

The Baron rang a small, brass call bell sitting on his desk. Within seconds, Luther was in the library.

"Luther, *bitte,*" said the Baron. "Go upstairs to Herr Schnabel's accommodations, put all of his belongings into his suitcase and then come downstairs with it."

"What are you doing, Baron? Why are you invading my privacy like this? Do you think I would lie to you?"

The question lingered in the air and went unanswered.

Luther came downstairs with the baggage quickly and asked the Baron if he should place it at the front door.

"No Luther. Please unzip the bag and empty all the contents on the floor. Right here. If you don't mind, take one of our butcher knives from the kitchen and cut open the lining of the suitcase as well."

Schnabel was now completely off kilter and went into one of his basket-case routines, like the captain of a submarine heading for a coral reef and couldn't stop in time. He hadn't told anyone where the disc was, and now he was in total fear that the Baron would back away from helping him and cause serious damage to his future – and his existence.

No longer could Schnabel continue the charade. "The truth is, Baron Rudfeld, the disc is hidden behind one of the zippered compartments. I am terribly sorry I was not more forthright with you."

"You're a leech on the body of society, an ardent follower of darkness. Everyone knows it except you, Schnabel!"

"Please, Baron, please. You must understand that I have lived in fear for the past several years under the Germans and that disc was the only way I would ever be able to fund my future."

You'll be lucky to have a future!

Baron and Ari knew he had to have had the disc somewhere handy. There was no possible way he would have left it in Germany or anywhere else because he trusted no one. Schnabel needed to keep it with him at all times so he could negotiate and conclude deals with Great Britain and the United States whose nationals' names were on that CD. His Swiss attorney, the one who made the deal with the Germans, knew he had it as well.

"How many copies of the disc do you have?" Ari asked. "Does your attorney have a copy?"

"No. I only have two. I swear to Jesus Christ only the two. I was saving one for the Americans and one for the British government. Those CDs were the keys to my financial salvation."

"You are probably going to hell anyway, Herr Schnabel." The Baron wasn't mincing words.

"So, you not only thought you could blackmail the Germans, the Americans and the British, but that you could get a split of some of the money that may be found in the LGT vaults!

"You seemed like such a nice man when I knew you at LGT, Franz, but now I find out you would actually sell your soul and everything else that's meaningful simply for money."

Luther returned to the library, emptied the contents of the suitcase on the floor, and proceeded to slice open the lining in the various compartments.

The two CDs had been hidden exactly where Franz said they were.

The Baron picked them out from the mess and slipped them into the side pocket of his jacket.

"I'll take these for safekeeping," he said. "Should anything you do in the future cause the royal family or any nation to be embarrassed or blackmailed, I believe you know what you can expect, Herr Schnabel.

"There are now three witnesses to this duplicitous and culpable behavior, Franz, so try not to do anything that will cause any of us to shatter your life!

"Remember, Franz. The prince is the master of this domain. He knows our people are depending on you to be honorable. If you disappoint him or them in any way again, there will be no way out for you or your family."

The Baron was finished giving Schnabel a lecture on honor and doing the right thing. The consequences, Schnabel knew, would be disastrous if he didn't heed the advice.

Ari knew the Baron had accomplished in two days what normally would have taken a month or more in almost any other country by a battery of lawyers.

Yes, the Baron's personal friendships and professional connections worked wonders. He had consciously established them for many years as a means of continuing his legacy as being one of the most venerated lawyers in Europe.

More importantly, he would not allow anything or anyone to besmirch the family name of Rudfeld. To him, that was who he was. And like Hirsch's dad who took great pride in his son, Rudfeld's father would have been quite gratified as well.

"Incidentally, I know about the demonstrations that will occur. This NAIL organization. Its members are not angry with you but at the United States government, Ari. Do not be concerned about your welfare. They are decent people and good citizens of our country. They want to maintain the status quo.

"I believe that's all for now. Gentlemen, dinner will be served at seven o'clock in the main dining room. In the meantime, if you would like to stroll through the private gardens or see some of my Arabian horses, the stables are about a five-minute walk on the road to the right of the castle. Luther will lower the drawbridge for you."

"Thank you, Baron," Schnabel said, "for taking such swift action and covering so much territory on our behalf. I will see you at seven."

Totally humiliated, Schnabel couldn't wait to get away and once again go into hiding, only this time within the confines of his castle bedroom.

After Schnabel left the library, the Baron turned to Ari. "I'm sorry I had to do what I did to Herr Schnabel, but I had no choice. Liechtenstein, I'm sure you know, has its own ways of dealing with corrupt, black marketeers like our little sociopathic friend.

"It took a bit of doing, but we've known about the second disc for a while. Please keep this to yourself, Ari, but we were able to reach out to an old friend of yours to get the information. We knew Schnabel had copied the disc, but I'm glad you were astute enough to elicit that information."

"Who in God's name did they contact?" Ari asked himself. It could have been one of any number of people. Dudu? Nunu? Geela? It didn't matter. As long as the job got done. "I thought you might have known about the additional discs, Baron. When Schnabel and I met in Florida, I purposely didn't question him about where the second disc was or how many copies there were. I suspected that information would come out soon enough. Brilliant job you did."

Now that the disc matter was settled, Baron Rudfeld changed the direction of the conversation.

"How is Jordan O'Banion, Ari?'

"He's doing fine. I'll let him know you asked about him."

"He seems to be a decent fellow, but there's something about him I don't quite trust. I usually don't impart that kind of information, but I have a strange notion about Mr. O'Banion. I cannot tell you exactly why. I had the same feeling twenty years ago when I first did business with him on your behalf."

"I'm somewhat concerned to hear you say that, Baron. Jordan is a good attorney and has been a wonderful friend for a number of years. Anyway, thank you for your kind hospitality and for locating the discs. God knows what would have happened if you hadn't. I'll see you at seven."

"I can't imagine why Baron Rudfeld said that about Jordan," Ari said to himself as he exited the library. "He's gotta be wrong."

But the Baron was almost never wrong when it came to reading people, especially someone like Jordan O'Banion. Ari would find that out soon enough.

After Hirsch went upstairs, the Baron went downstairs to the castle's wine cellar, which contained some of the most palatable and divine vintages from a dozen or more countries, all recommended by Baron Rudfeld's personal sommelier.

The cellar also contained a combination-locked safe hidden behind a seamless stone wall. The discs would stay there and would only be retrieved under dire circumstances. Dinner that evening was somewhat more than sumptuous. The executive chef, who had worked at the estate for twenty years and trained at a culinary school in the French region of Provence, prepared a seven-course meal that would have cost three bucks a bite at Paris' best bistro.

The wines between courses and mild cognac with a filthy-rich dessert were enough to mellow Hirsch and Schnabel.

The Baron, however, was naturally mellow. And he was as careful about his taste in clothes as he was in his food.

Midnight blue and ebony-black three-piece suits were his trademarks, and tonight he chose to wear the cobalt. Underneath, he wore an ivory-white, silk-and-cotton-blended, French-tailored shirt that he adorned with a conservative burgundy tie wrapped in a Double Windsor knot, the kind that made him appear confident.

His deep-red, jadeite-studded links he had received as a gift from a Chinese diplomat held his cuffs together. The pair of handcrafted red-coral cufflinks, the ones that had been presented to him by the prince and which bore a monotonic likeness of the Liechtenstein flag, were generally used for more formal occasions.

His calf-length navy socks matched his trousers, as did the color-coordinated, meticulously chosen, and pressed handkerchief that emerged slightly from the outside chest pocket of his jacket.

A butter-soft leather belt and shoes complemented each other. The gold, antique pocket watch and fob draped to the fourteen-karat chain running across his vest and chest created a regal finality to his garb. The only thing missing from his baronial aura was a monocle.

The Baron had maintained his one-hundred-eighty pounds on his almost-six-foot frame since he was a young man and was still as relevant and potent inside and outside the courtroom, including the society circuit.

The only noticeable physical change was his hair, which had gone from dark brown to grey in his late forties and had receded, but not enough to remove the illusion of aristocracy.

His deportment and vocal resonance immediately suggested one was dealing with a force that commanded recognition.

Conversation during dinner was limited to the taste of the cuisine, the global recession, and the melting of the polar ice caps. It was a rather uncomfortable and foreboding meal given that Schnabel's wine kept dripping from the sides of his mouth and soaking his shirt.

He also spilled a bowl of vichyssoise, half of which landed in his lap and the other half soaked and stained the Persian carpet beneath.

After dunking his dessert, a chocolate-covered éclair-in his coffee, Schnabel instinctually knew it was time to have a solid night's sleep, especially knowing a down-filled pillow was waiting for his greasy hair.

"Well, I must now go to sleep," he told the Baron and Ari. "Thank you for the delightful dinner. It was quite excellent." He retired to his quarters then listened for the Baron and Ari to head to their bedrooms.

Schnabel sneaked downstairs and walked into the library. He picked up the phone and made a call to his attorney to wire the $7.5 million to Baron Rudfeld's trust account Monday morning.

It would be a rather simple transaction since his lawyer was from Zurich and held the funds in, of all places, a branch of the LGT Bank. Extending his library visit became mandatory after the sneaky Schnabel found the Cherry Schnapps sitting in a liquor cabinet. He drank himself to dreamland while sitting upright on one of the chairs and couldn't quite flatten the speed bumps covering his brain.

Nor could he eliminate the thought of giving up all that money. Still half-dazed and reeking from a mixture of cherries, alcohol, and bad breath, he opened his eyes a bit past 5:00 AM, staggered upstairs to his guest room, and slept for another nine hours.

Ari woke up for a solo Sunday walk around the castle grounds while the Baron worked on some last-minute details preparing for the next day's duel.

Monday morning couldn't come soon enough. They might finally be able to get rid of the malodorous sot.

CHAPTER FORTY-SIX

"We have filled our prisons with drug offenders and diverted criminal justice resources and personnel away from serious crimes to wage the drug war. Washington's supply-side campaign was meant to stem the flow of drugs into the United States. But the evidence is glaringly clear-that campaign has not worked, is not working and given economic realities, will not work."

Ted Galen Carpenter, Author and Vice President of Defense and Foreign Policy Studies, Cato Institute

12 Hours Later - 2:15 AM (Switzerland Time), Sunday, July 13, 2008

ZANY ZURICH

By now, every Liechtenstein, Swiss and western Austrian newspaper, radio station and TV channel had reported on what they deemed to be the sensational story of how the U.S. government was attempting to undermine and decimate the financial security of Liechtenstein.

Editorials and commentary were in print and on the airwaves. The Internet was clogged with a mixed bag of accurate and inaccurate blogs and stories.

"LGT Bank Being Robbed by U.S. Authorities" read one tabloid headline.

"Liechtenstein Royal Family No Longer Banking On Privacy," shouted another.

Vaterland's online lead story was bannered with "Foreign Depositors to Pay Penalties; Prince Promises Protection."

The prince hadn't said anything of the kind. In fact, he wasn't even interviewed. When media attempted to reach him, the calls and e-mails were intercepted by the prince's long-time personal spokesman, Emil Osterhagen, who verbalized and typed "no comment" in at least six languages. The royal family considered issuing a Declaration of National Security but decided to defer to the judge hearing the case. They knew if they ran familial interference in a capitalist country, it might backfire politically.

The story was picked up by international wire services and appeared in financial periodicals and business sections of newspapers throughout the world. The story created an undercurrent in a number of countries and within large circles of wealthy investors, businesspeople, politicians, and organized crime.

Chaos ruled.

An LGT spokesman and its public relations department issued ex oficio statements every few hours on the activities occurring in Vaduz to keep its base of depositors from panicking.

The broadband phone lines in and out of Liechtenstein were so busy that callers waited hours to reach the financial institution and their personal bankers. For all practicality, the Principality's communications system became so overloaded that it nearly shut down. Liechtenstein wasn't the only place affected. LGT had twenty-nine branches around the world and bank representatives in every one of its offices were dealing with clients who thought their financial lives were ruined. The bank was under siege, as was the Principality.

None of the feds aboard had heard or seen anything of the story until a few minutes after the plane landed in Zurich.

One after the other their cell phones began to ring. Each was being called by colleagues from their respective agencies. Word had spread throughout the U.S. administration about the impending NAIL demonstration faster than the bubonic plague swept Europe in the 1340s.

"It's 2:00 AM over here. What could be so important?" questioned Rosselfellar. After being debriefed by the DOJ's public information officer, his face turned as white as the snow- capped mountain peaks surrounding him. All the others, except Buggy and E.F., went through similar telephonic experiences causing them to reach for their individual bottles of Zoloft and Prozac.

"Could this turn violent?" asked Rosselfellar.

"We've already infiltrated NAIL with one of our CIA guys. He doesn't think it'll get physical or turn into a courthouse riot but be careful and keep a low profile. Don't do anything that might be viewed as hostile."

There's that word again! Hostile or hostel? It didn't matter how it was spelled. They both sucked.

It wasn't simply what they heard from their Washington colleagues, but from the experience of the plane flight itself.

Other than Watts and Rappaport, none of them had a wink of sleep. The sound of the plane's engines was so loud and the noise insulation so poor that attempting to sleep would have been folly unless your last name was Watts or Rappaport.

Nothing not a single word about the case was discussed on the flight. Members of the group did manage to speak with each other at the refueling stop, but they were so discomfited by the journey that nothing notable was accomplished.

Besides, the aircraft's food, according to every federal "victim" who attempted to dine, tasted like what they thought might be government-sponsored recipes from a North Korean homeless shelter.

But all was not lost. There was a clean bathroom for the entire trip. It was most often used by Buggelshofer and Hutton during several bouts of airsickness from not only the victuals but their prescribed medicines. It was good their wives had taught them how to use Ty-D-Bol, which was a fixture on U.S. military aircraft, and to put the seat in the down position. Watts reminded them each time one of them came out of the head.

When they arrived in Zurich, each fed flashed a U.S. government identification badge and passport. They breezed past Swiss customs officers who had been notified by the White House Communications Office that a Task Force was on its way to Liechtenstein and to "please grant them diplomatic status." Hamilton and Ianucci didn't need the special arrangement since they already had their diplomatic credentials.

All thirteen strolled outside and were greeted by a light-skinned black man holding a cardboard sign that read "US Gummymint Pleece Heer." A wide smile on his face looked permanently painted.

"What does that say?" Smitherman asked.

"Could that be our welcome sign?" Rappaport answered Smitherman's question with a question and a cackle. "Man, your NSA credentials really have a lot of clout, don't they Smitherman?"

"Hey, mister, put down that sign!" yelled Whitfield. "We're here. You don't need to advertise it anymore!"

The man was wearing sloppy jeans, a white T-shirt, and a cardinal-red cardigan sweater. His blue-and-white New York Yankees baseball cap – Rappaport liked that – was set tight and backwards on his head. He held the sign high and continued politely to display his pearly white teeth.

"What the hell is wrong with you?" Even Watts was verbally crawling all over the poor guy. The man didn't answer...just kept on smiling. "Are you deaf?"

No response. Simply the same smile.

What nobody realized was that the man, Fethawi Tewolde, did not speak the first word of English. He was a twenty-seven-year-old immigrant from Eritrea in northern East Africa and one of more than a million and a half immigrants who now made up 20 percent of Switzerland's population.

In his quest for political asylum, Fethawi, who grew up in a village near the capital city of Asmara, had called a friend who worked for the American embassy in Bern to see if she could pull some strings to get him into Switzerland.

She had been in the Alpine country five years after fleeing the political and military problems of her homeland. The woman knew how tough a life it was for her and her fellow Eritreans and managed to somehow move Fethawi to the front of the immigration line. With some money he scraped together from some other African friends living in Zurich, he put a down payment on a twenty-seat jitney painted school-bus yellow and began a transportation business.

He had learned enough German in the few months he had lived in Switzerland but had a difficult time speaking any other languages except for his native tongues of Arabic and Tigrinya.

"Will you take that stupid grin off your face and tell us where to go?" Ianucci was seriously lacking "diplospeak" but that didn't bother Fethawi since he couldn't decipher what was being said anyway. Ianucci pointed and waved his finger at the bus. The young African put the sign to his side and rested it on the ground. He waved to the group as if to say, "Follow me. I'm your driver."

Everyone piled into the rickety jitney that read "FETHAWI TRANSPORTMITTEL" sloppily hand-painted in big red letters sloping at an angle across the sides of the vehicle. It was a retrofitted twelve-year-old Fiat that looked like it been decorated by a blind Swiss mountain goat.

Fethawi placed as many bags as would fit in an enclosed alcove on the passenger side of the vehicle. He pulled an expandable aluminum ladder from the same bay, climbed to the top of the jitney with one suitcase per trip, and tied them to the roof with heavy rope. He made sure to loop the line through each of the handles to protect them from falling off or being stolen.

As he pulled out of the airport entrance for the twenty-minute drive to the hostel, he heard a "thumpety-thump-thump," stopped the jitney and discovered the right front tire had lost its retread rubber. It had gone flatter than an out-of-tune fiddle.

"Watts, you did it again, you bitch!" Well, at least that's what the rest of the passengers were thinking but no one really said it.

It took about an hour after Fethawi made a call to get help and a spare tire for the jitney to once again head to his destination.

By the time they arrived at the youth hostel-a plain-looking five-story brick building with views of junkies shooting up across the street at Needle Park. It was 4:15 AM.

It was another fifteen minutes before Fethawi emptied the exterior alcove and got the roof baggage to the ground.

"How much do we owe you?" Rosselfellar screamed as though a loud voice would make him better understood.

Another big smile from their favorite tour director.

"Here's a hundred."

What a sport.

The Eritrean nodded his head up and down as though he appreciated the fare, hopped into the jitney, and motored off into the Zurich night.

They all needed to be up by 7:30 AM to freshen themselves, eat breakfast, and have a team conference prior to meeting with Herr von Stülpnagel. He was scheduled to arrive at noon in the lobby. Fat chance they'd have more than an hour or two of sleep. Trying to get into the locked building was another interesting event. They buzzed, banged, and blustered for another fifteen minutes before they got the attention of the front desk clerk who was sleeping in a lobby chair.

He slowly walked to the door after being awakened by thirteen mad maniacs hammering their fists on the plate glass window.

"*Ich bedaure*," he said as he unlocked the door.

"Do you speak English?" asked Watts.

"Yes, yes. I spik English. I zed I em sorry. You mahst be za Americans I vas expectink. You ah verry late, no?" The pensioner was a decent old fellow, but quite tired.

"We are. Please get us to our rooms right away." Hamilton was at least trying to be courteous to the man.

"*Willkommen*. Velcome. I vil get your rah-oom assignments now." He walked behind the desk to get his list of names and sets of keys.

"*Herren* Smitherman, Underman, Buggelshofer und Rappaport. You vil stay in rah-oom forr fawhty."

Was he trying to keep all the German names together? *Did he think that made a difference?*

"*Herren* Hutton, Bah-rown, Vitfield und Johnston. You vil be in rah-oom fife tventy.

Now he was picking out the Englishmen!

"Za rest of you gentlemen, bitte, pleece go to rah-oom fife fifty-two."

"Frau Vats, I belief?" he asked while looking straight at her.

"You believe correctly."

"I haf you in rah-oom thu-ree tventy nein, a puh-rivate accommodashun."

She fucked up the trip and she gets to sleep in a single room?

"Thank you."

All of them walked a few feet to the only elevator in the joint. It was too small to take more than four people with their belongings, so the group made four separate trips. Watts got to ride alone and was the first one on.

Finally, they got to lay their heads on somewhat uncomfortable cushions and their bodies on clean sheets although it wouldn't last very long.

They awakened two-and-a-half hours later. Rosselfellar, Hamilton and Brown never closed their eyes. They Crested their teeth, shampooed their hair, Dialed their bodies, had a quick pick-me-up continental breakfast with gallons of coffee, and gathered in the tiny meeting room off the lobby.

The conference area included a phony plant in one corner, a plastic-laminated table in the center and eight, cheap leatherette and anodized aluminum chairs. It would be standing-room-only for five of them, six when their attorney showed.

"Screw it," said Ianucci, "I'm sitting on the table." Three others followed suit, careful not to get splinters in their behinds.

Counselor von Stülpnagel, a well-dressed, bureaucratic type in his mid 50s, was as timely and dependable as the Nazi trains to Auschwitz.

He walked into the room precisely at noon, introduced himself to each of the feds, politely asked Buggy to remove his buttocks from the seat at the head of the table, and took over the meeting the way Hitler took Poland. Fast, efficient, and cocky.

As the day picked up speed, so did von Stülpnagel. By 3:30 PM, he had brought everyone up to date on various claims and motions he had prepared and already filed. He filled them in on what the Baron filed as well. Nuances of the Liechtenstein legal system followed.

Rosselfellar and Hamilton were doubly interested and enthused about the way things were progressing. They thought he had done a splendid job within the short window of time he had to get things accomplished.

"I'd be happy to answer any queries."

"Excuse me! What did you call us?" Buggelshofer was irritable and easy to provoke.

"He meant questions, Buggy. Why don't you and Hutton go back to bed?"

Rosselfellar knew he and Hutton were having a bad time of it. By now, both could have been typecast for two of the seven dwarfs.

Grumpy and Sleepy headed back to their "deluxe" accommodations and started snoring almost before they took off their clothes. After three trips each to the bathroom overnight, they awoke at 6:00 AM the next day. They met the rest of the crew for breakfast forty-five minutes later.

When the Task Force walked out of the hostel, there was Fethawi waiting for his group of American patriots to be shipped about an hour to Vaduz in the banana-colored jitney.

They were all thinking the very same thing. Should we have a group prayer and leave it in the hands of God, or should we find another way to get there? Crazy thought. They chose the former knowing there was no other transportation available because of the head-quacks' convention.

Once the feds boarded the bus, the smiley-face Eritrean took the road leading to Vaduz and sputtered his way through the glorious mountains. If he got there on time, his American passengers would not only be grateful but might even give him a healthy gratuity.

Or a complimentary course in "English as a Fourth Language."

CHAPTER FORTY-SEVEN

"The prohibition law, written for weaklings and derelicts, has divided the nation, like Gaul, into three parts - wets, drys, and hypocrites."

Dr. Florence R. Sabin, first female member of the American Academy of Sciences

29 Hours and 30 Minutes Later - 8:00 AM (Liechtenstein Time), Monday, July 14, 2008

COURT TIME

Helmut was behind the steering wheel of the black Mercedes limo when he came to a complete stop three blocks from the Court of Justice. The Baron, Hirsch and Schnabel were in the rear of the vehicle.

They couldn't help but notice through the back and side windows the hordes of Liechtensteiners displaying their feelings about this morning's hearing.

The streets were as crowded as New Orleans on Fat Tuesday.

Thousands of Liechtenstein citizens did not report for work that morning. Instead, they came from throughout the Principality to demonstrate against what they sensed was an assault on their financial system and the royal family.

NAIL was hammering the U.S. and what they perceived to be the injustices foisted upon American citizens who chose to bank in the Principality.

The people of Liechtenstein, mostly well-educated and aware of world events, knew about the widespread and growing corruption throughout the U.S. governmental structure caused by the War on Drugs. They were thoroughly familiar with the heavy tax burden placed on the average American because of decades of congressional waste, and why some chose to put their financial assets into secret bank accounts.

They had seen the American abuse of power on television, read it in print, and were experienced enough Internet users to keep up with current news. Yes, the planet was continually shrinking, not geographically but technologically.

Not only did the populace protest the American presence but there was a media onslaught the tiny nation had never seen before. Journalists arrived as early as 3:00 AM to set up their cameras outside the courthouse and guard what few square meters had been cordoned for reporters by the Ministry of Information.

They represented a multitude of multi-language media from throughout Europe, the U.S., Latin America, Asia, Saudi Arabia, and Australia, including mainstream and cable TV channels and wire services.

Many of those news outlets sent legal and financial reporters, correspondents, and stringers to cover what might well become a landmark decision involving tax havens and citizens of industrialized nations.

The initial story that appeared in banner headlines in the Vaterland newspaper a few days prior alerted most editors, wealthy investors, financial gurus, and even narcotics traffickers.

Instead of toting hunting rifles, axes, knives and blunt objects, the picketers held placards and posters. There were headlines scrawled on the signs. Don't Bank On Taking Our Money. Leave our Asse(t)s Alone. America: Stop The War On Money. The FBI Bugs Us. The U.S. Doesn't Knead Our Dough. We Have The Right To Remain Silent. Leave Liechtenstein Alone, and Just Leave Liechtenstein. Plus, a number of other insulting, homegrown phrases prepared for worldwide consumption.

Nevertheless, the head of *Landespolizei*, the National Police of Liechtenstein, prepared for any eventuality.

He called in every one of the force's eighty-five men and women officers, in addition to fifty-five auxiliary police personnel, to handle crowd control and protect the participants in the case. They put up barricades to keep the masses back, but some of them broke through anyway, including many of the journalists.

As media photographers and videographers grabbed images and sounds of infuriated citizens, print and broadcast reporters went through the legions of people capturing on-air interviews.

They took notes and quotes to write their stories in time to make their early editions and on-air deadlines.

Helmut couldn't move the limousine unless he wanted to run over or injure someone. So, he did the next best thing. He opened the door, stepped out of the vehicle, and whispered something into the ear of the man closest to the car who was less than two feet away.

As the chauffeur got back in the car, the demonstrator shouted loud enough to shatter quarter-inch glass. "It's Baron Rudfeld! Let him through! Move aside! Give them some room!"

He was able to outshout some of his fellow campaigners who by now were heaving indignant slurs against the United States government and shoving their fists into the air. "U-S-A, go a-way. U-S-A, go a-way. U-S-A, go a-way..." The mobs of people were chanting in unison as they vocalized their contempt for what they thought was a complete intrusion of Liechtenstein autonomy.

It was like Moses parting the Red Sea.

As word circulated among the throngs of Liechtensteiners that the Baron was trying to get through, people stepped aside and opened a broad lane, then applauded and cheered for their "savior" as the car slowly reached the courthouse entrance. Helmut opened the back door and out stepped Schnabel, Hirsch, and the Baron. Every Liechtensteiner and journalist recognized Baron Rudfeld, but who were these other two clowns?

Hirsch and Schnabel walked into the courthouse wearing floppy hats, sunglasses, faux moustaches, oversized windbreakers, and woolen scarves to hide their identities. The Baron had provided them with the outfits. Props would be needed, they thought, for any eventuality. Neither wanted their photos published in international tabloids or newspapers, nor did they want to be seen on TV or the Internet. That could have been much too hazardous to their health.

Many dissidents stood at the entrance to the modern but modest four-story courthouse, a rather stark contradistinction to the centuries-old buildings throughout Liechtenstein. Seconds after entering the courthouse, the three men peered out of a glass window and noticed the canary-hued jitney with black smoke belching from its exhaust system about two hundred feet away.

It was making a laggardly dash to the building entrance.

Damn thing looked like it belonged on a Caribbean island taking passengers on tours of banana and pineapple plantations.

Yes, it was Fethawi and the Feds, which might have sounded like a great name for a rock and roll group, but the only rocking and rolling was caused by a bad suspension system on the jitney. The Baron shook his head in disbelief and sauntered into the bailiff's office with his two clients.

As long as the human wave had been split in two, the jalopy was given enough leeway to reach the entrance mere seconds after Luther departed. The government parade began with Hamilton and Rosselfellar as its grand Marshals. Buggy and E.F. were the last to get off.

"Do you think these folks know what 'go fuck yourselves' means?" Buggy asked Hutton.

"Ignore it. We've seen lots worse than this. Don't you remember Sturgis when those nut-job bikers almost killed us with their Harleys? These folks are mad, but they're not gonna try to punch our tickets."

"Damn fools," thought Smitherman. "If it wasn't for us, these jokers would be clicking their heels together and shouting '"Heil Hitler."'

"Thank goodness Wazinski isn't with us." Rappaport contemplated that the presence of the bigot might have pushed the populace over the top with one of his infamous diatribes against anyone not Polish. The National Drug Intelligence Center nerd certainly didn't want to wind up being shipped home in a leg cast or carved up and fed to wildlife scouting the mountain habitats close to Vaduz.

Barrister von Stülpnagel, who had hitched a ride on the jitney in Zurich, gathered his money-mad group and promenaded inside. They made their way to the bailiff's office where the three rival claimants were already congregated and were relieved to get away from the angry swarm.

The teams of opponents remained peculiarly quiet, as did the clerks, secretaries, stenographers, and miscellaneous courthouse employees.

Everyone knew the importance of the case, and no one wanted to arouse the ire of anyone involved or give the impression they were partial to one side or the other.

Enemy lines had been drawn and no one wanted to cross them unless they wanted to take a verbal bullet. All had seen the discernible expression of discontent by the country's citizens and didn't want to add to the drama. It was enough the world's eyes might be focused on their miniscule homeland, which would give them more than the standard fifteen minutes of fame.

The case had been assigned to the Honorable Heinrich Albrecht Schallenberger whose ancestry dated back to fifteenth-century Liechtenstein.

The venerated jurist was a distant relative of the royal family, and in addition to his title of Chief Judge of the Court of Justice held the noble title of Count. He lived up to his blueblood designation.

He was a graduate of the Netherlands' Tilburg University School of Law, considered one of the finest schools of its kind in the world. There, he polished his knowledge not only of law, but economics and taxation as well. He used his education as intellectual instruments in helping shape the course of the banking system, financial structure, and well-being of his country.

His forty-five years of experience on the bench was virtually unequaled in that part of Europe. The seventy-eight-year-old judge knew everyone of importance in his country and neighboring Switzerland and Austria, including Baron Rudfeld.

None had ever questioned his honor or ability to hear cases and make decisions based on their merits, not friendships.

The courtroom gladiators and their witnesses signed in by 8:30 AM after which the bailiff, a mild-manner fellow named Bernhard, notified Judge Schallenberger all parties were present, and they could proceed with the hearing. Each lawyer had been handed a signed, official order of the court, which disclosed Liechtenstein civil rules of legal procedure. It stated that cases of similar facts and circumstances involving the same legal issues might be combined and heard as one case upon the sole discretion of the judge.

After reviewing the initial filings, the judge chose to merge these legal proceedings and consented to hear all matters pertaining to the Smith estates.

Witnesses were required to sign a document stating they were under oath and answer all questions honestly under penalty of perjury.

The courtroom typified most in the U.S. with one exception. The tables for the lawyers and their associates were placed in a semi-circle facing the judicial bench.

On the rim to the judge's left sat Baron Rudfeld, Ari Hirsch and Franz Schnabel. Further to the left was the witness box. To the judge's right was Reinhold von Stülpnagel. Three of the thirteen U.S. government agency representatives sat alongside their attorney while the rest sat in four rows lined up behind them.

Sitting in front of the judge was the court reporter who almost everyone visually and mentally rated as a ten. Watts thought the busty blonde was an eleven and would be a definite distraction to the unusually small number of people in the courtroom.

There was a perfectly legitimate reason why the audience attendance was limited. After a personal meeting with the prince, Judge Schallenberger had ordered the courtroom closed to outside parties, including spectators and the media.

He took the bold precautionary action after reading the initial newspaper leak. Nothing obligated him to divulge Liechtenstein banking laws, ones he had helped unify and integrate into the Principality's economic base that generated a sense of durability and validity. Additionally, the mood throughout Liechtenstein had turned as foul as a baseball hit into a third-base dugout. He refused to be a part of a hearing of such magnitude that could easily break down into a disorderly circus inside the halls of judicial authority.

A banner had been posted on the front door of the courthouse that read: Closed To The Public And Press Until Further Notice! Heavy security had been placed at the entrance and around the building to make sure nobody infiltrated.

Everyone who was supposed to be in the courtroom was awaiting the appearance of the judge. About fifteen minutes after they took their seats, he entered.

"Zis cohrt iss now in sesshun. All reiss for ze Honorable Judge Heinrich Albrecht Schallenberger."

Bernhard's proclamation encouraged everyone immediately to stand courteously. They waited for the white-haired justice dressed in his conservative black suit, white shirt, and grey tie to announce, "Please be seated" as he lowered his body into an overstuffed, high-backed leather chair sitting atop his podium.

He looked at the court reporter and directed her to "begin to chronicle the proceedings." After a slight pause, he continued. "This legal matter shall be recorded and referred to as the combined Estate Matters of Bobby Smith and Timmy Smith. This is case number 20081439, Probate, Court of Justice, Vaduz, Liechtenstein."

This was definitely not a case to be tried by Judge Judy.

CHAPTER FORTY-EIGHT

"The chemistry lesson from the last century is that no drug has ever caused as much problems as the attempts to rescue us from them."

Arnold Trebach, Professor Emeritus of American University, founder of Drug Policy Foundation, prolific author

5 Minutes Later - 9:05 AM (Liechtenstein Time), Monday, July 14, 2008

WHERE THERE'S A WILL THERE'S A WAY

"As we begin these proceedings, I would like to address some preliminary matters. For the record, please rise and identify yourself by name beginning with Baron Rudfeld and make the court aware of whom you are representing." Judge Schallenberger, politically astute as well as judiciously cautious, recognized several people, including Baron and Schnabel. Addison Hamilton, wearing his cowboy boots and western hat the way a Boy Scout shows off his merit badges, was also a familiar face because of his worldwide fame as the tough, resolute Chief of Staff of the White House.

"Baron Rudfeld. Please stand."

"Thank you, Judge Schallenberger, for hearing this important case." The Baron rose from his seat, turned his head in the direction of his rivals, stared, and said, "As you may know, I am Baron Julius ben Mendel Rudfeld and I am acting as Liechtenstein counsel for the estates of Bobby Smith and Timmy Smith. I am also serving as attorney-of-record for Aristotle Einshtein Hirsch and Franz Dieter Schnabel."

"*Danke*, Herr Rudfeld. Next please."

"Thank you, your honor." The Baron sat down and passed the floor to Ari.

"Aristotle Einshtein Hirsch, Executor and Trustee for the estates of Bobby Smith and Timmy Smith." Ari was up and down in less than three seconds.

"My name is Franz Dieter Schnabel of Liechtenstein. I will be a witness on behalf of the Smith estates. I am a former employee of the LGT Bank here in Vaduz and have been involved in many of the various elements of ---"

"That will be quite enough, Herr Schnabel," interrupted the Baron. "Your honor, because of the existential circumstances surrounding this hearing, Herr Schnabel will not be a witness to anything. I'm afraid he spoke out of turn."

He must be the designated court clown! Hadn't the bank thief heard what the Baron had told him? That he couldn't be a witness?

"Yes, Baron Rudfeld, I am aware of that. I was not planning to call Herr Schnabel to the stand."

"The court will allow him to be an observer only," Judge Schallenberger responded.

Ari fanned his hand over Schnabel's ear and whispered, "Shut up, you moronic simpleton. You'll be sitting in a cell if you don't!" The judge addressed the person in the seat normally occupied by the opposing attorney.

"Herr von Stülpnagel, I presume?" Although the Zurich attorney had heard of Judge Schallenberger, he had never appeared before him, nor had he ever met him.

"Yes, your honor. I am, indeed, Counselor Reinhold von Stülpnagel from Zurich." The pontifical barrister spoke like he was the epicenter of the legal universe. "I am pleased to be in your court. I am representing numerous agencies of the government of the United States. Sitting with me are representatives of those agencies, your honor."

"Excuse me, your honor, but would you have the counselor spell his last name for me?" The stenographer spoke in an undertone.

"Herr von Stülpnagel, please spell your last name for Fraulein Fuchs."

How much more appropriate could a name be for her? In English, Fuchs meant "fox."

"S-t-ü-with-an-umlaut-p-n-a-g-e-1." The diacritical mark of two dots over the "ü" was proper German and God knew Herr von Stülpnagel certainly fit the profile.

"*Danke*, Herr Stülpnagel." The "fox" thanked him with a slight growl as she showed some teeth with a smile.

"Please, Fraulein Fuchs. Place a 'v-o-n' in front of my last name. Small 'v'. I believe the judge did not include it when he asked for the spelling." There goes Herr Slick again.

"I already have that in the record but thank you anyway."

"Let's move on." The judge was eager to finish the intros. "Please make your introductions concise."

"Addison Hamilton representing the President of the United States, your honor. I serve as the White House Chief of Staff. I am also an attorney."

"John Rosselfellar. I am Chief Attorney for the Tax Division of the United States Department of Justice."

"James Whitfield. I am the Director of the United States Drug Enforcement Agency for the Southeast Region. It is my position that we are claimants under the estates of both Bobby and Timmy Smith. To that end ---"

The judge's gavel came down hard. "Please! No motions and no comments. All of you will have every opportunity to voice your legal positions, but not now. Proceed."

"Richard Johnston. I am a Special Agent for the U.S. Central Intelligence Agency, and an attorney for the CIA's International Financial Division."

"My name is William Patterson. I'm Chief of Operations for the U.S. Department of Homeland Security and an attorney-at-law."

"Wilson Brown, lawyer and Commissioner of the United States Internal Revenue Service."

"Wayne Underman, Chief of the Internal Revenue Service's Tax Evasion office. I am also an attorney."

"George Rappaport, Chief of Internet Technology of the U.S. National Drug Intelligence Center."

"Commissioner Bonita Watts of the U.S. Customs Department."

"Smitherman. Wilfred Smitherman. I am the Chief of the U.S. National Security Agency."

"Joseph Ianucci. Lawyer and Deputy Assistant to the Secretary of State of the United States."

"E.F. Hutton, U.S. Federal Bureau of Investigation. Also, an attorney."

"Robert Fenwick Buggelshofer. You can call me Buggy. I am a United States Federal Marshal and served in the Federal Witness Protection Program."

"You were a protected witness?" asked the judge.

"Sorry your honor. I meant to say I helped protect federal witnesses."

Judge Schallenberger thanked the group for its cooperation and began to tie up some loose ends prior to beginning the search for his impartiality.

If he had been appraised as a judge solely on his judicial deportment, he would have won by acclimation in any court in the world. His decisions were almost never appealed, and if they were, his decrees had never been overturned. Procedural knowledge and complete understanding of civil and criminal codes had always been the well-established core of Schallenberger's courtroom.

"I know that each of you has seen the large crowd of protesters outside," he said. "This is extremely uncommon in Liechtenstein. As a judge I find it quite disturbing and disheartening that I had to take the step of closing these proceedings to the media and the public.

"I cannot help but believe someone near the top of the food chain has leaked much information about this case. It wasn't only a matter of public record, in my opinion, that this lawsuit was revealed before we even began.

"Court matters in Liechtenstein are held at the highest level of secrecy similar to our financial and banking system. We are not out to win awards or certificates to grace our walls, or popularity contests as you might do in the States.

"We do not like publicity of any kind. So, I am issuing what you call a gag order. None of the parties involved in this case is permitted to make any public statement regarding these proceedings. I cannot urge you enough not to speak a word about what transpires in this courtroom.

"As of now, these proceedings are permanently sealed from public inspection and inquiry and will remain so. If anyone would like to object to these judicial rulings, please be recognized by the court and make your bone fide statement."

No one had any counterarguments, at least not that they overtly exhibited.

Hirsch was gratified. He thought Judge Schallenberger's ruling to keep the hearing in the closet was an excellent one. It would ensure secrecy not only regarding the facts of the case but any surprises that might surface regarding Bobby or Timmy. It would also protect Schnabel from any recriminations.

"Most of you have never appeared in my courtroom prior to today. I want all of you to know that I do not preside over cases in ways that might be similar to some of your American judges.

"I am not impressed with several of your politically oriented Supreme Court Justices nor am 1 comfortable with some of your made-for-television referees. I view this case as an exceedingly serious proceeding. The fates of many people are at stake and the consequences are high.

"All parties will be given ample opportunity to make valid legal arguments. Since I am the only arbiter of the facts, I will adjudicate this matter after listening to all of you and your claims. You will find I am a very easy judge to get along with.

"I want to attempt working with each of you to arrive at conclusions that are fair and just, ones that will be in the best interests of all concerned and consistent with the laws of the Principality.

"I have reviewed the briefs that have been submitted and based on their lengths I believe we can finish the case quickly. My ruling will be forthcoming after all presentations of the facts have been made.

"Court will be in session from 9:00 AM until noon, at which time we will break for luncheon. We will resume at 1:30 PM and work until 5:00 PM or until this matter has been fully concluded and resolved. Are there any questions?"

Seeing no hands raised and hearing no inquiries after ten seconds or so, the judge told the crowd, "Good. Then we shall proceed. Baron, please begin with your motions."

"Your honor, first I would like to file a motion requesting this honorable court to tentatively accept for probate proceedings these conformed, duplicate, executed copies of the last wills and testaments of Bobby Smith and Timmy Smith and accept jurisdiction to probate these wills.

"May I approach the bailiff your honor?"

"Certainly."

Baron Rudfeld walked over to Bernhard and handed him the copies of the last wills and testaments. In turn, the bailiff passed them to the judge. The only difference in the documents was the names of the decedents. Judge Schallenberger examined them with great interest and care. He noted several unique provisions, which caused him to lift his eyebrows and furl his forehead as though he had never seen anything quite like them.

"Your honor, while I am distributing copies, I would like to draw attention to several unusual phrases. May I ask all parties in the courtroom to spend a few minutes reading the document rather than my reciting it aloud?"

"Is that a motion, Baron Rudfeld?"

"A simple request, your honor."

"Request granted."

As he handed another copy of the originals to Fraulein Fuchs, he asked they be entered into the official record without objection.

"Mr. Hirsch and I served as witnesses when these wills were signed and notarized in the presence of Betty Amonds, whom I believe you know as a long-time and loyal employee of the LGT Bank here in Vaduz. It is our contention that every clause in this document disputes any and all claims that may be raised by the claimants representing the U.S. government.

"Moreover, since the decedents knew their identities might have been challenged, they not only signed their last wills and testaments but left their fingerprints on these documents in the very same manner we open bank accounts in Liechtenstein.

"I will vouch that these instruments are credible and truthful. All parties in this courtroom are surely aware of their authenticity. They certainly were not obtained by fraud or coercion."

Copies of the last wills and testaments were distributed by the bailiff to all the feds and their attorney. Ten minutes passed quickly when suddenly Reinhold von Stülpnagel arose and crowed his objection while the Task Force members fidgeted in their hard-backed chairs.

"Your honor, I request a thirty-minute recess to review the terms and conditions of these wills and testaments, and that Baron Rudfeld's remarks be stricken from the record at this time. I would like to confer with my clients about their positions on these documents. This is the first opportunity they have had to see them," said von Stülpnagel.

"I also move for the court to allow all claimants to read the documents prior to Baron Rudfeld's commentary on their stipulations."

With another pound of wood on wood, the judge granted the request and the motion.

"Remember, no one is permitted outside this building. I also caution everyone not to speak to anyone in the hallways or in the toilets. Court stands in recess for thirty minutes. And remember the dictate of this court. What happens in Liechtenstein stays in Liechtenstein!"

Almost as soon as Judge Schallenberger's wooden hammer fell and a recess declared, all stood while the man in charge headed to his chambers. Then, the Baron, Hirsch and Schnabel left the courtroom. The squad being led by von Stülpnagel turned their chairs into a full circle like an old-time football huddle and sat down to read and discuss Bobby and Timmy's final wishes.

LAST WILL AND TESTAMENT OF TIMOTHY SMITH

I, Timothy "Tim" Smith, currently known, at the time of the making of this, my Last Will and Testament and also have been known from time to time throughout my lifetime as Timothy "Tim" Jones, Tim Johnson, Tim Brown, and known also under such other names furnished from time to time by various agencies of the United States government and utilized by the undersigned during my lifetime as a former United States Special Operations Secret Agent assigned to "The Company," also known as the Central Intelligence Agency, and a current member of the Federal Witness Protection Program.
I do hereby make, publish, and declare this to be my Last Will and Testament, expressly revoking all wills and codicils heretofore made by me. The original of this will shall be placed in a safe deposit box at the LGT Bank in Vaduz, Liechtenstein, and a fully executed second copy placed in the possession of Baron Julius ben Mendel Rudfeld, Esq., of Galprin, Liechtenstein.

ARTICLE I

I direct my Executor to pay my judicially enforceable debts, funeral expenses, and the administrative expenses of my estate as soon after my death as practicable. In the event of my demise inside or outside the jurisdiction of the United States of America, I direct my Executor to exhaust all legal means to retrieve my body or remains and relocate my body/remains for proper burial in the Casualties of War section of Arlington National Cemetery.
Additionally, in light of my prior military service with the U.S. Special Forces in the Vietnam conflict and services rendered in Cambodia and Laos during the Vietnam Conflict while employed by "The Company," I am qualified for special burial with full military honors established by secret agreements between "The Company" and the U.S. government. I authorize my Executor to litigate with

the U.S. government to insure I receive the appropriate internment. Further, I direct that all Liechtenstein estate and inheritance taxes and other taxes in the general nature thereof (together with any interest or penalty thereon), which shall become payable upon or by reason of my death with respect to any property passing by or under the terms of this Will included in my gross estate for the purpose of such taxes, shall be paid by my Executor out of the principal of my residuary estate.

Notwithstanding anything to the contrary contained herein with regards to the payment of U.S. Income Taxes and/or U.S. Federal Estate taxes, with regard to all funds or types of assets, on deposit, in a Foundation, and/or Trust, held at the time of my demise at the LGT Bank in Liechtenstein, or, if said foundations or trusts are subsequently legally moved to another jurisdiction, due to the automatic transfer provisions of the legal site of trusts therein, being triggered by outside political events, and thereafter moved to another jurisdiction pursuant to other clauses contained therein and subject to specific written instructions delivered to the LGT Bank, in their possession. Accordingly, none of these assets or accumulations, in these accounts is subject to U.S. laws of taxation by virtue of secret agreements I have entered into with the U.S. government, wherever they may be situated.

I am instructing my Executor to not pay any U.S. income or estate taxes on these immediately aforementioned assets, and/or the income earned and accumulated thereon, as a result and pursuant to a secret, sealed employment agreement dated March 4, 1988, with the U.S. Central Intelligence Agency, the U.S. Drug Enforcement Agency, the U.S. Federal Bureau of Investigation, the U.S. Treasury Department, the U.S. Federal Witness Protection Program and signed by the undersigned and prepared in part by my Executor and personal attorney, Aristotle Einshtein Hirsch, who has personal knowledge of this sealed top-secret agreement and was present at the time of its execution.

No copy of this document was ever made available to me during my lifetime due to its highly secretive and sensitive nature. I direct my executor to follow these directions pursuant to the secret agreements previously entered.

ARTICLE II

I do give and bequeath to my Executor, in Trust, as provided for herein, all my personal effects and all my tangible personal property, including automobiles owned by me and held for my personal use at the time of my death to be used as he sees fit.

ARTICLE III
Directions to Executor and Trustee and Certification of Decedent

1. Directions: I have spoken at length with my Executor and Trustee as to my personal beliefs and desires as to the use of the trust funds and foundation funds I am establishing in Liechtenstein and leaving behind for a general trust purpose. This general purpose shall be broadly defined to permit without legal question my Executor to expend the total funds and income of these foundations and trusts in his absolute arbitrary and unilateral discretion in a manner that legally may bring about the stoppage of the war against drugs in the United States of America. Any unused funds not expended in this manner shall pass to Aristotle Einshtein Hirsch.
2. Certification: As to the uncertainty of my legal name, I would like to certify, by execution hereof, as to my best recollection as to the origin of my name. I was abandoned by my parents and dropped off at an orphanage in New Orleans, Louisiana. I stayed at the orphanage until I was adopted by two lesbian parents at age 12 (twelve). I immediately ran away from their home and began to live on the streets as a homeless runaway teenage child. Thereafter, I traveled to Chicago and lived in and out of reform schools and correctional institutions for minors. At age 17 (seventeen), I walked into an Army recruiting facility in Columbia, S.C., during the beginning stage of the Vietnam conflict and signed up to join the U.S. Army and its Special Forces Program. I used the name Tim Jones to sign up

for military service and lied about my age. Since that time, the U.S. government has furnished me with various fictitious names to use. I am presently in the Federal Witness Protection program and my name is subject to change from time to time as long as my life is in danger. At the time of the preparation of this document, I believe my life is in danger and will remain in danger for the balance of my natural life.

3. No Provision Made for Lifetime Best Friend: I have intentionally left none of my estate to my lifetime best friend Bobby Smith, who has left similar trusts and foundations in Liechtenstein and is in no need of income at this time in his life.

ARTICLE IV
Creation of Trust

All the rest and residue of the property which I may own at the time of my death, real or personal, tangible and intangible, of whatsoever nature and wherever situated, including all property which I may acquire or become entitled to after the execution of this Will, including all lapsed legacies and devises, or other gifts made by this Will which fail for any reason (but excluding any property over or concerning which I may have any power of appointment), I bequeath and devise to my Trustee, to be held IN
TRUST, hereinafter named "The Smith Trust Fund" for the following uses and purposes and upon the following terms and conditions:

1. Commencing with the date of the creation of this Trust, my Trustee, on an annual basis, shall disburse all of the net income derived from the Trust for the benefit of causes designed to end the War on Drugs in the United States of America.
2. In addition, my Trustee may pay to or apply for the benefit of accomplishing the general purpose of this trust such sums from the principal of the Trust as in his sole discretion shall be

necessary or advisable to the Trustee, from time to time, for carrying out the unique purpose of this trust.

ARTICLE V
<u>Presumption of Death</u>
In the event that I fail to contact in writing, either Baron Julius Ben Mendel Rudfeld, of Liechtenstein, Aristotle Einshtein Hirsch, of the U.S.A., or any bank officer at the LGT Bank in Liechtenstein for a continuous ten (10) years, then, and in that event, I direct the Court of Justice in Vaduz, to presume my death by violent causes and process the probate of my estate to carry out my last wishes and desires.

ARTICLE VI
I appoint Aristotle Einshtein Hirsch as my Executor. If he should not survive me or is unwilling or unable to complete the administration of my estate, I appoint Baron Julius ben Mendel Rudfeld, as my Executor. I direct that my Executor or Contingent Executor, whichever shall serve, shall not be required to post bond.

ARTICLE VII
I appoint Aristotle Einshtein Hirsch as Trustee of any trust created herein. If he should not survive me, or is unwilling or unable to serve, I appoint Baron Julius ben Mendel Rudfeld as Trustee of any trust created herein. I direct that my Trustee shall not be required to post bond.

ARTICLE VIII
I hereby grant to my Executor and to the Trustee of any trust established hereunder, the continuing absolute, discretionary power to deal with any property, real or personal, held in my estate or in any trust, as freely as I might in the handling of my own affairs. Such power may be exercised independently and without the prior or subsequent approval of any court or judicial authority, and no person dealing with the Executor or Trustee shall be required to

inquire into the appropriateness of any of their actions. Without limiting any of the powers that my Trustee or Executor may have under the laws of Liechtenstein or of any state in the United States, wherein the trust fund or assets of my estate may from time to time be situated, I hereby grant to my Trustee and Executor the following specific powers and authority in addition to, and not in substitution of, powers conferred by law:

1. To make distributions in cash or in specific property, real or personal, or an undivided interest in such property, or partly in cash and partly in such property, and to do so without regard to the income tax basis for federal tax purposes of specific property allocated to any beneficiary or to carry out the general purpose of this Last Will and Testament.
2. To sell, transfer or convey, at public or private sale and at such price or such terms and in such manner as said Trustee or Executor shall deem best, any property, real or personal, tangible or intangible, constituting a part or all of my estate or the trust, and to execute deeds or other instruments necessary to effect such sale, transfer, or conveyance. To compromise and settle claims in favor of or against my estate or the trust estates.
3. To hold and exercise any and all powers set forth Liechtenstein General Trust, Estate and Foundation Statutes as written on the date of the execution of this Last Will and Testament, and these powers are hereby incorporated by reference and made a part of this instrument and such powers are intended to be in addition to, and not in substitution of, the powers conferred by law. The powers shall be applicable in all legal jurisdictions. 4. The term of this trust shall be for a period of one-hundred years from the date of this, my Last Will and Testament, or the cessation of the War on Drugs by the U.S. Government and its various agencies, whichever shall first occur. Any remaining assets of this trust shall thereafter be donated outright, free of trust, to the Homeless Children's Society in New Orleans, Louisiana, U.S.A.

IN WITNESS WHEREOF, I sign, seal, publish, and declare this instrument to be my Last Will and Testament, this the 23rd day of March 1988.

Signature: *Timmy Smith*

I, Timothy Smith, the Testator herein, sign my name to this instrument this the 23rd day of March 1988 and being first duly sworn, do hereby declare to the undersigned authority that I sign and execute this instrument as my free and voluntary act for the purposes therein expressed, and that I am eighteen (18) years of age or older, of sound mind, and under no constraint or undue influence.

Witness: <u>Aristotle Einshtein Hirsch, Esq.</u>

Aristotle Einshtein Hirsch, Esq.

Witness: Baron Julius ben Mendel Rudfeld, Esq.

Baron Julius ben Mendel Rudfeld, Esq.

Witness: Betty Amonds

<u>Betty Amonds</u>

We, Aristotle Einshtein Hirsch, Baron Julius ben Mendel Rudfeld and Betty Amonds, the witnesses, sign our names to this instrument, being first duly sworn, and do hereby declare to the undersigned authority that the Testator signs and executes this instrument as his Last Will and Testament and he signs it willingly, and that each of us, in the presence and hearing of the Testator hereby signs this Will as witness to the Testators signing, and that to the best of our knowledge the Testator is eighteen (18) years of age or older, of sound mind, and under no constraint or undue influence.

City of Vaduz

Country of Liechtenstein

Subscribed, sworn to, and acknowledged before me by Timothy Smith, the Testator, and subscribed and sworn to before me by Aristotle Einshtein Hirsch, Baron Julius ben Mendel Rudfeld and Betty Amonds, witnesses, this the 23rd day of March 1988.

Betty Amonds

Notary Public (SEALED)

My Commission Expires: 8-18-10

Fingerprints of Timothy Smith

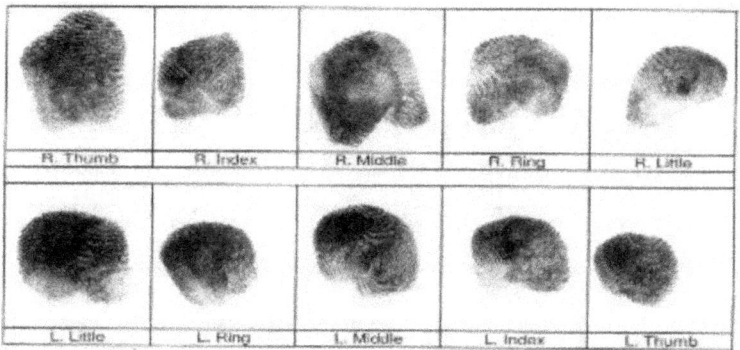

There would be no reason to eye-scan the second will. Bobby's and Timmy's were identical except for the first names and aliases.

CHAPTER FORTY-NINE

"If the zeal to eliminate drugs leads this state and nation to forsake its ancient heritage of constitutional liberty, then we will have suffered a far greater injury than drugs ever inflict upon us. Drugs injure some of us. The loss of liberty injures us all."

Gerald Kogan, Former Chief Justice of the
Florida Supreme Court

30 Minutes Later - 9:35 AM (Liechtenstein Time), Monday, July 14, 2008

FULL-COURT PRESS

"Cohrt iss beck in sesshun," Bernhard cried out as the judge re-entered the courtroom. All participants were in their seats and waiting for further instructions from the bench.

"Have your claimants reviewed the documents, Herr von Stülpnagel?" That was an obvious first question.

"Yes, your honor. We are ready to proceed."

"What is your position regarding the acceptance of these last wills and testaments for probate within the jurisdiction of Liechtenstein?"

The second question was almost as perceptible as the first.

Von Stülpnagel stood, paused for a moment, buttoned his suit jacket, and began to pace behind the table where he had been sitting. He twirled to the judge and faced him.

"This is for the record, your honor. On behalf of the U.S. claimants, we strongly object to the admittance of these last wills and testaments for probate under the laws of Liechtenstein."

"Fraulein Fuchs, bitte. Make sure you have included the word 'strongly' in the transcript." The alluring Liechtenstein lass jiggled her head corroborating the judge's order. He lowered his tortoiseshell, half-lens reading glasses on his nose, looked straight at von Stülpnagel and asked, "Based upon what legal premises, counselor? These documents were provided to you last week. Why didn't you file a motion at that time?"

"Because there was not enough time to do so, your honor. After careful review, we have collectively concluded that the court should not accept these wills and testaments of Bobby and Timmy Smith as original documents.

"Clearly, they are copies and should not be recognized by any court of law. We consider the copies deceptive. We further believe the opposing party has had enough time to provide the originals before a court of competent jurisdiction if, indeed, originals even exist.

"These copies should not be acknowledged at all. If the original documents are found later, we can address the issue at that time.

"It is also our position this court does not have jurisdiction of these probate matters. No proof has been offered to validate the demise of Bobby and Timmy Smith, and until proof of death can be established, we object to the acceptance of jurisdictional rulings taken by this court.

"Based upon our information, we contend that undue influence may have been exercised upon the decedents, if there are any, in the preparation of these last wills and testaments by both Aristotle Einshtein Hirsch and Baron Julius ben Mendel Rudfeld.

"If the original documents somehow are found, these individuals might well benefit from these proceedings. Therefore, both men should be judicially disqualified and barred from further participation due to an indisputable conflict of interest and multiple appearances of impropriety.

"Additionally, we affirm our opinion these documents should be dismissed as not being valid legal instruments. We maintain their signatures were obtained either by duress, trickery or deceit."

Baron Rudfeld got to his feet and assumed the position of a telephone pole: erect and immovable except by a crane.

"I forcefully object to these accusations and would appreciate the court's insistence that these types of factually unfounded outrageous comments not be allowed or be considered by this Liechtenstein court." The Baron was close to being incensed. "These kinds of words are more than provocative, your honor, and have no place in such a hearing."

Judge Schallenberger put an exclamation mark at the end of the Baron's lingual spanking.

"Do not show contempt for the opposition, Herr von Stülpnagel. That is not the way we conduct our legal proceedings in Liechtenstein."

The judge's words must not have registered with von Stülpnagel.

"We intend to show the court this legal proceeding is a big charade and a deceit perpetrated by Baron Rudfeld and Aristotle Hirsch!

"As for Herr Schnabel we all know he is a liar, cheat, thief, three-faced, despicable criminal who is a fugitive from justice by this very Principality!" The Zurich attorney began to raise the level of his voice by at least one octave.

"He has brought great disgrace to the legal and financial communities of Liechtenstein and has attempted to destroy their virtues and secrecy laws. There has been a strong undercurrent and rippling effect in Switzerland as a direct result of Herr Schnabel's misdeeds!

"We request that he not be permitted to even witness these proceedings. He should be banned from the courtroom and immediately arrested by Liechtenstein authorities!" By the time the tirade was over, von Stülpnagel's temples were visibly pounding, and white frothy droplets formed on the ridges of his lips. His attempt at speaking with a honey-lathered tongue was quickly squelched by his irascible persona.

The judge was as maddened as he had never been, well beyond accepting the attorney's malevolent behavior. He smashed his gavel three times almost breaking it in the process.

"You will not dictate to this court or any court in Liechtenstein how we should conduct our business, Herr von Stülpnagel. You will immediately cease and desist from this kind of behavior, or I will hold you in contempt of court! Please do not test me! Your penalty will be more than a simple fine!"

Had the pressure gotten to von Stülpnagel to the point where he couldn't even represent his clients properly? How could he assail Schnabel when it was the very same man who wanted to turn over tax cheats to the IRS? How could he argue on behalf of the agencies when they were the ones who stood to benefit greatly from Schnabel's information?

He couldn't.

"If it pleases the court, I would like to take a five-minute break to compose myself, your honor." Von Stülpnagel knew he stepped over his legal and professional limits. It wasn't a show. He meant every word, and displaying intolerance and anger was right up his righteously indignant alley. Without realizing it, he trapped himself and the U.S. government.

"Request denied," blurted the judge. "Move on with your arguments!"

Von Stülpnagel had still been on his feet but quickly sat down after the judge's brief but strong scolding. But that didn't stop him from continuing as though nothing had transpired, although at a more controlled and balanced pace.

The Swiss lawyer moderated his tone as he wiped his forehead with his handkerchief.

"In the event the last wills and testaments are admitted to probate, we are requesting the court to order Baron Rudfeld and Ari Hirsch to post substantial bonds.

"We have reason to believe assets in excess of $200 million U.S. could be in safe deposit boxes in the LGT Bank." It was a good thing for von Stülpnagel he had come to the end of his arguments. He might have regretted continuing on the implacable path he had taken.

"Did you say $200 million U.S. in the LGT Bank?" asked the judge.

"Yes, your honor. That's exactly what I said."

"Thank you, counselor." Judge Schallenberger was not only more cordial but didn't want to impart any bias. His mandate was to get as much information as possible so he could render what he thought was the correct and just verdict. "Your objections are noted for the record, and I will take them under advisement in the issuance of my final ruling." The judge then questioned Rosselfellar. "What is the Department of Justice's position in these matters? Please remember you are still under oath."

"Thank you, your honor." After his counselor's outburst and missteps, Rosselfellar knew he had to get things back on a happier track. He positioned himself behind his chair and began speaking.

"We agree with all of the stated objections and requests proffered by Herr von Stülpnagel but I would like to add several pertinent points.

"It is the belief of the U.S. government, including the President, that Mr. Hirsch represented the Smiths in the United States while they were engaged in illegal drug smuggling, and that Mr. Hirsch assisted them in laundering the proceeds from the sale of those narcotics.

"We further assert that collectively they have hidden a vast fortune in the LGT Bank and have purposely evaded paying federal income taxes to the U. S. Treasury. As you well know, these are criminal and felonious acts.

"The last wills and testaments, if accurate, are proof positive of their activities. Further, we have evidence that shows that Mr. Hirsch can execute a simple assignment of interest to himself or his assignees. That would give him ownership of the Liechtenstein trusts and foundations established in the names of Bobby and Timmy Smith.

"We deduce this has always been Mr. Hirsch's intention. It implies that he and the Baron are planning on misrepresenting the facts and implementing a devious scheme to gain control of a vast fortune.

"It is our position they are the criminal masterminds hiding behind a legal façade. We know how important credibility is to the Liechtenstein judicial system but because of their conspiracy to defraud the United States government this court's prestige will be permanently tainted if it finds in their favor.

"The fact that Mr. Hirsch has his fingerprints on all of the assignment documents to all of the trusts and foundations without including the names of Bobby and Timmy Smith at the time the foundations and trusts were created - well, your honor, isn't it plain that it was an intentional arrangement?

"As for Baron Rudfeld, we view him as a co-conspirator who has not entered this courtroom with clean hands. We are accusing him of acting in concert with Mr. Hirsch.

"Forgive me, your honor, but the LGT Bank is also complicit in hiding assets belonging to the United States. It continues to engage in conduct in direct conflict with the policies of the U.S. War on Drugs as well as international narcotics-trafficking statutes that legally provide for the seizure and forfeiture of assets of drug smugglers and dealers in foreign jurisdictions.

"That type of conduct aids and abets criminals in avoiding the payment of federal income taxes which are due on all income earned under Section 61 of the 1954 U.S. Internal Revenue Code.

"Thus, we are asking this court to add LGT Bank as a party to this litigation and to the jurisdiction of these court proceedings. We can justifiably assume the bank is a culpable participant in international tax evasion.

"Finally, the United States will not relent or surrender in its attempts to recover assets legally due its citizens."

At the end of that thorough oratory and pleading, Rosselfellar took his seat and a sip of alpine water from the glass sitting in front of him.

"Thank you, Mr. Rosselfellar. Your objections and profound words are well noted. I will respond to them at the appropriate time."

The judge realigned his glasses and scribbled some notes. He wanted everyone in the courtroom to know that he was being thoughtful about this case and hadn't made up his mind one way or the other regarding the final ruling.

He looked at Hamilton Addison and spoke directly to the Chief of Staff.

"Since you are here representing the President of the United States, I will most certainly give you the opportunity to voice any further objections or opinions."

"I appreciate your giving me some time and would like to thank the court on behalf of the President and all Americans," said Hamilton. 1

support the previously articulated objections and agree with their legal rationale, as does the U.S. administration. I do have additional objections and would like to enter those in the court record. Please consider these prior to your ruling."

"I will, Mr. Hamilton. Proceed, but please remove your rather large hat in the courtroom," Judge Schallenberger said as he pointed toward Hamilton's head.

"Sorry, your honor." The Texan completely forgot his scalp was covered. He politely removed his brown, beaver-fur cowboy hat and placed it on the table. Good thing he wasn't wearing his red bandana around his neck or a holster with a loaded six-gun strapped to his waist and leg.

"The U.S. government categorically denies the mere existence of Bobby Smith and Timmy Smith and refutes having any association, direct or indirect, with alleged activities associated with their conduct."

It was evident Hamilton had prepared a statement on the flight from Washington to Zurich.

"Any records in the possession of the President of the United States regarding the alleged actuality of the Smiths are sealed under my nation's Presidential Secrecy Act and cannot be disclosed for fifty years.

"To ensure fairness and proper distribution of any estate assets, I am entering a motion to have these proceedings delayed until the statute of limitations expires in the year 2058. At that time, the Presidential documents can be unsealed and offered to the Liechtenstein Court of Justice by whoever is the President of the United States at that time."

"Motion denied, Mr. Hamilton. I believe fifty years is a bit too long a time. By then I will probably be retired from the bench and relaxing peacefully in a garden somewhere, preferably beside a blight-resistant chestnut tree. Continue Mr. Hamilton."

"The President of the United States has been in contact with German Chancellor Gretchen Mitsch who has informed our Chief of State that Mr. Schnabel is not to be trusted,"

Hamilton offered as he quickly shifted the discussion.

"Certainly not in a court of law, your honor. He has been paid millions of dollars as part of an arrangement he has made with the Berlin government to sell the names of German nationals who have been hiding money in the LGT Bank.

"We are prepared to offer evidence of this concordance, in addition to proof that he has stolen monies from the bank. He is also a fugitive from Spanish authorities."

"Mr. Hamilton," commented the judge. "Did it occur to you that I might already know of these events? Herr Schnabel is quite well known to this court as well as to the royal family. Thank you for your cooperation. I will have your remarks added to the objections."

While Hamilton sat down, the judge twisted his chair so he could face Hirsch directly. "Mr. Hirsch, did you file motions with any probate court regarding these last wills and testaments?"

It was patently clear Judge Schallenberger was looking for answers as close to infallibility as attainable. He was judicious enough to know that absolute truth didn't exist, but he still was making every effort to find it.

"No, your honor, I did not. Unfortunately, I was out of the state of Florida for several years and was never able to file a motion anywhere. When I returned to Florida, it was my conclusion it was best to leave the situation as it was. I lost track of the Smiths for two decades and did not hear about their assumed deaths until quite recently. I knew of no assets they had in the United States or Liechtenstein. Because I represented them and prepared their last wills and testaments, I knew there were no heirs. The documents now in your hands are true and accurate.

"Your honor, with your permission I would like to disclose information that might infringe on my attorney-client privilege as recognized in all courts of the United States. However, I feel compelled to inform the court for the sake of providing a level of respect to the Smiths."

"Mr. Hirsch," said the judge, "I will allow it as long as the information entered is part of the permanent record of these proceedings."

"That's quite acceptable, your honor. I would welcome that." Hirsch knew all testimony would be locked away forever. "With all due respect to my native country, its government and its citizens, I must reveal that Bobby and Timmy Smith served in Special Operations for the Central Intelligence Agency and Drug Enforcement Agency of the United States.

"I'm quite certain Mr. Johnston and Mr. Whitfield" – Hirsch aimed a finger toward the two feds sitting at the arced table – can confirm this. Part of their negotiations with the Smiths included the two being placed in the U.S. Marshal Service's Federal Witness Protection Program. Marshal Buggelshofer can attest to that.

"The Smiths were operatives for a number of years before they were forced by the agencies into providing intelligence that would lead to the arrest of some of their own friends and associates who may have been importing and selling narcotics.

"In the course of many conversations with the Smiths, they informed me that the CIA and DEA threatened to put them in prison permanently if they did not provide them with times, dates and places of alleged narcotics crimes.

"The agencies wanted to make major arrests because millions of dollars were involved. The drug seizures occurred in many places, including Colombia, Mexico, and Peru.

"One such seizure amounted to 207 million U.S. dollars. Bobby and Timmy Smith both told me the two agencies split the money from the confiscations and paid them, for informant services rendered, 25 percent of whatever was seized.

"The collusion included highly secretive written agreements that contained provisions that the money was tax free, judgment proof and could not be taken away by the U.S. government for any reason. So, their compensation on that one raid alone was almost $52 million. I dictated certain facts in my files about secret agreements between---"

"*Twenty-five percent? Did he say a quarter of all that money was given to informants? Objection, your honor!*" Rosselfellar came out with his tongue swinging. "*This is pure hearsay and completely unproven! There is no way any agency of the United States would enter into this kind of an agreement with anyone!*"

Liar, liar, pants on fire.

"Au contraire, Mr. Rosselfellar," intoned the judge, as he lay back in his chair. "I have heard of many instances where similar arrangements have been stipulated by your government. What Mr. Hirsch says sounds quite plausible.

"Also remember, Mr. Rosselfellar, hearsay, unlike in many U.S. courts, is allowed in this Court of Justice and any decisions made by me will be based on the preponderance of the evidence, including plausible hearsay.

"Mr. Hirsch, is there anything else you wish to say?" the judge asked.

"Yes, your honor. I dictated certain facts in my files, which I have with me, and documented them in the event something like this might happen. I spelled out exactly what was told to me by the Smiths and I can assure this court they received the 25 percent as previously stated.

"That percentage was quite common. Many of my legal clients received that very percentage from the same agencies to testify against their acquaintances.

"For any U.S. agency to walk in now and attempt to break the agreement they had with the Smiths is, in my opinion, another casualty of the War on Drugs and the considerable greed so often exhibited by overly ambitious bureaucracies.

"The Smiths informed me their contractual obligations with the American government provided that the monies earned through those arrangements could not be touched by any governmental entity. For any U.S. agent, let alone thirteen, to fly to Liechtenstein and attempt to extort the wills is beyond what any reasonable person would consider equitable justice."

"Mr. Hirsch. I think I've heard enough for now. Court is in recess for fifteen minutes," declared Judge Schallenberger. "We will pick up where Mr. Hirsch left off when we come back."

Once again, remember all testimony in this case is confidential and sealed."

The judge took another swat with his gavel as though he was trying to murder a pesky fly.

CHAPTER FIFTY

"The drug war has arguably been the single most devastating, dysfunctional, harmful social policy since slavery."

Norm Stamper, Former Seattle Chief of Police and author

15 Minutes Later - 11:45 AM (Liechtenstein Time), Monday, July 14, 2008

RECESS OVER

"Mr. Hirsch, were you through or is there something else you wish the court to know?" Judge Schallenberger wanted to hear the rest of Ari's testimony, if there was any. The feds and von Stülpnagel were unprepared for the additional damage Hirsch would bring to their case.

"There is your honor. I would like you to enter into the court records that I, too, have negotiated a plea arrangement with the U.S. government. Less than one week ago, specifically on Tuesday, July 8, the Department of Justice granted me complete lifetime immunity from criminal and civil charges for helping the current administration solve a major international crisis."

Hirsch wanted a judge of Schallenberger's standing to have knowledge about the agreement in the event he was needed. Despite the sealed records of the proceedings, there might be a way, if necessary, to utilize testimony of what had been said in the Liechtenstein courtroom.

"The legally binding correspondence is not only signed by the head of the Department of Justice but by the Chief Justice of the U.S. Supreme Court, the U.S. Attorney-General and the President of the United States.

"Additionally, my government has negotiated immunity pacts on my behalf with foreign countries, which may be involved with any litigation, including this and future cases.

"I have electronic copies of the documents in my PDA" – Hirsch waved his red BlackBerry – "and I will gladly present them as evidence to the court. In addition, I have hard copies of the same documents with me, as does my lawyer in Florida.

"Fraulein Fuchs may be able to download the documents directly to her printer or photocopy the papers if you wish to see them now."

Once again, the fair *fraulein* bounced her head up and down in concurrence.

The fed's heads were now in assorted, contorted positions. Smitherman and Underman shook theirs from side to side. Hutton was tapping on his own with the curve in his cane. Ianucci's and Rappaport's were falling backwards off their necks. Buggy had the left side of his placed on the table. Hands were clasped on the back of Rosselfellar and Hamilton's.

Bonnie Watts rested hers on the palm of her left hand as if to say, "Oh, shit." The eyelids in the rest of them were closed.

"I really do not mean to interrupt your testimony, Mr. Hirsch, but from what I have gathered thus far, it would not be necessary to produce the instruments you have with the United States government.

"I believe I have heard quite enough. I will accept as factual the Smiths had negotiated exotic immunity agreements with the U.S. government. Those contractual terms and conditions shall be binding upon this court.

"Gentlemen and Fraulein Watts." Judge Schallenberger remained quite placid as he spoke. "I don't know where you are heading with all of your objections. I sense each of you sitting in the courtroom has even more objections to offer the court. And yes, it is understandable why all of you oppose admitting these documents to probate. But for so many lawyers and government agents to protest with such hubris and anger concerns me.

"This simple petition to enter into probate two almost identical last wills and testaments prepared jointly under the supervision of Baron Rudfeld and Aristotle Hirsch leads me to caution you about one of the local rules of civil procedure in this court. We have not amended the rule in more than two-hundred years other than to incorporate the fact that we also recognize the rights of women to sit as judges in our legal system.

"Simply, it states that the Chief Judge of the Court of Justice, in his or her absolute and arbitrary discretion, can determine that if one party protests too much he or she can expedite probate matters by summarily denying all objections.

"On that basis, all objections and motions by the United States and its representatives are hereby denied. Fraulein Fuchs, please enter my decision into the official records. In addition, I am admitting the last wills and testaments into probate, subject to the originals being located and presented to this court, so it is ordered."

There was another sharp bang of the gavel that followed another loud outburst of voices.

"What? Are we to believe all of our objections are summarily denied because we objected too much?" Rosselfellar felt cheated, stymied, puzzled. "How can that possibly be your decision, your honor? There is no basis of law in that conclusion!"

Von Stülpnagel stood up as quickly as Rosselfellar sat down.

"Judge Schallenberger. I must invoke my right to speak in your court and strongly protest this decision. This would be considered a legal travesty in any judicial venue in Switzerland, and I am asking you as a man of honor to reconsider this verdict!"

Von Stülpnagel was grandstanding. This was his routine, a petulant posture he always demonstrated when things didn't go his way. What was he thinking? Hadn't he already been warned by the judge to maintain his composure?

"Herren Rosselfellar and von Stülpnagel. If I hear another gust of verbal wind, I will dismiss this hearing and put you both in a cell to help you gather your thoughts. It seems that both of you protest too much and in a terribly confrontational manner.

"Financial matters in Liechtenstein are intertwined with laws, banking institutions, politics and Principality custom. Apparently, Mr. Rosselfellar, you do not understand what Herr von Stülpnagel definitively should understand but doesn't.

"Those four elements give our small country a sense of independence and economic freedom. Our system of laws calls for expeditiously distributing assets from foundations and trusts to the proper decedents and then on to the identified beneficiaries.

"We believe we have a major advantage in international estate planning and banking. We prefer our method over predatory estate tax laws such as those practiced in your country.

"I have heard many sad stories about probate litigation in the U.S. with cases being drawn out for many years. That is unfair to the deceased and their beneficiaries. Although you are one of the most developed nations on earth, we view your legal and economic system differently than you do. It is not a question of right or wrong, merely different.

"I am almost astonished that Herr von Stülpnagel has not explained these dynamics to you."

"If you're saying we are being penalized because of incompetent counsel," said Hamilton, "then we will most certainly appeal your decision to a higher court."

"You may do so, Mr. Hamilton, but may I remind you that this court has never had a decision reversed. Appealed, yes. Overturned, no. Spend your country's money freely if you feel you must take that course of action.

"However, what I am about to read to you, sir, is a document that is one of the fundamentals of our judicial system. If you wish, you may have a copy to take with you so that you may learn from this experience.

"Once again, I am not sure why you were not provided with this information and guidance, but that is a question you must deal with. Please listen to my words.

"In Liechtenstein, this is the minimum standard of a claimant's conduct as noted in section number 192.035 of our legal statutes."

The Liechtenstein Minister of Justice (and/or any claimant proceeding in a similar capacity) is the representative not of an ordinary party to a controversy, but of a sovereignty whose obligation to govern impartially is as compelling as its obligation to govern at all; and whose interest, therefore, in a criminal or civil prosecution is not that it shall win a case, but that justice shall be done. As such, he or she is in a peculiar and very definite sense the servant of the laws of the Principality of Liechtenstein, the twofold aim of which is that guilt shall not escape, or innocence suffer. He may prosecute with earnestness and vigor – indeed, he or she should do so. But while he or she may strike hard blows, he or she is not at liberty to strike foul ones. It is as much the judge's duty to refrain from improper methods calculated to produce a wrongful conviction or result as it is to use every legitimate means to bring about a just one. Thus, if any of the claimants' conduct in proceedings before the Court of Justice falls below this standard, then and in that event, they shall be required to pay a 5 percent judiciary fee on the amount of their claims, or, as adjusted upward by the Chief Justice of the Court of Justice, and in no event to exceed 50 percent of the total amount claimed based upon the act or acts of impropriety which fall below this standard of conduct."

After a few seconds, the justice said, "If there are no questions, we will continue. Mr. do you have any further motions?"

"Yes, your honor," Rosselfellar uttered with a certain disdain reflected on his face. "First, I want to thank the court for admitting the last wills and testaments under the probate laws of Liechtenstein. As such, we would now like to accelerate matters accordingly and move the proceedings into the Liechtenstein civil rules of procedure providing for prompt probate.

"That percentage represents withholding taxes on all funds revealed in the course of this proceeding and is within our purview to seize valuables of all American taxpayers pursuant to the jeopardy assessment provisions of the Internal Revenue Code.

"On behalf of the DEA, the FBI, Customs, and the CIA, I am requesting the court to accept the filing of a notice of interest in the proceeds of the estates of Bobby and Timmy Smith. These are separate claims and will be documented if the court grants the request."

Without the slightest flinch, Judge Schallenberger exhorted, "Your objections and motions are hereby denied under the Liechtenstein local rule of probate which ensures expediency for decedents and their loved ones via the rapid location and distribution of assets within the Principality of Liechtenstein."

"Surely you can see your way clear," Rosselfellar pleaded, "to allow us to discuss the amounts of money the United States Treasury and its agencies should be allowed to post if we determine that we have enough evidence to bring a lawsuit in an effort to collect our fair share."

Rosselfellar had paid attention to Judge Schallenberger's description of the appeals process, a copy of which he was now holding.

"Perhaps I incorrectly assumed you were not willing to deposit millions of U.S. dollars with the court in hopes of winning a filing of interest. If that is the case, let me officially withdraw my denial and give you time to determine what that amount might be based on the worth of the Smiths' assets, if any, in the LGT Bank."

"Do you have any additional items, Baron Rudfeld?" asked the judge.

"Yes, your honor. I have a motion to appoint Aristotle Einshtein Hirsch as personal representative of the estates of the Smiths and afforded all of the rights and powers associated with that legal position under the laws and jurisdiction of the independent country of Liechtenstein."

"Motion granted. Mr. Hirsch is hereby appointed personal representative. Please record that, Fraulein Fuchs."

"Yes, your honor."

Wow, she could speak.

"I would also ask the court not to require any bond." The Baron kept firing his pleadings.

"Motion granted."

"Objection your honor" said the Zurich attorney. "Liechtenstein's laws provide for the issuance of a bond to ensure the beneficiaries that the personal representative will not do something improper."

"Herr von Stülpnagel. It would be an unnecessary expense. I am familiar with Baron Rudfeld and the manner in which he governs financial matters on behalf of his clients. There is no one in Liechtenstein, this court believes, who is more trustworthy with large amounts of money.

"I will neither embarrass nor insult the ethics of the Baron or the personal representative with this matter. Objection overruled. Let's move on."

The courtroom fell silent. No more motions. No more objections. The one thing remaining was for Bernhard to arrange with the LGT Bank, under court order, to allow the inspection of the safe deposit boxes in the names of Bobby Smith and Timmy Smith.

"You will all meet at the LGT Bank at 5:00 PM," commanded the judge. "This will give the United States legal team the ability to determine the approximate amount of money it will need to deposit.

"After the authoritative count and currency conversions completed by a bank officer, we will arrive at an official number of U.S. dollars to be turned over to the Court of Justice to pursue your claims. I am also issuing a court order allowing both sides to witness the computations in the LGT Bank vault.

"In the meantime, all of you must be hungry. There are some charming eating establishments within walking distance, which the Clerk of Court's office can direct you to.

"You might want to *ess und fress* at the Restaurant Torkel. Try the filet goulash Stroganoff in Riesling sauce accompanied by one of our local sparkling wines. You won't be disappointed.

"In any event, please be at the bank at 12 Herrengasse, a short walk from the restaurant. Please be on time. I can assure you they will definitely be counting the assets either with you or without you.

"Court adjourned," said Judge Schallenberger as he once again thrust his gavel onto a round piece of wood. Everyone filed out of the room in less than a minute. Except for Rosselfellar. He couldn't believe he lost this part of the case. He needed some personal time to recover.

"I'll see you at the bank," he said to the others. "I'm in no mood to eat."

While the DOJ attorney fell into a giant funk, Schnabel and Hirsch put on their uniforms of the day which had been stowed in the court clerk's office. Yes, they were still dressing for the occasion.

They left the courthouse in the same outfits they had donned when they entered.

So, what if they felt like Emmett Kelley. Hadn't they just finished battling a bunch of clowns?

CHAPTER FIFTY-ONE

"...We are now in the twenty-first century. Perhaps we should have better reasons for depriving our neighbors of their liberty at gunpoint. Given the magnitude of the real problems that confront us terrorism, nuclear proliferation, the spread of infectious disease, failing infrastructure, lack of adequate funds for education and health care, etc. our war on sin is so outrageously unwise as to almost defy rational comment..."

Sam Harris, award-winning American author and philosopher

4 Hours and 41 Minutes Later-5:01 PM (Liechtenstein Time), Monday, July 14, 2008

BANK SHOT

The crowds of protestors had dissipated. They had met the objectives of having their opinions known and their voices heard. By early afternoon the leaders of the demonstration knew that attempting to get any information or a ruling on the case was elusive at best and hopeless at worst.

Everyone disappeared except for several diehards, and the streets of Vaduz were back to normal pedestrian and car traffic.

Almost.

Members of the media thought they could still dig out some answers and refused to give up their pugnacious efforts to "get the bank secrecy story at all costs."

This was especially true of the photographers and TV personnel who attacked with their cameras and bright lights. Without conscience, they followed the Task Force members, attorneys, Schnabel, and Hirsch like stalkers of Hollywood stars, sticking lenses in their faces and jostling them for interviews. Even CNN, ABC, CBS, and the rest of the American electronic media outlets had become dependent on paparazzi-like tactics. CNBC, Fox Business Channel, Al Jazeera, and other news organizations sent special bloodhounds dressed like humans to cover what they thought was an electrifying story. For them it meant viewership and readership; the more the viewers, the more the readers, the more the money would flow into the media conglomerates' strongboxes. Yes, it was always about the money.

The thirteen members of the U.S. Task Force, von Stülpnagel, Bernhard the bailiff, Fraulein Fuchs, the Baron, Hirsch, and Schnabel arrived at the bank at 4:55 PM and had attempted to open the door. It was locked and as stiff as its three bolts of steel keeping it closed. The coterie of news-hungry reporters joined the nineteen people peering into the glass windows and front doors of the LGT Bank. By now, the journalists had become angry, pushing their way through the feds, their attorney, and the court personnel.

They were attempting to spot anyone on the inside who might feed their gluttonous appetites for the "story" even if it meant shoving, kicking or screaming.

Some used their hands as blinders to keep out the glare of the sun to get a better view, and some used them to toss aside anyone in their way. The lights inside the bank were on but it was still difficult to get a glimpse of anyone.

Nobody was talking to anybody, and anybody was talking to nobody.

It was a few minutes later when the bedlam temporarily ceased.

At one minute past five o'clock one pair of armed security guards dressed in open-collared white, short-sleeve shirts and blue pants arrived at the interior lobby. In addition to their nametags and silver badges, they were wearing the embroidered logo patch of the bank on both sleeves; a simple gold crown and LGT spelled out in white letters against a diamond-shaped blue background.

At six-foot-three and dirty brown hair, one sentry looked like Arnold Schwarzenegger on steroids. His shirt had to be custom-made since the circumference of his arms wouldn't fit into off-the-rack armholes.

The other, at about five feet ten inches and weighing a hundred and twenty, could have been the recipient of the current Mr. Bulimia Contest.

"Conan the Barbarian" unlocked and opened the inside glass door and left "Mr. Matchstick" alone in the lobby. The hulk locked the inside door behind him and stepped into the vestibule between the inside and outside doors and unlocked the one leading to the street.

He opened it about one-quarter of the way and spoke. "*Guten tag*! Gut efternoon. May I halp you?"

"*Jawohl*. Yes. Vern't you expectink us, Engelbert?" yelled Bernhard from the back of the crowd. His big buddy was all booster and no payload.

"Yah, but I vasn't shurr it vas so menny menschen."

"Zere are nineteen auf uss," Bernhard answered, then motioned to Ari to walk to the front of the line. "Zis iss ze gentleman who hass propper identifikashun. Herr Hirsch, zis iss Engelbert."

Before anyone said anything else, the human giant motioned to the press corps to keep their distance. "*Achtung*! Kip avay frohm zees place! All auf you. Beck upp!" From sheer fright, the media obeyed. At this juncture, discretion was definitely the better part of valor. Besides, who wanted to deal with a Liechtenstein weightlifter?

"May I haf you kommen inside, Herr Hirsch? The rest auf you pleece vait heah."

Engelbert locked the outside door behind him so that both he and Hirsch were sandwiched between the set of entrances. On the wall was a ten-inch-by-ten-inch keypad with an aluminum cover, which the officer lifted from its bottom.

"Pleece poot your right hant flett, Herr Hirsch."

Ari put his right hand flat against the pad and less than ten seconds later Engelbert told him to remove it.

When the green light atop the fingerprint and palm print decoder flashed and the electronic instrument rang a pleasant-sounding, low-level "bing" the muscular chaperone reopened the inner door and walked inside with Hirsch. "Mr. Big" told his junior partner to let the "menschen" in one at a time and to make sure to lock the front door every time he let another one through. "Unt do nawt let ze *meshugganah* – crazy – media inside!"

"Mr. Toothpick" did as he was told and thwarted any improper entry.

Engelbert grabbed a board with a computer printout under its clip. As each person walked in, he enunciated, "*Namen, bitte*. Name, please."

"Whoever speaks this language should have their throats cut," E.F. said to Buggelshofer. "I can't stand the sound. It's scratchy and ugly."

"Exactly like you," snapped Buggy. "You're another Wazinski. Wanna join him?"

As the guard marked off their names, they were asked to wait in the reception area next to a small security desk. When everyone was through identifying themselves, he asked the crowd to follow him.

The string bean sentinel broke off from the single-line formation, walked over to a fingerprint pad on the wall next to another door, got the emerald signal, and entered. Other than Engelbert, no one knew he was resetting the alarm system for the entire building.

The herd walked past a long wall hiding three teller windows from view and headed straight for the one elevator that would take them to the basement. There was another fingerprint identifier above the "down" button where Engelbert stuck his right paw.

The stainless-steel doors split in half and hid themselves between the cab and the side walls.

The lift was too small for everyone to get on at once, something the feds had gotten used to at the Zurich hostel. They split into three groups of seven and took the one-flight journey down into the bowels of the building. "Big Foot" plus a party of six were the first to go down.

Upon arrival, they stepped off and waited for the other two groups. Engelbert made certain the pretzel-rod cop stayed upstairs until the final descent. A fingerprint profile was needed every time the elevator needed to be opened and he was the only one left who could play Ali Baba and babble "open sesame."

All twenty-one people marched in unison down a dimly lit hallway at the end of which was a steel door with more electronic security gizmos than Tel Aviv's Ben-Gurion Airport.

"Herr Hirsch. Ve neet your right hant vunce again." Ari put his hand on the high-tech pad and on came the light and the soft ringtone.

He would learn later the bank had scanned his prints from the original documents and had them transferred digitally so he could return to the bank without a glitch. Here he was, twenty years later, evidence enough that whatever method they used worked.

As the door opened wide, so did their mouths. They were looking at the largest, most behemoth vault they had ever witnessed. Movies didn't have them this big! The private polizei, the Baron, Schnabel, Ari and Bernhard had all seen it before, but to the thirteen feds, Fraulein Fuchs and von Stülpnagel it was an amazing sight.

Solid, twelve-inch-thick steel doors protected the vault entrance. Each was seven meters across and eight meters high. Both had four, three-movement electronic time locks, heavy fastening bars on the inside, and flawlessly slick, wheel-shaped opening mechanisms that outsized the helm on a supertanker. The depth of the vault – it was in effect a fortress – was eighteen meters and the width was fourteen, making the space more than twenty-two hundred square feet.

Safe deposit boxes were precisely arranged from floor to ceiling along each wall. There was a metal ladder on wheels with a large platform on top to enable someone to reach the highest row. Hundreds and hundreds of different boxes – from small to the jumbo economy size-that held everything from – well, who even knew except the people who rented them?

The entire vault was encased in sixteen-inch cement that could withstand seven-thousand pounds per-square-inch of pressure and had been reinforced with crosshatched, one-inch-diameter iron rebar, making the sealed chamber practically impenetrable. Even a rocket-propelled grenade would hardly make a dent in this monster of all money tombs.

There was a noticeable absence of photographic devices. "Kameras ahr *verboten*!" Engelbert exclaimed when the group first walked into the bank. Neither did LGT have any installed anywhere in the building.

If the institution wanted its patrons to believe in its total confidentiality and cautious discretion the bank claimed it exercised, there would be no capability of exposing sensitive information. That included photographs taken remotely or by an individual. Off to one side of the massive room was a small, secure conference room. It was almost always used by LGT's clients to open their deposit boxes in complete privacy, and big enough to hold a four-foot-by-eight-foot table. However, there were only four chairs. One was already taken by the bank treasurer, Wolfgang Eckhard, who reported directly to a member of the royal family. The stodgy codger had worked at LGT for forty-eight years and had been employed by the bank, including all of its branches worldwide, longer than any other worker.

"*Wilkommen* to LGT. Yes, I have been expecting all of you since I received a call earlier today from Bernhard. Also, Judge Schallenberger's clerk sent over the court orders, and we are now prepared to begin and complete the audit.

"Which one of you is Aristotle Hirsch?"

"That would be me." He walked over to Eckhard and shook hands. "Pleased to meet you, Herr Eckhard."

"Herr Hirsch, you do not remember meeting me twenty years ago?"

"Yes, I remember seeing you in the bank a couple of times. I am happy to see you again. I'm sorry I didn't remember you on first sight, Herr Eckhard. But now that I see you a bit closer, I do recall meeting you. It was so long ago, and I guess we have all changed somewhat. Nevertheless, it is wonderful to be back in Liechtenstein. I have never seen it more beautiful and the food at Restaurant Torkel is even better than before."

"When will this guy get on with the goddamn counting?" Wilson whispered to Underman, his IRS colleague. "This isn't a social occasion."

"What the fuck is wrong with Hirsch? His small talk is making me nuts! We won't get a count for a week if he keeps this up!" Johnston from CIA was engaged in extra-quiet conversation with Ianucci from State.

"Relax," Ianucci hissed. "It won't take much longer. We don't even know if there's anything in the boxes."

"Shall we proceed, Herr Hirsch?"

"Yes, I think this would be a good time to do so." Ari didn't want to rush him, mostly because he liked Eckhard and he didn't give a squat if he made the feds wait. Besides, it gave him a little more time to look at the near-perfect legs of Fraulein Fuchs.

"I have reviewed the list of boxes attached to the foundations and trusts that have been placed in the names of Bobby Smith and Timmy Smith. Earlier this afternoon, the Court of Justice sent LGT the order to do so.

"Our procedure to inspect the boxes is quite simple. Engelbert and his compatriot will bring one box at a time from the vault into the room.

"Herr Hirsch, as the Executor and personal representative, you may take this spare owner's key and authorize our security guards to access the correct boxes. It will be my responsibility, with the help of Bernhard, to make sure all the contents of each box are totaled correctly.

"If they are documents, they will be read aloud by Baron Rudfeld or Herr Hirsch. If they are financial instruments, we will identify them as such and carefully arrive at a sum for each of the boxes. If the assets are liquid and in the form of currency, we will identify the market value and ascertain their worth. We shall keep a running total as we progress through each container.

"Are there any questions?"

Everybody looked at one another with blank stares.

"Excuse me. May I sit down on one of the seats? It's been a very difficult journey for me." Hutton was truly fatigued, as was Buggy.

"But of course," Eckhard said politely.

"You may take a seat as well," he suggested as he glanced at Buggelshofer's noticeable weariness. Eckhard could easily show empathy with the older folks in the group.

"If you like, I can have one of the guards bring all of us some coffee. I suspect this might take a longer time than anticipated. There are twenty-seven boxes in the joint names of Bobby and Timmy Smith, and each is quite large and quite heavy."

"Twenty-seven boxes? Did you say twenty-seven boxes?"

"Yes, Herr, uh Herr--- excuse me, but what is your name?"

"Robert Fenwick Buggelshofer, but you can call me Buggy, Mr. Eckhard."

This was going to be a long night for everyone.

CHAPTER FIFTY-TWO

"Despite decades of warfare, every single proponent of the War on Drugs-bar none-admits that that war has failed to attain its purported goal-a 'drug-free' society. The best proof of this, of course, is that every proponent of the war wants it continued. If the war had been won, they would be calling for its end."

Jacob G. Hornberger, American journalist,
Founder/President of the Future of Freedom Foundation

30 Minutes Later - 5:31 PM (Liechtenstein Time), Monday, July 14, 2008

COUNTDOWN

Engelbert was almost as big a lug as the first metal container he and his scrawny subordinate dragged into the conference room.

Other than Buggy, E.F., Bernhard and Eckhard, everyone was standing. The guards had located box number 3436 at the very top of the right-hand wall. After unlocking it with the master and owners' keys, it took both men to yank it out of its rectangular hole, bring it down the steps, load it onto a dolly, and roll it to the conference room.

Herr Eckhard and Bernhard were sitting at the table when the IRS's Underman pointedly asked the banker, "When's the last time you saw the Smiths, Herr Eckhard?"

In an authoritative voice, the Baron interjected, "That is an extremely inappropriate question! You should know by now that is off limits. We all know why we are here, and it is not to locate Bobby and Timmy Smith. No more questions, please, unless they pertain to the immediate task."

Would that shut him up?

"Baron Rudfeld, you are not the judge and cannot tell me what I can and cannot say!" Underman wasn't buying it. It didn't shut him up.

"Bernhard," invoked the Baron, "please place a call to Judge Schallenberger and tell him what has transpired. We will need to have Mr. Underman removed from this process."

"Okay, okay. Call off the cops. We'll stop the questions. But that doesn't mean we won't pursue what's in our best interests." Underman was insistent upon getting in the last word.

He failed.

"Mr. Underman. You are now in Liechtenstein. Based upon your insufferable behavior and sanctimonious attitude, it will be most beneficial that you will soon be out of our country.

"Please do not believe for a single moment that while you are still here you will not be held liable for your lack of respect for our legal judgments and our sovereignty.

"Even though you were granted diplomatic status upon entering Switzerland, you do not have that standing in Liechtenstein. Do not assume you have license to speak as you please. You will pay dearly."

The different coins from different countries with different designs and different denominations were – well, different. Astonishingly different. From 1842 U.S. ten-dollar Liberty Heads to 1910 British Sovereigns with the likeness of King George V on the front and the mythical Saint George slaying the dragon on the flipside.

From Swiss, twenty-franc coins minted between 1897 and 1949, to Tonga's 1962 Queen Salote Pa'Anga with the island nation's coat of arms engraved on its back.

There were more species of meter money than any of them thought possible. There were enough coins from the C-section alone – Chad, Colombia, Cayman Islands, Costa Rica, Cyprus, Cuba, Canada, China – to make Long John Silver wish he'd changed his last name to Goldman. It was a lot more than your average pirate's booty. Indeed, it was in the millions of U.S. dollars.

The B-hive was also well represented – coins from Belize, Bhutan, Bolivia, Bermuda, Brazil, Brunei – even Byzantium – were part of the Smith boys' collection. By the time they got through all twenty-six letters of the English alphabet and the box was empty, more than three hours had passed. By then, a couple of the piles listed like miniature equivalents of the Leaning Tower of Pisa.

Eckhard carefully looked up the current market value of each of the coins on the Internet. Some of them were so rare that it took more than a cursory search of one or two websites, but numismatist catalogues as well. By the time the prices were hunted down, and the math was done to get the approximate total value of the contents, the feds were ready to throw in the towel.

"Are we out of our minds? Let's get out of here and come back tomorrow! At this pace, it's gonna take three more days to finish! Doesn't this guy know how to use a computer spreadsheet?"

Johnston was quietly complaining to the DEA's Whitfield.

Johnston almost always underestimated timing. The fact was it would take more than four additional days to finish the job even though Eckhard had been writing and calculating as fast as an automaton. Yes, the old gent knew how to use Microsoft Excel, but his do-it-by-hand method was seemingly as accurate and faster.

"That's it," said Rosselfellar when the clock hit 9:00 PM, "we're outta here. Mr. Eckhard, thank you for your services, but we're leaving. Our attorney, Mr. von Stülpnagel, will check with the court tomorrow to find out what the time frame will be to complete the inventory."

"Yes, that will be fine. The first box is usually the most difficult. You might like to wait until we open the second one. You never know what we might find."

"That won't be necessary. I'm sure whatever you find will be accounted for," Rosselfellar countered.

Finally, an official from the U.S. government had a sense of trust. Rosselfellar looked at Bonnie Watts. "Is our driver outside?"

"How the hell would I know?"

"Because that was your responsibility."

"What? Where did you get that from?"

"You found him. You lost him. You get him!"

Watts asked Engelbert to escort her to the outside of the building and walk her to the courthouse, which was where she last saw the yellow wonder bus.

The media provocateurs were still there pressing for any information they could wring out of their quarry, and Watts felt the full fury of their tenacity. Microphones, cameras, and a non-stop barrage of questions were hurled at her. She had been through this kind of situation many times, and she acted like a pro by not uttering a word or even stopping.

In German and in the name of "national security" Engelbert threatened to have the reporters arrested by the few military police officers who were still patrolling the streets. The reporters held their positions and didn't move as Watts and her security guard walked to the courthouse.

The Customs head couldn't help but spot the yummy-colored jitney on the now, near-quiet street leading to the Court of Justice. There she found Fethawi inside sleeping in the aisle.

She awakened him, had him drive to the bank with her and the Liechtenstein leviathan on board, broke through the shutterbugs and interviewers, and re-entered the bank with Engelbert's fingerprints. Watts made her way down to the basement where she announced, "Get your asses on the jitney 'cause we're heading back to Zurich." They complied, but not before their successful push through the line of reporters.

"Ari, let me take you and Herr Schnabel back to my home." The Baron used his cell phone to reach Helmut, the chauffeur, who had hours ago driven back to the estate. He had anticipated the call and arrived at the bank twenty minutes later.

"Fraulein Fuchs, may we drive you home?" asked the Baron.

"That would be delightful, Herr Rudfeld, but I need to stay until I get someone to fill in for me. *Danke schön.*"

Schnabel was more disappointed than the *fraulein*. He couldn't keep his eyes off her. He felt nothing but lust.

The Baron turned to Ari. "This financial reporting, I'm afraid, will not be finished until Friday evening. I believe we should leave now. I will come back tomorrow and exercise due diligence to make sure the accounting is correct."

The three men headed out of the bank and didn't even give the gaggle of correspondents a polite "no comment." Besides, Schnabel and Hirsch had once again put on their costumes and walked right past them. Now thinking that the case had been ended and no information would be forthcoming, the journalists headed back to their hotel rooms in Vaduz and Zurich. In the morning, the Baron went back to LGT to continue monitoring the coin count while Ari and Schnabel stayed back at the castle for fear of being recognized in and around Vaduz.

Even though he had been given clearance by the royal family to travel to and within Liechtenstein, Schnabel was taking no chances of being scrutinized by anyone who he thought might have less than virtuous intentions.

Some of those people, he knew, were out there. Even at that very moment. His assessment, he thought, might well be correct.

By this time Herr Eckhard brought in bookkeeping replacements for him and Bernhard, there was a changing of the guards, a fresh court reporter substituted for Fraulein Fuchs, and the counting didn't stop until late Friday evening.

The final number was mind blowing.

CHAPTER FIFTY-THREE

"The government was set to protect man from criminals-and the Constitution was written to protect man from the government."

Ayn Rand, Russian-American writer and philosopher

4 Days and 5 Hours Later - 10:01 PM (Liechtenstein Time), Friday, July 18, 2008

JUDGMENT DAY

None of the feds had any desire to go back to the bank prior to the end point. They knew it would be a frustrating exercise. They stayed in Zurich and bitched about everything-their accommodations, food, service, and language.

"Too damn guttural for me," said Ianucci of State whose Italian ancestors spoke a romance tongue that sounded nothing like the harsh sounds of German.

The Baron had kept a close watch over the tabulations and had visited the bank for two hours at a time, twice daily, since the count began.

In addition to the financial inventory, he wanted to know if the original last wills and testaments had been located. He would have been relieved if Eckhard had found them and knew it would be close to the end of the line for the opposition.

Once the counting was completed all parties to the case were notified by Bernhard who requested them to immediately report to the bank. Upon arrival, Engelbert met them at the front door and escorted them to the counting room.

The entire original cast was now in the room, with Buggy and E.F. again laying claim to the two empty seats at the table which by now was clear except for a few papers strewn about.

The safe deposit boxes had been carefully returned to their cubbyholes and locked. Everyone anxiously awaited Herr Eckhard's report, as the court had mandated, and the final number of the mother lode.

"Ladies and gentlemen," offered Eckhard, "before I give you our final report, I have come across two documents and an envelope. It is a shame you did not stay Monday evening because I located last wills and testaments of both Bobby Smith and Timmy Smith in the second receptacle we opened.

"Yes, the wills are authentic and contain the signatures and seals as required for probate in Liechtenstein."

"Shit! We can't catch a fucking break!" Those words, spoken aloud by IRS Commissioner Wilson Brown, were cacophonous. Even though the discovery of the wills was expected, Brown couldn't bear the thought of not having every piece of ammunition in his agency's arsenal.

"Herr Brown," said the Baron. "If that kind of speech and indignities continue, we will have you removed from these proceedings. I perceive that the Internal Revenue Service might be upset by the facts, but that does not grant you the right to recite such vulgarities.

"Your behavior is even worse than Mr. Underman's. If this is the way your agents conduct your audits and inquiries in your country, I feel quite embarrassed for the American taxpayer and the guarantees provided by the United States Constitution." Hirsch could unwaveringly support the Baron's perception. As a former IRS Special Agent, he was aware of the agency's abuse. It froze bank accounts and assets even before its human pigeons knew about an agency investigation and compounded its defilement by charging usurious interest and outlandish financial penalties.

Brown wasn't used to that kind of comeback. He was a bully to the bone and enjoyed the power he had, and used, to push people around until they succumbed to government clout. He was the kingfish of hostility and belligerence, the kind of qualities that served him well during his tenure as an IRS functionary working his way to the top. But now he was in a different spot and had as much power as a marathon runner with a pair of hamstrings and a collapsed lung. His race for the gold was now filled with more hurdles than he could jump, despite his high-steppin' nastiness.

"We have worked very hard all week to get to this point and I would like to move on," Eckhard affirmed. "Please save your arguments for Judge Schallenberger.

"The final figure we have based on the market value of the contents of the twenty-seven safe deposit boxes is approximately $240 million U.S. I say 'approximately' because as you know gold coins and platinum ingots and bullion vary in price every minute of every day.

"Yes, in addition to the tremendous amount of gold coins from almost every country that ever minted them, the Smiths also had thousands of ounces of platinum, which as you know is almost always priced higher than gold because of its scarcity."

"Two hundred and forty million dollars? Are you serious, Herr Eckhard? Are you sure you haven't made an error?" To Addison Hamilton, as well as almost everyone else in the room that figure was virtually incomprehensible particularly because almost all of it came from the 25-percent-of-the-profits pact the Smiths had made with the feds for drug-bust information.

"No, Herr Hamilton. No mistakes. However, I have one more item to discuss. We came across a large, sealed envelope addressed to Ari

Hirsch. We have left it unopened. If there is a document inside, Herr Hirsch must read it aloud as per the court's order. Herr Hirsch, would you please open the package?"

Hirsch walked over to Eckhard who handed him the envelope. He carefully unsealed the flap and removed a single sheet of plain white paper which appeared to be a letter. It had been cleanly typed on what might have been an IBM Selectric. Ari began to read loud enough for everyone to hear.

November 17, 1988

Dear Ari...

Other than what's in our last wills and testaments, we wanted to make sure that if you never heard from or saw us again, you'd know how much we've despaired over the ruinous War on Drugs...a war that's as devastating and ugly as any conflict our nation has ever fought. If we're no longer on this good earth by the time you read this, we want you to utilize whatever assets we have to fight this horrendous U.S. policy that has taken the lives, possessions and souls of so many of our fellow Americans.

It's bad enough that armed conflicts have taken their massive toll.

This drug war doesn't have to continue at the hands of our own government. Whatever you can do to lessen the injustices of what is supposed to be a just system then Bobby and I will at last be at peace.

Despite our constant travails, we love our country deeply, and as you know, we almost gave our lives any number of times to defend what we thought was worth saving. Yes, we made some mistakes along the way that we'll always pay for. But what we also did was create lifetime bonds with our military buddies who were sent into a very ugly conflict.

We both knew that one day you'd be standing in the vault of the LGT Bank making sure our worldly assets are safe, and our wishes fulfilled. The one person we could always count on was you, Ari. You were the only one who would and could understand why we lived the way we did, the one person we knew who was non-judgmental. We've never had a better friend. I once read somewhere that someone who finds a true friend discovers treasure. And to Bobby and me, you were worth much more than all the gold and platinum you've found.

The two of us lived every moment like it was our last, and oftentimes we thought it was. The hellishness of Vietnam, the work in Air America, the dangerous transportation of goods around the world through the Panama Canal and the waters of the Pacific and Atlantic Oceans-any of it could have claimed our existence.

Bobby and I survived in an impossible-to-understand way since we were kids. They weren't the kinds of childhoods we would wish for anybody, but we stayed alive knowing we'd have a hell of a run. We did. Now it's up to you to finish the race and help bring an end to the drug war. We've left enough money to put up one hell of a fight.

You knew our souls and we knew you cared about us, something we never experienced with anyone else other than Bobby and I taking care of one another. That was all we had, Ari. Sure, there were material things, partying with crazy women like Debbie and Lana, girlfriends all over the map but they never knew what Bobby and I truly felt. You did.

If you bump into Nunu and Dudu, please say "hi" for us. And make sure you use the money to battle for what we all know is the right cause. Sometimes, the good guys win. We love you, brother. See you on the other side.

Timmy Smith
Timmy Smith

P.S. Inside this envelope are two cases. One is mine and one is Bobby's, and both contain the same things. Please remember we're only a couple of guys who wanted to do the right thing, and we're not heroes. The contents of what's inside are yours now. Keep them safe. We want you to have them to remember us by. God bless.

Everyone in the room was as silent as faded memories. Tears slowly trickled from Ari's eyes as he read the letter. He removed and opened the two, clear plastic containers inside the manila envelope. One had "Timmy Smith" written with a black felt-tip pen on the outside, and on the other "Bobby Smith."

Inside each was a Purple Heart with oak clusters indicating both men had been wounded several times during combat. There were two additional medals, Silver Stars, the third highest military decoration in the U.S. Armed Forces awarded for valor in the face of the enemy.

Ari held up the medals for all to see. Every fed in the room now knew the Smiths were honored by their country for their gallantry in action. Yes, the recipients had distinguished themselves not by being drug traffickers or making deals with government bureaucrats, but by showing veritable, verifiable, and extraordinary heroism during the war in Vietnam. The agents were quiet, restrained, and noiseless, dumbstruck and non-communicative all. Buggy and E.F. got large lumps in their throats and could barely swallow. They and a few others choked up and bowed their heads in what appeared to be humble embarrassment.

There were a full two minutes of nothingness except for the people in that room who had to think their own thoughts and live with their own decisions of how they sought their own brands of redress.

Neither Bobby nor Timmy had ever shown their medals to anyone. Ari knew if they had, he would have already seen them. He surmised they thought that would have been too boastful, too self-aggrandizing, simply too foreign for them to have done.

"No," Ari thought, "you don't have to display your medals on your chest to be heroes. You simply have to think great thoughts and do things you thought you would never be able to do."

Baron Rudfeld broke the prolonged silence with an unshakable sense of finality. "This matter is concluded."

Not so fast, Baron, not so fast. What a shame you couldn't read Schnabel's mind.

CHAPTER FIFTY-FOUR

"The makers of our Constitution undertook to secure conditions favorable to the pursuit of happiness... They sought to protect Americans in their beliefs, their thoughts, their emotions, and their sensations. They conferred, as against the government, the right to be let alone-the most comprehensive of the rights and the right most valued by civilized men."

Louis D. Brandeis, U.S. Supreme Court Associate Justice
(1916-1939)

32 Minutes Later - 10:33 PM (Liechtenstein Time), Friday, July 18, 2008

DON'T COUNT YOUR CHICKENS

"All of you! Lie down on the floor! And don't make me tell you a second time or you will die from a bullet in your head!" screamed someone through the multiple holes of a black, fiberglass hockey mask as soon as the Baron said "concluded."

The camouflaged man was standing in the doorway of the conference room brandishing what looked like a serious killing instrument. It was an IMI Tavor TAR-21, an Israeli-built, fashionably sleek assault weapon that could wipe out everyone in the counting room in nanoseconds.

"Do it now! Now! Now! Get down, now!" The agitation in his voice became extreme as fear filled the room faster than a fire hose filling a two-gallon bucket.

No one believed he was being insincere, and no one was willing to test his mettle or doggedness. He took the barrel end of his weapon and jammed it hard and mean into Engelbert's ribs. As the security guard let out a loud moan and slumped to the floor on his back, his captor's voice became more and more intense.

"If you move even one eyelid you will never have children," he screeched as he aimed the rifle at the guard's groin, then sadistically kicked him in his right kidney and motioned to him to turn over on his belly.

If there was any hint of a hoax, it was undetectable.

Everyone fell to the ground faster than the flapping of a hummingbird's wings. Space was sparse, so much so that arms and legs intertwined and overlapped. Buggy and Hutton wound up under the table. Fraulein Fuchs lay next to Schnabel, tilting her head away from his face so she wouldn't have to inhale his wretched breath.

What started out to be serious international banking business wasn't over. Not by a long shot or a gun shot. And it would get a lot more threatening and menacing before the clock struck midnight.

To a person, each asked themselves if he or she was going to die from a high-caliber bullet to the head or perhaps two or three in the back.

As they lay there, three more men entered the room. Each was dressed head-to-toe in the same black uniform-pants, belts, long-sleeve turtlenecks, gloves, athletic shoes, socks, and goaltender facial protectors. They could have easily been hosts at a Johnny Cash memorial service. Especially if their prisoners could remember the words so they could sing *Help Me Make It Through The Night*.

The three additional men also carried the same type of weapon as the first invader. A 21st century innovation, the Tavors were equipped with normal metal sights plus an advanced red-dot reflex sight. It was the latest in Israeli military technology and included night-vision systems and a myriad of electronic devices.

These guys weren't exactly playing Cowboys and Indians. They were as serious as armed robbers got and were as professional as any legion of warriors. They probably could have given Lee Harvey Oswald a few lessons in not getting identified or caught.

As focused and as experienced as the feds and bank employees had been about security, somehow the foursome had made their way into the bank totally undetected.

And it marked the first time in Liechtenstein banking history that one of its financial institutions was invaded by a marauding group of armed bandits or even worse – human liquidators.

"These people must be from somewhere in eastern Europe," the Baron thought to himself after hearing the few words shouted by the first gunman. "They're either Czechs, Romanians, Hungarians, or perhaps Bulgarians." Because of his vast legal experience, friends, and decades of traveling throughout Europe, plus his linguistic talents, his ears were fine-tuned to various accents, especially those throughout the continent.

But their origination was yet to be determined. He hadn't heard a single word from anyone other than the head of the black-clad pack.

The trio of men who followed the leader into the room each had ten pairs of plastic handcuffs. Extras in case they were needed. As the head hood stood sentry the three others easily slipped the cuffs onto the wrists of everyone, who by this time were flat on their stomachs on the carpeted floor.

Stillness prevailed. The hostages were at the mercy of their captors. Everyone was too petrified to either speak or move. The black-bedecked men, who looked prototypical of a paramilitary group, didn't mutter a word. Flawlessly, they went about their business as though they had done it before many times over.

From where Ari was lying in a corner at the end of the room, shoes against the wall, he was able to see everyone by squinting his eyes and keeping his head rested to one side. He knew if he had been observed by any of the four gunmen his breathing days might well be over.

It wasn't as though he had never come into contact with these kinds of killer guerilla; it was simply the closest he came since his days in WitSec of getting himself placed on a stainless-steel table while a coroner conducted an autopsy.

Carefully, he counted the sets of legs of the people lying on the floor and the ones standing. Intuitively, Ari knew the men on their feet were either terrorists trying to fund clandestine missions against Western targets or mercenaries working for an underworld organization.

As he appraised the scene through quavering eyelids, he noticed Engelbert splattered on his stomach in his distinctive LGT uniform. How could he miss his massive body, the short-sleeve white shirt and the logo patch? Also easily identifiable were the feds, the Baron, von Stülpnagel, and all the bank and court attendants. Instantly, it dawned on him there was one person missing.

"Barney" the gaunt guard. "Where the hell is he?" Ari asked himself.

"Did he escape, and if so, how? Did he go undetected by the gunmen and flee the building?"

Or was he one of the nefarious louts holding an assault weapon pointed at the head of Herr Eckhard? What a way for the old man to end a banking career.

Not one of them had observed "Barney" slip out of the room during the recitation of Timmy Smith's letter. He had left to open the front door of the bank, let in his accomplices, and changed his uniform for clothes that appeared much more bellicose. Everyone else in the room had been too mentally absorbed and affixed as they listened to Ari read the passionate words.

Neither did Ari and the Baron know that "Barney" wasn't really a "Barney." They had never even been introduced. The security guard had pretty much stayed in the background and barely and rarely spoke to strangers or anyone else. "Just another bank guard," they thought.

They thought wrong.

His real name was Ilya Todor Chervenkov, a Bulgarian immigrant to Liechtenstein who had been in the country for almost nine months. Certainly, enough time to carefully develop and execute a plan to become a security guard at the LGT bank and to pull off one of the biggest bank heists in European history.

Getting into Liechtenstein by taking advantage of the Principality's new relaxed immigration laws via the Foreigners Act was easy. Not particularly well-educated, Chervenkov displayed a willingness to work hard and live quietly in a modest flat in Vaduz. He blended into Liechtenstein's mainstream society quite seamlessly, considering he not only spoke Bulgarian but German and English as well.

The 30-year-old had been born and raised in Pernik, a city of 85,000 southwest of the capital city of Sofia.

Timing for Chervenkov's career couldn't have been more perfect. When the Berlin Wall collapsed in 1989, he was ten years old. His alcoholic parents had tossed him into the streets at the point organized crime began to take a brutal hold of many provinces in the country. By the time he was eighteen, he was easily drawn into the underworld lifestyle. Four days before he turned twenty, he had carried out an assassination on behalf of one of the Sofia Mafia gangs. His victim was killed in broad daylight on one of the city's major avenues. It was but one of more than hundreds whose lives were cut short because of a communicable disease called barbarity.

The Reviled East became the Wild West.

Five minutes work for $30,000 American dollars was a profitable venture.

Although he didn't fit the physical description of Bulgarian Mafia operatives most members were menacingly enormous from their days as wrestlers and sportsmen – Ilya became one of the most feared assassins in Eastern Europe.

At five-feet-five and weighing less than most jockeys, he knew he couldn't play the part of a heavy. He was satisfied to keep a low profile and make as much money as he could in whatever odious niche he felt he could fit.

He refused to wear the typical black suit, sunglasses, and bling jewelry like so many of his criminal peers. Nor did he shave his head like many of his colleagues. He wasn't interested in looking mean and tough, and perhaps becoming a target himself. Rather, he thought it was more important to maintain an understated persona.

That didn't preclude him from becoming involved in narcotics trafficking, the sex-slave trade, extortion, and killing for large sums of money. But he wanted no part of setting up business enterprise "fronts" like so many others in the Mafia gangs had done.

Getting embroiled in paying off members of Bulgarian's judiciary and public safety officials wasn't his cup of vodka. Besides, Ilya knew his limits and felt much more at peace relishing the pure action of his criminal behavior.

He simply preferred to waste people rather than pay them.

And now it was the moment to execute.

One of the gunmen rolled Herr Eckhard onto his back, reached into one of his suit jacket pockets and pulled out the master key to the safe deposit boxes. The elderly banker was so thoroughly intimidated he kept his eyes shut during the entire humiliating and chilling experience.

Three of the gunmen walked into the vault while the leader made sure nobody on the floor moved as much as a muscle. One wrong twitch might be all it would take to get their brains splattered on the forest green carpet.

Blood, gray matter and verdant green don't mix so well.

All twenty-seven boxes were carefully removed and placed on a pair of industrial strength dollies: fourteen on one and thirteen on the other. They easily rolled them into the hallway, stopped, and returned to the vault.

The gunmen lifted the twenty-two hand-bound hostages to their feet and marched them one by one into the nearby metal sepulcher. Ari was last in line and was personally escorted by the chief mobster who distanced himself from the next-to-last person to enter.

Less than ten feet from the vault's entrance, the masked gunman cupped his free hand into Ari's ear and secretly whispered, "Regards from Debbie and Lana."

After Hirsch was inside the vault, the ambassador-of-bad snarled, "*Auf wiedersehen.*" The fun-loving dirtball and one of his fellow goons pushed the door shut and spun the two giant wheels that locked the impenetrable money mausoleum.

The four financial terrorists knew that cell phones were unusable inside the subterranean structure, and that their prey couldn't possibly be rescued until Monday morning when the bank reopened for business. That is, if they didn't run out of air first.

The captives, who quickly resigned themselves to spending a long and perhaps unsafe weekend in the safe, felt the fear of death.

At least the bastards left the lights on.

With no food, no water, no toilet, no fresh oxygen, and handcuffed, each of them thought they might well be entombed forever.

Except Ari.

Huddled in a corner with the Baron, Ari murmured confidently, "I have a hunch we'll be out of here sooner than you think."

The Baron simply stood there with a confounded look on his face.

The loot was wheeled to the elevator, hustled to the darkened main floor in two trips, and rushed outside the main glass doors to a waiting supersized panel-van painted dark blue.

It came fully equipped with a fifth member of the team at the wheel. Even on a weekend, the streets of Vaduz were as lively as a séance. It appeared there was no one around except the bank bandits.

And there were no cameras to even record what went on inside or outside the bank. Clearly, the bank's alarm system had been disarmed by the gang's mastermind, Chervenkov, who not only had access to the security system but every corner and hideaway in the bank.

The only witnesses to the massive theft were packed in a cold, unventilated storage bin.

Once outside, all the masks came off. It was too hot to be wearing them in July even in Liechtenstein. Plus, it made their jobs of lifting the boxes through the van's rear doors much easier; they could actually see what they were doing.

The moment the boxes were secured in the van the quintet of racketeers jumped in, and the driver headed north. Twenty minutes later, they arrived at their destination. A cleared area in the middle of one of Liechtenstein's many forests not far from the Baron's estate. Waiting for the scummy bandits was a Bell S-76C, a twin-engine helicopter that could accommodate not only the five thugs and its crew of two, but all of the safe deposit boxes.

The men off-loaded the containers and put them in the chopper, climbed aboard the craft, and gave each other high-fives as the captain started the rotor of the whirlybird.

All while the twenty-two weekend vault dwellers questioned each other as to who these marauders could possibly be. How could they know about the coins and the bullion? Why didn't the bank's security system alert anyone? Ari and the Baron knew this kind of operation could only be successfully undertaken by paramilitary forces, mercenaries, or a Mafia organization.

Time was running short to get those questions answered, and so was the oxygen.

As the helicopter gyrated east over the Austrian Alps to an unknown destination, it flew low enough to avoid radar detection and high enough to barely skim the mountain peaks. After five minutes aloft, Ilya slowly leaned over from his seat behind the captain and said softly and deliberately to the co-pilots, "We are all very rich men now, thanks to the both of you. By the way, Bobby and Timmy, I delivered your message to Ari."

About The Author

Ron Ruthfield is a former reporter for a CBS-affiliated TV station, newsman for The Associated Press, communications executive, novelist, and satirist. He grew up on Miami Beach where he attended South Beach Elementary School where he served as a distinguished member of the safety patrol in the 4th, 5th, and 6th grades and was awarded a special honor for allowing Dr. Stephen Hawking, who became one of the world's most foremost theoretical physicists and cosmologists, to cheat in class when he constantly looked at Mr. Ruthfield's test papers.

He makes his home in a happy hollow in the Blue Ridge Mountains of North Carolina and every now and then walks around aimlessly pondering how he ever wound up becoming a hillbilly.

Mr. Ruthfield's **Satire for the Soul** is one of a series of books which will have the same title but completely different content. We hope you'll begin a collection because they will be as important as your Family Bible, your diamonds and pearls, your financial legacy, all of which will go to your children, grandchildren and perhaps your ugly and avaricious cousins who constantly appear at your home at the very worst times like Easter Sunday, Thanksgiving and Christmas, and never help cleaning the table or washing the dishes. Don't even think about emailing them an invitation.

The books poke sardonic fun at real and fictional places, politicians, and elitists on an international, national, and local basis. Current events are particularly notable in the book. Nothing is out of bounds for the humorous mockery and lampoonery of not only the blowhard, high-brow

and stiff-necked globalists but your average person who might even be your neighbor. The author uses taboo and uncomfortable topics such as race, ethnicity, class, political systems, and illegal immigration.

The writing of this satirical collection of essays began when COVID-19 hit the world, and the author had absolutely nothing better to do with his time except take advantage of current events. So, he began to scribe and laugh at the people running – and sometimes ruining – our lives for their own benefit and bank accounts.

Using irony and exaggeration, **Satire for the Soul** was written particularly for those readers who love to laugh and smile at the world around them no matter how difficult or disturbing life might be. And the author dances with words as smooth as an Argentinian tango.

www.ingramcontent.com/pod-product-compliance
Lightning Source LLC
Chambersburg PA
CBHW020530030426
42337CB00013B/791